BATTLEGROUND
SCHOOLS

BATTLEGROUND

SCHOOLS

VOLUME 1 (A–K)

Edited by Sandra Mathison and E. Wayne Ross

GREENWOOD PRESS
Westport, Connecticut • London

Library of Congress Cataloging-in-Publication Data

Battleground : schools / edited by Sandra Mathison and E. Wayne Ross.
    p. cm.
   Includes bibliographical references and index.
   ISBN 978–0–313–33941–7 (set : alk. paper) — ISBN 978–0–313–33942–4 (vol. 1 : alk.
paper) — ISBN 978–0–313–33943–1 (vol. 2 : alk. paper)
1. Education—United States—History.   2. Public schools—United States—History.
I. Mathison, Sandra.   II. Ross, E. Wayne, 1956–
   LA212.B295   2008
   370.973—dc22   2007029589

British Library Cataloguing in Publication Data is available.

Library of Congress Catalog Card Number: 2007029589
ISBN-13: 978–0–313–33941–7 (set)
       978–0–313–33942–4 (vol. 1)
       978–0–313–33943–1 (vol. 2)

First published in 2008

Greenwood Press, 88 Post Road West, Westport, CT 06881
An imprint of Greenwood Publishing Group, Inc.
www.greenwood.com

Printed in the United States of America

The paper used in this book complies with the
Permanent Paper Standard issued by the National
Information Standards Organization (Z39.48–1984).

10 9 8 7 6 5 4 3 2 1

For Colin, who daily draws us onto the battleground of schools.

CONTENTS

Guide to Related Topics   *xi*

Preface   *xv*

Introduction   *xvii*

Entries

Academic Freedom for K–12 Teachers   1

Accountability   11

Afterschool Programs   19

Alternative Schools   27

Alternatives to Schooling   33

Art Education   37

Assessment   43

Bilingual Education   57

Bullying   64

Business and Corporate Involvement   71

Character Education   79

Charter Schools   85

Children's and Students' Rights   91

Citizenship Education   101

Civil Rights   110

Class Size   116

Clothing and School Uniforms   123

Commercialization of Schools   128

Compulsory Schooling   136

Creationism, Intelligent Design, and Evolution   147

Critical Pedagogy   156

Culturally Relevant Education   161

Curriculum   168

Desegregation   179

Discipline   187

Dropouts   194

Drug Use and Prevention   203

Early Childhood Education   213

E-Learning   221

English Language Learners   228

Evaluation   234

Finance   241

Foreign Language Education   249

Foundations and Schools   254

GED (General Educational Development) Credential   261

Gender   267

Gifted and Talented Education   274

Global Education   280

Government Role in Schooling   287

Grading Policies   294

Head Start   301

Homeless Children and Schools   306

Homeschooling   313

Homework   319

Human Development   326

Inclusive Schooling   333

Integrated Mental Health Services in Schools   340

International Comparisons of Student Achievement   346

Knowledge   357

Leadership   367

Lesbian, Gay, Bisexual, Transgendered, and Queer Youth   374

Literacy Education   381

Mathematics Education   391

Media and Schools   400

Mental Health   406

Middle Schools   415

Military in Schools   421

Moral Education   428

Motivation and Learning   437

Multiculturalism   445

No Child Left Behind (NCLB)   451

Nutrition in Schools   459

Parental Involvement in Schools   467

Pedagogy   473

Physical Education   483

Popular Culture and Schools   489

Progressivism   495

Purpose of Schools   502

Race, Racism, and Colorblindness in Schools   509

Religion and Public Schooling   514

Retention in Grade   520

Rural Schools   526

Safety and Security in Schools   533

School Choice   539

School Counseling   548

Science Education   556

Sexuality Education   562

Single-Sex Schools   569

Small Schools   579

Social Studies Education   586

Sports in Schools   595

Standardized Testing   599

Teacher Education   609

Teacher Knowledge   616

Teacher Licensure   622

Teacher Unions   628

Teaching   639

Technology and Schooling   649

Textbooks   655

Time in School   661

Tracking   671

Urban Education   681

Youth Activism   687

General Bibliography   695

Editorial Advisory Board   699

Contributor Biographies   701

Index   727

GUIDE TO RELATED TOPICS

LEGAL ISSUES AND LEGISLATION
Academic Freedom for K–12 Teachers
Accountability
Civil Rights
Desegregation
Finance
No Child Left Behind (NCLB)
Religion and Public Schooling
Textbooks

SCHOOL AND CLASSROOM PRACTICES
Accountability
Assessment
Class Size
Critical Pedagogy
Culturally Relevant Education
Curriculum
Discipline
E-Learning
Evaluation
Gifted and Talented Education
Grading Policies
Homework
Human Development
Inclusive Schooling

Pedagogy
Retention in Grade
Standardized Testing
Technology and Schooling
Textbooks

SCHOOL ORGANIZATION AND FORMS OF SCHOOLING
Afterschool Programs
Alternative Schools
Alternatives to Schooling
Compulsory Schooling
Early Childhood Education
Finance
Foundations and Schools
GED (General Educational Development) Credential
Head Start
Homeschooling
Integrated Mental Health Services in Schools
International Comparisons of Student Achievement
Leadership
Middle Schools
Parental Involvement in Schools
Progressivism
Rural Schools
Single-Sex Schools
School Choice
Small Schools
Time in School
Tracking
Urban Education

SCHOOLS AND SOCIETY
Bilingual Education
Business and Corporate Involvement
Civil Rights
Clothing and School Uniforms
Commercialization of Schools
Desegregation
English Language Learners
Gender
Government Role in Schooling
Homeless Children and Schools
Knowledge
Lesbian, Gay, Bisexual, Transgendered, and Queer Youth
Media and Schools
Military in Schools

Nutrition in Schools
Popular Culture and Schooling
Purpose of Schools
Race, Racism, and Colorblindness in Schools
Religion and Public Schooling
Youth Activism

SCHOOL SUBJECTS AND DISCIPLINES
Art Education
Citizenship Education
Creationism, Intelligent Design, and Evolution
Foreign Language Education
Global Education
Literacy Education
Mathematics Education
Multiculturalism
Physical Education
Science Education
Social Studies Education
Sports in Schools

SOCIAL, MORAL, AND EMOTIONAL DEVELOPMENT
Bullying
Character Education
Dropouts
Drug Use and Prevention
Mental Health
Moral Education
Motivation and Learning
Safety and Security in Schools
School Counseling
Sexuality Education

TEACHERS AND TEACHING
Academic Freedom for K–12 Teachers
Teacher Education
Teacher Knowledge
Teacher Licensure
Teacher Unions
Teaching

PREFACE

The *Battleground: Schools* volumes provide a historically situated description of the most salient controversies in schooling during the past century. Many of these controversies have persisted over this long period of time (such as what should be taught in the subject areas or the role of standardized testing in schools), and some are more contemporary (such as the role of technology in education or commercialization in schools). Controversial issues in schooling are topics about which there is no consensus of values or beliefs. By their nature, these controversial issues generate diverse opinions and debate on the distinctions between right and wrong, good and bad practice, justice and injustice, and on interpretations of fairness and tolerance. These are topics on which reasonable people sincerely disagree. Schools and education become sites of controversy because of their universality and the high expectations about what schools can accomplish. Controversies in schooling are driven by educational research, politics, courts, and grassroots movements.

Scholars and the interested public will find this collection helpful to gain a quick understanding of what is and has been happening in schools. Written in nontechnical language, this collection is easily accessible for high school and college students and an interested lay public, but scholars of education will find the collection useful as a reference on a wide variety of educational topics. Each essay concludes with suggested further readings for readers who wish to delve more deeply into a particular topic. In addition, many essays include graphs, charts, and illustrations that provide a quick sense of the magnitude or nature of the particular controversial issues.

We have selected 93 controversial issues to include in this collection, issues that have ebbed and flowed, or appeared sometime in the last 100 years of schooling in the United States. A thorough review of educational research literature, our own professional experience in schooling, and the assistance of an editorial board of prominent educational scholars aided us in identifying the topics to include in this collection. Indeed there are additional issues that might have been included, but the constraints of book length led us to choose these as the most central, both for their longevity and for the likelihood that these issues will persist well into the future.

The essays are authored by an impressive number of first-rate educational scholars. Never before has such a pre-eminent and diverse group of scholarly perspectives been combined in one collection. The authors each have demonstrated through their publications and research their prominence in their particular area. Many are award-winning scholars. Some are also practitioners. No single ideology prevails. Throwing a cocktail party for the 118 authors would be an intellectually exciting event—the room would brim with scholarly discourse and diversity of perspective and would reflect the cultural and ethnic mosaic of U.S. society. The reader can learn more about individual authors by consulting the alphabetically listed biographies included in this collection.

The essays are arranged alphabetically by topic. Each essay summarizes the nature of the controversy, including major players and events relevant to the topic. In a number of cases, timelines of critical events are also included. And each essay concludes with readings for further investigation of the topic. The complete volume concludes with a general bibliography of works that address the topics covered in this encyclopedia.

To give the reader further access to this volume, there are two helpful lists: An alphabetical list of the topics is included at the beginning of the volume, as well as a list of all the topics grouped under broad headings, called the Guide to Related Topics. Finally, the book ends with a comprehensive index.

It goes without saying that we could not have prepared this collection without the collaboration and cooperation of many people. We thank all of the contributors to *Battleground: Schools* who took on the metaphor of schools as a battleground with a keen eye for describing what has been happening in U.S. schools over the past century. We appreciate the help the Editorial Advisory Board provided in identifying the most salient issues to include and in identifying contributors. Thanks also to Marie Ellen Lacarda, whose idea this encyclopedia was—we appreciate her thinking of us as good stewards of the project. And thanks to Kevin Downing, our editor at Greenwood, who has provided the necessary supports and just enough encouragement to bring these volumes to fruition.

Neither of us has ever shrunk from controversy, and so we find ourselves in comfortable territory in these volumes. We would like to thank our many colleagues over the many years, on all sides of our own individually championed controversies, as well. While it is easy to thank those with whom you agree, as these essays suggest, those with whom we do not agree are equally important in helping us to reflect upon and give good reasons for the positions we hold. Without the counterpoint, our point is diminished.

INTRODUCTION

WHAT IS A CONTROVERSY?

Controversial issues in schooling are topics about which there is no consensus of values or belief. By their nature, these controversial issues generate diverse opinions and debate on the distinctions between right and wrong, good and bad practice, justice and injustice, and on interpretations of fairness and tolerance. These are topics about which reasonable people sincerely disagree. Schools and education become sites of controversy because of their universality and the high expectations about what schools can accomplish. Controversies in schooling are driven by educational research, politics, courts, and grassroots movements. The essays in this encyclopedia provide an historically situated description of salient controversies in schooling during the past century. Many of these controversies have persisted over this long period of time (such as what should be taught in the subject areas or the role of standardized testing in schools), and some are more contemporary (such as the role of technology in education or commercialization in schools).

WHENCE COMES CONTROVERSY?

Events and people have created, contributed to, and sustained controversies in schooling and education over the past century. Many social, political, and technological events occurring outside of schools have an impact on schools, and if there is disagreement about how and if schools should respond, controversy ensues. Some events are meant to solve controversies in schools, and while resolution sometimes occurs, just as often the attempts at resolution sustain disagreements and schools continue to be a battleground for different value positions. Court cases, legislation, and educational research are all such events. But individual people and their ideas also inhabit the battleground of schools and their ideas become the weapons in the ongoing struggle for power and control over schools both as an organization and an institution.

Events

Court Cases

Even before the 1900s the courts played an important role in schools. When value conflicts arise in schools the disputants turn to the courts to arbitrate those differences. Seldom do the courts settle matters for all times, although they do bring moments of quiet in controversies. The *Plessy v. Ferguson* decision of 1869 maintained that schools could be racially separate but equal, but *Brown v. Board of Education* in 1954 changed that ruling. And now, there are continued challenges to the Brown decision. The longevity of some court decisions is remarkable though, such as the *Scopes v. Tennessee* trial of 1925, which challenged the Butler Act passed to protect the teaching of divine creation and disallowing the teaching of evolution. Although Scopes was found guilty of teaching evolution, the court case created a public discourse that resulted in the repealing of the Butler Act. Throughout these essays readers will see that court cases are key weapons on the school battleground, in issues of children's rights, academic freedom, racial segregation and integration, gender relations, and many more. The courts have been and will continue to be used in an effort to quell controversy in schools, but in so doing they inevitably sustain and sometimes even sensationalize those controversies.

Legislation

As mentioned above, laws are passed that create or contribute to controversies in education. Whether to safeguard particular beliefs (like the Butler Act of 1925), to provide entitlements to redress injustices (like Title I, Head Start, or the Civil Rights Act), to direct educational policy and practice (like the National Defense Education Act, Education for All Handicapped Children Act, or laws that enable charter schools to be created), legislation is a key contributor to controversy in schools. When laws are enacted a problem is inherently defined and forms of redress prescribed. Inevitably there are disagreements with both. In part because it is contemporary, but also because of the unprecedented intrusion of the federal government into educational policy and practice, the No Child Left Behind Act (the reauthorization of the Elementary and Secondary Education Act—itself a source of controversy) demonstrates well the disagreements over what is wrong with schools and how they should be remedied. The fierce battle over the reauthorization of this legislation attests to its contribution to controversies that cut deeply into the nature of schooling in the United States.

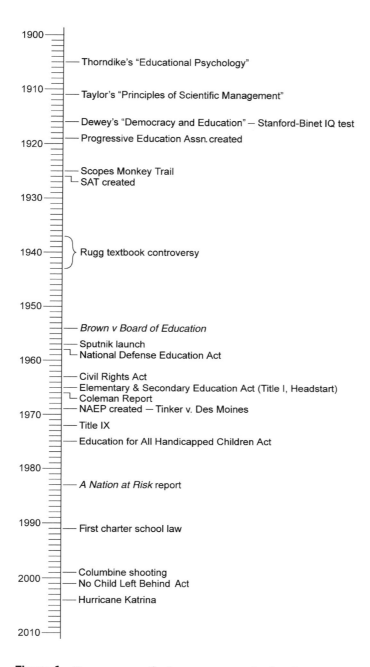

1900 —
    —— Thorndike's "Educational Psychology"

1910 —
    —— Taylor's "Principles of Scientific Management"

    —— Dewey's "Democracy and Education" — Stanford-Binet IQ test
    —— Progressive Education Assn. created
1920 —

    —— Scopes Monkey Trail
    └─ SAT created
1930 —

1940 — } Rugg textbook controversy

1950 —

    —— *Brown v Board of Education*
    —— Sputnik launch
    └─ National Defense Education Act
1960 —

    —— Civil Rights Act
    —— Elementary & Secondary Education Act (Title I, Headstart)
    └─ Coleman Report
    —— NAEP created — Tinker v. Des Moines
1970 —
    —— Title IX

    —— Education for All Handicapped Children Act

1980 —

    —— *A Nation at Risk* report

1990 —
    —— First charter school law

    —— Columbine shooting
2000 —
    —— No Child Left Behind Act

    —— Hurricane Katrina

2010 —

Figure 1   Key events contributing to controversy in education.

Educational Research and Scholarship

While some argue that educational research has little to contribute to schools and schooling, the essays in this volume suggest a different story. For example, John Dewey's influence on schools and education in the last century is remarkable. So too is the influence of Frederick Taylor, an engineer and not an educator, yet someone whose ideas reverberate in the organization and administration of every school. And the influence of psychologists on the many and competing conceptions of learning (whole language or phonics, behaviorism or constructivism, internal or external motivation, and so on) sustain controversies about pedagogy and human development (cognitive, moral, and physical). Specific works of educational scholars have also been the source of controversies in education—the development of the Scholastic Aptitude Test in 1926 was proffered as a solution to the need for greater efficiency in dealing with ever-larger numbers served by the schooling system. The use of standardized tests has always been a source of conflict, and there is no reason to believe this will change. Another example is the creation of the National Assessment of Educational Progress (NAEP) in 1969, a test developed for one purpose but one that has since been reformulated to serve some interests at the expense of others. Sometimes studies have had a profound impact on the definition of what matters in schools—James Coleman's *The Equality of Educational Opportunity Study* in 1966 is one such example. To this day, the Coleman report (as it is simply referred to) is used to support arguments about school finance, the nature of parental involvement, and a host of issues about the relative importance of schooling in determining life's chances.

Social, Technological, and Political Events

But it isn't just what happens within schools or the educational system that creates controversy and turns schools into a battleground. Events that are part of the cultural epoch have been key in drawing schools into larger controversies. The launch of Sputnik in 1957 set off alarms about American students' poor preparation in science and math, enough so that the National Defense Education Act (NDEA) was passed the following year; while its scope was wide ranging, the intent was to bolster American progress in the space race with the Soviet Union. Many technology advances, perhaps most notably the creation and uses of computers and digital information, produce skirmishes in schools: How

HISTORY OF AMERICAN EDUCATION PROJECTS

These on-line history projects are continually evolving; they include timelines as well as essays.

History of Education: Selected Moments of the Twentieth Century: http://fcis.oise.
utoronto.ca/~daniel_schugurensky/assignment1/index.html#90s
History of American Education Web Project: http://www.ux1.eiu.edu/~cfrnb/index.html
American Educational History: A Hypertext Timeline: http://www.cloudnet.com/
~edrbsass/educationhistorytimeline.html

should computers be used, can kids still learn arithmetic if they use a calculator, do computers keep kids from thinking for themselves, are digital sources of information better or worse than print sources, and so on. Recently, catastrophes (such as the Columbine shootings, 9/11, and Hurricane Katrina) have fomented disagreement about how schools should respond. The increased presence of the Religious Right in American social and political life has fueled the fires of old controversies (like the separation of church and state, including issues like the role of prayer or the teaching of evolution) and created some new (like the role of special interests in school boards). Schools do not exist in isolation, and indeed they are perhaps the common battleground for seeking resolution of differences of belief and value. The human right of all persons to education is widely accepted—and explicitly set out in international human rights instruments such as the Universal Declaration of Human Rights—and schools, as the primary manifestation of this right, provide a common context in which many differences are made public.

People

Many people's ideas and scholarship have contributed significantly to the nature of education and schooling in America, but a few scholars stand out for the extent to which their work fomented controversy in education, controversy that indeed has lasted throughout most of the twentieth century. These individuals' ideas are still at the heart of many controversies: Frederick Taylor's scientific principles of management are still evident in the ways schools are organized; the Progressive education movement, initiated by John Dewey and including Harold Rugg and George Counts, is alive and contested; and Ralph Tyler's hand can be seen in much of modern curriculum and assessment. These names recur throughout the essays in this encyclopedia, attesting to the foundational nature of their ideas and their sustaining qualities.

Frederick Taylor (1856–1915)

The publication of *The Principles of Scientific Management* in 1911 set forth the four basic principles of Taylorism: (1) replace rule-of-thumb work methods with methods based on a scientific study of the tasks; (2) scientifically select, train, and develop each employee rather than passively leaving them to train themselves; (3) cooperate with the workers to ensure that the scientifically developed methods are being followed; and (4) divide work nearly equally between managers and workers so that the managers apply scientific management principles to planning the work and the workers actually perform the tasks. Taylor, an engineer, was not himself interested in schools. His focus was on using scientific methods (like time and motion studies) to determine the most efficient way to produce goods. However, his ideas were appealing at a time when schools were grappling with too few teachers and classrooms and too many immigrant children to educate. If Taylor's principles were applied to education it was assumed there would be the same positive effect as in manufacturing, clerical work, and other production contexts. Schools became departmentalized, students began moving from teacher to teacher, and educational finance became a field. Over the years, Taylor's principles of efficiency have often prevailed in contexts such as the school consolidation movement, year round schooling, high-stakes testing, and educational-management organizations (EMOs).

John Dewey (1859–1952)

In stark contrast with the principles of Taylorism was the rise of the Progressive Era in public education. Born about the same time, John Dewey saw the world quite differently, and the influence of his ideas continues to this day. The publication of *Democracy and Education* in 1916 and the creation of the Progressive Education Association in 1919 mark the beginning of the Progressive Era, which ranged from 1880 to 1920, although the underlying ideas have long survived that period. While Taylor focused on efficiency to increase productivity, Dewey and the progressives focused on the effectiveness of schools in promoting democratic principles. Schools and education should be directed to: (1) helping each individual recognize his or her own abilities, interests, ideas, needs, and cultural identity, and (2) developing of critical, socially engaged intelligence, enabling individuals to understand and participate effectively in the affairs of their community in a collaborative effort to achieve a common good. This approach to education was and is referred to as child-centered and social reconstructionist. While these principles have probably never been manifest widely in American schools they have nonetheless prevailed throughout the century, providing the counterpoint to management principles. While the Cold War dampened the enthusiasm for progressive education, a number of recent educational reforms demonstrate that these principles live on, such as the Coalition for Essential Schools, the small schools movement, free schools, and whole schooling.

Harold Rugg (1886–1960)

In 1938, Columbia professor Harold Rugg's *Man and His Changing World*, a social science textbook, was published, and the controversy this sparked set the pattern for textbook publishing to the present. Rugg's text, in spite of its sexist title, reflected the principles of progressivism, including racial understanding, democracy, and social justice. The fact that he encouraged skepticism about business practices attracted the attention of the National Association of Manufacturers, the American Legion, and the Daughters of the American Revolution, among others. Rugg's textbooks were considered too critical of private enterprise, and the business community's campaign against the texts was highly successful: Sales in 1938 were 300,000 and by 1942 had dropped to 21,000, including book burnings in some communities. Lobbying by powerful groups has been a mainstay in determining what textbooks, library books, and curriculum materials are used in schools. Business interests continue to hold sway and have been joined by the interests of the Religious Right.

George Counts (1889–1974)

Continuing the progressive principles, George Counts published a slim volume, *Dare the School Build a New Social Order?* Teachers, he suggested, should be the leaders in society, taking an active change agent role in economics, politics, and morality. Education was the means for social change, he argued, and his argument was renounced by conservatives of the day. Counts understood the extent to which schools were a means for maintaining the status quo, and while he was clearly influenced by Dewey, Counts' faith in schools as sites for social and economic change had a more collectivist sensibility (society-centered rather than child-centered). Conservatives of the time labeled him a communist (which he was not) and the discourse of the day laid open an ongoing disagreement about who would control schools and toward what ends. Today, neoliberalism is the dominant discourse in schooling, but the refrain of George Counts' challenge to schools to build a new social order is still heard, especially in alternative schools, culturally relevant education, critical pedagogy, and liberatory notions of education.

Ralph Tyler (1902–1994)

Much of the modern era in American education (from the 1920s to the present) has been touched by Ralph Tyler's work. (Both Tyler and Counts were students of Charles Judd at the University of Chicago.) An advisor to six U.S. presidents, Tyler was the key figure in the development of many educational policies—as architect of the evaluation for the Eight Year Study he developed common and still prevailing notions of curriculum, evaluation, and student assessment. In 1949, Tyler's *Basic Principles of Curriculum and Instruction* was published, and "the Tyler rationale" became a mainstay in defining what curriculum studies is. Tyler was a key figure in the development of the Elementary and Secondary Education Act, and he initiated the National Assessment of Educational Progress (NAEP). Tyler likely served on more national policy-oriented committees and commissions than any other education scholar, and so his influence still rings through curriculum studies, pedagogy, evaluation, and assessment.

Modern Scholarly Contributions to Controversy

It remains to be seen who the lasting key contributors to controversies in education and schooling will be, but a number of possibilities recur through this collection of essays: Jean Anyon, Michael Apple, James A. Banks, William Bennett, Chester E. Finn Jr., Paulo Freire, Peter McLaren, Deborah Meier, Diane Ravitch.

SHOULD SCHOOLS BE A BATTLEGROUND?

Characterizing schools as a battleground may seem unnecessarily provocative. What the metaphor suggests, though, is a lively discourse about competing fundamental values and beliefs and how they are played out within schools. When controversies and struggles cease, schools will have become the agents of a single-minded indoctrination, a state that is singularly undesirable in a democracy. While today's controversy may lead to tomorrow's consensus, new and revived controversies will arise. That controversy is the steady state within education and schooling is a good thing, and what is to be guarded against are discourses, power relations, and institutionalized practices that disallow controversies to be debated in public and forthright ways. Deliberation in democracy (whether through legislation, courts, grassroots movements, or educational scholarship) does not guarantee particular outcomes, but it does set forth principles that insure that neither coercion nor brute economic power should determine how schools should be, and thus how American society should be. Deliberation is not, however, a guarantee for resolution. That schools are a battleground signals a healthy democracy.

Sandra Mathison and E. Wayne Ross

A

ACADEMIC FREEDOM FOR K–12 TEACHERS

Is there anything left of academic freedom for K–12 teachers? The *Hazelwood School District v. Kuhlmeier* decision removed the legal framework for defending teachers' academic freedom in the United States. Since that time, some conservatives have maligned academic freedom as "political correctness" and redefined it as student and parent rights to their viewpoints in classrooms and the curriculum. Lower courts have consistently relied on *Hazelwood* as a precedent, and the U.S. Supreme Court defaults to this 1988 decision to refuse to hear K–12 academic-freedom cases. The result of a long-term erosion of rights and professional autonomy is an increasingly difficult battleground of academic freedom for teachers.

Academic freedom for teachers is traditionally interpreted as freedom of expression. J. Kindred (2006) in the *Education Law Journal* defines the concept as "a right to raise new and controversial ideas in an effort to stimulate thought and the further pursuit of truth . . . a right to critically speak out against their [i.e., teachers'] employers" (p. 217). Clauses guaranteeing freedom of expression under constitutional law protect the freedom to acquire materials for teaching and more generally the professional autonomy to construct or select content, resources, and assessment or instructional methods that are responsive to courses, disciplines, and students. This includes the ability to make professional judgments without coercion or censorship. However, it is important to understand that the First Amendment basically stops at schoolhouse doors in the United States; teachers in Canada continue to be protected by section 2b in the Charter of Rights and Freedoms. Canadians have generally managed to address academic freedom at district and teacher union levels, or outside of the courts, but analysts describe an erosion of rights in Canada that parallels recent history in the United States, and Canadian judges invariably look south for legal precedent.

This discussion outlines the history of academic freedom for teachers and provides an overview of recent cases and trends. The neoconservative revival of academic freedom is juxtaposed against teacher activists who took a stand on academic freedom as fundamental to teaching in democratic systems of governance. Many believe that teaching controversial issues and promoting a collective sense of academic freedom have never been more important. This is the case for K–12 teachers as much as the university professoriate. Perhaps a statement on the times, educators of the current generation generally draw a blank when asked: "What is academic freedom for K–12 teachers?"

ACADEMIC FREEDOM FOR DEMOCRACIES

In many ways, mass education and academic freedom are synonymous, one requiring the other in democratic systems. Throughout the 1920s, the percentage of eligible students attending high school jumped from 31 to 51 percent. Average secondary school class sizes increased from 20 in 1915 to 31 in 1932. Mass education and the public schools had perennial critics, but during the 1920s criticism turned excessively alarmist. Conservative and liberal parents condemned the public schools and withdrew their children, reversing a 20-year downward trend in the percentage of students enrolled in private and sectarian schools. Control over the curriculum was particularly troubling, and in 1928, the National Education Association (NEA) reported that "a nationwide and insidious propaganda of prodigious proportions has been and continues to be carried on by the private power companies of this country [i.e., the United States], and . . . has attacked the entire public school and educational system" (p. 352). To defend against this, that same year in Minneapolis the NEA (1928) passed a "Freedom of the Teacher" resolution:

> Whereas, the classroom teachers are the ones who must use these censored text books and literature and are held responsible for the proper guidance and training of the youth, who are to become future citizens, therefore be it Resolved, that we most earnestly protest against the use of the public schools and educational system of our country by any private concern or organization in behalf of selfish class interests against the general and public welfare. (p. 352)

In 1935, the NEA expanded this to include the belief that schools and school personnel should have the opportunity to present different points of view on controversial questions to help students be better prepared for life.

Oppressive conditions reigned, and by the mid 1930s over 20 states required loyalty oaths, meant to effectively isolate and eliminate radical teachers. A little red rider law was passed in the District of Columbia in 1935, revoking salaries from teachers who "taught or advocated communism." The NEA and the American Federation of Teachers (AFT) fought against intimidation and for the repeal of loyalty and red rider laws. These were nevertheless heady days when it seemed like the schools really could play a lead in reconstructing the social order. In 1932, Teachers College professor George Counts challenged teachers with a resonant question: "Dare progressive education be progressive?" In the height of the depression, the effects of capitalism were horrific, and teachers generated a tremendous resistance to conservative governance, intimidation, and oppression. Academic freedom for teachers was part and parcel of democratic reform and social justice.

FIGURE A.1

Source: As first appeared in *Teacher Magazine,* September, 1995. Reprinted with permission from Editorial Projects in Education. Photo by Greg Goldman.

Similar conditions and sentiments prevailed in the late 1940s and early 1950s. The McCarthy era in the United States extended the loyalty oaths and red riders of the 1930s to a regressive practice of intimidation and red-baiting. The force of the schools as instruments of national security was tremendously challenging to teachers interested in defending academic freedom and fundamental rights to professional practice without coercion. The civil rights movement emerged from this context, demanding that teachers reject any pretense of neutrality. In his famous *Letter from Birmingham Jail* in 1963, Martin Luther King linked academic freedom to civil disobedience. He encouraged moderate professionals to get off the fence and speak out against injustice by exercising First Amendment rights. The day after King was shot in 1968, Riceville, Iowa, teacher Jane Elliott gave her third-grade students a lesson in racism that they would never forget. This and subsequent blue-eyed/brown-eyed experiments she conducted stand as extraordinarily meaningful expressions of academic freedom. In a later era, she would have been fired despite the lifelong lessons in discrimination the students experienced.

Inspired by civil rights and increasing activism, in December 1965 Beth Tinker and John Tinker, 13 and 15 years old, and Christopher Eckhart, 15 years old, decided to express their objection to the Vietnam War by wearing black armbands to school. Hearing of the plan, on December 14, principals of Des Moines, Iowa, schools adopted a policy that students wearing protest armbands would be asked to remove the symbols and, if they refused, be suspended. On December 15, Mary Beth and Christopher wore their armbands and were suspended. On December 16, John did the same and was suspended until after the New Year as well. The students' parents filed complaints in the district court, only to be dismissed. The circuit court appeal was split, affirming the district court's decision to dismiss the appeal. The Supreme Court eventually heard the case and in 1969 delivered its decision upholding the students' rights. "It can hardly be argued," the judges wrote in their opinion, "that either students or teachers shed their constitutional rights to freedom of speech or expression at the schoolhouse gate. . . . This has been the unmistakable holding of this Court for almost 50 years" (393 U.S. 503, 1969, sect. 1, para. 2). The opinion affirmed that administrators "do not possess absolute authority" over students and teachers. As a profound legal framework for academic freedom, this decision prevailed until the late 1980s.

At the time *Tinker v. Des Moines* was decided in the Supreme Court, academic freedom for teachers was fairly respected. Yet in 1969, only 55 of 2,225 school district contracts contained provisions to protect the right. Twenty-nine of these contracts were based on the Linden, Michigan, agreement stating that democratic values were best upheld

> in an atmosphere which is free from censorship and artificial restraints upon free inquiry and learning, and in which academic freedom for teacher and student is encouraged. B. Academic freedom shall be guaranteed to teachers and no special limitations shall be placed upon [teaching and learning] subject only to accepted standards of professional educational

responsibility. C. Freedom of individual conscience, association and expression will be encouraged and fairness of procedures will be observed both to safeguard the legitimate interests of the schools and to exhibit by appropriate examples the basic objectives of a democratic society. (NEA, 1969a, p. 9)

A year earlier, the Supreme Court ruled in favor of Township High School teacher Marvin Pickering's appeal that his board of education erred in firing him for publishing a letter critical of their budgeting process (391 U.S. 563, 1968). Given the *Pickering v. Board* and *Tinker v. Des Moines* decisions in addition to the robust statement in the Linden contract, the NEA (1969b) reaffirmed its resolution on academic freedom in 1969.

Censorship nonetheless persisted, and in 1980, the American Library Association reported that 62 percent of 910 censorship cases from 1966 to 1975 involved public schools. Increasing erosions of academic freedom prompted the *Education Digest* to ask: "Is academic freedom dead in public schools?" This was an ominous start to a decade that would, if not kill, nearly eliminate academic freedom for teachers. In 1983, three days before the April issue of a Hazelwood East High School (St. Louis, Missouri) student newspaper, the *Spectrum,* was to be printed, Principal Robert E. Reynolds censored the proofs and deleted two pages. He objected to the content of an article that dealt with teen pregnancy and another with the impact of divorce on students. The staff of the *Spectrum,* enrolled in a Journalism II course, objected, but the issue was published without the two pages. Upon encouragement from their previous journalism teacher, who transferred schools a month prior to the censor, three students (Cathy Kuhlmeier, Leslie Smart, and Leann Tippett) contacted the American Civil Liberties Union and filed suit in the district court. The censored articles were taken to the *St. Louis Post-Dispatch* and published in their entirety.

In 1985, the district court sided with the principal, but the appeals court decision upheld the rights of the students. On January 13, 1988, the Supreme Court reversed the lower court's decision with a five-to-three majority opinion that regressively shaped the future of academic freedom for K–12 teachers:

> school officials may impose reasonable restrictions on the speech of students, teachers, and other members of the school community ... Educators do not offend the First Amendment by exercising editorial control over the style and content of student speech in school-sponsored expressive activities so long as their actions are reasonably related to legitimate pedagogical concerns. (484 U.S. 260, 1988, sect. B, para. 4)

Those last three words—"legitimate pedagogical concerns"—subsequently provide the test for administrative intervention into curriculum and teaching and establish precedent for all legal deliberation to follow to date. Placing power over the curriculum in the hands of administrators, Justice White continued: "This standard [of legitimate pedagogical concerns] is consistent with our oft-expressed view that the education of the Nation's youth is primarily the responsibility of parents, teachers, and state and local school officials, and not of federal judges"

(484 U.S. 260, 1988, para 4b). With this default position, the Supreme Court has since refused to hear K–12 academic freedom cases. In dissent, however, Justice Brennan wrote, "the case before us aptly illustrates how readily school officials (and courts) can camouflage viewpoint discrimination as the 'mere' protection of students from sensitive topics" (484 U.S. 260, 1988, Dissent, sect. B, para. 5). He called the majority opinion a stamp of "brutal censorship" (sect. C, para. 2).

The *Duke Law Journal* immediately declared "the end of an era." Newspapers and civil liberties groups denounced the decision and accurately predicted

FIGURE A.2   Red Baiting School Propaganda from 1949.

the end of academic freedom for K–12 teachers and students. Looking back, Canadian legal analyst Nora Findlay (2002) aptly concluded: "With *Hazelwood,* everything changed ... Schools have the ability to censor material that raises 'legitimate pedagogical concerns' (i.e., the censorship can be justified educationally); this decision supports control of schools, not freedom of expression" (pp. 353–354). Indeed, trends in the history of academic freedom for teachers suggest a gradual erosion of activism and rights, marked by a vigorous defense in the 1930s and 1950s and a noticeable decline of support through the late 1980s and the current era.

SILENT NO MORE

Of course, prior to and between *Tinker v. Des Moines* and *Hazelwood v. Kuhlmeier* were numerous cases that tested or weakened academic freedom for K–12 teachers. But since *Hazelwood,* teachers have not had an opportunity in the U.S. Supreme Court to put the "legitimate pedagogical concerns" standard to test. Cases that in an earlier era would have gone to the Supreme Court were left with an unsettling feeling that the "myth" of academic freedom for teachers "dies slowly." Peggie Boring's and Cissy Lacks' cases are two such injustices that deserved a fair hearing in the high court. Their legacy is nonetheless significant, as both Boring and Lacks have been courageous in championing academic freedom and sharing their resistance narratives with teachers. Along with others, such as Nadine and Patsy Cordova, Releah Cossett Lent and Gloria Pipkin, they chose to be "silent no more."

In September 1991, Charles D. Owen High School drama teacher Peggie Boring and an extraordinary group of students chose the play *Independence* to rehearse and perform. *Independence* is fundamentally about love, care, and compassion, explored through intensely difficult relationships (divorced mother with three daughters: one a lesbian, one pregnant with an illegitimate child, and the third with street-sense vocabulary). Owen High School (Black Mountain, North Carolina) had just opened with a new theater, and the drama group was ecstatic over the facility. Both teacher and students were winners of prestigious awards and scholarships, and the group earned a chance to perform at the International Thespian Festival later that year. With script approval by the performers' parents and implicit approval from the school's administrators, their rendition of *Independence* was award winning and advanced to the state finals in competition. However, after a rehearsal in front of an English class in the school, a parent complained about the content of *Independence.* The principal intervened and insisted on censoring certain parts of the play. Boring reluctantly agreed, and the group went on to alternate winner at the competition. At the end of the school year, Boring was reassigned to a middle school for lack of compliance with the district's controversial materials policy.

Boring predictably lost an appeal of the dismissal at the school-board level but won her initial legal appeal in the Fourth Circuit court in 1996. A Fourth Circuit panel subsequently reviewed and in 1998 reversed the closely divided decision. Insofar as the principal and superintendent were acting on "legitimate pedagogical concerns," Boring evidently had no right to participate in creating the school curriculum through selection and production of plays (136, F.3d, 364; Daly, 2001; Russo & Delon, 1999; Zirkel, 1998).

In January 1995, English teacher Cissy Lacks, who had been teaching since 1972 and had a record of successes similar to Peggie Boring, was forced into the same battleground of academic freedom. Lacks drew on proven creative writing and poetry methods, including drama exercises accommodating the students' everyday "street" language. This method draws creative expression from reluctant and troubled students before moving to refinement of genre, technique, and style. For one assignment, the students wrote, performed, and videotaped short plays, which, all in all for the class, totaled to 40 minutes and contained 150 instances of profanity. Like most high schools, the tape represented a fair cross section of language and themes common to Berkeley High School (Ferguson-Florrisant School District of St. Louis). Following up on a student's complaint, the principal confiscated the tape from Lacks' locked classroom closet, reviewed it, and moved to suspend and eventually fire her for disobeying the school discipline code (i.e., no profanity). Lacks described her termination hearings before the school board as a kangaroo court. An appeal to the Federal District court won an injunction to have her reinstated, but the board rejected it. Her appeal trial in the Eighth Circuit court in 1998 trapped Berkeley High's principal on perjury, but the court nonetheless decided on behalf of the school district. Her claims to academic freedom in the selection of professionally proven methods and First Amendment rights to profanity in creative writing were summarily dismissed. Similar to the *Boring v. Buncombe* decision, the Eighth Circuit decision rested on *Hazelwood*—the board's prohibition of profanity was based on "legitimate pedagogical concerns" for acceptable social standards in the curriculum (147, F.3d, 718, 1998; Daly, 2001; Lacks, 2001, 2003; Russo & Delon, 1999). And like Boring, Lacks was denied a hearing by the Supreme Court. In Canada in 2003, Richard Morin's use of a video to teach resulted in a similar treatment and outcome.

Boring's and Lacks' cases are significant not only for constitutional and employment law, but for their power in reminding teachers of the relevance of academic freedom to everyday practice. As Lacks (2003) concluded:

> my story was the same as the myriad of stories like mine in schools everywhere. . . . Learning fields had become mined battlefields, but it was going to take my case, and some others, and a handful of catastrophic school violence incidents before most teachers would understand how vulnerable they were, and how ineffective this new censorship dogma would render them. (p. 113)

NEOCONSERVATIVE REVIVAL OF ACADEMIC FREEDOM

From the beginning of Boring's case, which quickly made headlines in local papers, conservative Christians rose up in moral outrage against the play *Independence* and the teacher's direction for the drama program. The "Friends and Supporters of Owen High School" took out a print ad in the local news-paper to chastise the teacher as an agitator for profanity, blasphemy, sexual promiscuity, adultery, and homosexuality. Although *Independence* and Boring's pedagogy may have drawn the wrath of conservatives in previous decades, it was no coincidence that this occurred in the early 1990s.

These nascent days of a neoconservative revival of academic freedom were punctuated by President George H. W. Bush's commencement speech at the University of Michigan on May 5, 1991. The president noted that "political correctness [PC] has ignited controversy across the land," declaring "certain topics off-limits, certain expression off-limits, even certain gestures off-limits." Chock-full of contradictions, the address set off a series of articles on PC in the *Atlantic Monthly, Newsweek,* and the *New York Times.* Nearly overnight, defenders of academic freedom were redefined to what Bush called "disputants" and sympathizers of PC. However, many educators including Henry Giroux reasoned that the PC battle was less a correction of bad educational practices and more a strategy for eliminating debate.

September 11, 2001, reinforced conservative backlash and made academic freedom for K–12 teachers ever more elusive. Parents and students with a range of political interests took it upon themselves to safeguard the patriotic curriculum. Civil liberties be damned, numerous corporate groups introduced curriculum to help buttress America's militaristic counter to terrorism. Even elementary and middle school students, such as 11-year-old Emil Levitin (pseudonym, see republicanvoices.org), began to patrol and report what teachers taught in classrooms and how well they entertained conservative or certain Christian viewpoints.

In September 2003, David Horowitz launched a campaign with parents and students to promote an academic bill of rights, effectively a manifesto for conservative viewpoints. A "Students for Academic Freedom" Web site and blog were created at the time, and a year later, a "Parents and Students for Academic Freedom" (PSAF) campaign and site was launched. The PSAF's *Academic Freedom Code for K–12 Schools* spells out a conservative agenda under a disguise of neutrality:

> Whereas parents and taxpayers have a right to expect that taxpayer resources will be spent on education, not political or ideological in-doctrination; Therefore be it resolved that this state's [board of education or other relevant regulating body] will promulgate clear regulations for appropriate professional and ethical behavior by teachers licensed to teach in this state; that these guidelines shall make it clear that teachers in taxpayer supported schools are forbidden to use their classrooms to try to engage in political, ideological, or religious advocacy. (Horowitz, 2004)

In response to Horowitz, an *Academic Freedom Bill of Rights* for post-secondary students was introduced into federal and state legislatures in 2004. In February 2005, the Florida House of Representatives, for example, passed the bill through the House Choice and Innovation Committee and the

Education Council. It died on the calendar in May 2005, but similar legislation across the United States has serious implications for both K–12 and post-secondary education.

In the midst of this neoconservative revival, in October 2005 a North Carolina high school student was turned over to police by a Wal-Mart clerk for photocopying an anti-President George W. Bush poster for a civics course assignment. Selina Jarvis, the Currituck County High teacher who gave the Bill of Rights assignment, was then questioned by the Secret Service. And in early March 2006, Aurora, Colorado, social studies teacher Jay Bennish was suspended after a student covertly recorded and circulated a tape of Bennish's in-class comparison of the arrogance of the Bush administration's policies with the arrogance of Hitler's Nazi Party. The Fox Network's coverage and the student's tape continue to be downloaded and circulate from YouTube.

CAVEAT PEDAGOGUE

On this battleground of surveillance, economic and military in/security, the commercialization of education, and neoconservative revival, academic freedom attenuates and censorship proliferates. There is no more important time for those who can to exercise and defend academic freedom as a viable, necessary form of activism. Are we not witnessing some of the worst fears of academic labor where power in the conception of curriculum is invested in administrators and a few appointed or elected officials while execution rests in teachers? As legal scholar Karen Daly (2001) cautions,

> the legal limitations that may be placed on an individual teacher's classroom speech encourage school boards and administrators to monopolize discussions about curricular and other pedagogical concerns, crowding out the voices of those on the front lines of education. This micromanagement of the teaching process reduces teacher morale, discourages innovative educational methods, and creates a disincentive for intelligent, independent-minded individuals to enter into the profession. (p. 3)

It should be clear that the cultural, historical, and legal dimensions of academic freedom for K–12 teachers only partially explain why we are at this juncture. Like education itself, academic freedom is profoundly political. Whether it remains a taken-for-granted discourse of the left is uncertain. What is for sure, however, is that the battleground of academic freedom for K–12 teachers can no longer be dismissed or neglected.

Further Reading: Clarke, P. T., 1998a, Canadian public school teachers and free speech: Part 1—An introduction, *Education & Law Journal, 8*(3), 295–314; Clarke, P. T., 1998b, Canadian public school teachers and free speech: Part II—An employment law analysis, *Education & Law Journal, 9*(1), 43–96; Clarke, P. T., 1999, Canadian public school teachers and free speech: Part III—A constitutional law analysis, *Education & Law Journal, 9*(3), 315–81; Cossett Lent, R., & Pipkin, G., eds., 2003, *Silent no more: Voices of courage in American schools,* Portsmouth, NH: Heinemann; Daly, K. C., 2001, Balancing act: Teachers' classroom speech and the First Amendment, *Journal of Law & Education,*

30(1), 1–62; Dolmage, W. R., & Clarke, P. T., 2002, Copyright ownership of teacher-prepared teaching materials: An examination of issues in the contemporary context, *Education & Law Journal, 11*(3), 321–341; Findlay, N. M., 2002, Students' right, freedom of expression and prior restraint: The *Hazelwood* decision, *Education & Law Journal, 11*(3), 343–366; Horowitz, D., 2004, February 13, In defense of intellectual diversity, *Chronicle of Higher Education, 50,* B12; Kindred, K., 2006, The teacher in dissent: Freedom of expression and the classroom, *Education Law Journal, 15*(3), 207–31; Lacks, C., 2003, Words can never hurt me, in ReLeah Cossett Lent and Gloria Pipkin (eds.), *Silent No More: Voices of Courage in American Schools.* Portsmouth, NH: Heinemann; Lacks, C. 2001, The teacher's nightmare: Getting fired for good teaching, in J. Daly, P. Schall, & R. Skeele (Eds.), *Protecting the right to teach and learn* (pp. 133–141), New York: Teachers College Press; National Education Association (NEA), 1928, Resolutions, *Proceedings and Addresses of the National Education Association, 66,* 351–352; National Education Association (NEA), 1969a, Negotiation agreements: Academic freedom, *NEA Research Bulletin, 47*(1), 7–10; National Education Association (NEA), 1969b, Resolutions, *Proceedings and Addresses of the National Education Association, 107,* 576; Petrina, S., 2006, Review of *School commercialism: From democratic ideal to market commodity, Teachers College Record,* retrieved Nov. 10, 2007 from http://www.tcrecord.org; Pipkin, G., & Cossett Lent, R., 2002, *At the schoolhouse gate: Lessons in intellectual freedom,* Portsmouth, NH: Heinemann; Russo, C., & Delon, F., 1999, Teachers, school boards, and the curriculum, *NASSP Bulletin, 83,* 22–29; Smith, H. L., 1936, Report of the committee on academic freedom, *Proceedings and Addresses of the National Education Association, 66,* 814–816; Violas, P., 1971, Fear and the constraints of academic freedom of public school teachers, 1930–1960, *Educational Theory, 21*(1), 70–80; Woods, L. B., 1980, Censorship in the schools, *Education Digest, 45*(5), 10–12; Zirkel, P., 1998, A uniform policy, *Phi Delta Kappan, 79,* 550–551.

Stephen Petrina

ACCOUNTABILITY

Accountability of schools is a relatively contemporary concern, dating probably to James Coleman's 1966 report *Equality of Educational Opportunity.* This report examined achievement of children of different races and shifted the attention toward outcomes and away from resources and inputs. That this report was followed closely by the development of the *National Assessment of Educational Progress* in 1970 meant that student test results were available to indicate the outcomes of schooling. Since then demands for schools to be accountable have been accentuated by the often-conflicting demands of policymakers and politicians who control the educational purse strings and professional educators with the knowledge and skills to educate children within a democracy.

THE MEANING OF ACCOUNTABILITY

Accountability is a means of interaction in hierarchical, often bureaucratic, systems between those who have power and those who do not. Complex hierarchical systems do not permit those in power to be everywhere and do everything at the same time to achieve what they consider to be desirable outcomes.

Consequently, authority must be delegated to others, which disperses power to lower levels of the hierarchical system. Those who receive this authority do not receive it in full, however. Power flows through them, but not from them. For example, the authority of accountable persons is limited to establishing the means by which the ends of power shall be achieved.

Specifically, accountability is an economic means of interaction. When power is delegated and dispersed to those within a hierarchical system there is an expected return from the investment of that power in others. Those to whom power has been delegated are obligated to answer or render an account of the degree of success in accomplishing the outcomes desired by those in power. Because of the diffuse nature of many hierarchical systems, accountability depends on both surveillance and self-regulation. The power of surveillance is borne out in part by the spectacle that may result from accounting by those to whom power has been delegated. In other words, the powerful in small numbers are surveilling the performance of many (through means such as standardized tests), which in turn become spectacles observed by the many (as in when schools test scores are reported on the front page of the newspaper). Self-regulation, that is the faithful exercise of delegated authority, is in part based on surveillance and the concomitant possibility of spectacle, but also on the perception of the legitimacy of those delegating power.

Within systems of accountability delegates of power must answer to some higher authority, but the identity of this authority is obfuscated when the interests of the public, "the American people," are used to obscure the special interests of the few. Additionally, the obfuscation of the identity of those in power and its purpose (i.e., being in the greater good) also serves to convince the many of the value of the interests of the few. The implication is that teachers, professors, public schools, and universities are accountable to the public, but the higher authority is more specifically the interests of the capitalist state, an inextricable conglomeration of business and government interests.

PUBLIC STATEMENT

Educational Accountability

American Evaluation Association
November 1, 2006

The American Evaluation Association (AEA) supports educational accountability systems that are methodologically sound and produce credible, comprehensive, context-sensitive information. Such systems can strengthen teaching, learning, and educational governance. With this statement, AEA hopes to contribute to the continuing public debate and evolution of educational accountability systems and, in concert with our *Guiding Principles for Evaluators* and our earlier statement on high stakes testing in education, to affirm and extend AEA's tradition of encouraging high-quality evaluation.

Good evaluation has much in common with good accountability systems, including responsibility for assuring the highest quality data and their most appropriate use.

Accountability systems are mechanisms by which (1) responsibilities and those responsible are identified, (2) evidence is collected and evaluated and, (3) based on the evidence, appropriate remedies, assistance, rewards, and sanctions are applied by those in authority. The relevance, accuracy, and completeness of the evidence are central to appropriate decision-making about policies, institutions, programs, and personnel and to the appropriateness of rewards and sanctions.

The research literature identifies several important concerns that may arise with educational accountability systems, including:

- over-reliance on standardized test scores that are not necessarily accurate measures of student learning, especially for very young and for historically underserved students, and that do not capture complex educational processes or achievements;
- definitions of success that require test score increases that are higher or faster than historical evidence suggests is possible; and
- a one-size-fits-all approach that may be insensitive to local contextual variables or to local educational efforts.

The consequences of an accountability system that is not accurately or completely measuring student learning can be significant. An over-emphasis on standardized tests may lead to a decrease in the scope or depth of educational experiences for students, if the tests do not accurately measure the learning of some. In addition, if resource allocations are based on difficult-to-attain standards of success, an entire educational system may suffer. Consider in particular those schools that are struggling to serve students who face the greatest obstacles to learning. These schools may be at risk for having resources unfairly underestimated or disproportionately withheld.

AEA is dedicated to improving evaluation practice and increasing the appropriate use of evaluation data. To encourage the highest quality accountability systems, we advocate approaches that feature rigor and appropriate methodological and procedural safeguards. AEA encourages movement in the following directions for educational accountability systems.

- *Multiple measures:* Empirical evidence from multiple measures, data sources, and data types is essential to valid judgments of progress and to appropriate consequences. For example, at the local level, if teachers' assessments as well as standardized test scores were incorporated into accountability systems, this could provide more detailed information regarding curriculum mastery by students.
- *Measurement of individual student progress over time:* Many traditional assessments examine current achievement levels only. Including longitudinal data on student progress over time would increase the sensitivity of the system to changes in learning made by individual students and could help identify the effects of services provided.
- *Context sensitive reporting:* Reporting systems that promote awareness of the many influences affecting outcomes are part of a complete and accurate assessment of school quality and student achievement. Findings from research and evaluations

should be reported and considered part of a comprehensive educational accountability system.

- *Data-based resource allocations:* If resource allocations take into consideration the needs and difficulties that are identified from comprehensive data of many types, the result could be greater equity in funding and increased support for teachers and schools that serve low-income and other high-risk students.
- *Accessible appeals processes:* The opportunity to appeal decisions enhances the fairness and transparency of an educational accountability system that is itself accountable for the appropriateness of its decisions and the accuracy, completeness, and relevance of its evidence.
- *Public participation and access:* Ideally, accountability systems should be developed and implemented with broad participation by many stakeholders. A system that is open to public involvement and scrutiny is likely to result in a more complete understanding of educational institutions, their contexts, the nature and success of their efforts, and the effects and appropriateness of the consequences of accountability systems.

Educational accountability has the potential to improve the quality of our schools and the experiences and achievements of our children. The concerns and strategies outlined above are intended to encourage educational accountability systems that fulfill that potential.

THE MANIFESTATION OF ACCOUNTABILITY IN SCHOOLS

Historically, external forces have often controlled schools: for example, the Sputnik era brought massive curricular reforms such as Man a Course of Study (MACOS), Biological Sciences Curriculum Study (BSCS), and others, and long before that accountability schemes such as the spelling tests proposed by Joseph Rice in Boston early in the 1900s to rid schools of undesirable headmasters. Still, the power of accountability in K–12 schools increased most dramatically in the early 1980s with the publication of *A Nation at Risk.* That report linked American educational performance to the decline in the perceived preeminence of the United States in science, technology, and overall global competitiveness.

The era of big curriculum reform lacked any widespread and sustained change in schools, in large part because local conditions mitigated efforts to create standardized content, pedagogy, and classroom processes. The curriculum reform era has been replaced by a standards-based reform era focusing exclusively on outcomes, a basic utilitarian approach that focuses more on ends (for example, test scores) than means, but that affects both. Much of the impetus and continued support for accountability comes not from educators, educational researchers, nor the public, but rather from corporate business. In fact, a main current in the history of education in the United States is the effort of corporate leaders and their allies in government to shape public education to the ends of business.

The National Education Summits

The four national education summits held since 1989 have been key events in the rise of the accountability movement in K–12 schools and intensified efforts to transform schools to meet corporate expectations. In 1989, President George H. W. Bush called the nation's governors together for the first national education summit in Charlottesville, VA. They set goals and developed ways to measure progress, but were stymied by resistance to federal interference in local school decisions. Seven years later, governors and top corporate leaders met at IBM's conference center in Palisades, New York, and developed an approach for states to accomplish what had eluded participants in the first summit, namely defining what should be taught in local schools and enforcing curriculum standardization through state mandated tests—what is called the "standards movement."

The most recent summits (in 1999 and 2001) aimed at consolidating "gains" that have been made in the corporate/state regulation and administration of knowledge in public schools, including the successful adoption of a national testing plan, which was President George W. Bush's top domestic priority when he took office in 2001. The 2002 reauthorization of the Elementary and Secondary Education Act (ESEA) is the most dramatic change in the federal role in local education since the early 1960s. Ironically, the Republican Party, which has argued for the abolition of the U.S. Department of Education, is now responsible for the greatest ever federal involvement in local schools.

This business-government alliance has, however, encountered public resistance to its agenda. At the 1999 Summit, Public Agenda, a public opinion research organization, reported that the movement to raise standards in public schools strikes a responsive chord with the public, but also warned that the issue of standards is not immune to the "normal controversies and complications that accompany any large-scale policy change."

What is noteworthy about this report, *Standards and Accountability: Where the Public Stands,* is its straightforward description of the agenda that must be pursued if the economic, political elite is to maintain legitimacy as they define the curriculum and pedagogy of public schools. The number one task according to Public Agenda is effective propaganda. While the authors of *Standards and Accountability: Where the Public Stands* make much of the "established and remarkably stable" support for standards-based educational reform in the United States, they are mindful of "pitfalls that could derail or unsettle support." First, the report warns that standards advocates should expect unhappiness when the rubber hits the road and students are retained in grade or denied diplomas. Pointing to the dramatic shift in public support for managed health care as people experienced drive-by surgery and denial of treatment options, Public Agenda warns standards advocates that delivering test score increases must be accompanied by the "appearance of fairness" in managing the reform effort. Now that, in the first decade of twenty-first century, thousands of students are being forced to repeat a grade or are denied a diploma, it is likely that the mere appearance of fairness will not be enough to stave off opposition to standards and the high-stakes tests that accompany them. Parents and teachers are the two groups most likely to derail the standards train.

The Public Agenda report—in a somewhat quixotic claim—declares that parents are insignificant players in the standards movement. While parents generally support standards-based reform, Public Agenda describes parents as, "not especially well-informed or vigilant consumers, even concerning their own child's progress." This claim conflicts with reports that the once-sporadic resistance to test-driven accountability is blossoming into a broader rebellion. For example, as a result of parent protests, Los Angeles school officials backed off a plan to end "social promotions," and in Massachusetts officials were forced to redefine cut scores on state tests that otherwise would have prevented as many as 83 percent of Latino and 80 percent of African American students from receiving high school diplomas.

While Public Agenda—and perhaps the corporate leadership of the movement—considers parents to be little or no threat to standards-based educational reform, politicians appear more sensitive to the growing antistandards, antitesting pressures. Test boycotts and other forms of resistance have moved the governors of Michigan and California to offer students money ("scholarships" of up to $2,500) for taking or scoring well on state-mandated tests. Indiana politicians are bracing for an enormous backlash against the state graduation test, which threatens to keep 50 percent of the seniors in urban districts and a quarter of seniors statewide from graduating this year.

Teachers are the most significant potential pitfall to the standards movement, according to the Public Agenda report. While many school administrators and the top leaders of the teachers' unions are solidly on the standards bandwagon, rank-and-file teachers' pivotal role is rightly acknowledged. Following the lead of Public Agenda, the top agenda item at the summit was teaching, in particular devising ways in which teacher preparation and pay can be tied directly to the standardized curriculum and tests developed by states.

In the end, the national education summits are a portrait of power relations in neoliberal democracy. Neoliberal democracy reflects our hierarchical society, where citizens are made to be passive spectators, disconnected from one another and alienated from their own desires, learning, and work. The spectacle of standards, test scores, and summits obscures the role of parents, teachers, and students in decision making in public education. This spectacle expresses what society can do, but in this expression what is permitted with regard to teaching and learning limits what is possible.

The Liberal-Conservative Alliance

The national education summits and the standards-based educational reforms they have nurtured should be understood both within the context of neoliberalism and the coalescing of historically liberal and conservative political and economic principles. A hallmark of the standardization craze is its remarkable capacity to unite seemingly disparate individuals and interests around the "necessity" of national and/or state educational standards—the standardization imperative. Ostensibly strange bedfellows, including for instance E. D. Hirsch Jr., Diane Ravitch, Chester Finn, Gary Nash, Bill Clinton, Edward Kennedy, both President Bushes, IBM chairman Lou Gerstner, the leaders of the American Federation of Teachers (AFT) and National Education Association (NEA), 49 state departments of education, and nearly all governors (Democratic and Republican), join to support standards-based reform and its concomitant "need" to implement systems of mandated, high-stakes testing. Somehow these "divergent" educational leaders manage to pull together around standards-based reform as the medium for "real" public school improvement.

In the past several years the Education Excellence Partnership, which includes the AFT, NEA, the Business Roundtable, the U.S. Chamber of Commerce, the National Alliance of Business, Achieve Inc., the National Governor's Association, and the U.S. Department of Education, have sponsored over 50 full-page advertisements in the *New York Times* promoting the standards agenda and, in particular, the use of high-stakes tests as means to both "motivate achievement" and retain children in grade.

Education policy is being crafted in a milieu distinguished by the pro-standards consensus among an array of both liberal and conservative players and exemplifies how elites manufacture crises (for example, the widespread failure of public education) and consent (for example, the way to save public education is through standardized schools driven by high-stakes tests). Accordingly, the commitments of the political-pedagogical Right—public school privatization, the reduction of national financial support for public education, the promotion of U.S. global corporate hegemony, "creationism," sociocultural homogenization around a few dominant "moral" themes, anti-immigration, the assault on organized labor, school prayer, and so on—blend with those of the Left—equality, expanded democracy, economic opportunity, social justice, diversity, and so on—to create a clever although fundamentally confusing admixture of contradictions and inconsistencies.

At its core the pro-standards accountability framework can be characterized by its commitment to a relatively few defining principles. Advocates argue first that standards-based reform is necessary vis-à-vis school improvement because the current educational "crisis" is rooted in the inability or unwillingness of "failing" schools to offer the same "high-quality" programs provided by more "successful" schools. Since the identified purposes, selected content, teachers, and modes of evaluation must be better in some (usually wealthy and majority white) schools than in others (usually less wealthy and majority Latino/a and African American), the implications are unmistakable. Elite educational leaders and policymakers are saying that "other" schools can indeed improve, but only to the extent that they become more like "our" schools. Hence, we see the promotion of a one-sided standardization imperative and the subsequent normalization of whiteness, wealth, and exclusionary forms of knowledge.

In short, the accountability alliance argues, in most cases without any evidence, that: (1) today's students do not "know enough" (no matter how knowing enough is defined); (2) curriculum and assessment standards will lead to higher achievement (although arguably many students achieve highly now—they just do so differently or in ways not easily quantified); (3) national and state standards are crucial in terms of successful U.S.-corporate-global economic competition; (4) standards-based reform should occur with federal guidance yet be implemented under local control (thus keeping both big government liberals and New Federalist conservatives happy); and (5) "higher" standards/standardization will promote equal educational, thus economic and political, opportunity.

SOME SPECIFIC EFFECTS ON SCHOOLS AND SCHOOLING

The national education summits and the standards-based accountability movement as a whole are quintessential examples of how neoliberal democracy works to thwart meaningful participation of the many by allowing the few to speak for all. The objective appearance of accountability schemes, which aim to reform schools by focusing on test scores, conceals (partially) the fact that these reforms are the result of the deepening economic inequality and racial segregation, which are typically coupled with authoritarianism. For example, in Chicago, many public schools have been militarized—six schools have been turned into military academies and over 7,000 students in 41 schools are in Junior ROTC—and teachers have been given scripted lessons, keyed to tests, to guide their instruction. In a dramatic shift away from democracy, urban schools systems are being taken over by states. In Detroit, a Democratic mayor and a Republican governor disbanded the elected school board and appointed a new board—whose members represent corporate interests and of whom only one is a city resident. In December 2001, another partnership between a Democratic mayor and a Republican governor resulted in a state takeover of the 200,000-student Philadelphia school system with the intention of giving Edison Schools Inc., the largest for-profit manager of public schools in the United States, a six-year, $101 million contract to become a district consultant and run 45 of the city's schools.

The primary justification for the seizure or closing of schools and/or the imposition of standardized curriculum has been poor test scores and high dropout rates. But standardized test scores are less a reflection of ability or achievement than measures of parental income. For example, someone taking the SAT can expect to score an extra 30 test points for every $10,000 in parental yearly income. Dropout rates are directly related to poverty, and none of the powers demanding the school seizure or standardization have addressed the broader question of poverty.

The accountability movement and its dependence on standardized testing is not only good for business, but also good business. While a sociopolitical agenda (of mixed perspectives) drives these reforms in education, they also present the opportunity for much enhanced profit making in textbook, educational materials, and test sales and increased stock values. These are corporate business interests intertwined with government officials in no less significant ways than other aspects of public life, such as energy or the environment. There are three major textbook/standardized testing companies in the United States (McGraw-Hill, Harcourt, and Houghton Mifflin), and all will see sales and profits skyrocket as

NCLB is implemented. George W. Bush's entanglement with Enron is rivaled by his entanglement with McGraw-Hill, one based on several generations of mutual support between a family of politicians and a family of publishers. Even not-for-profit organizations such as the Educational Testing Service (ETS) have ousted their academic CEO (Nancy Cole), replaced her with a marketing executive (Kurt Landgraf), and created a for-profit subsidiary, ETS K–12 Works, which will sell tests and testing services to elementary and secondary schools.

Accountability is not inherently bad—the public has a right to know that schools are educating the nation's young, and schools have a right to know that public officials are ensuring that the resources and capabilities to provide quality education are in place. Current forms of accountability are, however, one-directional and conceive of the purposes and outcomes of schooling in simplistic terms.

Further Reading: Carnoy, M., 2003, *The new accountability: High schools and high stakes testing*, London: Routledge Falmer Press; Dorn, S., 1998, The political legacy of school accountability systems, *Educational Policy Analysis Archives, 6*(1), retrieved March 4, 2007, from http://epaa.asu.edu/epaa/v6n1.html; Jones, K., ed., 2006, *Democratic school accountability*, Lanham, MD: Roman and Littlefield.

Sandra Mathison and E. Wayne Ross

AFTERSCHOOL PROGRAMS

Afterschool programs are a growing part of the educational landscape in the United States. While receiving broad support from parents, schools, policymakers, and the general public, there remains a great deal of controversy concerning the purpose of afterschool programs. Are they meant to boost school success, provide supervision for working parents, or prevent risky behavior?

There are three main arenas of influence for afterschool programs: education, child care, and prevention. Some supporters promote afterschool programs as an education strategy, designed to raise the achievement of students, especially those failing or at risk of failing high-stakes tests. Others point to the importance of adult supervision for children during the many hours when parents are working and school is out. Women's success in the workforce, including that of women transitioning off welfare, is dependent on having places for children to stay and caregivers to watch over them after school. Finally, there is a long history of programs designed to prevent problem behaviors in young people, especially adolescents, bolstered by evidence that most youth crime takes place in the afterschool hours.

AFTERSCHOOL: THREE PURPOSES, THREE HISTORIES

These various conceptions of the role of afterschool programs grow out of three disparate movements, each suited to a different purpose. The oldest afterschool programs began as part of a risk-reduction strategy, a way to keep young people out of trouble and constructively occupied. This approach was popular during the immigration waves of the early twentieth century, when settlement houses "Americanized" youth, providing recreation and social services to help them and their families acclimate to a new nation, and by the 1980s had resulted in funding for pregnancy prevention, drop-out prevention, drug-abuse prevention, and so on.

While prevention represented an improvement over a purely interventionist approach to youth problems, practitioners realized that the narrow funding that drove their work needed to be linked, as it all focused on the same group of "at-risk" students, ignored the larger societal framework that led to their vulnerability, and assumed that economically disadvantaged young people had nothing to offer but trouble. The youth development movement has worked to transform the "at-risk" approach to one of "at-promise," focusing on building the strength and engagement of young people, often with a focus on the arts or community change.

In the meantime, white, middle-class mothers were joining their African American and immigrant peers in the labor force in increasing numbers, beginning back with "Rosie the Riveter." As their child aged out of early care and into the school years, there often was nowhere to go and no one to take care of them during the many hours when parents were working and schools were not in session, leading to the birth of "school-age child care."

More recently, in an era of high-stakes testing and intensive accountability for schools, afterschool programs have emerged as a promising strategy for promoting academic achievement. As a relatively low-cost and easy to institute educational reform, afterschool programs have the ability to extend children's learning time and to do so in innovative ways, since they are less encumbered by institutional structures and requirements. While decades of attempts to reduce the achievement gaps between races and classes have had only incremental results, there is strong evidence that most of the gap is due to experiences and influences from outside of school, including caring adults, access to extracurricular and enrichment activities, and social capital. Afterschool and summer programs are increasingly seen as a potential way to "level the playing field," providing economically disadvantaged, African American, and Latino students with access to the same opportunities enjoyed by their middle-class and white peers.

THE PROGRAM LANDSCAPE TODAY

Despite the existence of programs in the education, child care, and youth development sectors, there are still many children left unserved. According to a survey by the Afterschool Alliance, more than 14 million K–12 youth are responsible for taking care of themselves during the afterschool hours. African American and Hispanic youth spend significantly more time unsupervised. Nearly four million (26 percent) of the children in self-care would be likely to participate in an afterschool program if one were available in the community.

National household surveys indicate that approximately 6.5 million children (11 percent of the 57 million youth in grades K–12) participate in afterschool programs. Younger children make up the largest segment of afterschool program participants. Afterschool programs serving youth and families are offered through many types of organizations including not-for-profit, for-profit, and public agencies. Programs take place in public schools, libraries, parks, sports/recreation facilities, faith-based organizations, community centers, housing development centers, cultural organizations, and private schools/agencies. While each historical strand of afterschool—school-age child care, youth development, and education—encompasses a wide diversity, there are also features that distinguish these prototypes.

By 1991, over 50,000 school-age child care programs were serving 1.7 million children. These programs, sponsored by a wide variety of providers from national organizations such as the YMCA to small churches, often depend on child care subsidies from CCDF or other state child care funds as well as parent fees to provide supervision after school hours, during school vacations, and in the summer. Children who attend school-age child care programs are generally in early elementary years and often find an environment similar to that of an early childhood program, including "soft" reading or resting areas, time for free or outdoor play, and relatively close connections between staff and parents.

Youth development programs include an extremely wide diversity of models, ages, and missions. Some are prevention-oriented programs focused on reducing risky behavior such as drug and tobacco use, while others bring teens into the arts or social action projects. Programs tend to be focused on older youth, including middle school and especially high school, and have a broad array of developmental goals for youth, often with a focus on strong mentoring relationships between staff and youth. While there is no nationally representative data on participation in such programs, it has been estimated that youth-serving organizations serve nearly 40 million children and adolescents each year.

The prototypical education-oriented afterschool program consists of teachers and paraprofessionals from the school day working extra hours to help with homework and provide remedial instruction. However, while many school-run programs may follow this model, others, including those funded by state and federal community learning center grants, often collaborate with community resources to offer a wide variety of activities and opportunities. Programs serve a wide age range, typically only open after school on days when school is in session. Whatever the model, though, these programs share a common goal: enhanced achievement in core academic subjects.

THE POLICY LANDSCAPE

The two major sources of federal funding for afterschool programs reflect—and contribute to—the segmented nature of the afterschool field. Child Care and Development Fund (CCDF), federal block grant subsidies from the Department of Health and Human Services and Twenty-First Century Community Learning Centers (21st CCLC) grants from the Department of Education are the largest providers of school-age child care and educational afterschool programs, respectively. The Finance Project estimates that in 2005, the federal government invested 1.2 billion dollars in CCDF funding for afterschool programs for children ages 5–12 and one billion dollars in 21st CCLC grants to afterschool programs.

The Child Care and Development Fund (CCDF) represents a significant public investment—$4.8 billion in federal dollars and an estimated $2.2 billion in state funds in FY2003. In addition to these figures, many states are transferring significant amounts of Temporary Assistance for Needy Families (TANF) funds to CCDF, and are directly spending TANF on afterschool programs and child care. Federal law mandates that CCDF funds may be used to provide child care support for children up to the age of 13 (the age may be extended to 19 in certain circumstances). In FY2001, 36 percent of 1.8 million children receiving CCDF subsidies were school-aged; another 10 percent of the subsidies were for kindergarten-age children.

The CCDF block grant supports subsidies, in the form of contracts with providers or vouchers for families, to low-income families with work-related child care needs, including those transitioning off welfare. As long as the family maintains income eligibility, the child is able to continue receiving care until he or she reaches the age of 13. Programs gain a relatively stable revenue stream in exchange for meeting state licensing guidelines and providing services that meet the needs of working parents (that is, until 5:30 or 6:00 P.M. on school days and eight to ten hours during school holidays and vacations).

The Department of Education had little formal involvement in afterschool programs until the mid-1990s. Prior to the 1990s, some local school districts and schools used a portion of their Title I dollars to support extended learning opportunities for low-income children. In 1994, the 21st Century Community Learning Centers Act (21st CCLC) was introduced; and in 2003, 1.4 million children and youth were attending these programs in approximately 6,800 schools in 1,597 communities across the country. Federal funding for the 21st CCLC program began at $750,000 in 1995 and had grown to nearly one billion dollars in FY 2003, where it has remained nearly level.

The 21st CCLC program has been referred to as the fastest-growing grant in U.S. history and has created a vast new system of school-linked programs across the continent, which has resulted in the development of models, professional development, research, recognition, and curricula that benefits the broader field. At the same time, 21st CCLC funding comes in the form of grants that last for a limited duration, typically three to five years, and sustainability has been a major challenge. Few programs are open during school vacations or summers, and children may only attend a few hours or days per week, causing challenges for working parents and limiting the effects on participants.

Many states and cities have also joined the afterschool bandwagon, whether for purposes of reducing juvenile crime, moving mothers from welfare to work, or boosting academic test scores. Many states, including Georgia, Maryland, South Carolina, Washington, D.C., New Hampshire, and Delaware, use state dollars to supplement funding for programs, while Californians passed Proposition 49 in 2002, which promises to boost state funds by as much as $550 million. Most large and medium-sized cities have also launched significant afterschool initiatives, including Los Angeles; Columbus, Ohio; Charlotte, North Carolina; Kansas City, Missouri; New York; Detroit; and many others.

Table A.1   The Afterschool Program Landscape

	Education After School	**School-Age Child Care Programs**	**Youth Development Programs**
Major Goals	Improve academic achievement Decrease achieve ment gaps	Supervision for children of working parents Support child development	Promote youth development Prevent risky behaviors
Accountability Framework	State 21st CCLC evaluation measures Changes in test scores	Licensing Accreditation	Outcomes-based evaluation
Primary Staffing	School teachers Paraprofessionals	Child care staff	Youth workers
Major Funding Sources	21st Century Com munity Learning Centers	Child Care Development Fund Parent fees	Philanthropic funding Public crime and drug prevention funding
Primary Population Served	Elementary and middle school students; low-performing students	Elementary school children with working parents	Middle school and high school age youth; often low-income
Hours	Open on days when school is in session; range from 5 days to just a few hours per week	Open 3 or more hours all days when school is in session, full days (8–10 hours) during school holidays and vacations	Typically a few days per week or on weekends/evenings

THE EFFECTS OF PARTICIPATION IN AFTERSCHOOL PROGRAMS

What changes for young people who participate in an afterschool program? One thing is clear from existing research: spending time without adult supervision during the hours after school puts children at risk. Especially likely to end up in trouble—whether in the form of substance abuse, behavioral problems, or school truancy—are young people who are "hanging out" in neighborhoods with their peers.

Beyond safety and reduction of risk, it is less clear exactly how youth benefit from participation in afterschool programs. Despite the expectation that attending an afterschool program will boost student performance, research on the academic effects of afterschool programs has been mixed, with some studies finding benefits for youth in math, reading, and other scores while others find no positive outcomes. In addition, the wide variety of program types, outcomes measured, and methodologies employed make comparison exceedingly difficult.

The major national study of educational afterschool programs, Mathematica's evaluation of the 21st Century Community Learning Centers, had disappointing results for those in the field who promoted afterschool programs as a "silver bullet" answer to low student performance. Seeking evidence of academic effects, the study found little support for afterschool programs as an achievement-booster, although parent involvement did increase, which may lead to positive outcomes in the long run. However, these weak results have been questioned in light of many other studies indicating positive educational outcomes, whether on direct measures such as achievement in reading and/or math or on school-linked outcomes such as attendance and attitude toward school. Researchers attribute this discrepancy to a number of methodological problems, but perhaps most importantly, the fact that the Mathematica study did not take into consideration variations in quality and quantity (hours of service) between programs.

While studies examining the academic effects of afterschool program participation are somewhat mixed, the research literature suggests that afterschool programs are especially suited to promoting the social and emotional skills of young people. Studies have found that participation in afterschool programs can lead to a stronger sense of competence, better social skills, closer connections with adults and school, and enhanced work habits. The youth development literature emphasizes the importance of these attributes for healthy development, while education researchers note the foundational aspect of engagement in learning to long-term school success.

While research points to the potential of afterschool programs to benefit young people, there is less evidence that these positive outcomes are likely to be experienced by most of the young people currently participating such programs. Afterschool programs face daunting challenges in meeting their promise for youth. Given the many challenges, including lack of sustainable funding, low wages, and the part-time nature of afterschool employment, many programs are barely beyond crisis management and have little capacity to plan and implement effective curricula.

ATTRIBUTES OF EFFECTIVE AFTERSCHOOL PROGRAMS

What makes an afterschool program "work?" Research on the quality of effective programs is of very recent origin. It is common sense that low-quality programs are unlikely to produce positive outcomes for youth. Many studies may be mixing low- and high-quality programs and therefore finding little evidence of program effects.

In two studies of elementary school children, Deborah Vandell found that positive interactions between staff and children, as well as between children and peers, were related to successful functioning. A team of researchers from the RAND Corporation reviewed all existing studies of afterschool program quality in 2001. While concluding that there were few studies emulating high scientific standards, the RAND researchers found a number of program practices that the data supported as good indicators of program quality, including a high level of staff training, education, and compensation, low child-to-staff ratio, age-appropriate activities, positive emotional climate, communication with school and families, and community partnerships.

In 2002, the National Research Council published *Community Programs to Promote Youth Development,* which identified eight features of positive developmental settings: physical and social safety; appropriate structure; supportive relationships; opportunities to belong; positive social norms; support for efficacy and mattering; opportunities for skill-building; and integration of family, school, and community efforts. While the National Research Council book bases its recommendations on knowledge about child and adolescent development, an accumulating series of afterschool program research and evaluation studies have been adding to our understanding of how program quality leads to positive outcomes for youth.

More recently, several important studies have attempted to disentangle the complex levels and features of programs that produce positive outcomes for children and youth. The Massachusetts Afterschool Research Study (MARS) obtained information on program characteristics, program quality, and youth outcomes from nearly 4,000 youth between kindergarten and eighth grade attending 78 diverse afterschool programs across the Commonwealth of Massachusetts. Through the use of multilevel modeling, a sophisticated statistical strategy, the researchers found that staff engagement led to youth engagement, which in turn was the critical pathway to youth outcomes. The five youth outcomes included in the study were: increased initiative, better quality homework, stronger relationships with adults, stronger relationships with peers, and better behavior. Programs with highly qualified staff were most successful in producing the high-quality programs that led to good outcomes. Strong leadership in the form of an experienced, educated site director, higher staff compensation, strong connections to schools, good communication with families, and more staff training were also linked to higher program quality in the study.

A six-year evaluation by Policy Studies Associates of projects under the auspices of the After School Corporation (TASC) in New York City included 96 afterschool program sites serving 52,000 participants in a school-based model. A substudy examined the characteristics of 10 afterschool programs that had particularly strong contributions to student's academic performance. Interestingly, these programs were not ones with the greatest focus on academic outcomes, but rather programs that used effective strategies to promote children's development in all areas. The evaluators note five especially important characteristics of such programs: (1) a broad array of enrichment opportunities; (2) opportunities for skill building and mastery; (3) intentional relationship-building; (4) a strong, experienced site manager supported by a trained and supervised staff; and (5) administrative support from the sponsoring agency.

A study sponsored by the Collaborative for Academic, Social, and Emotional Learning (CASEL) provides new insight into the important role played by appropriate, well-implemented curricula. In this meta-analysis of existing high-quality studies, positive outcomes for youth in the areas of personal and social skills were associated with programs' use of four research-based approaches to skill development: sequential, active, focused, and explicit. That is, there is a sequential set of activities designed to build skills, the skills are developed through engagement in active learning, there is at least one program component focus on developing social or personal skills, and the targeted skills are explicitly communicated to all those participating.

Together the MARS, CASEL, and TASC studies provide important insights into characteristics of effective afterschool programs. Programs must have staff with the knowledge and capacity to carry out well-planned, intentional learning activities with youth. Not only that, but they must be able to develop strong relationships with children that build and strengthen over time. Interestingly, the findings for academic and nonacademic outcomes are very similar. In the TASC study, programs that did *not* have a strong academic focus were most successful in raising school performance. What this research suggests is that strong staff and good curricula is necessary for all programs, whatever their intended outcomes.

MANY PURPOSES—ONE PROGRAM?

Many afterschool programs are moving to combine the "best of both worlds," in recognition that if children are to succeed in school, they need strong relationships with adults, motivation to learn, positive behavior, and a sense of mastery, which are all outcomes of high-quality afterschool programs. Afterschool programs that look and feel too much like school aren't likely to benefit children very much, in part because children will have little reason to attend. On the other hand, purely recreational or custodial programs may succeed in keeping children safe, but are otherwise unlikely to benefit them developmentally or academically. Research suggests that the very same qualities promote positive outcomes in all areas of development: highly qualified staff; small group sizes and low ratios that permit the development of strong relationships; and active, intentional, well-planned curricula.

Recent research on how people learn supports these evaluation findings. Learning isn't just a matter of taking in new information; knowledge is organized into conceptual frameworks based on past experience and understandings. Children (and adults) learn by fitting new information into a framework that they have already developed. Afterschool programs, with their relative flexibility in scheduling, content, and accessing community resources, at their best provide fertile ground for building children's background knowledge, deepening their understanding, and broadening their horizons.

The strongest evidence to date suggests that afterschool programs can play a powerful role in children's development, but it is not necessarily the same role that is played by schooling. Afterschool programs rely on different staff, have different hours, and have a great deal more flexibility than schools. The fact that youth often attend programs over several years creates opportunities for strong relationships to develop with adult role models, a key factor in educational success. In addition, the relatively flexible circumstances of afterschool programs can support the best of informal learning modalities, including project-based learning, community service learning, experiential learning, science inquiry-based learning, and the arts. At the same time, in order to reach this potential, programs will need adequate, sustainable financial and institutional resources, which are not typical at this time.

Further Reading: Birmingham, J., Pechman, E., Russell, C. R., & Mielke M., 2005, *Shared features of high-performing after-school programs: A follow-up to the TASC evaluation,* Washington, DC: Policy Studies Associates; Durlak, J. A., & Weissberg, R. P., 2007, *The impact of after-school programs that promote personal and social skills,* Chicago, IL: Collaborative for Academic, Social, and Emotional Learning (CASEL); Halpern, R., 2003, *Making play work: The promise of after-school programs for low-income children,* New York: Teacher's College Press; Miller, B. M., 2003, *Critical hours: Afterschool programs and educational success,* Quincy, MA: Nellie Mae Education Foundation; National Institute on Out-of-School Time and Intercultural Center for Research and Education, 2005, *Pathways to success for youth: What counts in afterschool?* Boston: United Way of Massachusetts Bay; National Research Council, 2000, *How people learn: Brain, mind, experience, and school,* Washington, DC: National Academy Press; Vandell, D. L., Pierce, K. M., & Dadisman, K., 2005, Out-of-school settings as a developmental context for children and youth, in R. Kail (ed.) *Advances in Child Development and Behavior,* Vol. 33, Cambridge, MA: Elsevier Press.

Beth M. Miller

ALTERNATIVE SCHOOLS

We are approaching 50 years since the first alternative schools were launched, and one can point to a number of reforms adopted by mainstream institutions that are fairly directly traceable to alternative schools. Yet these schools have still not attained institutional legitimacy within education, and snide comments are still often tossed their way. For example, the Brooklyn Free School, one type of alternative, earned an Associated Press story in late November 2006. But the title one newspaper gave it was *Free Schools: Anarchy at Work*—hardly a respectful characterization, and particularly for a school that prides itself on being a democratic community. So after almost half a century, the genre—if not all its practices—remains a field of pedagogical contention. Its advocates include some of today's leading names in education, and the same can be said of its detractors.

BACKGROUND

The first alternative schools were sired by the 1960s and carried many of the themes and emphases of that tumultuous decade. Many of these first alternatives, which began outside the public schools, sought to free and liberate children from the stultifying, oppressive institutions in which they claimed to labor, and instead to make schools inviting, fascinating places. Other alternatives focused explicitly on the poor and minority children of the cities and the South and sought to extend the benefits of education to this population. Still others were not so much interested in benefiting individual children as in rebuilding all of society. And people with all three visions of what the fundamental mission of a school should be were starting what came to be called "alternative schools" in the 1960s.

As the 1970s dawned, public school systems began launching their own alternative schools, and although each was unique, they tended to differ systematically according to their locations and circumstances. Those established in affluent communities, for example in suburbs, tended to be the kind of alternative schools created to attract, challenge, and engage able students. They often had innovative curricula and creative teachers who, like their students, wanted something more than traditional schools appeared to offer. These schools often attracted some of the ablest of students, and many were able to claim remarkable achievements on the part of their students and graduates.

The alternatives begun in the inner cities were quite another story. Their mission was to try to bring education to populations that schools customarily had failed. As a result, they were often dealing with students who had little support at home and who needed a great deal of remedial work. These were the first schools for the "at risk," although the appellation didn't come until later and even today is rather rarely claimed by genuine alternative schools, which are more likely to prefer a heterogeneous student population and to share the stance of the principal of one such school who insisted, "It is our school and its way of teaching that is alternative, not our students."

Both sorts of alternative schools sketched above were likely to be launched by people with progressivist leanings. If they were politically inspired, the inspiration was likely to come from the political Left, and if solely pedagogically inspired, from the "pedagogical Left," such as John Dewey or such then-recently emerged gurus as A. S. Neill, John Holt, and Paul Goodman. Not surprisingly, then, it was not long after public schools began establishing alternatives in the late 1960s and early 1970s, before educational conservatives began asking for their own alternatives.

Two books appearing in the early 1970s lent considerable, though indirect, support to the establishing of alternatives of both types—indeed, of all types. Mario Fantini's *Public Schools of Choice* was welcomed in 1973 by espousers of the 1960s sorts of alternatives (of which Fantini, himself, was one). It argued that different youngsters need different kinds of school environments in order to succeed. A year later, David Tyack's *The One Best System* (1974) underscored the arbitrary nature of the assumption that there is any single best way to organize and deliver education. Both books were invoked to urge that alternative schools become the norm and that every public school in effect become the alternative to all the others. The new "best system," in other words, would be marked by enormous diversity as well as by choice, with families selecting the school program and environment they found most compatible.

The alternative schools idea rather quickly proved adaptable to a variety of purposes beyond the several rather diverse ones for which these schools had originally been established. In the early 1970s, the federal government, seeking ways to refashion entire school systems, set up the Experimental Schools Program, which funded three school districts to create multiple alternative schools. Under the program, whole sets of alternatives were established as models for school change, in Minneapolis, Berkeley, and Tacoma.

In 1976, the federal government offered a broader, major stimulus to the alternatives and options idea when it began funding magnet schools under the

Emergency School Aid Assistance Act. Although magnet schools and alternatives are not synonymous, some people tended to see magnets as alternatives created to stimulate voluntary racial desegregation. Despite important organizational differences—with magnets typically inspired by and often controlled by the central office, and alternatives more typically grassroots generated and operated—a number of alternative schools have been funded as magnets.

There have also been a number of federal and state initiatives for alternatives in the interests of preventing school vandalism and violence, juvenile crime and delinquency, and truancy and dropping out. In Hawaii, alternative schools were begun for a somewhat different reason: to address the needs of secondary, at-risk students. Then, in 1994, when a federal court ordered the state's public schools to improve their provisions for children needing mental health services, that served to impose a particular slant on the alternative schools. The State Department of Education rushed to expand what had been a pilot program for special education students into a statewide program for all students, in order to take advantage of the funding opportunities opened by the court order. The pilot program had been designed by a mental health expert, and across the state, today's alternative schools still bear that influence.

TODAY

Alternative education is not as prominent today as it was three or four decades ago. One does not hear as much about it or hear the label as often. Yet it is certainly here. In addition to numerous state organizations, there are two national organizations of alternative school educators, the Alternative Education Resource Organization (AERO), with almost 400 member schools and organizations and an e-newsletter with 7,000 subscribers; and the International Alternative Learning Association (IALA). For the last several years, AERO has held an annual conference with the last one drawing about 350 people from the United States and elsewhere. There is also an annual IDEC, or International Democratic Education Conference, drawing a very similar audience, since "democratic education" is a variant of alternative education, as will be seen below. The IDEC conference, which this year drew 300 attendees, is truly international, being sponsored by a different school, in a different country, each year. So far, the annual meetings have been held in Israel, Japan, Germany, India, the United States, New Zealand, England, Ukraine, Austria, and Australia.

But despite such a widespread following, it appears that alternative schools around the world are often in difficulty. Nowhere, it would seem, have they arrived at institutional legitimacy, and they still often have to struggle against local authorities to remain open.

Why is this the case, with an educational genre that is far from new, and which has, over the years, received tremendous support from foundations and numerous government agencies? One reason is that after almost half a century we still have no accepted definition of alternative schools or alternative education—and a wide range of institutions identifying themselves this way, with the result that failures of one type of "alternative" are erroneously and unfairly attached to a school or program of another sort altogether. This is too bad, because there are striking differences and even contradictions among schools that go by the name "alternative."

ALTERNATIVE SCHOOL TYPES

Three distinct archetypes—with different sources, different missions, and different audiences—can be used to describe alternative school types. The alternatives designed to provide a more challenging and compelling education to students and teachers seeking it are termed Type I alternatives. These are the schools that are likely to be found in affluent communities and populated by middle-class and upper-middle-class students (although perhaps the best known Type I alternatives are among those established in District 4, Manhattan's Spanish Harlem, in the 1970s, where it was the explicit wish of the founder, Deborah Meier, to provide for poor children the kind of education she had enjoyed as a child attending a private progressive school). Education in these schools is highly invitational, with strong emphasis being placed on motivation, and accordingly, it is likely to feature strikingly innovative curricula and instructional methods.

In tone, Type II alternatives are the exact opposite of Type I schools. Whereas those of the Type I variety work at being chosen by those who want to affiliate with them, students (and perhaps sometimes teachers) are "sentenced" to Type II alternatives. Variants of Type II programs include in-school suspension programs, "cool-out" rooms, and longer-term placements for the behaviorally disruptive. Type II programs are assumed to be temporary—at least if successful—and typically offer time off (i.e., a shortened sentence) for good behavior. Behavioral modification is usually the Type II program's focus, and instead of any attempt at a novel educational program, these alternatives often try to have students perform the work of the regular classes. Since many of the students assigned to these programs may be behind academically, Type II alternatives sometimes offer a heavily "basics-oriented" curriculum emphasizing factual knowledge, elementary skills, and rote learning.

Type III programs are typically nonpunitive and more positive and compassionate in orientation. They are designed for students thought to need extra help, remediation, or rehabilitation—academic, social, emotional, or all three. If jail is an apt metaphor for Type II alternatives, therapy seems appropriate for Type III programs. In theory, after sufficient treatment, successful students will be able to return to the mainstream and continue in the regular program. There is no special sort of academic program that is specific to Type III schools, but most reflect an emphasis on the school as community, since such a focus is thought to stimulate social and emotional development. The Hawaii alternative education program described above calls for Type III schools.

Alternative schools are usually identifiable as one or another of these three types, although particular programs may be something of a mix. A compassionate staff, for example, can give a Type II program overtones of Type III, despite official purposes. Or a committed Type III staff may undertake a bit of the programmatic innovation that distinguishes a Type I alternative. But even so, the fundamental type goes far in determining such central features of an alternative school as how its students arrive there (by choice, sentence, or refer-ral); how long they stay and whether or not they can remain to graduate; and how the alternative school itself will be evaluated.

Perhaps most basic of all the differences among the three types is the relation-ship they assume between student behavior and performance and achievement on the one hand, and school program and environment on the other. Type I programs assume that by changing the school, student performance and accom-plishment can be changed. In contrast, both Type II and Type III alternatives assume that the reasons for student misbehavior and failure lie within the in-dividual; so it is the student who must be changed, not the school, in order to bring about improvement.

RECORDS OF THE THREE

Not surprisingly, the track records of the three types of alternatives differ. It is difficult to find any positive evidence for Type II alternatives. They seem to serve no positive purpose for those sentenced to them, only perhaps for rid-ding conventional classrooms of disruptive youngsters. A now classic study of a Florida program assigning students to in-school suspension programs con-cluded that the almost 58,000 such assignments made during one school year had accomplished no positive purpose whatsoever. Comparisons with districts without such programs demonstrated that there was no correlation between having them and lowering dropout, referral, corporal punishment, suspension, and expulsion rates—the problems that Type II alternatives had been launched to solve.

The record of Type III programs is better. Student behavior and accomplish-ment usually improve under the compassionate, supportive conditions these programs provide. However, the improvements are likely to fade once the stu-dent has been returned to the regular school. The studies documenting such outcomes typically conclude that the alternative school the student attended has failed—has failed, that is, to successfully remediate the student—rather than what has been documented, that the student can succeed in an alternative envi-ronment. (Thus, the very evidence documenting the need for such school vari-ants is sometimes read as testimony to their failure.)

The record of Type I programs is quite a different story, sometimes traced all the way back to the famous Eight-Year Study of the 1930s, when the college suc-cess of 1,500 students attending progressive schools was compared with that of 1,500 graduates of conventional high schools. The progressive school graduates earned better grades and more academic honors and displayed more intellec-tual curiosity, higher levels of critical-thinking ability, greater resourcefulness in responding to challenges, and more concern for the world around them. Psy-chologists have also established that autonomy-supportive environments, which Type I alternatives typically constitute, are associated with greater conceptual learning than are more structured and directive environments.

One of the Type I alternative school success stories that is often cited is Central Park East Secondary School (CPESS) in East or Spanish Harlem—a neighborhood where crime, drugs, and violence abound. In the 1990s, five years after its establishment, this school enrolled a population that was 90–97 percent minority, with 60 percent of its students coming from poverty homes. Yet its attendance rates were above city averages and its suspensions below. Ninety-two percent of those who began the school year at CPESS completed it there, compared with 71 percent in other high schools, and there were *no* dropouts from the class that graduated in June 1994. In the 1990s, approximately 90 percent of the school's graduates were going on to four-year colleges.

Although CPESS is clearly an outstanding case, it would appear that a number of Type I alternative schools are outstanding even if less renowned. It is not unusual for researchers and evaluators to receive testimony of amazing individual transformations that such schools have brought about—with youngsters who had detested school suddenly anxious to attend, and poor students suddenly transformed into well-performing ones.

And what is it about a Type I alternative school that could account for such changes? Different advocates tend to locate the crux of success in different features. Thus, some alternative school educators insist it lies in the freedom such schools permit, others attribute their success to their holistic preoccupation, while still others claim it lies in their democratic orientation. There are many varieties of alternative schools. A recent list assembled by the new editor of *Education Revolution* included the following: Montessori, Waldorf, Democratic schools, Quaker or Friends schools, Reggio Emilia schools, charter schools, magnet schools, progressive schools, folk schools, and holistic schools. Core principles for an alternative school are:

- Offers a personalized education for each student with a focus on the academic, social and emotional needs of each, and has systems in place to address those needs as part of daily practice.
- Is chosen by families, students, and staff for its distinct philosophy, culture, mission, and practices.
- Employs authentic assessment of student learning, without sorting or stratifying.
- Has a strong identity shaped by the community it serves.
- Articulates and models shared values.
- Includes and responds to the voices of all its constituents by distributing leadership.
- Is less bureaucratic and more personal than schools generally are.
- Introduces and experiments with pedagogical practices.

If some of these principles sound familiar, it is because they have been picked up and featured by a number of other educational movements. So ironically, although alternative schools themselves may still be the object of battles, considerable parts of what they stand for have been incorporated as features of programs that have won wide acceptance and approval.

Further Reading: Fliegel, S., with MacGuire, J., 1993, *Miracle in East Harlem: The fight for choice in public education,* New York: The Manhattan Institute; Mintz, J., ed., 1994, *The alternative education handbook,* New York: Macmillan; Raywid, M. A., 1995, Alternatives and marginal students, in M. C. Wang and M. C. Reynolds (Eds.), *Making a difference for students at risk: Trends and alternatives* (pp. 119–155), Thousand Oaks, CA: Corwin Press.

Mary Anne Raywid

ALTERNATIVES TO SCHOOLING

The history of deschooling is necessarily tied to the history of compulsory state schooling in the West, which has a surprisingly short trajectory, especially in North America.

The idea that the State should take responsibility for what children must learn has its origins in Platonic theory. In the *Republic* Plato suggested that in an ideal State philosopher-kings would have total control of education, streaming students based on collective needs and perceived abilities. Plato's scheme was entirely theoretical, but at least one Athenian lawmaker, Solon (638–558 B.C.) had already tried to legislate that all freeborn boys would have to learn to swim and play the lyre, but to little avail, and Greek education was a private matter, left to families, tutors, and lyceums.

Throughout the span of the Roman Empire, various emperors attempted to institute mandatory educational reforms, hoping to replicate Athenian intellectual vitality, but with little success. Hadrian (76–138 A.D.) and Marcus Aurelius (121–180 A.D.) were two notable examples who attempted to create common schools for children of peasants and the poor, with mandated curriculums, but these initiatives too fell short, in large part due to jurisdictional diffusion. After the fall of the Roman Empire, there were few significant Western efforts to compulsorize children's education, and it was largely left a private, and typically religious, matter for a millennia.

It is during the Enlightenment that the first real roots of our modern school system find soil. As Western European culture began to pull itself out from the weight of religious hegemony, many prominent intellectuals and writers began to posit that State control of education was the only way to forge a citizenry whose loyalty would be to the nation, not the church. Voltaire, Diderot, Condorcet, Rousseau, and many others began to devise schemes by which the State could direct and organize its subjects, inculcating them with progressive and humanistic ideals and a fidelity to the national good.

Progressives who argued that only with compulsory schools could ideals of equality and equity be disseminated carried much of the argument for what was called national education. The most prominent early opponent was William Godwin, who is also often called the first anarchist. He suggested that governments would hardly fail to use compulsory schools to entrench their power and domination.

One person who was forcefully affected by the arguments for national schools was Napoleon, who set out to transform the French educational system. He began to reorganize schools and universities into replications of military structure, in regiment-sized classes, with work done to the sound of a drum and uniforms for authorized teachers. His argument was that a strong and loyal population could be made, not just hoped for.

This line of thinking was confirmed during the wars of 1806 when Napoleon's army swept through Prussia and destroyed German forces with surprising and humiliating ease. In defeat Prussian leaders began pointing to the French efforts towards national education as one of the key reasons for their humiliation, particularly the comparative cohesiveness and discipline of Napoleon's forces. Prussian intellectuals and leaders quickly began designing a compulsory State-organized education system, which would ensure a knowledgeable, loyal, and compliant citizenry.

Alongside the establishment of a Prussian national school system, the German industrial economy began to recover exceedingly quickly from the ruins of the war, and the first decades of the nineteenth century saw a rapid revival of Prussia: militarily, economically, and culturally. Impressed by the stunning growth, young aristocrats and academics began streaming to Prussia to study the resurgence. Among them was Horace Mann, a young official from Massachusetts who returned to the United States a national education convert and immediately began proselytizing for the establishment of state schooling in America.

Mann was eventually successful, and in 1852 Massachusetts passed the first compulsory education laws in North America. By the 1880s every state in the union had passed similar laws. Compulsory schooling took effect a little more haphazardly in Canada, with Ontario passing legislation in 1871 and BC by 1873, while Quebec and Newfoundland held out until 1943. Since the introduction of national schooling in North America, the system has been founded on four basic premises suggested by R. Koetsch (1997), which remain largely intact today:

1. The State has a responsibility to educate all of its citizens.
2. The State has the right to force all parents to send their children to school.
3. The State has the right to force the entire community—including citizens without school-age children—to support by taxes the education of all children.
4. The State has the right to determine the nature of the education it offers.

This is what we have in front of us in North America: a 150-year-old, Platonically rooted, Prussian-inspired model that is built to support and augment nationalist rationales. It is little surprise then that not only have the best and most coherent critiques of compulsory state school come from anarchists, but also the most compelling alternatives.

RESISTING STATE POWER

Leo Tolstoy in *Tolstoy on Education* once famously claimed that the imaginary characters of his books were far less interesting than real children. A Christian anarchist, Tolstoy established a school in 1859 for peasant children on his estate called Yasnaya Polyana and a journal of the same name, and much of his thinking around education foreshadows contemporary deschooling thought.

Education is the tendency of one man to make another just like himself ... Education is culture under restraint, culture is free. [Education is] when the teaching is forced upon the pupil, and when the instruction is exclusive, that is when only those subjects are taught which the educator regards as necessary. (Tolstoy, 1967, p. 76)

The connection between forced education and state power was made more clearly by Francisco Ferrer, a Spanish anarchist who was interested in building an institution where children were free of hegemonic teaching, state dogma, and religious sentiments. Ferrer was very clear that schools were designed to provide the state with industrial workers, and the intent of his Modern School was to allow children to develop free of race and class prejudice in an atmosphere of free expression as a precursor to a just society. Ferrer founded his school in 1901, and it quickly spread with branches around Spain.

Ferrer's critique of schools was an explicit attack on State power, for which he was executed in 1909, after founding the *International League for the Rational Education of Children* as well as a journal. In 1911 a Modern School was established in Manhattan, with classes during the day for children and lectures at night for adults. Prominent activists including Alexander Berkman, Voltairine de Cleyre, and Emma Goldman were founders, Will Durant was an instructor and principal, and people like Margaret Sanger, Jack London, and Upton Sinclair gave talks. Eventually the school moved to Stelton, New Jersey, and more than 20 similar schools were established around the country.

As the last of these schools was closing its doors in the 1960s, the free school movement, spurred by A. S. Neill's book *Summerhill: A Radical Approach to Child Learning,* was beginning to explode in North America. Neill founded Summerhill in 1921 believing that children need an atmosphere free of fear to genuinely thrive, and that their days should be free of external compulsion. Thus students at Summerhill, which is still running in southern England, are permitted to play as long and as much as they wish and only participate in classes and activities of their own choosing.

Neill's famous line is that children have "freedom, not license" at Summerhill, and the whole school community is governed democratically. That means that all rules and decisions governing daily life are made by the whole group of students and staff together in school meetings. Each person has a single vote, regardless of age, and meetings are run by strict rules. Disputes and individuals who break the rules can be brought in front of the school meeting to have their grievances and/or transgressions heard out and resolved.

This is the basic model of a democratic free school, and its introduction to North America caused a remarkable proliferation; by 1971 there were more than 1,100 free schools across Canada and the United States. There were many variations on the theme, but all built upon Neill's basic recipe of personal autonomy and collective self-governance. The movement did not last long, and by the end of the 1980s there were no more than a few dozen remaining. Interestingly however, there has been a contemporary resurgence of interest in democratic schools, with international networks linking schools across the globe and multiple schools popping up in Russia, Israel, Europe, India, Japan, and Korea, as well as all over North America.

The energy of the free school movement did not evaporate in the 1980s; it transformed itself in new configurations, largely morphing into progressive homeschooling or unschooling, and the creation of learning centers. Much of this was fueled by the writings of John Holt (1923–1985) and Ivan Illich (1926–2002). Holt began his career as a teacher and slowly radicalized, eventually coming to believe that education was the project of people shaping, and that he was against it entirely. Instead he advocated for "self-directed, purposeful, meaningful life and work, and against 'education'—learning cut off from active life and done under pressure of bribe or threat, greed and fear" (Holt, 1976, p. 2). In 1977 Holt started *Growing Without Schooling* magazine to describe and support a kind of homeschooling that wasn't simply parents replicating school curriculums in the home. Thus the term unschooling was born.

Illich articulated the larger cultural repercussions of a society where learning is assumed a scarce resource administered by professional teachers. Illich's critique of modern development took a number of directions, and in *Deschooling Society* he called for the disestablishment of schooling and the deinstitutionalization of learning, calling for self-directed learning occurring in fluid, informal, and local webs. Illich also critiqued notions of schooling itself, suggesting that alternative schools were simply more pleasant routes to the same end: the professionalization of knowledge and the undermining of people's capacity to run their own lives.

Illich's analysis has been the catalyst for many unschoolers, drop-outs, and activists to create community learning centers, or free schools, places built not on a school model, but more like a library, where people of all ages can come together to share resources, take classes, and develop projects without official curriculums or coercive authority. Deschoolers argue that noncoercive learning, that is, learning that is motivated by people's own energy and enthusiasm, leads to deeper academic and intellectual engagement, develops self-reliance, and supports people's confidence in their own capacities, all of which compulsory schooling erodes.

CONTEMPORARY DESCHOOLING MOVEMENT

The contemporary deschooling movement is built on this historical and philosophical ground. Deschoolers represent a wide range of political and philosophical perspectives, and thus their resistance takes equally varied forms, but deschoolers in general support the displacement of monopoly state schools with a wide range of community-based alternatives that might include, but is not limited to: charter schools, alternative schools, learning centers, homeschooling and homelearning, community learning networks, and even traditional and religious schools. The point is not to legislate a certain mode of schooling, but to allow a vast range of options to develop, including the possibility of children and families rejecting schooling altogether. Potential alternatives are intertwined, building and supporting one another to develop a genuine alternative to compulsory schooling.

There is certainly a libertarian thread to the unschooling movement that repudiates any government involvement in schools whatsoever, often coming with calls for a voucher system. Deschoolers are largely disinterested in vouchers, however, believing that they would only replicate existing class inequities. Instead, deschoolers look to community control of resources, whereby public funding would be retained, but with a much wider array of possibilities and clear local control over funding decisions. There is recognition that a broad array of possibilities is needed in a diverse society and that individual children may well shift and move through a variety of scenarios over the years.

Pedagogically, deschoolers seek to deconstruct contemporary conceptions of learning, arguing instead for an equally broad and fluid understanding of how people acquire knowledge, skills, and capacities. Instead of asking how we can accumulate and deposit information in students, we should be asking under what conditions children will thrive, and not the abstract children of theory, but the kids we see and work with every day. And necessarily, those answers are always shifting and contingent, questions that look much closer to parenting than professionalized teaching. Deschoolers question dominant Western beliefs about teaching, building on Paulo Freire's critiques of the "banking method of education" and looking to approaches that emphasize self-direction, often arguing that "the only thing you can teach is yourself," which has a double-edged meaning.

Deschooling is also closely linked with other social movements: ecological, antiglobalization, queer rights, antiracism, vegetarian, vegan, and animal rights, native self-determination, anticolonialism, and much else. Deschoolers tend to see these connections not as ancillary, but as fundamental to deschooling. Resistance to compulsory schooling cannot simply be reduced to an individualist politics or it will simply reproduce or entrench inequality. Deschooling has to be about genuine social freedom: a freedom *to* something, not just from. That something has to be a social vision of collective freedom, which can only be achieved when compulsory state schooling and its attendant pedagogical imperatives are abandoned.

Further Reading: Gatto, J., 2002, *Dumbing us down: The hidden curriculum of compulsory schooling*, Gabriola Island, BC: New Society Publishers; Holt, J., 1976, *Instead of education*, Boston: Holt Publishers; Illich, I., 1999, *Deschooling society*, London: Marion Boyars Publications; Koetzsch, R., 1997, *A Handbook of Educational Alternatives*, Boston: Shambhala Publications; Llewellyn, G., 1998, *The teenage liberation handbook: How to quit school and get a real education*, Eugene, OR: Lowry House Publishers; Tolstoy, L., 1967, Education and culture, in L. Weiner (Trans.), *Tolstoy on education*, Chicago: University of Chicago Press.

Matt Hern

ART EDUCATION

A relatively decorous battle, as school battles go, is being played out among art educators concerning the definition and selection of the art content in K–12 art curricula. It's a battle that has been evolving in its most recent form since the mid-1980s, when art education was helped by considerable infusions of financial support from the Getty Center for Education in the Arts to reconsider the disciplinary boundaries—content and attendant methods—of art education. That late-twentieth-century battle has largely been won—there now seems no question that art teachers should be teaching art history and criticism (and even aesthetics) in addition to how to "make" art. The current battle is more focused on the kinds of imagery appropriate to teaching these disciplines and, behind all of that, the reasons why we should be teaching art at all.

Some observations follow on the issues reflected in the current deliberations and on their implications for both why and how we educate young people to examine their own culture as well as the cultures studied in other subject areas such as literature and social studies. Much of K–12 education is aimed not only at building immediately useful skills but also, ultimately, at developing a lifelong commitment to learning, learning that can be continued both deliberately and accidentally at museums of all kinds. The current battle over art content reflects fascinating differences in the art education community's conceptions of what in today's culture is worthy of our attention.

THE EARLIER BATTLE FOR DISCIPLINE-BASED ART EDUCATION

The argument to move art education from a production-focused, "creativity"-focused, emphasis to a broader definition of education in the arts was articulated by proponents of discipline-based art education, or DBAE, a conception developed by a number of scholars beginning in the 1980s and distilled into some cogent, thoughtful, and often free and broadly disseminated publications funded by the Getty. DBAE seemed revolutionary at the time, a broadening of the conception of "art" that required of art teachers a stronger foundation in art-historical inquiry and in the purposes and techniques of criticism than many had received in their preservice teacher training. DBAE was threatening to many, invigorating to some, but so well endowed by Getty funds that it was able to spread and be learned, tried, assessed, and reported on in print and at small and large conferences. Art educators arguing for a DBAE approach argued that making art, alone, was an inadequate approach to convey the importance and rewards of the language of the visual arts, that in order to make art well, students needed also to have a strong art-history background, be adept in critiquing and assessing art, and be comfortable in discussing issues of aesthetics. Thus, the four disciplines of (in no particular order) art history, aesthetics, art criticism, and art production were the "disciplines" of discipline-based art education. DBAE was promulgated in an astonishingly rich array of resources coming from the Getty—policy publications, handbooks, curriculum guides, and how-to guidelines, presentations at state and national conferences, regional workshops involving K–12 art teachers, practicing artists, art historians, critics, and aestheticians. Sessions at annual meetings of the American Educational Research Association, for example, included K–12 art teachers who had been trained more traditionally as art-production teachers, testifying with slides and curricular examples to the richer and more meaningful art their students were able to produce when able to understand, decode, appreciate, and move beyond the art of mature artists from our own and other times and places. Over the years it became apparent to established art teachers that young children could, in fact, understand and interpret serious art from many cultures, and that their art projects could be far more sophisticated than the worst examples of what a colleague of mine calls the "sparkly bunnies" approach to art-making, a kind of playing with materials that results in representations that may have little or no meaning behind them. Children could indeed respond to Renaissance portraits, Matisse paper cutout compositions, Chinese landscapes, African masks, Native American weavings, and pre-Columbian ceramics with interest, insight, and invention. By the end of the century that just ended, it seems safe to say that the battle for a redefinition of "art education" to include a variety of disciplines exercised in an intertwined and enriching way has been won. Sometimes an art teacher might suggest that students "paint a landscape" without first studying excellent mature examples of landscapes, but that is now, fortunately, quite rare.

TODAY'S BATTLE: "VISUAL CULTURE"

The debate is no longer over whether art criticism is appropriate for the K–12 art curriculum, but rather about what kinds of visual images are worthy of our attention in that curriculum—what kinds of images should be included in the "art history" we address, and what kinds of interpretive skills are required to address whatever imagery we do admit? We are, as another colleague of mine said a few years ago, "beyond DBAE." The current debate is phrased in terms of the role of "visual culture" in the art curriculum, and on what actually constitutes the "visual culture" in "visual culture studies." Freedman, in *Teaching Visual Culture: Curriculum, Aesthetics, and the Social Life of Art*, offers an excellent summary of the argument for using the visual culture in art education, and a large number of current thinkers at the forefront of art education have addressed the topic in various public forums including the NAEA and state art-education meetings as well as NAEA's journal addressed to K–12 teachers. A number of small-group meetings have attempted to define visual culture and to identify what does and does not fall within its purview; generally it has been agreed that the visual culture that merits inclusion as the object of serious study by children includes print advertising, billboards, product packaging and other commercial design, television commercials, television shows, movies, buildings, shop window design, zines, animé and Manga, Web sites, even pop-up ads on the Internet—in short, the consciously designed visual environment. It has been debated whether, in laying out the visual-culture studies field, "garbage on the street" might be included—it is, after all, a visual event, and might be memorable even in terms normally applied to the fine arts (color, area of emphasis, etc.)—but most visual-culture scholars are content to focus instead on more deliberately designed visual experiences.

The current struggle to identify what kind of imagery is appropriate in the school art curriculum takes the form of debates over whether children most need exposure to the fine arts or whether they need skills for interpreting visual compositions of all kinds. Some of the now-convinced DBAE supporters are so fully comfortable with using the fine arts in school that they fear that including contemporary advertising in the art curriculum threatens to dilute the impact of art instruction; adamant visual-culturalists can easily see this adherence to established and traditional art forms as elitist and limited. But it is the success of DBAE that has liberated art educators to think this broadly about the content of the art curriculum, and the most effective use of popular-culture imagery explores this content through precisely the disciplines that DBAE freed us to trust children to be able to master. Thus, we can approach popular-culture imagery with a trained critical eye, can assess its aesthetic value, and can see its place in the history of imagery—can even make insightful comparisons and contrasts between popular-culture imagery and the images from art history textbooks.

We could not have gotten to this point without first having had the success of DBAE: The current interest in visual-culture studies is a chance to apply DBAE methods of inquiry to a body of content that goes well beyond the "art history" defined by DBAE. DBAE's disciplines are now freely used as filters for examining our contemporary visual environment. This extension of the content of art education to include billboards, shop windows, and Web sites is exciting. It is the logical extension of a conception of education that—in all fields—includes children's own everyday experiences as well as the records and experiences of people and civilizations long dead.

WHY THIS BATTLE IS IMPORTANT

The battle for art content is more important than it might seem to non-art educators, whose conceptions of "art" may fit the popular stereotype (things in gold frames or on pedestals), for whom the content of art may have always seemed to be "art" as defined by what museums value, and for whom the notion of a battle for content might seem rather odd, even unnecessary. There is, after all, so much "art" in the world that we scarcely seem to need an even broader range of choices for teaching. There are more fine examples of cultural artifacts than we could ever fully use, and the art in museums reflects a range of media and purposes (celebratory, decorative, ritual, everyday) broad enough to cover virtually every subject connection we might make. That a battle rages over broadening this resource to include advertising and comic books might seem strange, given the serious crises of funding, violence, religious incursions, the distortions fostered by an emphasis on testing, and other quite immediate dangers that face schools.

But the battle over art content is important, and the following are four reasons why, phrased as arguments *for* broadening the content to a definition of "visual culture" that includes popular culture and other sources of compelling visual compositions.

1. *Curriculum content carries signals about the relative value of the content of everyday life.* In other words, the potential "elitism" of a focus solely on Great Art is dangerous not only because students need to know more than

some predetermined canon of great art, but also because including images from their own lives honors their own everyday experience as something worth taking seriously. To exclude familiar images from the study of imagery is to move contemporary imagery to some other, undefined and unstudied, realm.

2. *The visual content of everyday life is rich, stimulating, compelling, and heavily imbued with meaning: It offers rich content in itself, and it demands interpretation.* It is new, ever-changing, looks quite different from the Mona Lisa or Asian landscapes, and needs a language for analysis and critique. But this language already exists in the language of art criticism, which can illuminate the meaning of contemporary visual content partially by making connections between today's visual environment and the vestiges of past visual environments now visible on museum walls. In short, serious exploration of visual culture calls on the skills of assessing fine art and can create useful connections to it.

3. *Most art now considered "fine art" once had another life, and not all fine art started life as fine art.* Much of it started life as decorative embellishment, soup tureens and upholstered chairs, ritual objects, family portraits in private rooms, and burial objects never intended to be seen at all. To study today's practical, public visual design is to study exactly the kinds of objects that could later be declared "art": to study these things is to accord respect to today's objects and to people willing to take them seriously—students themselves. The study of visual culture honors the potential status of familiar things as things that might be valued by future generations for reasons we don't now intend for them. It honors the true life story of things.

4. *The language of the visual arts is a language to which all students should have access, just like the languages of words and numbers, and the visual culture offers countless examples of both effective and less-effective uses of this language: Students need to know how to assess the difference if they are to be responsible consumers of design and visual content.* They can learn this language by studying fine art, but if they limit themselves to fine-art content they can (depending on how teachers define "fine art"—some courses stop decades ago, with the advent of "modern" art) miss the opportunity to learn the contemporary language of art. Just as they read contemporary novels and study current events, students need guidance in learning the contemporary language of the visual.

The current battle over art content, when it takes the form of "fine art" versus visual culture, is also a battle about the purpose of art education itself. Do we teach "art" because we want students to master a repertoire of great images from the past, and some of the skills that those artists used, as a kind of canonical approach to what knowledge is of most worth? Or do we want students to study art because art refers to the rich array of visual choices made by artists and designers throughout time and including the students' own visual environments, and because we want students to have the skills to understand, assess, respond intelligently to, and be able to participate in their own world?

AN INTERPRETATION AND A PREDICTION

The difference between the two approaches is sometimes phrased in those stark terms. However, what we are seeing in this decorous battle is, instead, not a battle so much as an evolution, a metamorphosis of sensitivity on the part of art educators regarding what art images are worth our attention. An art-history textbook once widely in use turned out to be (as was appreciated, much later) focused almost entirely on art by dead white males—painting and sculpture from Europe and America—and "art" was symbolized by a gold-gilt frame. That has changed. Art history, even in high school, now routinely includes what we used to call "non-Western" art (though pre-Columbian Mexico is plainly in the "west," as are Native Americans), and DBAE, for all that it has been criticized as elitist, always did include art from non-EuroAmerican cultures. The debate is now presented as a choice between "museum-quality" imagery and objects (allowing for all kinds of cultures and media), and imagery that includes—without rejecting the things in museums—today's popular culture as well. "Visual culture" will probably win this quiet battle, and someday we may wonder that we ever considered excluding children's real lives from the study of artfulness and its techniques.

The lovely thing about this battle over art content is that if visual-culture studies wins out, the other alternative still exists. Teachers will still be able to focus their attention on the Mona Lisa and Asian landscapes, for these of course will always (we hope) exist. What these more old-fashioned teachers will inadvertently benefit from, of course, is that time keeps marching on, the stockpile of imagery keeps growing, and the Mona Lisa continues to be part of an ever-lengthening and ever-modernizing tradition, one that is available to teachers if they want to use it. And very probably they will indeed want to use it, for the Mona Lisa becomes even more fascinating when she can be compared to a fashion model today, especially since the fashion portrait isn't necessarily "better," only more contemporary, more familiar, more accessible to interpretation. We can always have both.

One last note: This battle over art content may be referred to as a quiet one, a decorous one. This should not imply that the battle isn't vociferous, or heart-felt, or fraught with anger and frustration on both sides—all of these qualities are discernible in the articles, the conference presentations, and especially the private conversations on the subject, on both sides. And art should not be stereotyped as especially decorous or gentle, either, for some of the most powerful visual imagery studied today, especially by visual-culture enthusiasts, is violent and disturbing, including images of war, or natural disasters, of racist perceptions, or graffiti—the world of art is not a decorous world, though the museum setting can make it seem so. What seems decorous in this battle is the shared values behind the deliberative, articulate, impassioned, and well-reasoned cases being made on both sides. Both sides see the art curriculum as a place where students learn essential skills and perspectives not available through other subjects, and both sides agree that a school without art is an incomplete and barren place in which to ask children to spend 12 years. Both sides delight in the visually wonderful, and all seem to agree that the skills promulgated by that earlier battle (over teaching four disciplines of art rather than just one) are skills an educated person should have. The disagreements are not over such fundamentals, and because of this, they seem calm, decorous, more interesting than violent.

Today's battle over art content is one battle in a series of many, the future ones of which we can't now envision. The joy of working in art education lies partly in the joy of constant discovery of new visual forms and of students' abilities to respond to them—and time will not stop this story of change. It is an art educator's job to stay current with the imagery that our and other cultures produce. Cultures produce visual culture, and if we agree that art is a language we need to master, it seems clear that we need to master it completely. Today's battle for a visual-culture definition of art content is a beautiful example of the task that faces all educators—that of teaching our children well about the world they live in now, and preparing them for the world they will live in later, as adults, when today's battling adults have retired and are no longer guiding them.

Further Reading: Boughton, D., Hausman, J., Hicks, L., Madeja, S., Smith-Shank, D., Stankiewicz, M. A., et al., 2002, *Art education and visual culture,* Reston, VA: National Art Education Association; Dobbs, S. M., 1992, *The DBAE handbook: An overview of discipline-based arts education,* Los Angeles: The Getty Center for Education in the Arts; Freedman, K., 2003, *Teaching visual culture: Curriculum, aesthetics, and the social life of art,* Reston, VA: National Art Education Association; Wilson, B., 1997, *The quiet evolution: Changing the face of arts education,* Los Angeles: The Getty Education Institute for the Arts.

Elizabeth Vallance

ASSESSMENT

Classroom assessment in the United States has been strongly influenced by standardized testing. One hundred years ago, "objective tests" were developed for classroom use to correct the problem of unreliability in grading, and for many decades, teacher candidates took courses in tests and measurements to learn how to make classroom tests in the image of standardized tests. Eventually subject-matter experts, troubled by the limitations of objective formats for capturing important learning goals, began to develop alternative assessment strategies that were much more closely tied to ongoing instruction. They also reconceptualized the purpose of classroom assessment to be less about grading and more about improving student learning.

Unfortunately, in recent decades, efforts to improve classroom assessment, such as the "authentic assessment" movement of the early 1990s, have been persistently thwarted by escalating demands from external, high-stakes testing. When teachers feel pressured to "teach to the test" in response to high-stakes accountability tests, one of their most frequent strategies is to make their own tests, quizzes, and worksheets imitate the high-stakes test as much as possible. Moving now into the new century, a research-based reform focused on "formative assessment" in classrooms runs the risk of being subverted because it is easier for school districts to purchase commercially available standardized tests labeled as formative assessments than to invest in curriculum-embedded assessments and necessary teacher professional development.

HISTORIC INFLUENCE OF STANDARDIZED TESTS

The first standardized achievement tests were invented by educational reformers who believed that schools were failing and who wanted scientific measures to force school improvement. Joseph Rice launched the school survey movement and was credited with the invention of the "comparative test," but it was Edward Thorndike who became the "father" of educational measurement because of his far greater influence. Thorndike and his students created the first standard tests, in arithmetic and handwriting, with the intention that the principles of scientific measurement would be used to overcome the "scandalous" unreliability of teachers' examinations found in numerous studies. Thus, Thorndike worked to bring standardized, objective formats into the classroom. At the same time, he was also working to develop the statistical machinery underlying IQ testing and contributed to the measurement of individual differences. It is no surprise, then, that the formats of standardized achievement tests shared much in common with IQ tests.

A TIMELINE OF IMPORTANT EVENTS IN THE DEVELOPMENT OF CLASSROOM ASSESSMENT

1908: Edward Thorndike published the first standard test, the Stone Arithmetic Test, to overcome the "scandalous" unreliability of teachers' examinations.

1929: G. M. Ruch published *The Objective or New-Type Examination*, which became a model for tests and measurement textbooks for teachers to learn about classroom tests.

1983: *A Nation at Risk* and the Back-to-Basics Movement intensified the use of standardized test formats in classrooms as teachers began to "teach to the test."

1985: Marie Clay developed "running records" to assess decoding errors and comprehension during oral reading. Other subject-matter experts also developed alternatives to standardized tests for classroom purposes.

1989: The National Council of Teachers of Mathematics emphasized the importance of conceptual understanding in mathematics learning and refocused the purpose of assessment on diagnostic feedback and the improvement of instruction.

1989: Grant Wiggins used the term "authentic" test to argue that assessments should more fully represent the intended outcomes of a discipline.

1989: In Australia, Royce Sadler introduced a model of formative assessment, arguing that students needed feedback that would help them internalize the features of quality work.

1998: Paul Black and Dylan Wiliam published their famous review of research showing that formative assessment can be an effective intervention to improve student learning.

2000: Lorrie Shepard argued that formative assessment would not work unless classrooms could move from a "grading culture" to a "learning culture."

2001: The No Child Left Behind Act has exacerbated the negative effect of standardized testing on classroom practice, making it more difficult to support teachers in developing new formative assessment strategies. Test publishers have worsened this problem by selling interim standardized tests to districts and calling them "formative assessments."

From the beginning, critics complained that objective tests measured facts instead of reasoning, but measurement experts, who had the upper hand, countered by saying that there was a strong correlation between measurement of information in a field and the ability to think in the material of that field. Thorndike himself acknowledged three criticisms to be answered. First, it was feared that official measurements would cause students to work for marks instead of real achievement. To solve this problem, he argued that we should have measures worth working for. Second, it was said that teachers should be working to improve achievement rather than measuring it, but Thorndike argued that all but the most gifted teachers are aided, not hindered, by instruments to measure progress. Third, he acknowledged the fear that only the "baser parts of education can be counted and weighed." Thorndike called this fear groundless, however, and answered with his famous article of faith, "Whatever exists, exists in some amount," and therefore can be quantified.

From the early 1900s through the 1980s, Thorndike's view of what teachers should know about testing predominated in teacher-preparation programs. Teachers took "Tests and Measurement" courses with a heavy emphasis on statistical procedures and the skills needed to construct formal tests for the purposes of grading. Although measurement textbooks included a chapter on essay tests, greater attention was paid to objective formats—true-false, matching, and multiple-choice. Item analysis and technical aspects of test construction were emphasized. Traditional measurement textbooks affirmed the need to design tests to reflect instructional objectives, but because tests were intended to be administered at the end of instructional units, no attempt was made to connect them to instructional activities or to help teachers know what to do when students performed poorly.

AUTHENTIC ASSESSMENT AND REFORMS
BY SUBJECT-MATTER EXPERTS

In the 1980s, subject-matter experts began to develop alternatives to standardized tests for classroom purposes. These efforts can be seen as a revolt against the increasing strong influence of standardized tests following *A Nation at Risk* and the basic skills movement. However, more fundamental changes were also taking place at that time in conceptions of learning and achievement. Because of the "cognitive revolution" there was a growing awareness of the need for sense making on the part of learners and the need to connect instruction to students' developing understandings. Real-time assessments would play a key role in helping to make these connections.

In reading, researchers working from an emergent literacy perspective, focused much more on observing and supporting children's developing skills during normal activities, rather than on measuring isolated skills under standard conditions. In place of old theories, which saw learning as the accumulation of small, decontextualized bits of knowledge, new theories of learning suggested that children come to understand what reading is for and how to participate in literacy activities *before* mastering specific skills. For example, a child demonstrates important pre-literacy skills if she scribbles and then tells her mother what the scribbles "say" or turns an upside-down book right-side-up and opens it from the front. Instead of using readiness tests to determine the fit of children to a pre-specified school program, informal observations in the context of real-world tasks can help the teacher see what each child is ready to learn based on emerging skills. Marie Clay, a well-known teacher and researcher from New Zealand, developed a note-taking technique called "running records" that teachers can use to record specific types of errors and self-corrections during normal reading groups or in periodic one-on-one sessions. By analyzing the patterns of errors, teachers can determine whether a child needs help with medial vowels or should be reading an easier text with a focus on comprehension and meaning making.

In the mathematics community, learning mathematics was redefined as a process of inquiry and reasoning that involves looking for patterns, formulating and representing problems, making connections, and applying a variety of strategies to solve problems. In 1989, The National Council of Teachers of Mathematics (NCTM) developed *Curriculum and Evaluation Standards for School Mathematics* to move curriculum and instructional practices away from memorization and mindless use of algorithms toward conceptual understanding and discourse practices that would engage students in explaining their thinking. Correspondingly assessments needed to change to capture the kinds of thinking processes and application of skills envisioned by the reforms. The contrast between test questions from early in the twentieth century and the assessment tasks, which appeared in the Dutch National Mathematics Exam in 2002 (see pages 48–49), reflect the significant changes that have occurred in both the conception of mathematics and the character of assessment tasks. NCTM reformers also refocused the purpose of assessment, emphasizing the need to provide rich diagnostic feedback and evidence to improve instruction rather than merely evaluating achievement.

Table A.2 Examples of Test Questions from Standardized Achievement Tests Published Early in the Twentieth Century

Cooperative General Mathematics Tests for College Students, Form 1934

28. How many axes of symmetry does an equilateral triangle have?   (   )
29. Eight is what per cent of 64?   (   )
30. Write an expression that exceeds M by X.   (   )
31. Solve the formula $V = \dfrac{Bh}{3}$ for h.   (   )

Sones-Harry High School Achievement Test, 1929

SECTION G. MATHEMATICS
IMPORTANT THEOREMS IN GEOMETRY

Directions: In the parentheses after each geometric condition given below in Column 2, write the number of the results in Column 1 that can be proved by it.

COLUMN 1 (RESULTS)	COLUMN 2 (CONDITIONS)	
1. angles equal	66. If two opposite sides are equal and parallel	( )
2. triangles congruent	67. If perpendicular to the same line	( )
3. triangles similar	68. If the sides are proportional	( )
4. lines perpendicular	69. If they have equal arcs	( )
5. lines parallel	70. If side-angle-side equal side-angle-side respectively	( )
6. quadrilateral is a parallelogram	71. If they are parallelograms with equal bases and altitudes	( )
7. parallelogram is a rectangle	72. If their central angles are equal	( )
8. two arcs equal (in same or equal circles	73. If a tangent is drawn to the radius at a point of contact	( )
9. two chords equal (in same or equal circles	74. If corresponding parts of congruent triangles	( )
10. areas of polygons equivalent	75. If one angle is a right angle	( )

In 1989, Grant Wiggins introduced the term "authentic test" to refer to this idea that tests should more directly "embody" and "evoke" desired outcomes in their real-world contexts. Building on examples from the arts and athletics, Wiggins argued that it would be legitimate to teach to an authentic test because then we would be coaching or supporting students to engage in the actual performances that we want them to be good at. Wiggins was most interested in changing classroom assessment practices by using projects, portfolios, exhibitions, and the like so that students would be engaged in the actual work of the discipline and would learn to internalize the criteria of excellent work. Other reformers at the same time applied the idea of authentic performance assessments to external accountability tests because of their significant impact on classroom practices. Lauren Resnick coined the phrase "You get what you assess" and demonstrated the harm to instruction of using indicators that only correlate with the real learning goals. For a short time in the early 1990s, a number of

A SAMPLE MATHEMATICS ASSESSMENT TASK FROM THE DUTCH NATIONAL MATHEMATICS EXAMINATION USED IN MATHEMATICS REFORM WORKSHOPS IN THE UNITED STATES

A campground has a large lawn with a soccer field that measures 100 × 50 meters. The park manager decides to keep the field open at night.

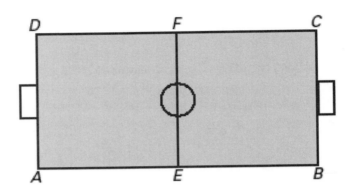

Therefore, a decision needs to be made about where to place some light posts. Standard lamp posts are 13 meters high and light a circular region with a radius of 50 meters.

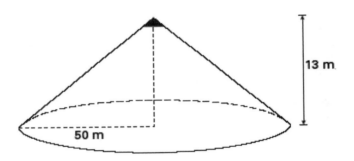

1. The diagram below shows the lighting of the field when lights are placed at points D and B. What is the area of the soccer field that is NOT lit when these two light posts are used? Show your work.

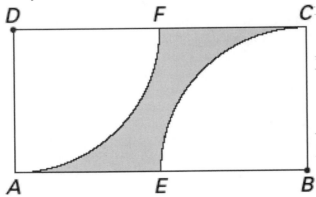

For soccer tournaments, the entire field must be lit and so more lights are needed. However, the Figure below shows that even with four lights the soccer field is not completely lit. The radius of each "circle of light" is too small.

2. How large must the radius of the "circles of light" be to light the entire soccer field with four light posts?

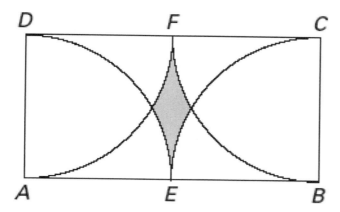

3. A decision is made to increase the height of the lampposts rather than purchase extra lights. To light the entire field with four lights, what height should be used for the light posts? (If you were not able find an answer to question 2, use a radius of 58 meters.)

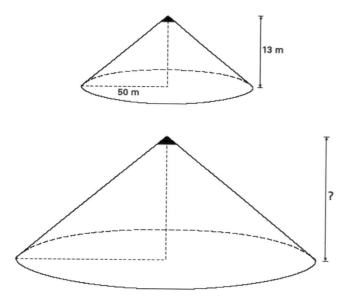

Note: Cito, 2002, Verlichting op het voetbalveld (Lighting on the football field), in Cito (Ed.), *Wiskunde Examen VBO-MAVO-C (National Mathematics Exam: Level VBO-MAVO-C)*, Arnhem, The Netherlands: Cito. Reprinted with permission.

states developed more open-ended and challenging assessments. Many introduced writing assessments. Two states even implemented portfolio assessments. However, many of these reforms have since been eliminated because of their greater cost and the mandate to test more subjects and more grade levels.

RESEARCH-BASED FORMATIVE ASSESSMENT

Subject-matter experts in the United States understood that assessment reforms required changes not only in the content and form of assessment tasks but also in the way that assessments are used. To policymakers and the majority of educators, however, authentic assessment reforms looked mostly like a change in the content of high-stakes tests and a shift from norm-referenced to standards-based reporting metrics. In contrast, reformers in other countries looked to the research literature on learning and motivation to identify features of classroom assessment that were known to support student learning; and they made a concerted effort to convince policymakers that improving "formative assessment" in classrooms could be an effective tool for increasing student achievement.

Again in New Zealand, in 1988, Terry Crooks conducted an extensive review of research in educational measurement, motivational psychology, cognitive science, and research on teaching to determine the effect of classroom evaluation practices on students. To no one's surprise, he found that classroom tests and grading practices shape students' judgments about what is important to learn and affect students' self-perceptions of competence. More significantly, Crooks also reached the following conclusions from his research synthesis: (1) Greater learning occurs when assessments focus on deep learning rather than surface or memorization approaches to learning; (2) Feedback that helps students see how to improve is much more important for learning than is maximizing the reliability of summative assessments; (3) Cooperative learning contributes to students' active engagement and helps to develop valuable peer and self-assessment skills.

In Australia in 1989, Royce Sadler developed a model of formative assessment in classrooms. Sadler was trying to show why students so often failed to improve even when teachers provided accurate feedback. He argued that it was insufficient merely to point out what students had done wrong. For assessment to be *formative,* literally to *form* new learning, a student must:

- Come to hold a concept of quality roughly similar to that of the teacher.
- Be able to compare the current level of performance with the standard.
- Be able to take action to close the gap.

Sadler addressed both the cognitive aspects of learning, that is, helping the student understand the qualities of good work and how to make changes in their own work to move closer to the goal—but he also emphasized that successful learning required that students develop intelligent self-monitoring skills and take increasing responsibility for their own learning.

In England, Northern Ireland, Scotland, and Wales, also in 1989, a task group of the British Educational Research Association was formed, initially to study new national testing programs and their impacts on schools and classroom practices. Later this group became the Assessment Reform Group and focused much more on the link between assessment in classrooms and teaching and learning. The Assessment Reform Group commissioned the now famous review by Paul Black and Dylan Wiliam on formative assessment, published in 1998. In their comprehensive review, Black and Wiliam brought together research from a wide variety of areas including motivational research on self-perception and goal orientation, discourse, teacher questioning, and mastery learning. They focused especially on studies demonstrating the characteristics of effective feedback, namely studies where feedback was focused on features of the task rather than the goodness or badness of the individual and where it gave students specific information about how to do better. They also identified student self-assessment as a critical component of formative assessment. Self-assessment in the studies with positive outcomes did not mean helping the teacher with grading. Rather, self-assessment is beneficial for learning, following Sadler's ideas, when it helps students develop a clear understanding of the learning targets and helps them gain experience evaluating their own work in light of quality criteria.

Impressively, Black and Wiliam showed that formative assessment, used in the way described by the research, produced positive learning improvements compared to controls of .4 to .7 standard deviations. (Because studies use a variety of different outcome measures, it is helpful to report results in standard units. These standard units compared to controls are called *effect sizes*.) An effect size of .4 standard deviations is a large effect compared to other educational interventions designed to improve achievement. It would mean, for example, that an average student at the 50th percentile would instead be performing at the 64th percentile because of the improvement in teaching and learning. Black and Wiliam worked to convince policymakers that formative assessment could be used to improve student learning in contrast to national testing programs, which merely document rather than help school achievement. They published *Inside the Black Box: Raising Standards through Classroom Assessment* in an effort to help policymakers understand that tests aimed at outcomes would not ensure gains unless supports were also put in place to improve what goes on in classrooms.

There are additional elements of effective assessment practices identifiable from the cognitive science literature. For example, we now know that learning occurs when students make sense of new experiences and ideas and connect them to existing understandings. Therefore, effective instructional strategies build on what students already know, which requires assessment of *prior knowledge*. Rather than a score on a pretest, however, prior knowledge assessment may be invisible to students. It involves questioning or other classroom routines to draw out students' relevant knowledge; and it requires that teachers develop a *qualitative* understanding of students' existing conceptions. Teaching for *transfer* also has implications for assessment. When students first begin to understand a new idea, their knowledge is superficial and fragile. Teachers foster limited and nonrobust learning when they rely on repetitive formats and only ask students to demonstrate their learning in one, familiar way. To build deeper and more principled understandings, teachers should regularly ask students to extend what they just learned to a new context and should engage them in conversations about the underlying principle that let them generalize from one application to the next.

Beyond specific, cognitively based strategies, is the call for a fundamental shift in the purpose of assessment and how assessment insights are used. To move from a "grading culture" to a "learning culture," we have to change the social meaning of evaluation. Because of the paramount importance of grades, students worry about what will be on the test rather than thinking about learning. They finish assignments to "be done" and don't expect to use knowledge again. They have learned to pretend competence and hide their confusion from the teacher. The older the students, the more ingrained these negative habits have become. To change these cultural practices requires a consistent refocusing of classroom activities to be explicitly about learning. For example, a well-known prior-knowledge assessment tool is Donna Ogle's K-W-L technique, where teachers ask students to post on a chart what they already *know* (K) and, through discussion, establish what they *want* (W) to learn. At the end of the activity students discuss and summarize what they have *learned* (L). Perhaps it seems obvious, but classroom routines such as this help students think about the learning purpose of an assignment, and over time can help students develop self-monitoring skills. Similarly, the research on feedback shows that feedback is effective when it is specific about ways to improve. This means, however, that classroom practices have to allow regularly for students to use the feedback they receive either by redoing an assignment or by attending to the same features in the next assignment. Feedback given only at the end of a unit of study is more about justifying grades than about fostering improved performance.

Lev Vygotsky was a Russian psychologist who lived from 1896 to 1934. His cultural theory of development has had great influence on present-day learning research, and it provides a coherent way of thinking about the cultural shifts needed in classrooms to enable effective formative assessment practices. Children develop their abilities to think and reason in the same way that they learn language, gestures, interpersonal behaviors, and attitudes—through their social interactions with family and community. In various learning contexts—talking at the dinner table, helping in the kitchen, doing math in classroom—learners have both expert models and supports from adults or peers to enable them to participate in that activity and increase their competence. This theory from Vygotsky of socially mediated learning and internalization has had a profound effect on reforms in nearly every field of study. Mathematics and science reforms have students explain their reasoning to develop deeper conceptual understanding but also to help students practice reasoning from evidence. In literacy instruction, classroom routines like "author's chair" help students think about ways to improve their story, but also help them try out the roles of author and critic. An important aspect of today's sociocultural theory based on Vygotsky's insight is that motivation and cognitive development are no longer separated. At the same time that they are developing specific skills, children are also taking on the identity of an author, a scientist, and a capable learner.

Vygotsky also developed the concept of the *zone of proximal development* to help describe how it is that adults and peers help support a learner in becoming more competent. The zone of proximal development is the space between what a student can do independently and what he or she can do with assistance. Teachers are now familiar with the term *scaffolding,* which refers to the supports teachers provide to the learner during problem solving to enable successful completion of a task. The teacher or adult does not do the task for the student but may modify the task or ask leading questions to help the student complete the task in a meaningful way. Consistent with apprenticeship models of learning, these supports are gradually removed so that eventually the student can perform independently. Sadler's model of formative assessment can be thought of using these same ideas. Formative assessment provides insights about a learner's current understanding and involves the teacher and learner jointly in figuring out how to close the gap between the learning target and current performance. According to Sadler, the teacher could help the student internalize quality criteria by translating them "from latent to manifest and back to latent again" until these criteria become "so obviously taken for granted that they need no longer be stated explicitly." As was stated previously, Sadler saw that the ability to self-monitor was an important aspect of developing competence in a field of study.

RESEARCH-BASED GRADING PRACTICES

Summative assessment and grading pose a serious threat to the learning purposes avowed for formative assessment. As we have already seen, if tests diverge from valued goals, students focus only on the graded portion of the curriculum. Thus it is essential that the work and tests that determine students' grades be conceptually aligned with rich and authentic learning tasks and criteria that have been a part of ongoing classroom instruction. Summative assessments used for grading can be thought of as important milestones on the same learning continua that undergird formative assessment. These can be thought of as *achievement-based grading* to distinguish them from grading practices based on effort or improvement. Unfortunately, a quick Google search indicates that many educators use the term achievement-based grading as a synonym for norm-reference grading, which has well-known negative impacts on student motivation. Perhaps a better term is *standards-based grading,* requiring that grades reflect attainment in relation to substantive standards of performance. A commitment to standards-based grading would mean doing away with compliance grading used to control student behavior and extra-credit points unrelated to learning goals. Other ways to soften student and parent worries about grades can be allowed as long as they provide opportunities for students to demonstrate mastery, for example, by using replacement assignments or throwing out test scores when mastery of a particular learning objective is verified by later assessments.

Of equal importance to the substantive basis for grades is their impact on students' motivation to learn. In the research literature on motivation, an important distinction is drawn between intrinsic and extrinsic motivation. We know that extrinsically motivated students work toward "performance goals"— to get good grades, to please the teacher, and to appear competent. In contrast, intrinsically motivated students, or students with a learning orientation, work toward "learning goals"—to feel an increasing sense of mastery and become competent (as opposed to appearing competent). Learning-oriented students are more engaged in schoolwork, use more self-regulation, and develop deeper understanding of subject matter. Importantly, learning versus goal orientations are not fixed student attributes but can be created or elicited by different learning environments. In her major review of motivation research completed in 1996, Deborah Stipek concluded that normative grading practices and the use of grades as rewards contribute to the development of a performance orientation. She cited in particular a series of studies undertaken by Ruth Butler in which normatively determined grades resulted in lower interest, less willingness to persist, and lower performance compared to students who received substantive feedback. Thus, there are strong parallels between the types of feedback that improve both cognitive development and student motivation.

CONCLUSION

Formative assessment holds great promise for significantly improving student learning. A compelling body of research shows us specifically how it works—by eliciting and building on prior knowledge, by helping students internalize the features of good work, by providing specific guidance about how to improve, and by engaging students in a classroom culture focused on thinking and reasoning and becoming more competent. Despite the best efforts of curricular reformers, however, new research-based conceptions of subject-matter learning have not easily displaced traditional teaching practices. Thus, teachers will clearly need consistent support to develop the knowledge and skills needed to carry out formative assessment practices in the ways envisioned by the literature. Marie Clay's literacy assessment practices, fully embedded in instructional routines, are an encouraging example because they illustrate how a substantial rethinking and shift in practice can occur. Efforts to improve teachers' classroom assessment practices are most likely to be effective and coherent if they are closely tied to standards-based curriculum and instructional reforms in each subject area.

Authentic assessment and formative assessment reforms represent significant efforts intended to correct the negative effects of standardized testing. Unfortunately the forces that work to maintain the dominating influence of standardized testing are quite powerful. The passage of the No Child Left Behind Act in 2001 only exacerbated the negative effect of standardized testing on classroom practice and has left very little room for the development of formative assessment expertise. As before, the high stakes attached to test results encourage teachers to ignore subjects that aren't tested and to teach reading and mathematics in ways that closely imitate the test. Most recently, test publishers have invented new products to help in the flurry to raise test scores. Interim or benchmark assessments can now be given three or four times per year to identify students at risk of failing to meet the proficiency standard at the end of the year. By design, these official instruments imitate the end-of-year test but for ease of scoring use only multiple-choice questions. From the sheer amount of testing we might imagine students' images of subject matter shifting toward the knowledge conceptions evident in tests 100 years ago. Sometimes publishers use the term "formative assessment" to refer to these interim or benchmark tests, but that would be a misnomer because they reflect none of the features of formative assessment described in the research literature. Investments in this type of product only exacerbate the effects of standardized testing on classrooms and undermine the chances for truly important research-based reforms to occur.

Further Reading: Black, P., & Wiliam, D., 1998a, Assessment and classroom learning, *Assessment in Education: Principles, Policy, and Practice, 5*(1), 7–74; Black, P., & Wiliam, D., 1998b, *Inside the black box: Raising standards through classroom assessment,* London: Department of Educational and Professional Studies, King's College; Clay, M. M., 1993, *An observation survey of early literacy achievement,* Portsmouth, NH: Heinemann; Crooks, T. J., 1988, The impact of classroom evaluation practices on students, *Review of Educational Research, 58*(4), 438–481; National Council of Teachers of Mathematics, 1989, *Curriculum and evaluation standards for school mathematics,* Reston, VA: Author; Sadler, R., 1989, Formative assessment and the design of instructional assessments, *Instructional Science, 18,* 119–144; Shepard, L. A., 2000, The role of assessment in a learning culture, *Educational Researcher, 29*(7), 4–14; Stipek, D. J., 1996, Motivation and instruction, in D. C. Berliner & R. C. Calfee (Eds.), *Handbook of educational psychology* (pp. 85–113), New York: Simon & Schuster Macmillan; Thorndike, E. L., 1922, Measurement in education, in *Twenty-first yearbook of the National Society for the Study of Education, Part I* (pp. 1–9), Bloomington, IL: Public School Publishing; Wiggins, G., 1989, Teaching to the (authentic) test, *Educational Leadership, 46*(7), 41–47.

Lorrie Shepard

BILINGUAL EDUCATION

Miriam Amanda Ferguson, known as Ma Ferguson, the first woman governor of Texas some 75 years ago, became involved in a debate about which languages should be used in teaching Texas school children. "If English was good enough for Jesus Christ, it's good enough for me," she said. This statement characterizes the seemingly irrational view many Americans have of English. Just like motherhood, justice, freedom, democracy, and apple pie, it seems that English has become a central symbol of American culture.

Many view English, especially reading and writing, as the prerequisite that allows both native-born and immigrant students' participation in schools, socialization into society, ability to learn, and academic and professional success. Many believe that the learning of English is a basic requirement of citizenship for immigrants; their democratic responsibility. Many secondary teachers argue that English should be a prerequisite for entrance into their classes and are convinced that English should be a prerequisite for immigration. Issues relating to the use of languages other than English in the United States have become both contentious and politically charged. English has become so central that some states have passed English-only laws, and the group called U.S. English has organized to lobby for an amendment to the U.S. Constitution that would establish English as the official language. In 1998, 63 percent of the voters in California supported an anti-bilingual proposition called Proposition 227. Arizona has also passed a similar law. In the mid-term election of 2006 voters of Arizona voted 849,772 (66 percent) to 295,632 (26 percent) in favor of Proposition 103 to make English the official language and businesses to enforce the measure. (See http://englishfirst.org/ for an interesting view of English.)

The passage of the law in California in 1998 neither made the advocates of English-only happy nor did it eliminate bilingual education.

> The bilingual lobby is now simply defying the law. A front-page story in the *San Francisco Chronicle* headlined "Educators Working Around Prop. 227" reports that "in many Bay Area school districts, bilingual education lives." When kids got back to school "they found bilingual education waiting for them." The bilingual-education director in Contra Costa County defiantly said, "If a child is very limited in English proficiency, we will offer [native] language instruction. It's essentially the same as what we offered last year. (Amsell & Moore, 1998, p. 2)

The mere mention of bilingual instruction disturbs many Americans. Those who speak English as a Second Language (ESL) are seen as the culprits of lower reading scores in many jurisdictions. Unfortunately, students who speak languages other than English at home are less likely to succeed in schools. Spanish-speaking students are less likely to complete high school than English speakers and are also less likely to go on to university. Immigrants enrolled in secondary school English-only programs do not do well academically, and they drop out at alarming rates. Such students could be helped in their studies by some kind of support in their first languages. The political climate is such, however, that the use of languages other than English or bilingual instructional programs causes general societal and governmental angst. History, however, reveals that the United States is a country of diversity that has welcomed people who speak many different languages. How then, has it transpired that English-only is considered by so many as the only way; the American way?

NOT ALL OF THE FOUNDING FATHERS WERE ENGLISH SPEAKERS

The earliest European colonists to America were English speakers. However, by 1776 there were thousands of German settlers in what became the states of Pennsylvania, Maryland, Virginia, New York, and Ohio. The Continental Congress produced German versions of many of its proclamations. H. Kloss, in *The American Bilingual Tradition* (1998), notes that "the most important German publication of the Continental Congress was the German edition of the Articles of Confederation, which had the title: 'Artikel des Bundes under der immerwährenden Eintracht zwischen den Staaten'" (p. 28). And the recognition of the German language was also a recognition of "a strong and enthusiastic participation of most of the German minority in the armed rebellion" (p. 28).

According to Kloss, the Third Congress was asked in 1794 by individuals from Virginia to print copies of federal laws in German. This issue did not come up for a vote until 1795, when it lost, 41 to 42. Kloss notes these events gave rise to the "Muhlenberg legend." The legend is that the Congress wanted to make German rather than English the official language of Congress, and Muhlenberg, the Speaker of the House, "thwarted" the action (p. 30). Kloss concludes that this is not true. It is true, however, that the first Constitutional

Convention in the State of Pennsylvania on July 26, 1776, published records in German. Therefore, the use of German in state business is as old as the state itself.

BILINGUAL INSTRUCTION: AN AMERICAN TRADITION

The State of Ohio first authorized German-English instruction in 1839. Laws authorized French and English programs in Louisiana in 1847 and Spanish and English in the territory of New Mexico in 1850. By the end of the 1800s nearly a dozen states had established bilingual programs in languages such as Norwegian, Italian, Cherokee, Czechoslovakian, and Polish. Reports revealed that about 600,000 students were receiving some or all of their education in German. During the years before the First World War there were thousands of students enrolled in bilingual classes. Subjects such as mathematics and history were taught in students' first languages. However, it appears that the First World War signaled a hardening of attitudes toward instruction in languages other than English. This negative view appears to have been solidified during the Second World War and did not change substantially until the 1960s. It is important to note that immigrant students did not do so well in their studies by being immersed in English-only programs. During the later 1800s and early 1900s immigrant students did considerably worse than their English-speaking classmates.

> Immigrant groups did much worse than the native-born, and some immigrant groups did much worse. The poorest were Italians. According to a 1911 federal immigration commission report, in Boston, Chicago, and New York 80% of native white children in the seventh grade stayed in school another year, but 58% of Southern Italian children, 62% of Polish children, and 74% of Russian Jewish children did so. Of those who made it to the eighth grade, 58% of the native whites went on to high school, but only 23% of the Southern Italians did so. In New York, 54% of native-born eighth-graders made it to ninth grade, but only 34% of foreign-born eighth-graders did so. (Olneck & Lazerson, 1974, pp. 453–482)

By the mid-1940s bilingual education had become unpopular in general, and it seems that an anti-German response was likely responsible.

THE EXCITING 1950S AND 1960S

The space age was launched on October 4, 1957, by the Union of Soviet Socialist Republics (USSR). This first successful launching of Sputnik I was followed by the launch of Sputnik II on November 3. A great feeling of failure became part of the American "psyche," and a general angst focused Americans' attention on how Russia could have been first. The schools became the target for critics who believed they were not producing the scientists required to keep America first in technology and science. In 1963, H. G. Rickover wrote *American Education: A National Failure.* As a result of his efforts, a focus turned to developing students trained to be scientists. However, in the early 1960s hundreds of thousands of Spanish-speaking Cubans arriving in Florida resulted in a resurgence of and a refocus on bilingual education in an environment of the drive for civil rights.

BILINGUAL EDUCATION REDUX

Systematic bilingual programs in the United States appeared in Dade County in Florida after the influx of thousands of Spanish-speaking Cubans. These bilingual programs were designed to be transitional; that is, the first language was used to support students until their English skills developed and they could learn in English. The majority of students' early education in this model was conducted in first language, with a daily "period" reserved for English instruction. Students began to transition to English after they had attained a degree of English proficiency. These programs came to be known as transitional bilingual education, or TBE. It is interesting to note that in 1968 Governor Ronald Reagan signed into law California Senate Bill 53 that allowed the use of other instructional languages in California public schools. Like other Republicans in the 1960s he was a proponent of bilingual instruction.

Congress passed the Bilingual Education Act (known as Title VII) in 1968. The act specified that individuals who "come from environments where a language other than English has had a significant impact on their level of English language proficiency; and who, by reason thereof, have sufficient difficulty speaking, reading, writing, or understanding the English language" should be provided bilingual programs. All programs had to provide students "full access to the learning environment, the curriculum, special services and assessment in a meaningful way." Congress did not provide funding for Title VII. However, subsequently it provided support, and 27,000 students were served by Title VII–funded programs. The bill encouraged instruction in a language other than English, primarily Spanish.

BILINGUAL PROGRAMS GAIN SUPREME COURT BACKING

The U.S. Supreme Court in 1974 concluded that all students had the right to access to educational programs in schools and that an individual's first language (L1) was a key to such access. The decision is referred to as *Lau v. Nichols*. The decision included a number of comments, however, and one significant one was, "Basic English skills are at the very core of what public schools teach. Imposition of a requirement that, before a child can effectively participate in the educational program, he must already have acquired those basic skills is to make a mockery of public education." Title II of the Educational Amendments Act of 1974 mandated that language barriers were to be eliminated by instructional programs. School districts were required to have bilingual programs. The new teachers were told was that any group that had 20 or more speakers was to be provided bilingual programs.

The situation was tense. Budget cutbacks forced some school districts to lay off teachers. However, bilingual teachers were exempt from being laid off. Many were minimally qualified and were hired on "emergency" certificates, without the required teaching qualifications. There was the perception that the least-qualified teachers were Spanish and Tagalog speaking. The San Francisco district in general was in continuing distress, a distress that was confounded by the assassination of Mayor George Moscone and city councilman Harvey Milk. There were significant negative views and perceptions of bilingual programs. It cannot be concluded that these negative views formed the foundation of what appears to be a widely held negative view of bilingual instruction. It seems, however, that sometime in the 1980s a powerful pessimistic view of bilingual education became widely held across the United States. It may also be a coincidence that the Reagan presidency was also a feature of the 1980s. Unfortunately, research hasn't helped much.

BILINGUAL EDUCATION: THE RESEARCH BASE

Researchers became interested in exploring bilingual education beginning in the late 1960s and found evidence that a student's initial reading instruction, for instance, should be in their "mother tongue." The belief was that students should learn to read in their L1s first as the "native-language literacy axiom." Some early researchers, particularly those who looked at French-immersion programs in Canada, concluded that students don't necessarily learn to read best in their L1s. This is an argument that continues. Generally, however, the students in these early studies were from families in which both English and French were highly valued and the dominant language was English.

There are two kinds of language proficiencies to be learned: basic interpersonal communicative skill (BICS), the language of ordinary conversation or the manifestation of language proficiency in everyday communicative contexts, and cognitive academic language proficiency (CALP), the language of instruction and academic text. These labels might lead to a misinterpretation of the complexities they seek to describe and imply a deficit model of language. CALP has been likened to "test-wiseness" and is sometimes referred to by an additional acronym; SIN, or "skill in instructional nonsense," a term coined by C. Edelsky in *With Literacy and Justice for All: Rethinking the Social in Language and Education.* The two labels have generally, however, come to represent two categories of proficiency; one associated with face-to-face conversation (BICS) and the other with learning in the context-reduced cognitively demanding oral and written environment of the classroom (CALP). Older students use knowledge of academic material and concepts gained studying L1 to help them in L2, and the acquisition of L2 occurs faster. A number of researchers found that BICS requires about two to three years to develop and that CALP takes about five to seven years.

Cummins and Swain (1986) proposed a "Common Underlying Proficiency" (CUP) model based on the notion that "literacy-related aspects of a bilingual's proficiency in L1 and L2 are seen as common or interdependent across languages" (p. 82). Literacy experience in either language promotes the underlying interdependent proficiency base. This view suggests that "common cross-lingual proficiencies underlie the obviously different surface manifestations of each language" (p. 82). There is evidence to support CUP; however, there is only modest evidence of transfer of language skills. Common underlying proficiency has also been referred to as the interdependence principle, and some research provides powerful long-term evidence that common underlying proficiency or interdependence does exist.

The 1990s brought a focused research effort to investigate bilingual education but resulted in little definitive evidence that transitional bilingual education (TBE) is a superior strategy for improving language achievement. Bilingual immersion programs were designed to introduce minority students to English during the early years by integrating second-language instruction with content-area instruction. Immersion students showed an early significant advantage at grade four that disappeared by grade seven. One major difficulty in evaluating bilingual studies is that there are so many variations in programs across studies. A second major difficulty is that many studies are neither well designed nor well evaluated. A third difficulty is that authors often take for granted that what other authors claim is true of their findings is, in fact, true.

Dual-immersion programs were an alternative to TBE programs that gained popularity in the 1990s. Two-way immersion programs are defined as the integration of language-majority and language-minority students in the same classrooms where: (1) language-minority and language-majority students are integrated for at least half of the day at all grade levels; (2) content and literacy instruction are provided in both languages to all students; and (3) language-minority and language-majority students are balanced. The support for dual-immersion programs, like other bilingual programs, is limited.

The Director of the National Institute of Child Health and Human Development (NICHD) established the National Reading Panel (NRP) in 1997 as a result of a congressional request (http://www.nichd.nih.gov/publications/nrp/intro/htm). The issue of second-language learning was not included in the panel because it was to be addressed by a different research review. An additional National Literacy Panel was established to conduct a literature review on the literacy of language-minority children and youth. In August 2005 the U.S. Department of Education declined to publish the report of the National Literacy Panel reportedly "because of concerns about its technical adequacy and the degree to which it could help inform policy and practice."

Research has found that secondary students in English-only schools disappeared from academic classes at about a 60 percent rate, and there were significant differences in disappearance rate among ethnolinguistic groups. The relatively high socioeconomic status (SES) students who were Mandarin speakers achieved at higher rates and had lower disappearance rates than did the low SES students who were Spanish and Vietnamese speakers. Other research shows that structured English immersion resulted in higher success for English Language Learners (ELLs).

There is a constant debate between advocates of English-only and advocates of bilingual programs. The claims that one instructional approach is superior to any other appear to be founded on limited or questionable evidence. At best, inferences about best approaches appear to have limited empirical support. It is likely impossible to conduct scientific research in a typical school because there are too many confounding variables to control.

Unfortunately, hundreds of thousands of ESL (ELL) students are failing to learn in school and are dropping out. In the United States, Spanish-speaking students are less likely to complete high school than English speakers and are also less likely to go on to university. The 2005 National Assessment of Adult Literacy report states that, "Perhaps most sobering was that adult literacy dropped or was flat across every level of education, from people with graduate degrees to those who dropped out of high school" (accessed on December 22, 2005, at http://www.nifl.gov/nifl/NAAL2003.html). They also report that those who have higher literacy levels made about $50,000 a year, which is $28,000 more than those who had only minimal literacy skills. It is estimated that the loss of potential wages and taxes in the United States alone over the lifespan of the total number of dropouts in a year is approximately $260 trillion. For countries like the United States that are striving to have a technically trained work force and to remain technically superior, dropouts are a serious difficulty. It is a significant problem that seems to be ignored in favor of arguments about language of instruction.

BUT WHO'S ON FIRST?

The struggle to learn English and to learn academic content is extremely difficult. ESL students deal with the trials and tribulations of growing into adulthood while trying to master English and multiple sets of expectations from their schoolmates, their friends, their teachers, and their parents. Many hundreds of thousands drop out. Proponents and opponents of bilingual education argue their viewpoints vehemently, often referring to research or to political views to support their beliefs. Most bilingual research is focused on younger students, and what happens in secondary and post-secondary situations has had little attention. Much like Ma Ferguson, modern-day critics often make statements that are not always logical. Bob Dole, for instance, argued that "We must stop the practice of multilingual educations as a means of instilling ethnic pride, or as a therapy for low self-esteem, or out of guilt over a culture built on the traditions of the west." The former Speaker of the U.S. House, Newt Gingrich, concluded: "Bilingualism keeps people actively tied to their old language and habits and maximizes the cost of transition to becoming American" and "Without English as a common language, there is no such civilization." He also has stated, "When we allow children to stay trapped in bilingual programs where they do not learn English, we are destroying their economic future."

The scandalous situation is that ESL students are not learning the academic skills to allow them to enter into our technological society and they are dropping out at high rates; some groups more than others. In the meantime, educators, researchers, politicians, and others seem intent on proving that their views of English-only or bilingual instruction are right rather than on searching for the best programs to assure that all students, including ESL students, learn the vital skills they need to participate in this technologically based society. Is learning English in a bilingual program so evil? It seems time to wake up to history. Diversity has worked well for the United States in the past; one wonders, why not today?

Further Reading: Amselle, J., & Moore, S., 1998, North of the border—Mexico lobbies for specific U.S. educational policies—Includes related article on California's Proposition 227, October 12, *National Review* 50, 22–24; Crawford, J., 1999, *Bilingual education: History, politics, theory and practice*, 4th ed., Los Angeles, CA: Bilingual Education Services; Cummins, J., & Swain, M., 1986, *Bilingualism in education.* New York: Longman Group; Gunderson, L., 2007, *English-only instruction and immigrant students in secondary schools: A critical examination*, Mahwah, NJ: Lawrence Erlbaum Associates; Kloss, H., 1998, *The American bilingual tradition*, McHenry, IL: Center for Applied Linguistics and Delta Systems (originally published in 1977 by Newbury House); NCES, 2004, *Language minorities and their educational and labor market indicators—Recent trends*, Washington, DC: U.S. Department of Education, Institute of Education Sciences, #2004–009; Olneck, M. R., & Lazerson, M., 1974, The school achievement of immigrant children: 1900–1930, *History of Education Quarterly*, Winter, 453–482; Ovando, C. J., 2003, Bilingual education in the United States: Historical development and current issues, *Bilingual Research Journal* 27(1), 1–24; Stritikus, T., 2002, *Immigrant students and the politics of English only: Views from the classroom*, New York: LFB Scholarly Publishing.

Lee Gunderson

BULLYING

The animal kingdom, as well as an extended view of human history, demonstrates how biological and sociological forces interact to produce and temper dominance and submissive behaviors. Charles Darwin first taught about how natural selection identifies dominant individuals for long-term survival of the species. Societies create norms designed to temper the more powerful in order to promote the society's survival needs over the desire for individual domination. The continuing tensions between these forces can be seen in many segments of society. One of these segments is schools, where bullying is a problem reflecting domination and socialization forces as students grapple with learning to balance individual and societal needs.

The continual collision of individual dominance pressures with socialization demands creates a fluctuating pattern of aggression and reactions as people seek, but never quite find, the perfect balance for themselves and others. The pattern is so historically consistent that until recent history, schools accepted bullying as a problem to be dealt with individually and scholarly attention was minimal. The topic of youth bullying was virtually absent from the major medical, education, social science, and psychology journals prior to 1980. Even by 1990, less than two dozen scholarly articles were available. All that changed in the following years, so that now more than 1,000 manuscripts can be easily identified and the research continues to expand.

The focus of theory, research, and practice around school bullying has been more one sided than the human experience itself, and therein lies the seeds for conflict. Scholarly works and professional application models generally emphasize the harm in bullying, societal needs for order, the human right for a sense of safety, and caring for others. These are highly moral and reasonable issues that emphasize sensitivity and cooperation. Only by emphasizing such behaviors can families, schools, societies, countries, or cultures maintain strength and ability to control their fates.

What professional exploration has given less emphasis to is the human drive to assert oneself and demonstrate superiority over others. Individuals and societies know this drive well, giving it recognition in many ways. Across cultures, people struggle to win at games, compete for resources, acquire the best mating partners, and secure positions of authority. All these victories provide individuals or groups with a source of pride and security in the knowledge that they control people in their environment that might otherwise control them. This individual drive to control others in order to achieve a sense of security and superiority is a normal part of human existence.

CONFLICTING PRESSURES

Domination Pressures

The support for demonstrating dominance has always been visible in many aspects of society, even though scientists and educators have shied away from publicly supporting its virtues. Those who dominate take pride in it, are rewarded for their control of others, and seek to maintain or increase these pleasurable results. Those dominated are hurt by their one-down position and either attempt to strengthen themselves in some way so they can win back power, find another who they can dominate, or drop out of the competition. These processes can provide strength and growth leading to more productive ways of being as supporters would say, or they can lead to deterioration and loss of hope as detractors would emphasize. Two common situations provide examples of how societies indirectly demonstrate and teach the value of dominating behaviors.

Games that get the most public attention require one person or team to gain control of their destiny by dominating another. Winners take pride and the motivation to continue their status while losers must decide how to cope with diminished status. The desire for victory can become so extreme that it can carry over to violence that goes beyond the rules of the sport or the norms of public decorum. Academic achievement is also commonly measured by what one has accomplished more than others. Students, schools, and even countries are given grades and percentile ranks that clarify how well they are doing in comparison. Those who do the best are rewarded with superior grades, prizes, and the support of peers and those in authority. Those who do less well miss out on the rewards and, in some combination, feel bad, work harder, or drop out of the competition.

Socialization Pressures

Just as individuals strive to control themselves and others to achieve rewards and security, so do groups of individuals such as families, schools, communities, and countries. To approach these goals, they attempt to make the best use of the varied individuals in their group, which requires discouragement of excessive dominance by one component over another because such a situation reduces the number and value of resources. Children, for example, can be seen as highly vulnerable and least immediately valuable to a society. If individual dominance and survival of the fittest were the only component in operation, children might be eliminated as a drain on resources with no immediate value. It is the society that recognizes the need to protect children because of their long-term value and essential role in producing future generations. It is this societal role of protecting the weak from over-control by the dominant that creates pressures against bullying.

Social pressures attempt to control domination by a few without eliminating the desire for dominance altogether. Rules are created in games to emphasize fairness, sportsmanship, and the value of the competition itself being as important as identification of the victor and loser. Schools try to balance academic achievement pressures with caring and attention to the needs of all students regardless of their success level, and governments reinforce this by providing funding designed specifically for those with the greatest needs.

INCREASING ATTENTION TO BULLYING

Schools have been hit particularly hard since the mid-twentieth century with the conflicting pressures for domination and socialization in ways that have increasingly highlighted issues of bullying. One significant point at which pressures to identify outstanding individuals and promote their achievement came about in the late 1950s when U.S. president Kennedy concluded that there was a crucial need to produce more scientists and mathematicians. Fear of scientific and technological domination by the Soviet Union, who had recently won the race to put the first man in space, provided the emphasis to win the race to the moon. Money and energy flowed to training programs and schools to identify high achievers, guide them toward critical careers, and track the success of individuals and programs. What followed was a huge surge in standardized testing, emphasizing where people stood in comparison to others. The most recent decade has seen another surge in testing highlighted by the No Child Left Behind Act designed to identify the best schools from others. These are examples of how society was increasingly rewarding the best and improving or eliminating the weakest through academic competition.

Expanding technological advancement and the demand for people who can compete intellectually both demonstrate how emphasis on winning, achieving, and having value in school can become largely determined by being better than others and maintaining that position. This domination of others is reflected in society by greater distances between the economic and social haves and have nots at all ages. So it is not surprising that various forms of bullying and harassment among individual students and groups have also increased during these times.

The Vietnam War symbolized, for many, a time of human consciousness raising in the mid-to-late 1960s and early 1970s. The negative aspects of dominating and winning at all costs became highlighted during these times and pushed society to seek more humane ways of dealing with others. The U.S.

Supreme Court ruled unanimously in 1971 that forced busing was an appropriate vehicle for integrating schools in order to equalize educational opportunities and help diverse groups develop better relationships by learning and sharing together. Values clarification and helping all students achieve at their own pace with lessened pressures were core to the models for schools into the 1970s. More attention was being paid to student social skills, relationships, and helping those most in need. How to get along and accommodate others gained a more equal focus of attention with the press to demonstrate superiority. This time frame was virtually absent of literature on bullying.

One form of bullying did increasingly receive major attention during the 1970s, 1980s, and early 1990s and would later become a model for recognizing and dealing with bullying in the schools. Sexual harassment in the workplace became a significant social issue as women became more assertive about being treated as equals. Businesses and societies in general were pushed to recognize that, because women had generally less physical and authority power in the workplace than men, they were vulnerable to domination in various forms of abuse and particularly sexual harassment. Eventually sexual harassment policies and legislation gave focus to the primary abuse characteristics that would later become the core definition of bullying: Harm was defined from the victim's perspective; a significant power differential put the victim at a disadvantage; and repetition of such acts increased the harm done. These abuse characteristics would become integral in defining severity of various issues including sexual abuse, discrimination, and bullying in schools.

Scholarly and public discussion of school bullying as a problem began to gain visibility in the late 1980s and early 1990s. It was again a time of building societal pressures for success and winning. A good business or farm was no longer one that produced a profit and provided jobs for employees. Success was increasingly identified as continually getting bigger and better by beating competitors. Schools faced the same pressures from societal trends, policies, and laws fostering private schools, charter schools, and school vouchers. Schools now had to compete academically or lose the best students and funding. Pressures built to limit the more physical and social aspects of schools from recess time to physical education, the arts, and psycho/social development programs. Increased academic pressures and limiting social development opportunities gave a clear message to administrators, teachers, parents, and students that what mattered was demonstrating your superiority over others. These times of increased pressures to outperform others was reflected in the increased visibility of gangs, cliques, and bullying, which are opportunities to show dominance in nonacademic ways.

The first serious scholarly work on bullying came in the late 1980s and early 1990s from Dan Olweus in Norway and Peter Smith in England. Numbers of students involved and the impact students reported on them began to receive attention in the United States as concerns about the safety of individual students began to grow. This type of research is important to understanding, but it was public events in the mid-1990s that created major movement.

A 15-year-old student named Brian Head went to his Georgia classroom as usual, pulled out a gun, and shot himself to death in front of his classmates. The year was 1993, and his notes, poetry, and drawings made it clear that this suicide was because he could no longer take the bullying and teasing he had endured in school. Brian's actions caught the attention of the national media, and it was becoming clear that he was not alone. Suicides related to being bullied at school received increasing attention, and bullying became raised to the level of a potentially life-threatening danger.

Violence in the schools and the role of bullying in it were raised to another public level in 1997 when a 14-year-old in Kentucky came to school and shot eight students in a prayer group, killing three. It was not the first of its kind, but it included more people and got more press. These killings were followed up in the next year by similar high-visibility school shootings of multiple students in Jonesboro, Arkansas, Edinboro, Pennsylvania, and Springfield, Oregon, among others. Then there was the Columbine High School shooting in 1999, where 13 were killed and 24 wounded. Each of these very public events had one particular thing in common; the perpetrators had made it clear that their harassment and bullying by others was the central motivation for taking violent revenge.

The public visibility of bullying's relationship to youth suicides and murders of peers continued to shock people who viewed schools as places of safety. The result was an increasing concern about the safety of students in schools and the need to deal with it directly. Brian Head's father was among the earliest individuals instrumental in pressing for legislation around bullying in schools. His efforts and those of others continue to find success in establishing local policies and even state laws around bullying issues. Major educational, medical, psychology, and social work organizations have all since taken major stands on the dangers of and need to deal with bullying in schools. Laws and policies that direct practices or prevention efforts to reduce bullying in schools have been passed in countries around the world, including over half the states in the United States. Prior to 1990 catalogs of school programs, videos, books, and other materials contained virtually nothing on bullying. Since that time, the same types of materials have been among the fastest-growing types of educational products, and schools have been given a major responsibility for reducing bullying even as the pressures of individual and school competition continue.

The conflicting domination and socialization pressures placed upon schools by nature and society have become too visible and problematic to ignore. Two examples of how the conflict plays out in schools are zero tolerance and legislating bullying prevention in schools. These two issues highlight the pitfalls faced by school personnel and laypersons as they work to create a safe environment for all students while allowing for natural developmental issues that result in students making mistakes.

Zero Tolerance Policies

Zero tolerance policies gained popularity with the recognition that deadly school violence could emerge from bullying, harassment, and the anger and frustration they can cause. Policies set forth predetermined consequences to be applied to students and situations regardless of the seriousness of deemed inappropriate behaviors or mitigating context. The consequences are generally punitive, sometimes harsh, and result in punishments to students whose behavior has some degree of potential to create an unsafe environment. Studies have shown that controversy and public outcry arise when similar punishments are doled out across a wide range of incidents.

While violence against others, like bullying, cannot be condoned by schools, some incidents of implementing zero tolerance policies have people saying enough is enough. One of many examples is the 2001 case of two second-graders being suspended and charged with making terroristic threats after pointing a piece of paper folded in a crude approximation of a gun at fellow classmates and saying, "I'm going to kill you all." School personnel justified their strict interpretation of zero tolerance policy and consequential actions as appropriate in light of actual school shootings that have occurred elsewhere. Others were incensed with the thought that taking two second-graders to the police station and charging them with making terrorist threats was enormously bad judgment.

Promoters of zero policy actions believe that the inflexibility of the utilitarian policy is the significant deterrent. Applied to the case of the second-graders, the school's policy was designed to teach both boys as well as an entire community that no matter how or why you threaten others, the fact that you broke the rule causes the penalty to be enforced. Detractors believe it is definitely wrong and counterproductive to frighten students into conformity and that more socially appropriate prevention and treatment models are available. This type of controversy found its way to a joint effort by the U.S. Secret Service and the U.S. Department of Education, which came to the conclusion that zero tolerance policies are not recommended as a vehicle for dealing with bullying, harassment, and potential school violence. While zero tolerance polices are unproven and may carry the potential for serious harm as a result of the use of such policies, they continue to have supporters even in the face of lawsuits.

The threat of legal action against implementers of zero tolerance policies has moved some states to provide legislative protection for school personnel required to adhere to school policies. One such state is New Hampshire, where mandatory reporting directly to the school principal is required for any bullying incident. Staff members who initiate the bullying report are immune by state law from any liability that might occur after the reporting. People opposed to zero tolerance reject this dominance-based model and believe that the answers to dealing with these interpersonal problems in schools are prevention efforts designed to help promote empathy, communication, and social skills to reduce peer abuse and foster a safer environment.

Bullying Legislation

Many state legislatures have proposed laws requiring schools to have antibullying policies and programs in an effort to create safer schools. Currently more than half the states have laws related to school bullying and harassment, with additional bills being presented in other states and even the U.S. House of Representatives.

Individuals who endorse a legislative approach to keeping students safe from bullying in schools point to previous reporting statutes like mandated reporting of child abuse and neglect that have been successful in helping to safeguard the welfare of children. Supporters also recognize that incentives for schools to deal with abuse and violence can come from state and federal laws and policies. Prime examples of such initiatives are funding for Drug and Alcohol Free Schools and No Child Left Behind, which have provided funds for research and programs on school violence. State bullying statues have been used to support training for school employees to increase their ability to recognize and intervene in peer-abuse situations before they can escalate into deadly peer violence.

Several state legislative bodies require local schools or school boards to develop and implement bullying policies. In these cases, involving appropriate stakeholders within the community and the school including students is seen as optimal for community/school buy-in and sense of shared ownership of the issues and their solutions. Promoters believe that sustained programmatic effort integrated into the curriculum, the school's discipline policies, and other violence-prevention projects can create a learning culture that is productive and safe for all. The U.S. Department of Education supports this view and has developed a five-day on-line course to provide quality information to school districts for developing and implementing effective bullying-prevention programming.

Not everyone is a proponent of bullying legislation. Many cite the problems associated with attempting to implement such forced policies. School personnel often discuss (1) lack of time in the school day, (2) inadequate support within the school and community, (3) staff inadequately trained to effectively implement policy, and (4) lack of financial support. Administrators report frustration that state legislators impose such demands as unfunded mandates. Others suggest that the law simply forces schools to deal with yet another "new" program that creates a sense of burden due to increased paperwork and hoops through which teachers, students, and administrators must jump. Some detractors believe that bullying programs stigmatize students by categorizing them as a bully or victim, thereby giving them a label that might make it more difficult for students to escape their role within the bullying dynamic.

Another category of individuals who oppose mandated approaches refer to them as feel good popular legislation, not the meaningful legislation necessary to meet the educational and safety needs of schools. They see bullying as something that has always occurred and that a skewed focus on it creates a situation where responses to other potential school issues are not given their due attention.

Bullying in schools is viewed differently depending on time, place, and individuals involved. Natural pressures interact to influence individuals and school in ways that promote both the domination and socialization thinking and behaviors. The result is that how the problem is viewed fluctuates with the pressures and events of a given social climate as well as the individuals and communities involved. The expansion of research on the issue over the past two decades will likely continue in its attempts to sort out the complexities of these interactions.

Further Reading: For additional information on zero tolerance policies, see: Skiba, R., Reynolds, C. R., Grahan, S., Sheras, P., Close Conoley, J., & Garcia-Vazques, E., 2006, *Are zero tolerance policies effective in schools? An evidentiary review and recommendations,* Alexandria, VA: American Psychological Association. Available at: http://www.apa.org/ed/cpse/zttfreport.pdf; for additional information on bullying legislation and prevention programs, see: Limber, S. P., & Small, M. A., 2003, State laws and policies to address bullying in schools, *School Psychology Review, 32*(3), 445–455; U.S. Department of Education, 2006, *Exploring the nature and prevention of bullying,* Washington, DC: Author. Available at: http://www.ed.gov/admins/lead/safety/training/bullying/bullying_pg3.html; A five-day Web course offered by the U.S. Department of Education is an excellent resource on bullying prevention through which participants can examine state-of-the-art research, policies, and practices from the field to assist schools in developing well-informed programs, policies, and practices. The five-day Web course is taken on-line with a commitment of one hour per day.

JoLynn V. Carney and Richard J. Hazler

BUSINESS AND CORPORATE INVOLVEMENT

Perhaps the most fundamental question underlying public education is its purpose. Why do we mandate compulsory education, raise taxes to fund it, and gather the vast majority of our nation's youngsters in public schools? In the mid-nineteenth century, Horace Mann promoted public education as a way of promoting stability during times of turmoil. Additionally, he touted it as a means of increasing the value of labor in the economy. John Dewey, a founder of the Progressive movement in education in the early twentieth century, saw two purposes of education: the development of intelligence in the individual and the creation of a thoughtful electorate in a democratic society. And, in the early 1900s, leaders of the new world of corporate business promoted the idea that in order to strengthen America's position in an era of global economic competition, public schools needed to prepare children for their future roles as workers. It is a vision of education that has remained powerful for more than 100 years.

At the very same time that Dewey and the progressives developed their educational philosophy and practice, a competing vision of education was put forth by a coalition of men who held power and authority in American society: businessmen, presidents of prestigious universities, and many superintendents of the recently formed urban school districts. University professors in the newly developed specialty of educational administration joined this coalition. Together they presented a consensus of experts on the needed reorganization of American schooling. These reformers based their program for school reorganization on the model provided by the modern business corporation, along with its innovative mass production processes and its use of the principles of scientific management. Their vision could not have been more different from that of the educational progressives. It valued efficiency more than democracy in the schools. These reformers eschewed the progressives' notion of organizing the classroom and the school around the needs of developing children. Rather, it aimed at achieving efficiency in schools by establishing external or environmental controls through organizational techniques. It is no surprise that 100 years ago it was the business community's vision of education that took root across the nation and, to a large degree, endures to this day. Business has long held a position of prestige and influence in our country. Business leader's values, beliefs, and opinions are both listened to and often admired. Their emphasis on "the bottom line" and efficiency has held allure for much of the populace because of its apparent practicality and efficacy.

Corporate power and influence has been used for over 100 years to promote the idea that the primary purpose of our schools should be to prepare children for their future roles in our economy. In fact, a reading of the business community's call for school reform from 100 years ago sounds eerily familiar today. Much was made then of America's precarious position in comparison with its international economic competitors, particularly Germany. American schools were blamed for not preparing children for their roles in a newly industrialized economy. At that time, vocational education was seen as being key to improving the nation's schools. This was a novel idea, since up to that point, training for the workplace had been done by employers through apprenticeships. However, leaders from the world of business and commerce were united in their belief that the public schools should assume this responsibility.

Beyond vocational education, the National Association of Manufacturers (NAM) and other business groups championed the argument that unless the educational system was entirely revamped, the United States would have to surrender its place as a leader among the manufacturing nations of the world. Should you think you have heard this argument more recently, you are correct. In 1983, *A Nation at Risk* asserted, "Our once unchallenged preeminence in commerce, industry, science, and technological innovation is being overtaken by competitors throughout the world." The report warned of a "rising tide of mediocrity" in our nation's schools. The message to the American people at the beginning and end of the twentieth century was the same: Unless we radically overhaul our school systems to take account of economic exigencies we are, in essence, sealing our own doom.

How, exactly, education should be reformed has, time and again, been strongly influenced by the latest industrial management models of the day. Throughout the twentieth century, business leaders promoted the idea that schools would become more productive if they used "universal" management principles first developed in industry. For example, the corporate form of organization, a management revolution that swept the United States at the close of the nineteenth century, was heralded as critical to improving efficient operation of early twentieth-century schools. Ninety years ago, Ellwood Cubberley, one of the most influential school reformers of the time, confidently recommended consolidation of small rural and urban neighborhood schools into large, bureaucratic organizations. Cubberley promoted a governance structure that mimicked that of the corporation: a president, board of directors, and full-time administrative staff.

The president, known as the superintendent of schools, would have total control over the school organization. The school board would have an advisory role, with all professional functions left to the "captain of education," i.e., the super-intendent. Just as the corporate board of directors had little power to direct the day-to-day operations of a firm, the school board would defer to the educational executives. As Cubberley wrote in 1916, it was in the "interests of efficient administration for the board to leave all executive functions to carefully chosen executive officers, who act as its representatives. In this regard the evolution of city school control has kept in touch with the best principles of corporation management and control."

Reform of the school organization was the first step in a two-step process to make schools function more like successful corporations. Once in power, the professional school administrator could apply efficient, mass production principles developed in manufacturing. The introduction of departmentalized instruction, similar to the division of labor in a factory, made this possible. Departmentalization was coupled with the principles of "scientific management," which were imported into the schools in the early part of the twentieth century. Frederick Taylor, the inventor of scientific management, disapproved of improvisation by people throughout an organization. Rules, developed by management, needed to replace improvisation. The rules had to be based on the "science" of the particular job to be done, whether it be making a widget in industry or teaching arithmetic to schoolchildren. It was postulated that conformity and obedience by people at all levels of the bureaucratic pyramid, from the child in the classroom to the teachers, principals, and central office administrators, was essential for the school organization to operate efficiently. An order, once given, was to go without question "through the works" of the school organization. Of course, this stripped teachers of the power to innovate or adapt curriculum for their students. It was the belief that any decision made by a classroom teacher would be inferior to those made by the men at the top of the organizational pyramid; men who understood the "science" of the job to be done.

This education reform movement was based on the idea that once industry made clear what educational products were necessary for its competitive operation, the science of education would allow school managers to devise the one best way of teaching the curricula and skills necessary to deliver the desired end. Here is how Elwood Cubberley (1916) delineated the efficient way to meet society's demand for educational output:

> Our schools are, in a sense, factories in which the raw products (children) are to be shaped and fashioned into products to meet the various demands of life. The specifications for manufacturing come from the demands of twentieth-century civilization, and it is the business of the school to build its pupils according to the specifications laid down. This demands good tools, specialized machinery, continuous measurement of production to see if it is according to specifications, the elimination of waste in manufacture, and large variety in output.

The wide variety of output was needed to prepare children for the four layers of "civilized society" described by Harvard president Charles Eliot in 1908: the narrow upper layer of the managerial and intellectual class, the layer of skilled workers, the commercial or merchant class, and finally, the "thick fundamental layer engaged in household work, agriculture, mining, quarrying, and forest work." Andrew Draper, first commissioner of education in New York, used a military analogy, promoting his idea that the mass of society was suited for the rank of corporal. These corporals were important to society because they supplied labor "for the great manufacturing and constructive industries" in the country. Education, accordingly, had to be designed by the elite to get the masses ready for their participation in these industries. Children had to be tested, sorted, and prepared for their future roles in society.

Although progressives such as Jane Addams protested having the schools do the training for work that she and others felt was the responsibility of employers, this vision of education prevailed. Accordingly, educational tracking, much in keeping with the layers outlined by Charles Eliot, was ubiquitous throughout the twentieth century. It was only at the close of the century that a demand for a new type of employee led to a call for reform of the educational system instituted nearly a century earlier.

The 1980s brought recession and the rise in the intensity of global economic competition. Manufacturing jobs began to be sent off-shore to countries where workers were paid a tiny fraction of the wages and benefits paid to American employees, particularly those in unionized industries. The alarm sounded by *A Nation at Risk* led to one call for school reform after another. But in the case of nearly every call for reform, the "economic imperative" was the driving force behind it. This led to unanimity on the following assumption: *All* students, not just those from Eliot's top tiers of society, would now have to be educated, not merely trained for a trade or vocation. This education should prepare them for "knowledge work" in order to allow the United States to compete economically. Every student would now need strong math, science, and reasoning skills. Robustly supporting, and often directing these calls for reform in the contemporary period, is the business community. It brings to bear its vast array of resources, networks, and influence on discussions about how education should proceed.

After *A Nation at Risk* there was some effort to inject an element of autonomy and professionalism into teaching. The idea, borrowed from the business management model, Total Quality Management (TQM), was that in order to improve the quality of a product or service, the people closest to the actual production or service provided should be empowered to make decisions about how their work should proceed. Site-based decision making was touted as the best way to get our children ready to compete with children from nations such as Japan—the home of TQM—who surpassed American youngsters in international comparisons. CEOs from Fortune 500 companies and the National Alliance of Business encouraged school districts around the country to follow their lead and adopt the TQM management model.

However appealing this idea was to teachers, i.e., that they should have the autonomy to decide how educational services ought best be delivered, it was less appealing to those at the top of the bureaucratic pyramid, who feared a power shift downward. Within a decade of its introduction, site councils were either abandoned or stripped of any authentic power to control how education was carried out in their schools. And by the turn of the twenty-first century, centralized decision making was back in vogue—more vigorous than it had been prior to the wave of site-based decision-making councils. In fact, some reformers proposed doing away with local school boards and having states control schools directly, i.e., mandating curricula and programs, hiring teachers, funding schools entirely from their coffers, and turning over the day-to-day operations of schools to private contractors.

The impetus for the renewed faith in and popularity of centralized power is the two-sided coin of "standards" and "accountability" that has dominated the debate about education since the turn of the twenty-first century. The argument is that schools need to be held accountable for turning out students who are fit for the workplace or college. The standards movement is closely tied to the "specifications for manufacturing" that Cubberley discussed so long ago. Though those specifications have changed, the utilitarian vision of the schooling remains a constant. This is due, in great measure, to the influence of the Business Roundtable, the U.S. Chamber of Commerce, the NAM, and the Conference Board. These business groups have been key players in the development of what the new specifications for educational "output," that is, graduates, ought to be. Schools that are highly productive create those graduates efficiently. Accountability is assessed by quantitative measures, for example, standardized test scores and graduation rates. These aggregated data are regarded as representing objective, value-free truth.

Big business has pulled out its big guns to shape today's education reform agenda. It has pushed for nation-wide *high-stakes testing* via the No Child Left Behind (NCLB) legislation, serving the dual purpose of imposing one-size-fits-all standards as well as opening rich, new markets in testing, test preparation, supplemental tutoring, and curricular programs that promise higher test scores. New *partnerships between business and education* have been developed in an attempt to import business-based management principles into the schools. As was seen in the early part of the previous century, business management models are viewed as being universally applicable to the school setting. TQM and other data-driven management systems have been imported into school administration. Harvard, Stanford, and other elite universities have programs developed jointly by their schools of business and education to help school district superintendents work more like corporate executives. The U.S. Chamber of Commerce sponsors the Business Education Network aimed at building partnerships between business and education. Business philanthropy helps to advance its reform agenda, including the sponsorship of favored curricular packages and programs. It has also supported the break up what has been deemed the public school "monopoly" through its vigorous support of charter schools and "educational entrepreneurship."

As involved as it was in setting the school reform agenda in the early part of the twentieth century, business rarely got involved in the day-to-day operations of schools. However, today's business reform agenda parts company with that of the past in its drive for the private, for-profit takeover of public schools. Beginning with Education Alternatives, Inc., and followed by the Edison Project (now Edison Schools, Inc.) in the early 1990s, private management companies have marketed themselves as the means of improving student outcomes as measured by higher test scores. In 2006 these education management organizations (EMOs) operated in 28 states and the District of Columbia, enrolling nearly 240,000 students. The EMOs argue they can do a better job of running schools than traditional school administrators; this, despite the fact there is no research to indicate that private management does, in fact, improve student achievement. EMOs have generally been brought in by school boards to take over troubled schools in urban areas. NCLB allows for state takeover of schools that fail to meet annual performance goals for five consecutive years. One option for this takeover is contracting with an independent entity to run the school. It is assumed that private management, aligned with the best principles of business administration, will improve educational outcomes. The students most often enrolled in the schools run by EMOs are children of color who come from families of the working poor.

How has business continued to be so successful in getting its agenda for school reform adopted over the last century? The argument that children should be able to earn a living after attending school is an appealing one to most parents. In addition, business embodies much of what is esteemed in our nation. But business is powerful not only for this reason. It has behaved proactively, using its influence and vast economic resources in attempts to sway both the public and the legislatures to its way of thinking on school reform. For example, business has been perhaps the strongest proponent of the No Child Left Behind Act. In 2001 the Business Roundtable and the U.S. Chamber of Commerce formed a coalition of 50 other business groups and companies to support the passage of NCLB. The coalition worked to ensure that the law's testing requirements concentrated on reading and math and required annual testing of students. In addition, business groups endorsed the accountability requirements, for example, allowing students to transfer from "failing" schools to other schools, including those run by EMOs. Congress adopted the approach favored by the business coalition.

NCLB has been lambasted by a variety of critics. Modern-day progressives disagree with the emphasis on annual testing as the only measure of education success. Teachers' unions argue that insufficient funding accompanies the mandate to get all children on track for high math and reading achievement, regardless of their knowledge of the English language, the difficult lives they live, or their learning problems. Commentators such as Richard Rothstein question whether the goal of having every child master high academic standards by 2014, regardless of his or her academic talent, is achievable even with the best funding, curricula, and teaching. As 2007, the time for reauthorization of the law, approaches, critics clamor for radical changes in the legislation. In 2006, sensing a fierce challenge to the law, the U.S. Chamber of Commerce and the Business Roundtable formed a new coalition to prevent substantive changes to NCLB. They hired lobbyists to protect their interests. These business groups say that as the biggest consumer of American educational products, it is only natural that they be involved in making sure that students learn the skills that will make them capable employees in tomorrow's workforce. Why should Congress listen?

The answer is clear: to make American workers of the future economically competitive, and ensure America's standing in the world.

Further Reading: Cubberley, E., 1916, *Public school administration,* Boston: Houghton Mifflin; Dewey, J., 1900, *The school and society,* Chicago: University of Chicago Press; Hoff, D., 2006, Big business going to bat for NCLB, *Education Week, 26*(8), 1, 24; New commission on the skills of the American workforce, 2007, Washington, DC: National Center on Education and the Economy; Tyack, D., 1974, *The one best system: A history of American urban education,* Cambridge: Harvard University Press; U.S. Department of Labor, 2000, *What work requires of schools: A SCANS report for America 2000,* Washington, DC: U.S. Department of Labor.

Denise Gelberg

C

CHARACTER EDUCATION

Except for parents who occasionally want to know whose values are to be taught to their children in public schools, the public generally is unaware of the controversy that colors what has become known as "character education." Yet it is telling that the nation's only endowed chair for character education (c.e.), University of Missouri's professor Marvin W. Berkowitz, begins his chapter for William Damon's book, *Bringing in a New Era in Character Education,* as follows:

> The field of character education is rife with controversy as debates question whether the focus should be on virtues, values, behaviors, or reasoning capacities. Controversy swirls around varied approaches of implementing c.e.: experiential learning, peer debate, indoctrinative teaching, community service, participatory governance, reading about character, and so on. Many of these debates have strong roots in theoretical and philosophical differences. (2002, p. 19)

The most significant debate in c.e. relates to Berkowitz's last sentence. It is this philosophical arena where the most passionate battles in c.e. are fought. (The irony in using such militaristic language to describe virtue education is noted.) A chapter in volume three of the Praeger Perspectives text, *Defending Public Schools,* places the various philosophical ideas about c.e. into conservative, liberal, and spiritual categories. The conservative model wants children to be socialized to conform to status quo, authority, and employment market needs. The liberal model focuses on questions of power in reaction to the injustices that result from the dog-eat-dog ethic of capitalism, although it still tends to view the world as competitive in nature. In the spiritual model, conceived by way of indigenous worldviews, relationships are neither intolerant of nor competitive with others, but are seen as inherently symbiotic and rooted in nature. In this latter model, virtues originate not in cities as human constructs, but in nature as lessons from the observation of nonhuman forms of life.

It is the conservative model that dominates most c.e. programs in public and private schools today. These are generally aligned with assumptions that are embraced by both Democrats and Republicans, including the Protestant work ethic, nationalism, corporatism, and the absence of an emphasis on ecological sustainability and its relationship to character. The assertion that a conservative orientation dominates c.e. in America is supported by Smagorinsky's and Taxel's research as presented in *The Discourse of Character Education: Culture Wars in the Classroom.* They analyze c.e. proposals of 31 states that were funded by the U.S. Department of Education's Office of Educational Research and Improvement. (A good way to get a feel for the passionate debate that surrounds their conclusions regarding their claims about the authoritarian and didactic approach that they believe defines many c.e. programs is to look at the amazon. com reviews of their book.)

In any case, both the conservative model, and to a lesser degree the liberal model, are essentially rooted in traditional Christian religiosity. This alone has been a cause for controversy. Educational critic Alfie Kohn, in his 1997 article for Phi Delta Kappan, entitled "How Not to Teach Values: A Critical Look at Character Education," goes as far as saying that modern character education is little more than a pulpit for Christian religion. In fact, much of the federal and state funding for c.e. programs has resulted from the federal government's 1999 Ten Commandments legislation. In an effort to improve the moral character of American youth, the federal government in 1999 gave states the right to choose if they want to mandate posting the Ten Commandments in public schools. Only a few states have implemented such mandates in their schools, and there have been many challenges.

Many had hoped for a resolution to this church/state issue when the Supreme Court agreed to hear two related suits in 2005. Unfortunately, the Court bowed out in essence by giving a "split decision" that has kept the fires of debate hot and allowing for the continuation of what First Amendment senior scholar Charles C. Haynes calls the Bible wars—the longest-running argument in public school history. In November 2005, the Kansas Board of Education passed a resolution allowing for intelligent design to become an alternative to the theory of evolution. The same year saw censorship of books on sex education and on gay or lesbian issues. In July 2006, legislation to bar federal courts from ruling on constitutional issues surrounding such religious references as the Pledge of Allegiance's "one nation, under God" passed the House of Representatives 260–167, after lawmakers argued that the pledge is linked to the nation's spiritual history.

Although some of the precepts behind contemporary c.e. may have their roots in pre-Christian ideas about moral education that came from Aristotle, these ideas were incorporated into the early Christian church. In 350 B.C.E., his book, *The Nicomachean Ethics,* explained that only teachers possess the expertise for developing character in others; that the natural world does not contribute to character (only life in the cities can do this); and that children are basically blank slates when it comes to character development. These assumptions continue to be reflected in c.e. as well as in religious orthodoxy.

By the time the first formal schools of America emerged in 1635, however, the Bible and its representatives became the "experts" for teaching character." The Olde Deluder Satan Act of 1647 in the Massachusetts Bay Colony mandated Bible reading in the schools. Scripture was used for most reading, and early primers contained verses such as "In Adam's Fall, we sinned all" as a way to teach literacy and the virtues of Christianity. In 1636, Harvard College was similarly founded with the goal of assuring that scripture and Puritan religious perspectives would define society. By the mid-1800s through the early twentieth century, *McGuffey's Readers* continued to use Christian values as a way to socialize immigrants from diverse cultures to a citizenry that reflected the Puritan values of obedience, hierarchy, and industriousness that would support the nation's economic system.

Religious debates emerged in the 1840s between Horace Mann's ideas for the first public schools, or "common schools," and the growing Catholic minority. Mann imagined the schools as teaching a common morality based on nonsectarian Christianity. His goal was to homogenize immigrants into this Christian way of thinking. Mann and the common school idea won the debate, and the Catholics began building the parochial school system. The Bible, in both cases, remained the foundation for studies.

By the 1930s, the overt reliance on Christian doctrine as a basis for character education began to disappear. This was not because the core ideas about obedience, hierarchy, and industriousness were being questioned, but because the social gatekeepers were afraid they would be lost. These ideas were threatened by their affiliation with increasing challenges to religious orthodoxy as well as by communism, bootlegging, labor unions, and increasing calls for social justice. Progressive educators like John Dewey eloquently challenged the idea of using divine authority as the centerpiece of education. Science also played a growing role in questioning this authority, as evidenced in the famous John Scopes trial of 1925.

To maintain an economic system based on hierarchy, authority, and industriousness, the policymakers who feared for capitalism's future wove a more generalized set of Christian values into the "character education" curriculum. Now, overt nationalism and an uncritical view of the United States replaced the emphasis on orthodoxy. The Bible was still read, but without the overt interpretations that were now subject to scrutiny.

By the 1960s, however, Americans began losing faith in nationalism as well while schools started losing faith in their ability to find common ground. Faced with the Vietnam War, racial tensions, and growing student unrest with authoritarianism, educators began to avoid controversy of any kind. Educators like John Holt, Paul Goodman, Charles Silberman, and Ivan Illich wrote that schools were little more than enforcers of conformity to authoritarian institutions that smothered creativity. As a result, all curricula, including character education or "citizenship" training, were now being designed so as to offend as few as possible.

By 1963, the courts ruled against reading the Bible in public schools at all, and religion became the province of "Sunday schools."

Throughout the 1960s and 1970s, the influence of Christian orthodoxy on public schools remained low. Then, in the 1980s, the current resurgence in Christian-based c.e., as marked by the events described earlier, such as the 1999 Ten Commandments legislation, the 2005 Supreme Court decisions, and the 2006 legislation, began. One reason for this may have been the introduction of tax breaks for attending religious schools. These contributed to a drastic increase in private religious schools, eventually culminating in the 1998 federal legislation allowing for vouchers to pay for religious schooling. Gallup polls by 1986 were reporting that 3 in 10 Americans felt comfortable referring to themselves as evangelicals or born-again Christians, and the percentage has grown significantly since. Educational policy, textbook selection, and curriculum all became influenced by Christian traditional values. Once a fringe element, the "Religious Right" became a mainstream influence on policymaking, resulting in such "character education" offerings as the U.S. Department of Health and Human Service's "Silver Ring Thing," a multimillion dollar federally funded abstinence-only program that involves virginity pledges and Bible quoting.

At this time in history we must seriously question the ability of religion to successfully contribute to the good character of people. In Sam Harris's (2004) recent *New York Times* bestseller, *The End of Faith: Religion, Terror and the Future of Reason*, he describes the dangers and absurdities of organized religion and suggests that there is a terrible price to pay for "limiting the scope of reason in our dealings with other human beings" (p. 21) that comes from tolerating religious faith. Of course, this criticism is not new. Thomas Paine, in his famous *Age of Reason*, wrote as much in his chapter "The Effects of Christianism on Education."

This connection between rational thinking and spirituality is an important link for understanding the c.e. controversy. Aristotle even admits that rational thinking is a prerequisite for character building. Being a person of good character involves making good choices in life, therefore critical thinking should be a vital component in c.e. At the same time, a spiritual dimension is equally vital. Harris understands that humans cannot and should not live by reason alone. This does not mean, however, that humans must be irrational to engage a spiritual reality or a sense of the sacred.

In their survey of c.e. programs funded by the USDE, Smagorinsky and Taxel found that although rhetoric regarding the importance of critical thinking was in some of the proposals from the upper Midwest, even these did not address the ways in which critical thinking alone may lead to immoral acts. Nor did anyone address how critical thinking may be a threat to authoritarian educators who might find that someone who challenges authority is lacking in character.

Teaching Virtues: Building Character Education across the Curriculum (Jacobs & Jacobs-Spencer, 2001) offers an indigenous approach to c.e. that connects practical reflection on experience with a sacred awareness that all things in the seen and unseen universe are interconnected. This spiritual perspective is about universal questions regarding the meaning of life, rather than an arrogant assertion that a particular religion can answer the questions for everyone. Traditional indigenous education sees character development as a continuation of the nurturing that must be done for the inherent sacredness of the child. Smagorinsky and Taxel (2005) truly understood this approach, saying: "Such a belief about human nature runs counter to that of Headmaster Jarvis's view that people are by nature mean, nasty, brutish and selfish. It is also distinct from Rousseau's view of the young as noble innocents who become corrupted by the effects of society, a view potentially available in the reflective approach to character education (rather than the conservative one) we have reviewed" (p. 57)

Thus it may be that, in the final analysis, the greatest controversy in character education has yet to be engaged in the public forum as it was briefly introduced in *The Discourse of Character Education*. It will come from a dialogue that considers the possibility that character education will find authenticity, not in the Eurocentric orientations initiated by the Greeks, nor in any religious orthodoxy, but in the spiritual understanding that pervades the diverse approaches to transformative learning that have been practiced by many indigenous cultures for thousands of years. This transformative process is not defined by any particular book or set of precepts. It is not driven by extrinsic reward systems that ultimately lead people away from generosity, courage, patience and other character traits. It is a complex, experiential journey that Gregory Cajete, in his book, *Look to the Mountain: An Ecology of Indigenous Education* (1994), calls the endogenous dynamic of Tribal education (p. 209).

Cajeti describes this process or this dynamic as involving seven stages. The following brief interpretive synopsis is included to allow the reader to actively engage in the character education controversy by contrasting them with what they may know to be happening in a local school district and considering which one may best allow for improving the health of ourselves, our children, our fellow creatures, and the planet upon which we live.

The first stage requires a deep respect for the spirit of each child from before the moment of birth. It is about learning how to integrate one's personal identity into that of the community and ultimately into that of the natural landscape in which the community dwells.

The second stage is about how children can learn to live in harmony with their natural environment on a day-to-day basis and how this way of living is informed by both one's ancestral wisdom and by the local geography.

The third stage is a focus on coordinating the needs of the child with the needs of the group through the processes of initiation, ritual, and ceremony.

The fourth stage finds the individual person moving toward what the Lakota call "Wolakokiciapi," a high degree of peace of mind and personal empowerment. This, however, is only the mid-point of the c.e. program.

The fifth stage involves searching for a life vision while at the same time gaining what Toni Gregory refers to as a mature understanding of diversity in her writings and work involving grounded theory.

The sixth stage involves a time when the individual suffers through a rebirth and understands at long last how to heal the wounds of life through an enhanced awareness of the unconscious. This stage is referred to in the book *Primal Awareness: Survival, Awakening and Transformation with the Raramuri Shamans of Mexico* as coming from the CAT-FAWN connection, which shows how one's take on fear, authority, words, and nature during trance-like states of consciousness serves to guide or misguide healthy actions.

The last stage represents "the place the Indians talk about." It is about the deep healing that comes when we ultimately find our center and recognize our multiple connections to all things of body, mind, spirit, place, community, and cosmos. It is not about creating this center. We were born with it. It is about contacting it and knowing it through one's own experiences and reflection. When we understand that the culture wars in the classrooms of America are little more than what Daniel Wildcat thinks of as abstract disagreements between antiseptic ideologies, perhaps we can enter into this place. In his book, *Power and Place,* co-authored with the late Vine Deloria Jr., Wildcat argues that by reducing success to competitive perspectives, rather than to a profound sense of place and all it represents for those who inhabit that place, Western civilization will continue a downward spiral in all matters pertaining to authentic health and relationships.

In the same vein, as long as the character education controversy is reduced to Western liberal or conservative ideologies that ignore the possibilities that exist in indigenous approaches to c.e., it will contribute not to generous citizens who are genuinely concerned with the well-being of all, but rather to self-serving consumers who remain victims of their own fears and who feel alienated from the places in which they live.

Thomas Paine learned from observing American Indian people that many European ideas about character were flawed. Paine's study of the American Indian way of life helped him realize a number of ideas that are reflective of good character development. For example, he learned that caring for the elderly should be a responsibility of the society. He became a champion of public education and a guaranteed minimum wage. He advocated for many other radical ideas that stem from a citizenry characterized by what are generally the stated goals of character education—generosity, caring, honesty, humility, courage, and respect—traits he saw the native people practicing without the need of legal repercussions for acting otherwise.

Character education, even according to Aristotle, was ultimately about the pursuit of happiness. The idea of happiness was substituted for property in the Declaration of Independence largely because of the influence of American Indian societies on Paine and Jefferson. Perhaps a similar influence can make a difference in the character education controversy.

Further Reading: Cajeti, G., 1994, *Look to the mountain: An ecology of indigenous education,* Durango, CO: Kevaki Press; Damon, W., ed., 2002, *Bringing in a new era in character education,* Palo Alto, CA: Hoover Institution Press; Four Arrows, 2006, *Unlearning the language of conquest: Scholars expose anti-Indianism in America,* Austin: University of Texas Press; Harris, S., 2004, *The end of faith,* New York: W. W. Norton; Jacobs, D. T., and Jacobs-Spencer, J., 2001, *Teaching virtues: Building character across the curriculum,* Landham, MD: Scarecroweducation Press; Smagorinsky, P., and Taxel, J., 2005,

The discourse of character education: Culture wars in the classroom, Mahwah, NJ: Lawrence Erlbaum and Associates.

Four Arrows, aka Don Trent Jacobs

CHARTER SCHOOLS

Charter schools have become one of the most sweeping school reforms in the United States in recent decades. Charter schools seek to reform public education through a blend of elements found in public schools (universal access and public funding) and elements often associated with private schools (choice, autonomy, and flexibility).

While the definition of charter schools varies somewhat by state, essentially they are nonsectarian public schools of choice that are free from many regulations that apply to traditional public schools. The "charter" agreement establishing each charter school is a performance contract that details, among other things, the school's mission, program, goals, and means of measuring success. Charters are usually granted for three to five years by an authorizer or sponsor (typically state or local school boards). In some states, public universities or other public entities may also grant charters.

Authorizers hold charter schools accountable for meeting their goals and objectives related to their mission and academic targets. Schools that do not meet their goals and objectives or do not abide by the terms of the contract can have their charter revoked or—when it comes time for renewal—not renewed. Because these are schools of choice and receive funding based on the number of students they enroll, charter schools also are accountable to parents and families who choose to enroll their child in them or choose to leave for another school.

The charter school movement has grown rapidly from two charter schools in Minnesota in 1992 to nearly 4,000 schools in 40 states and the District of Columbia as of 2007. In spite of this impressive growth, charter schools enroll only a few percent of the public school students in the United States. Some estimates suggest that charter schools enroll close to one million students in 2007. While the impact of charter schools appears minimal at the national level, a few states and several cities have seen the proportion of charter school students rise to capture a quarter of all public school students.

Beyond the United States, charter school reforms can be found in Canada and Puerto Rico. The charter school concept is also very similar to reforms initiated in other countries at approximately the same time. In the U.K., we saw the creation of grant-maintained schools, and in New Zealand and Sweden independent schools were initiated. These various reforms are part of a larger set of national and international trends that have sought to restructure public education. Attempts to restructure schools in the 1980s focused largely on decentralization, site-based management, small-scale choice reforms, and the use of market mechanisms. Proponents argued that restructuring public education would make it more efficient and responsive. One of the main reasons for the rapid and widespread growth of the charter movement in the 1990s was that it provided a vehicle to pursue many or most of the goals related to school restructuring. Another reason for the growth of charter schools is that this reform has been championed by a wide range of supporters, from those who saw these schools as a stepping stone to vouchers to those who saw charter schools as a compromise that would avoid vouchers.

HOW AND WHY CHARTER SCHOOLS WORK

The simplest and most direct way to explain the theory and ideas behind the charter school concept is to provide an illustrative model. Figure C.1 illustrates the charter school concept and highlights some structural changes as well as the intermediate and long-term goals or expectations of charter schools.

Structural Changes

The figure contains three parts. On the left are a set of policy changes—brought about mostly through changes in state law—that alter the legal, political, and economic environment in which charter schools operate. These are *structural changes* because they seek to fundamentally alter the conditions under which schools operate. The structural changes provide an opportunity space in which charter schools may experiment. Thus, the charter concept is rather different from other education reforms in that it does not prescribe specific interventions; rather, it changes the conditions under which schools develop and implement educational interventions.

One of the most important ways in which the charter concept seeks to change schools' external environments is through *choice*. Charter schools are schools of choice in that, with some exceptions, students from any district or locale may

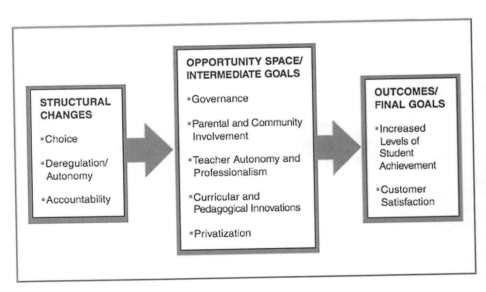

Figure C.1   Illustration of the charter school concept.

attend any charter school. Advocates of school choice argue that choice will lead to sorting by preferences, which will reduce the amount of time schools spend resolving conflicts among school stakeholders, leaving them more time and energy to devote to developing and implementing educational programs. Advocates of school choice also argue that the very act of choice will leave students, parents, and teachers disposed to work harder to support the schools they have chosen.

Another theoretical argument for charter schools is that *deregulated and autonomous* schools will develop innovations in curriculum, instruction, and governance that will lead to improvements in outcomes. Traditional public schools could also improve by adopting the innovative practices that charter schools are expected to develop.

At the heart of the charter concept lies a bargain. Charter schools will receive enhanced autonomy over curriculum, instruction, and operations. In exchange, they must agree to be held more accountable for results than other public schools. This new accountability holds charter schools accountable for outcomes—many of them articulated in the charter contract—and then employs deregulation to allow them to choose their own means for arriving at those goals. If charter schools do not live up to their stated goals, they can have their charter revoked by their sponsor, or they may not be able to renew the charter when it expires. Another form of accountability charter schools face is market accountability. Since these are schools of choice, and since money follows the students, charter schools that fail to attract and retain students will, in theory, go out of business.

Opportunity Space and Intermediate Goals

The autonomy granted to charter schools provides them with an "opportunity space" to create and operate schools in new ways. One important opportunity that charter schools have is to create their own governing boards. Charter school governing boards function much as local district school boards. Unlike district school boards, however, charter school boards are appointed rather than elected. Depending on the state, the board members are selected by the sponsor of the school that granted the charter or they are selected according to specific bylaws approved by the sponsor. This process helps ensure that the charter school can obtain a governing board that is focused and responsive to the specific needs of the school.

Charter school laws limit—to some extent—the opportunity space in which the schools operate by defining a number of "intermediate" goals. One such intermediate goal found in many states is the enhancement of *opportunities for parental and community involvement*. Parents who choose schools can be expected to be more engaged than those who do not. Beyond that, proponents of the charter concept contend that such involvement is a valuable resource that will ultimately lead to higher student achievement and other positive outcomes.

Another intermediate goal in most charter school laws is enhanced *professional autonomy and opportunities for professional development for teachers*. Charter schools are schools of choice for teachers as well as for parents and students. The charter school concept suggests that allowing teachers to choose schools with educational missions and approaches that closely match their own beliefs and interests will create school communities that can spend less time managing value conflicts among school stakeholders and more time implementing effective educational interventions. School choice can also promote a shared professional culture and higher levels of professional autonomy, which the literature suggests lead ultimately to improved levels of student achievement.

While it is true that many important regulations are not waived for charter schools, a few of the key freedoms charter schools are granted deal with teachers; for example, teachers are at-will employees, and most states do not require all charter school teachers to be certified. These provisions allow charter schools more flexibility in recruiting and structuring their teaching force to suit the specific needs of the school.

A third intermediate goal for charter schools is to develop *innovations in curriculum and instruction*. Put another way, proponents argue that charter schools can function as public education's R&D sector. As such, the benefits of charter schools will extend to noncharter students as traditional public schools adopt and emulate these innovations.

Finally, some charter school advocates hope the schools will be laboratories for experiments in the use of *privatized services*. According to these advocates, schools will run more efficiently by contracting out part or all the services they provide. Charter schools, as it turns out, have provided a quick and easy route for privatization as many states allow private schools to convert to public charter schools, and most states allow charter schools to contract all or part of their services to private education management organizations (EMOs). While some states have no charter schools operated by EMOs, others such as Michigan have more than three-quarters of their schools operated by EMOs. In total, it is estimated that between 20 and 25 percent of all charter schools in the United States are operated by EMOs.

The research base to support many of these theoretical arguments is largely borrowed from market research and remains unproven within the education sector. Nevertheless, proponents continue to argue that increased school choice and privatization will bring a much-needed dose of entrepreneurial spirit and a competitive ethos to public education. While the research base is still somewhat limited, in recent years more and more sound evaluation and research has replaced the rhetorical or theoretical pieces that earlier dominated the literature on charter schools.

Outcomes

Accountability is the price that charter schools pay for their autonomy—specifically, accountability for results rather than accountability for inputs and processes. This, however, begs two additional questions. The first is "accountability for which outputs and outcomes?" That is, which outcomes shall serve as the primary indicators of charter school quality? The second question is "accountability to whom?" In other words, who will decide whether charter schools are making sufficient progress toward their goals?

The most commonly noted "final" outcomes for charter schools are student achievement and customer satisfaction, which are the two constructs on the right-hand side of Figure C.1. There is some controversy over how policymakers and citizens should balance the values of student achievement and customer satisfaction. While many charter advocates argue that both are important, some libertarians and market conservatives view customer satisfaction as the paramount aim of public programs and agencies. Advocates of this position hold that a policy decision or outcome is good only if its customers think it is good and continue to "vote with their feet" for the service. Proponents of this position also maintain that it is the customers—parents and guardians—and not public officials who are best suited to know what is good for children. Interestingly, while most studies or evaluations of charter schools find that parents and students are generally satisfied with their charter school, the growing body of evidence indicates that—on the whole—charter schools are not performing better on standardized tests than are traditional public schools. Although there are a few successful states, the overall results are mixed at best.

THE FUTURE OF CHARTER SCHOOLS

Charter schools are here to stay. Few will question that. However, two unanswered questions are of particular interest to the future of charter schools: What will be the likely rate of growth of charter schools? Will charter schools remain a distinct and separate school form, or will they be dragged back into the fold and come to resemble and operate like traditional public schools? Answers to these questions will depend greatly on how charter schools respond to a variety of potential threats that are both external and internal to the movement.

External threats to charter schools include state deficits and re-regulation. School systems are under increasing pressure due to large budget deficits at local, state, and national levels. In times like these, governments will need to focus on core education services and are less likely to start or expand reforms such as charter schools. Although some may argue that charter schools can be more efficient, to date there is insufficient evidence to support these claims. Another potential threat to charter schools is re-regulation. Requirements that charter schools administer the same standardized tests and have the same performance standards as traditional public schools mean that they cannot risk developing and using new curricular materials. New mandates regarding outcomes pressure charter schools to conform and restrict the autonomy they were intended to enjoy.

There are also a number of internal threats that charter schools face that come from within the movement. These include the following:

- Growing school and class size that is now approaching the sizes found in traditional public schools.
- Unchecked expansion of private EMOs. Claim that EMOs can make charter schools more effective have not been substantiated by research.

While charter schools were originally intended to be autonomous and locally run schools, increasingly they are being started by EMOs—rather than community groups—and steered from distant corporate headquarters.

- Lack of innovation and limited diversity of school options. True school choice requires a diversity of options from which to choose, but charter schools are becoming increasingly similar to traditional public schools.
- Lack of support and standards for authorizers. Many authorizers have no funds allocated for oversight activities. Also, many authorizers are unprepared and sometimes unwilling to be sponsors of charter schools.
- Attrition of teachers and administrators is extremely high in charter schools. A number of studies suggest that annual attrition of teachers ranges from 15 to 30 percent. The loss of teachers leads to greater instability in the schools and represents a loss of investment. Some of this attrition may be "functional" as charter school administrators exercise their autonomy in determining which teachers to hire and fire.
- Rapid growth of reforms. As with any sound reform process, it is important to test charter school reforms on a small scale in order to make adjustments before implementing it on a large scale. Some states have implemented and expanded their charter school reforms very rapidly, resulting in a backlash of resistance as shortcomings in oversight and other neglected aspects of the reform become apparent.

EVALUATING SCHOOLS OR EVALUATED SCHOOLS

Charter schools—by their very design—were intended to be evaluating schools. The charter school concept is based on providing greater autonomy for charter schools in exchange for greater accountability. This implies that charter schools would be actively involved in evaluating their outcomes and reporting these outcomes to state agencies, the authorizer or sponsor, parents, and the public at large. Another reason that suggests that charter schools would be "evaluating schools" is that they embody site-based management, so there are no bureaucracies to deal with. Also, the smaller size of these schools and self-selection by teachers and staff should lead to higher levels of interpersonal trust and better collaborative relationships and professional culture. Reasons such as these suggest that charter schools would be more likely to use and incorporate evaluation into regular operations at the school.

Nevertheless, charter schools face a number of obstacles in using evaluation or fulfilling their obligations for accountability. These include vague, incomplete, and often unmeasurable goals and objectives included in the charter contracts and the overwhelming start-up issues that charter schools face. Given the enormous start-up challenges related to facilities, staffing, and recruiting students, it is no surprise that charter schools place evaluation low on the list of priorities. Further obstacles include the often new and inexperienced school leaders and the high turnover of teachers and administrators. Another critical obstacle is the weak signals that the schools might receive from oversight agencies.

While there are tremendous differences between and within states, it generally can be said that evaluation conducted by individual charter schools is weak and limited in scope. Because of demands for accountability and because they are not sufficiently proactive in demonstrating success, charter schools have largely become "evaluated" rather than "evaluating" schools.

AUTONOMY FOR ACCOUNTABILITY

As noted earlier, the academic performance of charter schools is mixed at best. Defenders of charter schools rationalize or justify this less-than-expected performance by pointing out that many traditional public schools are also failing; and thus it is unfair to hold charter schools to high standards when other schools are not.

Nationally, between 6 and 7 percent of all charter schools have closed, which is surprising given their relatively weak performance. One reason for the lack of closures is insufficient evidence about school performance from which authorizers can make renewal, nonrenewal, or revocation decisions. Political and ideological factors can also explain—in part—why many authorizers are closing so few poor-performing charters.

Closing poor-performing charter schools will strengthen charter school reforms in two ways. First, removing these schools from the aggregate results for charter schools will increase their overall results. Second, closing such schools sends a strong message to other charter schools that the autonomy for accountability agreement is real.

While many traditional schools do perform far below established standards, this should not be used as a justification for excusing charter schools from the standards agreed upon in their contracts. The idea behind charter schools was not to replicate the existing system, which many argue suffers from a lack of accountability. Rather, they were envisioned as a means of pressuring traditional public schools to improve both by example and through competition. If charter schools are to serve as a lever for change, they must be better than traditional public schools, and they must be held accountable for their performance.

Further Reading: Bulkley, K., & Wohlstetter, P., eds., 2004, *Taking account of charter schools: What's happened and what's next?* New York: Teachers College Press; Finn, C., Manno, B., & Vanourek, G., 2000, *Charter schools in action. Renewing public education,* Princeton, NJ: Princeton University Press; Fuller, B., ed., 2000, *Inside charter schools: The paradox of radical decentralization,* Cambridge, MA: Harvard University Press; Miron, G., & Nelson, C., 2002, *What's public about charter schools? Lessons learned about choice and accountability,* Thousand Oaks, CA: Corwin Press.

Gary Miron

CHILDREN'S AND STUDENTS' RIGHTS

We live in a world where conflict is a constant reality of our day-to-day existence. The images of violence in the context of our homes, schools, communities, and across national and international settings bombard our senses so that no one is immune from these horrific cruelties. Although we are witnesses to this violence throughout society, the pervasiveness of these events across time and settings has often buffered our shock and muted our response to atrocities against the most vulnerable, including the children who bear the brunt of abuse and exploitation.

Children are the historic victims of ill treatment. Infanticide was an accepted practice to manage population growth, selectively limit female births in favor of preferred male offspring, or eliminate physically deformed children. Infanticide became less accepted as a practice, but communities condoned the sale and abandonment of children. Throughout the Middle Ages children as young as five years old worked alongside adults, wore fashions that mirrored adult dress, and were treated as miniature grown-ups. In England, sexual relationship with a child under 12 years of age was only a misdemeanor, and it was lawful to engage a child aged 12 or older in sex. During the nineteenth century in the United States the privacy of the family superseded the state's interest in protecting the rights of the young. Sexual abuse was largely ignored as a crime until the 1970s, and even in the new millennium, stories of child abuse abound in the newspapers, on television, and in radio broadcasts. These stories may elicit a visceral response, but the pervasiveness of these acts may evade our sense of duty to act.

The history of childhood chronicles the intensity and expansiveness of abuses suffered by children throughout time and delineates the necessity of protecting the young who are at risk for the most toxic effects of destructive acts against their well-being. The universal pervasiveness of children's exploitation highlights the challenge to policymakers and child advocates to intervene on behalf of the young and to uphold their civic obligation to protect the most vulnerable individuals in society.

Tragically, our desensitization towards others' despair has contributed to a minimization of the social connectedness within our communities. The social capital of a community relies on the civic engagement of its members and gauges levels of trust, socialization, and interaction with others. Recent studies have suggested that social capital can predict the quality of life and contribute to greater happiness and well-being.

Despite the importance of social connectedness, it has experienced a decline during the past half-century. Nonetheless, efforts to transform the status of children have fostered the evolution of child advocacy. Through social action, political agendas, and organizational policies, a universal obligation to protect children's rights and engage youth has been nurtured and disseminated.

It requires a significant transformation in society to not only listen to children's voices but to also take children's issues seriously, regardless of the diverse perspectives on how to respond. Childhood, a socially constructed concept that has proliferated through Western views of personality and society, has contributed to the evolution of an international human rights initiative and nation-specific responses. Although there is not agreement on what is harmful to children, internationally there is a legislated expectation that children will be protected.

The ideal of applying human rights to children's issues through legal enforcements is a recent development and is considered controversial. Divergences in cultural responses to violence and maltreatment, including its definition, necessitate a complex response, and some perceive the universal application of children's rights to be a mandate for culturally specific solutions based on assumptions about childhood.

Although infringement of children's rights is a global and endemic problem, culture affects not only the definition of abuse and exploitation but also the response to child victimization. Our conceptualization of child protection and maltreatment reflects the beliefs, tensions, and injustices of the surrounding society. Although these social constructs are culturally defined, the universal dictates support an undefined practice of protecting children and upholding their right to safety and well-being.

Within a cultural context some practices are deemed exploitative while others are encouraged as a necessary component of the socialization process into adulthood. Yet the unifying cause of protecting the well-being of our youth joins the world in a universal obligation to acknowledge violence against the young as a fundamental violation of human rights, regardless of the extent of condemnation or tolerance for the victimization of children. As a result, every child in the global community has a recognized right to protection and safety.

A child embodies the future while reflecting the past. The history of family traditions, social expectations, political policies, religious dictates, and cultural mores partially defines the experience of each child. Abuse occurs in the context of these social and cultural foundations. Consequently, there is a need to adopt critical and cultural approaches to pressing social issues.

Although child advocacy can serve as an integral component of developing students' understanding of participatory citizenry, these social concerns are more than just of academic consequence. Child advocacy is pertinent to public policy, since children who are victimized or exploited are more likely to be arrested as a juvenile, engage in adult criminal behavior, abuse drugs, and experience other adverse effects on their health and mental health.

FOSTERING ADVOCACY AND PROMOTING SOCIAL JUSTICE

Standing up for those who have no voice—the weak, the powerless, the young—is a challenge. Threats to children's well-being have persisted through time, and although universal principles and international frameworks have guided efforts to safeguard children, an effective response to infringements of children's rights requires the active support of young people. The transformation of the response to child maltreatment and exploitation necessitates a focus on youth whose voice can shift participatory citizenship to an emphasis on children and children's issues. The active participation of young people can improve the policies, structures, and mechanisms that are created to protect them. Participatory citizenship is a component of civic education in which students engage in discussions and activities to address critical social issues and serve the public good. This focus on social issues connects the scholastic emphasis of a content area with real world issues.

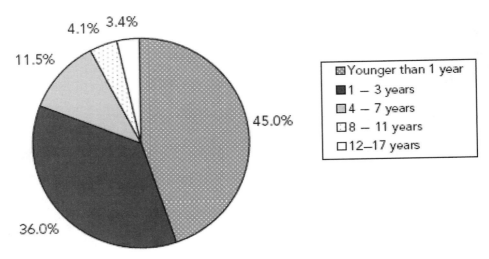

Figure C.2 Child abuse and neglect fatalities victims by age, 2004.

Source: Child Welfare Information Gateway. 2006. Child abuse and neglect fatalities: Statistics and interventions.

The broad issue of children's rights extends to the global community as technological networks overcome geographic boundaries, foster communication, and draw attention to the interrelatedness of people across nations. Young people can become social actors who contribute to part of the solution by championing changes that not only enhance their own lives, but also promote the need to protect and defend other vulnerable individuals.

The Convention on the Rights of the Child (CRC) has highlighted the challenges of implementing and monitoring public policies that are designed to advocate for children. Although the CRC was unanimously adopted by the United Nations General Assembly in 1989 and subsequently ratified by 192 countries, developing mechanisms to overcome child fatalities, promote quality health care, foster educational opportunities, and prevent maltreatment and exploitation is difficult when child-friendly policies are underfunded or a low priority amidst complex political agendas and economic instability. The momentum for achieving children's rights must be driven by an informed citizenship with the skills and knowledge to recognize the interrelationships between national, cultural, familial, and individual factors associated with child victimization. Child well-being has drawn the attention of policymakers and researchers, yet the education community has been relatively disconnected from the significance of the CRC for their own practice and focus of work with children in schools. In addition to helping shape program development, young people can serve effectively as peer educators and advocates for children's rights.

CHILD ADVOCACY

Although nations may differ on the social policies and professional practices that frame community responses to child abuse, there are commonalities in the

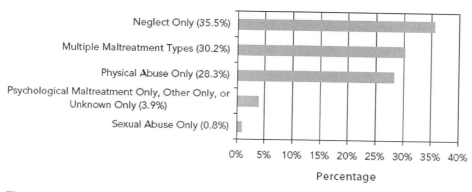

Figure C.3 Child abuse and neglect fatalities by maltreatment type, 2004.

Source: Child Welfare Information Gateway. 2006. Child abuse and neglect fatalities: Statistics and interventions.

underlying issues that guide the implementation of interventions. Child advocacy is based on a conceptualization of schools as prosocial support systems for children and families in which educators are active participants in multidisciplinary, community-oriented intervention efforts. Despite global awareness and widespread support, implementation of an advocacy role is an ominous task and can have controversial aspects. In the United States, concerns over intrusive influences into family life have blocked ratification of the Convention on the Rights of the Child, and even in other countries where the CRC is ratified, specific policies and solutions to the dilemma of protecting children are not resolved.

Although the international laws clearly dictate as offenses the abuse of children, many individuals in the United States, where the treaty has not yet been ratified, remain unaware of its existence and the right of each child to protection. The culture of the United States encompasses diverse languages, ethnicities, religious principles, gender roles, political orientations, views of class, and family structures. Each of these components contributes to a unique perspective on how to regard issues of violence and abuse. In addition to the divergence of perceptions, the response to child maltreatment is further confounded by the variations in state definitions of abuse. The federal statutes stipulate a minimum set of behaviors, but states define what constitutes abuse and the exceptions, which are often based on variations in parenting practices due to cultural, religious, and socioeconomic diversity. Confusion over the definition of maltreatment may affect practice in responding to and intervening in abusive behaviors. This imprecision and variability in defining abuse may be a barrier to drawing valid and reliable comparisons between cultural groups and national entities.

American schools primarily have been involved in violence prevention as part of a mandated role to intervene on behalf of children at risk for abuse and neglect. The public interest in child protection dates back to the 1800s, when separate juvenile courts were established to address children's unique legal and judicial needs. In 1865 the Society to Prevent Cruelty to Animals was founded in the United States and addressed children's issues. Nine years later the Society to Prevent Cruelty to Children was formed. However, it was not until the 1960s that nationwide interest in child maltreatment spurred the implementation of statutes to protect the physical and mental well-being of children. Today, every state in the United States has enacted laws requiring the reporting of suspected abuse and neglect.

Educators in school settings across the United States serve as a critical first line of defense in assisting with the identification and prevention of child abuse and neglect. Due to the extensive interaction between school personnel and students during the school day, educators have an important opportunity to observe children, establish a reasonable level of suspicion, and report suspected incidents. Educators in this process may play an integral role; however, they tend to lack confidence in their range of knowledge of abuse and their ability to provide appropriate intervention services to victimized children and their families. Consequently, as society struggles to address the serious social and public health problem of child abuse and neglect, educators often find themselves inadequately prepared to assist child victims in the classroom.

A CIVIC RESPONSIBILITY TO ADVOCATE FOR CHILDREN

Although recognizing when a student is at risk increases the potential for intervention that can assist abused and neglected children, educators in the United States have a great opportunity to facilitate the growth and development of children by presenting strategies that decrease the likelihood of abuse and exploitation occurring and provide support for children's disclosures. Child abuse outcomes are impacted by the chronicity of the maltreatment, suggesting that early recognition and intervention may optimize the child's functioning and promote resilient behaviors.

Barriers that stifle attempts to help children compromise the well-being and potential of students; however, the interplay of teacher education programs, school systems, and the community can challenge this difficult social issue and secure resources that promote best practices. The schools are an ideal setting to foster connections between isolated families and the community. In the school setting, social networking can create a stable environment where consistent daily interaction can foster natural community-based supportive services. A program in Pennsylvania accomplished this objective by developing an intervention curriculum that trained resilient parents as cofacilitators and included topics that focused on parent needs for themselves (i.e., establishing trust, identifying strengths and weaknesses, focusing on stressors and coping skills, and addressing goals and barriers); parent needs in managing parent-child relationships; and parent needs to engage with the school community. When programs are implemented to create collaborative initiatives addressing children's rights, a supportive focus can readily be embraced by school personnel as they subsequently increase their sensitivity to the identification of children and families who could benefit from a multidomain array of services.

Many school districts have established procedures for reporting, but the intent of the legal mandate is not just to legislate a report, but also to reinforce action for the protection of children. With regard to schools, action can extend to monitoring the intellectual, physical, and social-emotional functioning of children; creating a supportive and caring climate in the classroom; and offering interventions in conjunction with community agencies. Despite their extensive access to children, many education professionals have not realized their opportunity to intervene on behalf of a maltreated child.

Overall, education professionals report a limited understanding of ways to work with abused children in the classroom. Formal training is infrequent and limited. Moreover, it tends to focus on indicators of abuse for identification and places little emphasis on intervention skills for dealing with families in crisis. Not surprisingly, there is widespread interest in additional training to supplement current incomplete levels of knowledge. This identified need presents an opportunity to introduce developmental interventions to educators that empower abused and neglected children with constructive problem-solving skills and build on their strengths, interests, and capacity to cope with stress. The skills needed by professionals include strategies to provide consistent messages of worth and safety to children in schools.

With the focus of the schools on the promotion of academic standards, many teachers have obscured their awareness of the daily trauma of abuse and neglect and undermined their authority and role as advocates and protectors of children's well-being. In fact, many policies contribute to the systemic oppression and violence against children. The failed response of educators to address trauma and abuse with caring and therapeutic interventions will require further perpetuation of policies of containment and control as the social stressors take their toll on fragile children. Confusion over appropriate responses to victimized children has resulted in a pervasive failure of significant adults to protect children and ensure their safety.

Teachers need to create a classroom environment that is safe, nurturing, and responsive to the needs of an abused child. In this context, educators will find many opportunities to attend to children's basic needs for warmth and security. Children's ability to achieve is impacted by fulfillment of these basic needs and can be accomplished by communication and conflict-management strategies to provide alternatives to rage, violence, and despair. Overall, the classroom should foster a strength-based orientation and approach, and as a result academic success will contribute to resilience.

These findings note the importance of the interplay between legal mandates, personal experience, and institutional response and demonstrate the need to involve educators in training and collaborative initiatives. Presently, systems for monitoring the maltreatment of school-age children and the manner in which the school system and staff address maltreatment are lacking. The full implementation of policies with multiple program components that address school-facilitated prevention and intervention can enhance outcome efficacy.

The necessity of involving educators in the response to child maltreatment is supported by evidence that indicates that child abuse or neglect can contribute to educational and behavioral difficulties in the classroom. School-based interventions, which are structured without regard for complex family problems, fail to optimize the coordination of assistance and support. It is critical that educators understand the multidimensional symptoms and effects of child maltreatment. Moreover, the contributions of educators to an interdisciplinary response to abuse and neglect are essential to facilitating detection and prevention. The following recommendations describe changes that can reinforce the role of educators in meeting their civic role as advocates for children.

PREVENTING AND INTERVENING IN THE VICTIMIZATION OF CHILDREN

Schools are often relied upon to be the center of prevention and intervention efforts. Personal safety programs are implemented in many school sites; however, these programs are not mandated in all schools, and they tend to be infrequent. There remain a number of opportunities to improve practices in the schools that will identify and support children who have been abused and neglected.

The focus in schools on high-stakes testing does not negate children's needs for support and prosocial skills. We are faced with the conundrum of teaching what we measure. But there is no state or national test for effective survival skills. Nonetheless, educators need to incorporate into the curriculum resilience training and measurements of effective functioning. This can be accomplished by integrating communication and conflict-management strategies into instruction.

Specific prevention programs in schools need to focus on teaching appropriate behavior that can counter the learned abusive interactions. Punitive responses are not sufficient in moderating discipline problems and violent behaviors that may be associated with abuse and neglect. The critical component of successful intervention is a uniform structure and consistent expectations. Peer mediation, which is currently incorporated into many schools, demonstrates an evolving school-wide culture that is supportive of socially responsible behavior. Continued initiatives that involve a whole-school response to conflict and a commitment to open communication and problem-solving skill development enhance the schools' role in providing a safe and supportive environment for children at risk. Teachers and administrators also have an opportunity to model for students their roles in a community of caring by listening to children's issues and responding in a responsible and respectful manner. To ensure that all schools in the system have an effective and caring approach to intervention, community-wide planning is recommended that involves families and neighborhood agencies in forming comprehensive plans and coordinating interagency services.

Educators need guidance in recognizing the broader response needed to respond to suspected child abuse and neglect. Obligations of educators extend beyond the legal mandate of reporting and include the professional dictate of fostering intellectual and emotional development by observing a child's strengths, skills, interests, talents, and methods of coping with distress to assure appropriate interventions that respond to the child's academic challenges and demands. Effective intervention offers empowerment of young victims with constructive problem-solving skills and caring and supportive contexts. Beyond the legal responsibility to report abuse, teachers have opportunities to create classroom environments where all children feel safe, valued, and respected. This can be best facilitated by clear classroom expectations and predictable routines that assist students in regaining control of their environment. Instruction in social skills helps students feel confident in their role as valued contributors to the class setting and assist them in achieving a sense of control.

Interventions that may be designed should incorporate multilevel strategies that serve the needs of parents and children in creating safety in their homes and the community. School-based prevention programming should include a focus on child development, protection, and linkages with community resources and supports. These interventions could include outreach activities that promote prosocial parent-child interactions through school-based parenting services, supportive parent networks, and social skills training in which parents serve as volunteers in the school and assist in evolving the social effectiveness and support of child victims.

FOSTERING INTERSYSTEM COLLABORATION

An important skill for educators is when and how to seek outside assistance in order to address issues related to victimized children. By reinforcing the role of educators in a multidisciplinary partnership between school, community, mental health, medical, social service, and law enforcement professionals, teachers may experience increased levels of certainty in their identification of abuse and more lenient decision criteria for reporting. This can be accomplished by minimizing the perceived costs of reporting and maximizing benefits.

Presently, the trauma from abuse and neglect exceeds the capacity of school systems to respond to child victims. Schools should work to coordinate a collaborative and productive response to abuse by facilitating communication between school faculty, parents, the child, protective services, and community agencies. This includes follow-up after a suspected case is reported. To initiate this partnership, a forum for discussing the public-policy implications of school involvement in child-maltreatment intervention should be initiated.

School-community programs and partnerships can promote training and staff-development programs, public awareness initiatives, and access to school facilities and resources. This may include parenting education and initiatives to make children aware of their rights and supports to protect their safety. It is also important that children and adolescents have opportunities to participate in creating safety at a developmentally appropriate level. This promotes confidence and competence as they learn to shape solutions to critical social issues. A community-wide multidisciplinary response involves critical stakeholders in identifying the most effective ways to achieve sustainable social outcomes for children.

HELPING CHILDREN BY STRENGTHENING FAMILIES

Although school-based responses to child maltreatment are necessary, they are not a sufficient remedy to the trauma of abuse. Children's rights promotion needs to be addressed through integration into school policy and programming.

Schools are an important system in child well-being initiatives; however, proactive prevention efforts are receiving little resource allocation. In the United States, less than 10 percent of the funds allotted for abuse and neglect are designated for prevention. Although interventions may be valuable, implementation requires a financial capacity to involve families and communities while facilitating collaborations. Resources are needed to forge partnerships and build the schools' capacities to address their responsibility to violence prevention.

Some nations have already integrated comprehensive plans for the prevention of abuse, abandonment, and neglect of children. However, the capacity of schools to facilitate this role cannot be actualized until additional financial resources are provided to fund training and partnerships between educators and the communities in which children live. Policymakers should be encouraged to provide funding that supports the current provisions of existing statutes. An emphasis on preparation of educators to promote children's rights will contribute to a standardization of practice, intensified training, and better accountability of practices in schools to stem the tide of abuse and exploitation.

PLACING THE CHILD AT THE CENTER

In order to sustain positive change for children, communities need to commit their support to children's rights by actively modeling participatory behavior and creating safe environments for children to grow and develop. Child-led advocacy creates a context in which children's voices are heard and valued. Young people are actively engaged in efforts to transform policies and laws by providing them with developmentally appropriate and child-friendly knowledge and relevant information to help shape outcomes and the process. It is the responsibility of the adult community and governments to contribute to the development of resilience in children and young people, enabling them eventually to assume responsibility for their own lives and achieve their full potential by actively contributing to decisions to enhance their lives.

Every child has the right to be loved and cared for and to feel safe both at home and away from home. One aspect of this is the provision of education and child welfare services that are more responsive to the voices of children. Moreover, the development of initiatives that allow children a voice and work towards the increasing democratization of schools are necessary components. But as a society we need to consider how we empower all children. Empowered children speak out and do not become alienated. They reject bullying, racism, and abuse. Evidence shows that disempowered children are more frequently the victims of abuse. While citizenship education may be part of all our curricula, it will not make the citizens of tomorrow unless they feel they have a valued role in that society—first as children and subsequently as adults. Children and young people who know they can talk about their experiences, who feel their views and fears are listened to and respected, and who are given explanations of events that impinge on them are more likely to understand the extent of their own obligations in the various aspects of their lives. We know this is not the experience of many children in their own homes, so as a society we are obliged to have structures in place that support all children and keep them safe.

The inclusion of children's voices in the promotion of children's rights affirms children's human dignity and physical integrity. Children are not just social actors in their families and communities; they are the holders of rights and the key to ending the violence that is perpetrated against our young.

Further Reading: Berson, I. R., & Berson, M. J., 2001, Galvanizing support for children's issues through awareness of global advocacy, in Ilene R. Berson, Michael J. Berson, & Barbara C. Cruz (Eds.), *Research in global child advocacy: Cross cultural perspectives,* Greenwich, CT: Information Age Publishing; Berson, M. J., & Berson, I. R., 2000, An introduction to global child advocacy: Historical action, contemporary perspectives, and future directions, *The International Journal of Educational Policy, Research, and Practice, 1*(1), 1–11; Block, A. A., 1997, *I'm only bleeding: Education as the practice of violence against children,* New York: Peter Lang Publishing; Dudley-Marling, C., Jackson, J., & Stevens, L. P., 2006, Disrespecting childhood, *Phi Delta Kappan, 87*(10), 748–755; Petit, M. R., 2006, *Homeland insecurity: American children at risk,* Washington, DC: Every Child Matters Education Fund, retrieved December 15, 2006, from http://www.democracyinaction.org/dia/organizationsORG/ECM/www/homelandinsecurity/.

Michael J. Berson and Ilene R. Berson

CITIZENSHIP EDUCATION

Citizenship education is the fundamental premise on which the whole public school experience functions. Schooling in all societies aims to teach students the knowledge, skills, and dispositions needed to act effectively as citizens within the parameters of what each society deems worthy. In a democratic society, key curricular goals include knowledge of the community, nation, and world; skills of critical mindedness and political action; and democratic dispositions of cooperation and tolerance.

Schools in the United States, unlike their counterparts in many other countries, operate independently of a national authority. However, national controversies over citizenship education, especially as it relates to patriotism, abound. These controversies include the clash between unfettered free market economics and social justice, the problems of pluralism and national unity in a context of modernization, and the struggle over the meaning of patriotism in a democracy. Each of these controversies stem from the American sociopolitical and economic context as it developed over the past 125 years.

A SOCIETY IN FLUX

Democratic citizenship education both reflects and aims to improve society. In the United States, varying states of sociopolitical and economic flux influenced the course of the public school experience. Prominent among these include trends related to immigration, modernization, and free market economics.

IMPORTANT EVENTS IN CITIZENSHIP EDUCATION

1889: Jane Adams opens Hull-House to help immigrants gain citizenship.

1903: W.E.B. Du Bois' The *Souls of Black Folk* attacks Booker T. Washington's "accommodationist" approach to African American education.

1905: Thomas Jesse Jones establishes "The Social Studies in the Hampton Curriculum" for developing African American citizenship.

1916: *Report of the Social Studies Committee of the National Education Association.*

1921: David Snedden's *Sociological Determination of Objectives in Education* lays out differentiated instruction for producers and consumers.

1923: Supreme Court overturns teaching foreign language bans in *Meyer v. Nebraska.*

1929–1940: Harold Rugg textbooks capture social studies market.

1936: Attacks begin on popular Rugg textbooks for "anti-competition" content.

1940: National Association of Manufacturers "educational assignments" curricula disseminated to promote free market system and citizenship.

1942: Historian Alan Nevin characterizes the teaching of American history in schools as unpatriotic.

1958: E. Merrill Root's *Brainwashing in the High Schools* attacks textbooks in civics and social studies as divisive and unpatriotic.

1964: Establishment of over forty Mississippi Freedom Schools intended to promote and expand African Americans' citizenship education.

1969: Supreme Court rules in favor of "symbolic" free speech in schools in *Tinker v. Des Moines Independent Community School District.*

1994: Controversial national history standards released and attacked.

2002: Florida enacts Celebrate Freedom Week in all public schools and requires portions of Declaration of Independence to be recited daily.

Following the Civil War, events in Europe and Asia launched a massive trend of immigration to the United States. Between 1876 and 1926 alone, some 27 million immigrants entered the United States. Moreover, the world wars brought large populations of African Americans looking for work to urban centers in the northern states. The lure for many of these immigrants and migrants was the opportunity to obtain jobs during a time of massive industrialization. These immigrants and sons and daughters of former slaves brought cultural traditions and religious beliefs with them that ran counter to the pre-existing white, Anglo-Saxon, Protestant belief system that was most prevalent in schools. This trend fluctuated over the last century, but a steady wave of immigrants, particularly people from Latin America who now comprise the largest minority population in the country, continues to see the United States as a viable economic alternative to their homelands.

Modernization spurred massive immigration to the United States and migration to its largest cities. This trend, sometimes known as the Industrial Revolution, shifted the workforce from a rural agrarian base to urban centers, where the growth of large public schools assisted newcomers in seeking economic success and also built a competent workforce for the benefit of business and industry. With modernization, government began to grow in size and regulatory power, establishing bureaucratic, highly organized systems of maintenance such as school systems. The secularization of knowledge—a trend motivated by the faith in scientific endeavor—brought about the belief that societal ills produced by modernization could be cured via the methods of science that brought about these ills.

Laissez-faire, free market capitalism has been lurking in the background throughout the multicultural growth and modernization of American society. The valorization of rugged individualism free from government regulation has winnowed its way in and out of education in the United States for more than a century. Sometimes overtly taught as an aspect of patriotism and at other times assumed to be a part of the hidden curriculum of personal success, free market capitalism has been a major player in the struggle over citizenship education in America's classrooms. As the catalyst for massive immigration and migration, as well as the fuel that fired the engine of modernization, free market capitalism has a great stake in what it means to be a citizen in this democracy.

THE FREE MARKET AND SOCIAL REFORM

The lack of government regulation on expansive industrial growth and cheap immigrant and migrant labor brought about an extreme disparity in wealth following the Civil War. The "robber barons," as they were known, took advantage of this situation by accumulating fortunes of astronomical size, often at the expense of immigrants and migrants flocking to urban centers. The turn of the twentieth century experienced a backlash against the inhumane treatment of workers and the extreme power put in the hands of the wealthy few during the Progressive Era. Social reformers and critics such as John Spargo, Edward Bellamy, and Jane Addams engaged in projects that gave visibility to social and economic disparities. Nonetheless, huge waves of immigrants flooded the urban North, and schools faced the task of educating millions of immigrants and their children in democratic citizenship. This situation led to the ongoing clash between free market capitalism and the goals of social reformers in the education of democratic citizens.

Citizenship education during the Progressive Era fell largely into two camps using the same term—"social efficiency." Education sociologist David Snedden envisioned schools that would educate children as either "producers" who would constitute the working class or "consumers" who would assume the mantle of economic and social leadership in society. His view of a socially engineered society, where everyone found and accepted their social situation, received high praise from the business world. In opposition to Snedden's idea of social efficiency was the view of philosopher John Dewey. Dewey believed that schools should be agents working to assist students in developing a socially efficient mind through reflective thinking. Thus, the school, far from acting as an agent for the corporate status quo, aimed to eliminate social barriers through experiences designed to enlarge the human sense of community.

Influenced heavily by Dewey's ideas, the landmark 1916 *Report of the Committee on Social Studies of the Commission on the Reorganization of Secondary Education of the National Education Association* placed the responsibility of citizenship education squarely on the shoulders of the social studies curriculum. The notion of community civics, forwarded by this report, appealed nationally to schools. The report's capstone course for high school students, titled *Problems of Democracy*, laid the foundation for more aggressively critical citizenship curricula during the Great Depression. From this point forward, the struggle over citizenship education took place primarily in the field of social studies.

World War I and the 1920s diminished the quest to seek a more socially and economically equitable curriculum for citizenship education. Patriotism spawned by the war and economic growth throughout the "Roaring Twenties" masked social ills and rekindled the urge to socially engineer society. Organizations such as the National Association of Manufacturers (NAM) championed vocational curricula that sorted students into their most fitting roles as citizens in a free market. The exultant tide of economic boom swamped the causes of social reform and social justice. Even many progressives believed that vocational training in the schools, if conducted in an inclusive and comprehensive setting, held the best hope for a competent, happy citizen workforce.

The Great Depression, however, adjusted this sort of thinking. A movement began under the banner of "social reconstruction" that rekindled the reform spirit of the Progressive Era and rained a torrent of criticism on the free market system. In education, a group of scholars and school personnel known as the "social frontiersmen"—drawing from Dewey's version of social efficiency—led the way. Emblematic of this group was Harold O. Rugg, a professor at Teachers College, Columbia University. Titled *Man and His Changing Society*, Rugg's wildly popular series of social studies textbooks brought into question the assumption that unfettered free market capitalism was a necessary foundation for democracy. Attacks on Rugg began in 1936 when his books were criticized for "sovietizing" students with "anti-competition" content. School book burnings of his curriculum ensued.

In 1940, NAM again joined the citizenship education fray with an explosion of curricula known as "educational assignments" to combat the social-reconstructionist movement in citizenship education. As the Depression came to a close, NAM commissioned a professor of banking at Columbia University, Ralph W. Robbey, to develop abstracts of social studies textbooks so that businesspeople could be armed with knowledge to address and combat negative free market curricula in their communities. Scholars and educators as diverse as Charles Beard and Henry Steele Commager in history and Harold Rugg and Edgar Wesley in social studies education came under severe criticism for their treatment of the free market system.

World War II and the ensuing Cold War brought heightened interest in the business community to link free market capitalism to patriotism within the

THE RUGG SOCIAL-SCIENCE COURSE SERIES

Up to 1931

The Reading Books

Volume I: An Introduction to American Civilization
Volume II: Changing Civilizations in the Modern World
Volume III: A History of American Civilization: Economic and Social
Volume IV: A History of American Government and Culture
Volume V: An Introduction to Problems of American Culture
Volume VI: Changing Governments and Changing Cultures

The Workbooks

Volume I: Pupil's Workbook to accompany An Introduction to American Civilization
Volume II: Pupil's Workbook to accompany Changing Civilizations in the Modern World
Volume III: Pupil's Workbook to accompany A History of American Civilization: Economic and Social
Volume IV: Pupil's Workbook to accompany A History of American Government and Culture
Volume V: Pupil's Workbook to accompany An Introduction to Problems of American Culture
Volume VI: Pupil's Workbook to accompany Changing Governments and Changing Cultures

The Teacher's Guides

Volume I: Teacher's Guide for an Introduction to American Civilization
Volume II: Teacher's Guide for Changing Civilizations in the Modern World

curriculum. Massive public relations campaigns brought various forms of pro-free market curricula (e.g., Junior Achievement programs) into America's classrooms from organizations such as NAM and the U.S. Chamber of Commerce. Social reformers also contributed much to the struggle over citizenship-education curriculum after World War II via renewed vigor drawn from *Brown v. Board of Education* (1954), the War on Poverty, and protests of the Vietnam War. The Citizen Education Project at Teachers College, Columbia University, represented a growing movement during the 1940s and 1950s that advocated citizenship development through an ambitious, participation-oriented curriculum. Other curricula involving social problems and public issues (e.g., the Harvard *Public Issues Series,* Brown University's *Choices for the 21st Century,* and *Rethinking Schools*) continued the spirit of social justice and reform through the study of pressing social problems since the Vietnam War era. Additionally, service learning as a graduation requirement has moved students throughout the country to a heightened awareness of issues in social and economic justice and how, as citizens, they can address these issues through action.

PLURIBUS AND UNUM

Immigration and emancipation mark a century-long debate over the definition of citizenship, as well as the makeup of the citizenry. An expanding inclusiveness in the meaning of citizenship brought about clashes between the forms of citizenship education best suited for the United States.

Constitutional amendments expanding citizenship to include African Americans and women and the Snyder Act of 1924 (making Native Americans citizens), coupled with child labor laws and compulsory schooling regulations, increased school enrollments tremendously during the early twentieth century. Today, more than 90 percent of school-age children (approximately 50 million students) attend public schools in the United States. Given this growth in public education's vastness and diversity, the fundamental mandate of citizenship education experienced much tension over the past century.

This situation—the tension between ethnic and racial pluralism and national unity—continues today. Immigrant waves and heightened patriotism clashed during the Progressive Era as the United States entered the stage of world powers and experienced the infusion of myriad cultural mores. Citizenship education from both the conservative and liberal perspectives saw the enlarging pluralism brought about by immigration as a threat to democracy. Nativism in the schools manifested in bans on foreign language instruction by some state governments (overturned by the Supreme Court in *Meyer v. Nebraska,* 1923) and the attempt to denationalize immigrants from their cultural heritage in order to assimilate them into the Anglo-American tradition. Progressives addressed the cultural influx by gently assimilating immigrants into the principles of democracy without stripping immigrant students of their heritage.

Post–Civil War constitutional amendments ensuring citizenship for former slaves brought about African American public education on a large scale. The Supreme Court decision in *Plessy v. Ferguson* (1896) kept local enforcement of racial segregation intact, especially in the South. Efforts at citizenship education for African Americans under these conditions came to rest largely within two opposing camps. Booker T. Washington, architect of the Tuskegee Institute, and Thomas Jesse Jones of the Hampton Institute looked upon the plight of African Americans as one that could only be surmounted through service to white Americans via hard work and exemplary moral behavior. Washington seemed to care little for African American civil rights outside the realm of economic contribution and achievement. Jones, who developed one of the first known courses in "social studies," viewed citizenship education for African Americans as something that would bring them into closer alignment with "the essentials of civilization." Opposing this subservient point of view was William Du Bois. He championed civil rights as essential to the situation of minorities, especially African Americans, through his teachings, writings, and lectures. His attack on

Booker T. Washington in *The Souls of Black Folk* (1903) and his co-founding of the National Association for the Advancement of Colored People—with, among others, John Dewey—made him a leader in socially active citizenship education for African Americans.

CITIZENSHIP CURRICULUM FOR MISSISSIPPI FREEDOM SCHOOLS (1964)

Unit I: The Negro in Mississippi
  Statistics on Education, Housing, Income, Employment and Health
  The Poor in America
The South as an Underdeveloped Country
Unit II: The Negro in the North
  Triple Revolution
  Chester PA
Unit III: Myths about the Negro
  Guide to Negro History
  In White America (excerpt)
  History addendum I
  History addendum II
  Negro History Study Questions
  Development of the Negro Power since 1900
Unit IV: The Power Structure
  Mississippi Power Structure
  Power of the Dixiecrats
  Nazi Germany
Unit V: Poor whites, Poor Negroes and Their Fears
  Hazard, KY
Unit VI: Soul Things and Material Things
  Statements of Discipline of Nonviolent Movements
Unit VII: The Movement, Part 1, Freedom Rides and Sit-Ins
Unit VII: The Movement, Part 2, COFO's Political Program
  Readings in Nonviolence
  Rifle Squads or the Beloved Community
  Voter Registration Laws in Mississippi
  Civil Rights Bill
  Nonviolence in American History
  Behind the Cotton Curtain
  Teaching Material for Unit VII, Part 2

Source: http://www.educationanddemocracy.org/FSCfiles/A_03_Index.htm.

The Washington-Jones view of the African American in citizenship education lasted throughout the twentieth century in spite of such gains as *Brown v. The Board of Education* (1954) and the Civil Rights Act of 1964. Occasional and important challenges to the status quo came with the Tennessee Foxfire movement and the 1964 Mississippi Freedom Schools, where recognition of existing inequities in citizenship and thoughtful activism highlighted the curricula. The National Council for the Social Studies, a leader in citizenship education theory and practice for thousands of teachers and teacher educators since 1921, championed the plight of unequal citizenship for both ethnic minorities and African Americans throughout the latter half of the century, and depictions of minorities in textbooks began to take a dramatic turn toward integrating, rather than denigrating or ignoring, the role of minorities in the development of American democracy. Growing multicultural perspectives on the social studies and citizenship education in recent decades by scholars such as James Banks produced a backlash from conservative scholars Diane Ravitch and Arthur Schlesinger, among others, who warned of the dangers inherent in undermining the *unum* for the sake of the *pluribus.*

The general response in schools, however, has been to teach English skills to ethnic minorities and to steep all students in a basic understanding of government. In spite of progressive ideas embedded in the aforementioned 1916 NEA report on the social studies and the many advances in teaching for and about cultural difference since then, little has changed in the school curriculum with regard to citizenship education for and about immigrants and minorities.

PATRIOTISM: BLIND FAITH OR CRITICAL THOUGHT?

The history of American citizenship education is filled with battles over the meaning and manifestation of patriotism in the curriculum. Issues concerning patriotism are a persistent subtext of the struggles between free market economics and social reform, as well as disagreements over the proper place of culture and race in citizenship education. Joel Westheimer points out that patriotism is a struggle between unquestioning faith in and total allegiance to the policies and decisions of the government (authoritarian patriotism) and loyalty to the basic principles of democracy (democratic patriotism). The events of the past century pushed the debate on which of these two types of patriotism is most beneficial to citizenship education.

National hubris brought about by manifest destiny and World War I pressured the school curriculum to raise the United States to a level of unparalleled superiority throughout the first half of the twentieth century. Coupled with the influx of immigrants, schools were looked upon as the agent of Americanization necessary to convert various immigrant cultures to this form of authoritarian patriotism. Embedded in this notion of patriotism was the edification of a laissez-faire approach to free market capitalism as the bedrock of the American way of life.

The 1916 NEA report on the social studies, Charles Beard's 1932 American Historical Association Commission on the Social Studies, and the Rugg curriculum represented attempts to establish a more democratic form of patriotism in schools. Although the Great Depression ignited a backlash against authoritarian patriotism in schools, these and other attempts at promoting a social reconstructionist, active view of citizenship came under severe attack. The Hearst newspapers labeled Beard and his associates as a "red menace," the Federal Bureau of Investigation kept a watchful surveillance on Rugg, and the NAM textbook survey decried the anti-American stance of many social studies curricula to which the task of citizenship education was assigned. Even though curricula with a focus on the discussion of social problems during the 1930s gained credence in many publications for teachers, surveys found that less than 12 percent of teachers deemed discussions on social problems appropriate for their students. The fact that 21 states required loyalty oaths for teachers by 1936 may have contributed to this sentiment on the part of teachers.

World War II ignited further assaults on an issues-centered, critical approach to teaching democratic values. Historian Alan Nevin's attack on attempts to scrutinize the United States through the basic principles of democracy appeared in the May 3, 1942, edition of the *New York Times Magazine*. Emblematic of the authoritarian onslaught, Nevin's article, titled "American History for Americans," excoriated public schools for neglecting to teach American history as a means to preserve unity and promote patriotism, especially in times of war.

This theme—the importance of patriotism in times of war—ran throughout the century and into the present. Education critics E. Merrill Root and Vice Admiral Hyman G. Rickover continued Nevin's theme during the Cold War. Shocked by the Soviet Union's success in its 1957 launch of Sputnik, these critics again assailed the teaching of history (and all subjects, for that matter) as being intellectually soft and anti-American. Root's 1958 *Brainwashing in the High School* managed to pull together the strands of immigration, free market capitalism, and patriotism in his reading of textbooks that, in his analysis, fomented class struggles, questioned free market capitalism, and denigrated patriotism. Amidst this struggle over patriotism in the curriculum, Maurice Hunt and Lawrence Metcalf published a social studies methods book in 1955 that offered the analysis of American society's closed areas (e.g., economics, race, social class, and religion) as a way to develop democratic habits of mind. Indicative of democratic patriotism, this methods book for prospective high school social studies teachers lived on into the early 1970s.

The Vietnam War era reopened the conflict between authoritarian and democratic patriotism in schools. One Supreme Court decision, in particular, highlighted this struggle. The *Tinker v. Des Moines Independent Community School District* (1969) case concerned a 1965 incident over free speech carried out by students in three Des Moines schools. Disciplined by the school district for wearing black armbands to protest the Vietnam War, the students took the case to the Supreme Court, which, by a seven-to-two vote, supported the students' right to free "symbolic" speech as long as it did not disrupt the educational process.

Struggles over the type of citizenship education best suited to the development of patriotism continue. During the 1990s, authoritarian patriots argued staunchly against the proposed history standards as being negative toward the American story and diminishing the importance of loyalty to the government and its processes. After September 11, 2001, states and school districts heightened the importance of pledging allegiance to the nation's struggle with terrorism. The Florida legislature, for example, passed a bill in 2002 creating Celebrate Freedom Week, during which time students are required to recite daily a portion of the Declaration of Independence. Although educational organizations and individual teachers continue to promote the notion of democratic patriotism through issues-centered curricula and open inquiry, the Florida law is indicative of the trend toward authoritarian patriotism at this point in America's educational history.

CONCLUSION

The education of democratic citizens is the core mission of public schooling in the United States. Sociopolitical and economic trends, as well as unforeseen events at home and throughout the world, have fueled controversies over how citizenship education should be conducted in schools. These controversies involve the role of free market capitalism, social reform, pluralism, and patriotism in the education of students as citizens.

Further Reading: Butts, R. F., 1989, *The civic mission in educational reform: Perspectives for the public and the profession*, Stanford, CA: Hoover Institution Press; Evans, R. W., 2004, *The social studies wars: What should we teach the children?* New York: Teachers College Press; Ross, E. W., ed., 2006, *The social studies curriculum: Purposes, problems, and possibilities*, 3rd ed., Albany: State University of New York Press; Westheimer, J., 2006, Politics and patriotism in education, *Phi Delta Kappan 87*(8), 608–613.

Gregory E. Hamot

CIVIL RIGHTS

In December 1963, the Student Nonviolent Coordinating Committee (SNCC), a civil rights group comprised mostly of young black college students and graduates, conceptualized several projects to involve white volunteer college students in assisting African American communities during what became known as the Summer Project of 1964 in the State of Mississippi. One of the various projects created was the notion of freedom schools—an alternative elementary/secondary educational program. Freedom schools were designed to dramatize the inadequacies of the Mississippi public schools and to encourage African American students to participate socially and politically in their communities, linking education to their personal experiences. In March 1964, a two-day curriculum conference, sponsored by the National Council for Churches, was held in New York City. Conference participants recommended numerous progressive, democratic instructional methods that emphasized self-discovery and self-expression, encouraging students to think critically, to question Mississippi's oppressive social order, and to participate in instituting social change. Traditional teaching in Mississippi had been a form of oppression. Authoritarian in approach, it had relied on rote learning in which a teacher lectured and then tested solely on the lecture. Students were expected to be passive and subservient. Black students had little or no opportunities in their Mississippi classroom to talk about, much less act upon the many problems that they faced in their daily lives.

Under this oppressive form of education, African American youth learned to accept inadequate conditions as unchangeable facts of their lives, not to trust others (particularly whites), to be cynical, and to expect to be ill-prepared to function in their society. The possibility that students should someday function as active agents for social change was unheard of—and undesired. This was the mentality of the black public education system, indeed the mentality of the Mississippi society at large.

SCHOOLS FOR QUESTIONING

In contrast, the freedom schools were to reject these traditional teaching practices, to rely on progressive methods designed to promote student participation, worth and equality among students, and a connection between school and life. These were to be schools for questioning, for exposing students to meaningful discussion experiences, for helping them understand the social forces influencing their lives, hopefully enabling them some management of social conditions under which they lived. Students would be encouraged to ask questions about their experiences and their personal situations. Asking a question was a first step toward overcoming the pattern of passive acceptance of authority: toward learning to think, to inquire, and, ultimately, to convert learning and inquiry into action.

SNCC leaders believed that Mississippi students had vital and unique ideas to contribute both to their communities and to the movement. It was hoped that by learning to question freely and thoughtfully in an open environment of group learning and discussion sessions, students would challenge views of society and find alternatives. Freedom schools were to enable students to articulate the desire for change awakened by the questions they were being empowered to ask. Asking questions was to be the means for converting attitudes from passive to active—helping students to understand themselves, their society, and the need to change it.

How to Design "Questioning" Lessons: Notes on Teaching in Mississippi

To help the volunteer-teachers in encouraging students to question, the Freedom School Committee compiled a number of the teaching suggestions from the various curriculum outlines emerging from the curriculum conference into a teaching manual entitled *Notes on Teaching in Mississippi,* which are part of the collected SNCC papers. The purpose of the manual was to prepare the volunteer-teachers for the specific situations they would encounter and to instruct them on how to respond to and teach the black students who would be in their freedom schools.

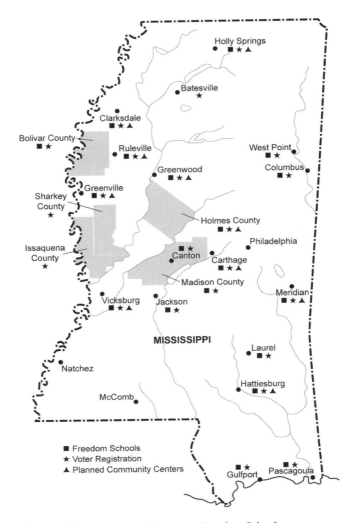

Figure C.4 Location of Mississippi Freedom Schools.

Promoting students to ask questions was to be built around the method of meaningful and reflective class discussion. Discussion was to enable students to learn to listen to others, to explore their own views, to ask questions in a sincere attempt to understand conflicting views of others, to make up their own minds about which ideas had better justification, and, in the end, to possibly improve their own lives and the lives of others in their community. Discussion would make ideas, beliefs, and experiences accessible to analysis, criticism, and new insights. Embedded in the freedom school's concept of discussion was that a successful discussion included a problem or issue topic that involved students' views, clarifications, and analyses; that through discussion students would learn the obligations of civility, as well as strategies for moving a discussion forward; and that policy conversations would focus toward decision and community action.

Notes on Teaching in Mississippi stated that the discussion method was encouraged above other methods because it allowed for encouraging expression; exposing feelings; permitting participation of students on various levels; developing group loyalties and responsibility; and permitting the sharing of strengths and weaknesses of individuals. On the simplest level, students needed to learn to talk and share ideas in the classroom. Through student talk, the conversion from passive to active was to be accomplished, thus facilitating the primary belief of the freedom schools.

Notes on Teaching in Mississippi provided a number of "teaching hints" and "discussion-leading techniques" that defined the role of the freedom school teacher as a moderator. The role was not passive; it required active participation. As moderator, the freedom school teacher was responsible for establishing the open environment needed for students to exchange views and for contributing to the discussion at key points to clarify issues, aid analysis, and initiate evaluation. Teachers were to promote thoughtful, personal inquiry and to avoid using their "authority" to influence students' actions.

Discussion usually followed a three-step pattern. The teacher would first ask introductory questions: "How do you feel about...?" or "How would you feel if...?" After the students had had a chance to express their feelings, the teacher would then ask probing questions: "Why do you feel this way?" or "Why would anyone feel this way?" Finally, as the discussion progressed, the teacher would draw more critical thinking from the students: "How do you feel about his idea?" or "How do you feel about her experience?" The purpose of these questions was to show that the teacher was interested in the students and their independent ideas and to encourage the students to respond emotionally or intuitively and then to reflect upon those responses thoughtfully, even analytically, rather than to solicit some particular answer from the students, trick them into following the teacher's own line of thought in the Socratic manner, or force them to second-guess in order to please the teacher.

What to Teach: The Civic Curriculum

The classroom connection that would bring together the questioning, the students' real life experiences, the solutions, and the direct action was a progressive curriculum based on student-teacher talk. It was designed both to raise students consciousness as a self-determining "minority culture" and to educate students to be active agents of social change for a more just and equitable existence.

The curriculum was organized around a question-answer format to facilitate the freedom school teacher to be "a concerned questioner." Two sets of questions were the foundation of the Civic Curriculum.

THE BASIC SET OF QUESTIONS

1. Why are we (teachers and students) in freedom schools?
2. What is the Freedom Movement?
3. What alternatives does the Freedom Movement offer us?

THE SECONDARY SET OF QUESTIONS

1. What does the majority culture have that we want?
2. What does the majority culture have that we don't want?
3. What do we have that we want to keep?

IMPLICATIONS FOR CURRENT EDUCATIONAL PRACTICE

Much of current educational practice seems to be steeped in a technocratic and procedural methodology that looks for a "one-size-fits-all" approach to solve the academic malaise of all students. Focusing on their own experiences as freedom school teachers, Florence Howe and Paul Lauter argue that the discussion format is an approach that exemplifies "a politically charged way of thinking about the relationships of teachers to students, students to learning, and of education to the struggle for social justice." Discussion of students' experiences can generate visions of social change in students' lives, empowering them to alter the tasks that society in general and schools in particular have demanded of them.

The pedagogical orientation of the freedom schools was centered in key questions. The role of the teacher was to create an "open" environment in which discussion began with the experience of the students. Thus students in a class may express themselves, explore their feelings and assumptions, share with others, and eventually come to understand their experiences. From these experiences, common intellectual ground can be established for further analysis. From the discussions based on the "open" questions and on the students' experiences, the class could engage in collective decision making, planning and pursuing activities with shared goals. The teacher and the students would leaven the entire process with new and additional information gleaned through further discussion and analysis. The entire learning experience would have students and the teacher working together in the educational classroom for the mutual benefit and enlightenment of all.

The freedom school educators realized that to implement what they called a "liberatory pedagogy" would be difficult in light of the dominant rigid curriculum and authoritarian teaching. However, they believed that individual teachers, either in isolation or collectively in the public schools, can indeed make a difference in the lives of their students. To do so they must change fundamental curriculum tasks and encourage new curricular developments, with provocative questions, liberated student voices, greater understanding of student experiences, and then possible societal change. To be sure, the ideal in the freedom schools was not always implemented, but it presented an alternative.

CONCLUSIONS

Reflecting upon the 1964 freedom school experience, Liz Fusco, the coordinator of the freedom schools in Indianola, Mississippi, wrote a summary of the impact freedom schools had on the Mississippi students and, consequently, on their society. Freedom schools became a font of real activity during the Mississippi Project. Students began to have a sense of themselves as people who could be taken seriously. They were encouraged to talk, and their talk was listened to. They became articulate about what was wrong and what changes should be made. Connections between curriculum and personal experience were made as students studied the realities of conditions in Mississippi and the effects of those realities on their lives. Students discovered that they were real human beings and that they could alter realities by taking action against the injustices, which kept them "unhappy and impotent." The visible results were in the transformations of who they were able to become "as discussion leaders, as teachers, as organizers, as speakers, as friends, as people." Fusco claimed it was asking questions about real problems that led to students' transformation from passive bystanders to active community citizens.

The organizers of the freedom schools wanted a certain type of community of students—active, participating student-citizens who would make positive changes in the Mississippi social fabric as opposed to being passive "good little n.....s." We should want nothing less for students today. Freedom school organizers created a discussion-based curriculum to accomplish their transformative goals. The objective of this discussion-based curriculum was to strengthen self-esteem, build cultural identity, promote critical thinking and problem solving, and provide opportunities necessary for students to take control of their personal lives. Therefore, this discussion-based curriculum motivated students to become agents for change in improving existing conditions in their community; promoted learning as a foundation for democratic living when focused on useful knowledge and meaningful tasks; promoted an appreciation for human diversity, acknowledging the dignity and worth of each individual; and encouraged equality and social justice for all humankind. The discussion-based curriculum was also related directly to the students by examining the existing conditions, situations, and experiences in and outside of their communities. Students participated in serious in-depth examination and discourse concerning problematic political, social, and economic issues; mastering relevant information, relating the new information to what they already know, and applying new insights to current problems. In addition, public presentation of meaningful student work provided opportunities for students to participate actively in evaluating their own and their fellow students' projects, thus building skills of critical examination and experiencing personal growth. And finally, discussion-based curriculum emphasized a team approach, with learning experiences that created a dynamic, participatory, collective consciousness-raising educational environment in a democratic partnership. The focus was on both group responsibility and community involvement, with genuine respect for and trust in students, allowing them the freedom to express their feelings and ideas. Students were guided in constructing, ordering, and making sense of their experiences and in putting those experiences into action; they were encouraged to discover, engage, and evaluate their own existing values, attitudes, and beliefs in relation to other people, to their community, to society at large, and even to themselves.

Educational classrooms could follow the example of freedom schools by providing democratic classroom laboratories where students encounter, rehearse, cultivate, and apply the skills and practices of participating citizens. The public discourse should not be passive, rather it should be active in exploring the meanings of self-determination and activism within the context of problems and conditions that face students in their own society. Freedom schools gave to African American students within the context of a repressive society that seemed to hold no democratic possibilities the opportunities to realize that they had a voice and that through their collective voice real changes could be made. Educational classrooms in today's society should provide similar opportunities where students can engage in a civic curriculum for democracy, sitting face-to-face in discussion circles; student citizens committed to questioning, to active give-and-take dialogue on everyday issues, discussing authentic problems focused on the potential of real social change.

Further Reading: Lauter, P., & Howe, F., 1970, *The conspiracy of the young,* New York: World Book; Perlstein, D., Teaching freedom: SNCC and the creation of the Mississippi freedom schools, *History of Education Quarterly 30* (Fall 1990); The Student Nonviolent Coordinating Committee Papers, 1959–1972, 1982, Stanford, NC: Microfilming Corporation of America.

George W. Chilcoat and Jerry A. Ligon

CLASS SIZE

Class size reduction seems a simple idea, something that would be easy to define, implement, and evaluate. Put fewer students in a classroom with a teacher and achievement should go up. But like so many things in education, class size reduction has been anything but simple. It is a source of frequent argument among researchers who debate its critical attributes, designs for research, and the meaning of outcomes. It is a flashpoint for legislators who are hesitant to vote against an incredibly popular reform. It is little wonder, because the public commitment to class size reduction is stunning. The public favors investment in class size reduction over vouchers by a seven-to-one margin. Most new teachers and the majority of adults favor reducing class size as a way to improve teacher quality. In 2006, 33 states had some kind of legislation limiting class size. In this context, class size reduction is a puzzle for policymakers who work to develop a policy that will fit into today's cash-strapped schools.

Contentious debate surrounds this reform, its definition and history and the methods and evidence used to support or refute its use, and there are several dimensions of the discourse and practice of class size reduction:

- *How big is small?* Under the label of class size reduction, reforms have limited class sizes to 20 in California, to 15 in Wisconsin, but to 30 for 4- to 7-year-olds in England.
- *What do you mean reduced class size?* Sometimes class size is calculated in terms of group size by capping the upper limit of the number of students

assigned to a teacher. In other cases, class size reduction is taken as pupil-teacher ratio, premised on the ratio of students to adults in the classroom or school.

- *Choosing targets of investment:* Although any policy is a choice of relative investment, class size reduction is often pitted against teacher quality as a strategy for improving student achievement.
- *The power of the individual:* Class size reduction might be seen as a Western concern, based on assumptions about the needs of individual children in the context of schooling. While seen as a valuable investment by many U.S. educators, parents, and policymakers, educators in China and Japan prefer larger classes so that children learn to be a part of a group.

DEFINITION

A simple definition of class size reduction is that it is a reform that limits the number of students assigned to a teacher within a given classroom. The limit set by a class size reduction policy varies by the context—in some cases it is relative to empirical evidence on class size reduction and in others it is relative to prevailing practice or what is affordable. Embedded within the definition are assumptions about *how* class size reduction works to support student learning.

For those who take a strict constructionist view of class size reduction, its power comes out of changes in instructional and assessment practices. With smaller groups, it is assumed that teachers do more intense assessment, they have more direct interaction with individual students, their instruction matches student need, they develop closer relationships with students and families, and they spend less time on behavior management. Students are thought to learn the culture of schooling more easily, they connect with their teachers and peers in productive ways, and they are supported in their behavior as teachers can identify problems more quickly. This theory of action rests on increasing the intensity of educational practice and experience and is based on research that has examined the linear relations between group size and student outcomes. More moderate approaches set class size at a politically expedient limit (smaller than current practice) and reachable within budget resources. These programs, which in the United States set class sizes to approximately 20, use the concept of class size reduction without the idea of a threshold for improving practice. Instead, it operates from a generic notion of the relationship between group size and student outcomes.

In contrast to instructionally focused approaches to class size reduction, administrative or economic approaches attend to the ratio of students to teachers at either the classroom or school level. Pupil-teacher ratio (PTR) is persuasive to those interested in educational costs, and the ease of calculation makes it a quick and dirty proxy for estimates of class size. Its logic is conceptualized in terms of relative investment (class size vs. teacher salary vs. teacher quality) or in terms of general allocation of units of educational expertise (the addition of staff, any kind of staff, provides students with a greater proportion of adult support). The problem is that PTR is tangentially related to classroom practice and as a result, student learning. Dividing the number of students by school staff can factor in both certified staff (speech and language clinicians, psychologists, special education teachers, etc) and noncertified staff (secretaries, janitors, foodservice) that support students but indirectly. At the classroom level, pupil-teacher ratio approaches might include the use of paraprofessionals or pairing large groups of students with more than one teacher. These classroom practices are difficult to translate to increased student achievement.

HISTORY

There are two related but separate histories in this story. The first is the history of class size reduction practice, most typically at the state level. The second is the history of class size reduction research, told through analyses of student outcomes, teacher practice, and economic costs. This research history has two components—the research on class size and the research on programs that specifically aim to shape teaching and learning by having teachers work with smaller groups. These histories sometimes develop in parallel; sometimes they intersect, with actors referencing the other strand to advocate, repudiate, and substantiate work. The practice of class size reduction policy only vaguely relies on the research on class size, and the research on class size reduction goes on separately from the work on class size as a whole.

Although researchers and policymakers have been interested in class size for years, the most recent scholarship and policy development have come out of the opportunities created by new research methodologies and the economic bubble of the late twentieth century. Research methodology supported the trend with the development of meta-analysis, a tool that allowed powerful statistical synthesis of quantitative studies on a topic. Class size was one of the first topics chosen to showcase the method. Following foundational meta-analyses by Glass & Smith, states took up class size reduction as a tool to enhance student achievement. From the start, there was a conflation of class size reduction and pupil-teacher ratio in research and practice, tangling up interpretations. The first major initiative, Indiana's Project Prime Time, added paraprofessionals to classes, making it a PTR approach. It was soon followed by Project STAR in Tennessee, a field-based experiment that randomly assigned students and teachers to regular-sized classes, regular-sized classes with an aide, and small classes of 13–17 students. Despite some weaknesses in the design, STAR was touted for its methodological rigor, and its results were widely disseminated, reanalyzed, and discussed. Its results, combined with an economic upturn that allowed states to explore new policy investments in education, prompted other states to develop class size reduction programs. Wisconsin developed the Student Achievement Guarantee in Education (SAGE) program, initially designed to support communities in poverty and later expanded to approximately 500 schools. SAGE calls for class sizes of 15:1 in K–3, rigorous curriculum, professional development and teacher evaluation, and increased connection between home and school. California took a different approach, providing funding for universal class size reduction. In contrast to SAGE, which provided $2,000 per low-income student, California provided $650 per student regardless of income status. The federal government had a short-lived class size reduction program that infused 25,000 teachers into the teaching ranks, and through the 1990s and early part of this decade, other states implemented limited class size reduction programs. A class size reduction program in Britain focused on an upper-end estimate of effective group size by setting a limit of 30 on the early groups in schools. More recently Florida voters approved a constitutional amendment that phases in a sweeping class size reduction program by 2010. Students assigned per teacher in core courses will be limited to 18 in Pre-K–3, 22 in grades 4–8, and 25 in grades 9–12.

In addition to analysis of specific reforms, researchers looked to existing databases to understand class size effects. This work analyzed existing data, correlating class size information with outcomes as diverse as student achievement, teacher salary, and placement in special education. More narrowly constructed database analyses used large-scale data collection opportunities like the National Assessment of Educational Progress and the Early Childhood Longitudinal Study. These database analyses often expanded attention to class size reduction beyond the early elementary years, where the bulk of the reforms have invested funding. This resulted in an interesting asymmetry—the student outcomes could be most easily available at the later elementary or secondary level while the class size reduction programs were at the early elementary level.

DOES CLASS SIZE REDUCTION WORK?

The most typical question asked about a reform is "Does it work?" Class size reduction is no exception, and the first-generation research posed that question simply, comparing students who had attended reduced-sized classes with students who had attended more typical groups. Rather than a single answer, researchers qualified their responses. In research on specific class size reduction implementations, class size effects could be identified in programs with sufficiently small groups, with best outcomes in classes smaller than 20. These achievement effects were seen across all students but were more pronounced for African American and economically disadvantaged students. Low-achieving students and English language learners did not receive *extra* benefit from class size reduction beyond their peers in smaller classes. Students who experienced small classes maintained their advantage over their larger classes peers in later grades, and the longer they stayed in small classes, the better the outcomes. The addition of teacher aides, purported to reduce pupil-teacher ratio, did not improve student achievement.

Analysis of surveys and other databases about class size are inconclusive, with some analysts arguing that it is a good investment and others denying its utility. Much of the scholarly argument centered on methodology chosen for analysis, with more global strategies generating less-positive findings.

Recognizing the complexity of classroom practice, researchers also looked beyond student outcomes. How does class size reduction change how participants feel about schooling and shape what teachers do? Student and teacher attitudes are improved in smaller classes, less class time is spent on discipline, and students receive more individualized instruction. In higher-achieving classrooms, the teaching is more explicit and more directly related to student needs. Although there is an implicit assumption that teacher activity will be different in smaller classes, researchers have not always found that to be the case. Differences in practice are more likely in early primary than later school grades.

The California implementation provided a window on systemic effects of a universally provided class size reduction program. The introduction of this reform stressed an already pressured system, with an increase in the number of underqualified staff and expansion of classroom sections without adequate space, with these problems most acutely experienced in the most challenged schools. These problems were experienced to a lesser extent in Wisconsin, where many schools implemented class size reduction in buildings with insufficient space, placing 30 students with 2 teachers.

How Does Class Size Reduction Work?

As researchers pondered the mixture of outcomes uncovered in first-generation research, a number of people shifted their attention to the question of *how* class size reduction produced, or did not produce, changes in student outcomes. This work came out of a growing recognition that *how class size reduction works depends on how it is implemented.* This should come as no surprise—class size reduction is an educational treatment used to change the conditions in classrooms to increase student achievement. The variability of implementation, however, implies that there is little consensus and/or little recognition of the parameters of the treatment or the mechanisms at work. The following section will examine several ways we can interpret the mechanisms at work in class size reduction and will explore conceptualizations used in prevention science, ideology and culture, and developmental effects as potential explanatory factors.

Treatment Fidelity

When a treatment is tested in medicine or intervention science, there is careful attention paid to treatment fidelity—the degree to which it was implemented as it was designed and intended. While it is certainly the case that any educational intervention or reform will have a local implementation that reflects the history, needs, and politics of its context, extreme variation changes the basic meanings of a treatment. If we thought of class size reduction in this way, we would look carefully at how stakeholders implement class size reduction in terms of three specific elements: *timing, intensity, and duration.* Timing describes *when* a treatment is applied—is it best to reduce class size in the early grades, later, or both? Intensity describes *how* the treatment is enacted and would address issues such as how small a class needs to be to have an effect and the types of instruction that makes smaller classes most potent. Duration relates to *how long* students need to experience small classes (a) to have an effect and (b) to sustain an effect. Implementations of class size reduction have typically ignored these elements, particularly related to the issue of intensity, with little attention to preparing teachers to take advantage of CSR. An example of this comes from evaluation of the SAGE project, which has within the reform provision for professional development (PD). In action, schools can define *any* professional development as meeting the policy's PD requirements. This played out in interesting ways in SAGE's 30:2 classrooms, where many pairs of teachers used tag-team teaching, a strategy where one teacher took charge of 30 students while another teacher did other classroom work such as going through folders or contacting parents. This strategy effectively *increased* class size in a reform that promoted smaller groups, reducing the intensity of the treatment. Analysis of class size research needs to take these elements into account if we are going to have a more nuanced understanding of the mechanisms underlying class size reduction. Policy construction and enactment should address these elements to ensure that investments are made on dimensions that are scientifically based.

Developmental Mechanisms

There is more investment in CSR programming in the primary grades and more evidence of efficacy with younger students. The public is more likely to invest in class size reduction, believing in early intervention and the needs of younger students to work in smaller groups. Is class size reduction more effective for younger students or do we just have more data on it? Several researchers have suggested mechanisms that produce the effects in early grades. Ehrenberg, Brewer, Gamoran, & Willms (2001) suggest that CSR has a latent effect in two related dimensions. CSR has an ability to change the cognitive, psychological social development through its intensified instructional practices. This in turn changes the future developmental context for students, improving their chances of success. By intervening early these changes accumulate positively over time.

Is it more amenable to the practices of teachers in the primary grades? More focused on small group instruction, teachers in grades K–3 may already have in their practice the seeds of class size reduction strategies. However, little specific attention has been paid to fostering these strategies. It seems that there is a belief that teachers will naturally change their practice to take advantage of smaller classes, and researchers and policymakers have not described the changes. The research community seems stuck in the description that teachers don't change.

Ideology

The ideology of CSR (or its poor cousin PTR) shapes the nature of implementation and research in every dimension. The politics of achievement drive this reform, with a simplified view of educational practice. Although there has been attention paid to other elements of implementation and practice, most frequently CSR is isolated as an input that will magically change both the processes and the outcomes of education. If we just change the number of children in a class, achievement goes up. But achievement is nested in many contexts. In the early grades CSR's effects can be seen across student groups but are most profound for African American and economically disadvantaged students. CSR's promise, however, has a powerful pull for the middle class who advocates for universal implementation. Unfortunately, this results in scarce resources being spread across schools in generic ways, without attention to differential needs of students or teachers. The cost of increasing staff is so formidable that other concerns like space or support for teachers cannot be addressed. CSR is implemented in an educational context where teachers are socialized to work in particular ways, ways that come out of histories where larger groups were much more prevalent. These histories also have developmental assumptions about the needs of children to become increasingly independent over time, making small group work less likely for older students. And they are histories where one-teacher:one-class is the norm rather than forms of team teaching or sharing students. Some frame CSR as pork barrel politics, a bone thrown to teachers who see it as making their life easier. When education is viewed in terms of bodies to process through a system, CSR makes teaching look like a cushy job, particularly if it's asserted that teachers don't change what they do with smaller groups. This makes it very easy to blame teachers if CSR does not produce the outcomes implicit in this considerable investment. It allows us to ignore the more troubling structural elements that limit student and teacher resources. These simple conceptualizations of CSR apply linear thinking to a nonlinear world, isolate cause in a multidimensional model, and reduce the possibilities that CSR will have positive effects.

CONCLUSION

What would be a reasonable justification for class size reduction? And how would we enact it in policy, practice, and research? In the current political context, any justification has to highlight student achievement. But a singular focus on student outcomes, without attention to the contextual dimensions of teacher practice, the physical realities of school space, and the tradeoffs of competing investments will undermine the potential impact class size reduction might have on teaching and learning.

Further Reading: Blatchford, P., 2003, *The class size debate: Is small better?* Maidenhead, UK: Open University Press; Ehrenberg, R. G., Brewer, D. J., Gamoran, A., & Willms, J. D., 2001, Class size and student achievement, *Psychological Science and the Public Interest,* 2(1), 1–30; Finn, J. D., Pannozzo, G. M., & Achilles, C., 2003, The "whys" of class size: Student behavior in small classes, *Review of Educational Research,* 73(3), 321–368; Graue, M. E., Hatch, K., Rao, K., & Oen, D., in press, The wisdom of class size reduction. *American Educational Research Journal.*

Elizabeth Graue

CLOTHING AND SCHOOL UNIFORMS

In contemporary American society, it has become increasingly important to understand the debates surrounding school clothing, educational dress codes (defining what may *not* be worn to school), and school uniforms (defining what *must* be worn to school). Such an understanding requires traversing the complex paths of history, culture, and politics to take stock of the ways these have structured the contestation over dress in schools. The cultural anxieties of "appropriate" school clothing and the practices stemming from such ideologies have taken varied forms, for assorted reasons, in a myriad of contexts, for some time. Indeed, in the last quarter of the twentieth century, the majority of public schools had some form of dress code, while only a handful of public schools had mandatory school uniform policies. By the turn of the century, fully one-quarter of our public elementary and about a tenth of our public middle/high schools had a mandatory uniform policy. It is upon these shores that the battle over school clothing is being waged.

The history of pre-industrial educational dress is difficult to pin down. In general, it is accepted that our current dilemmas have their roots in the confluence of secular and religious influences that contextualized early universities in Germany, France, and England. The *cappa clausa* is the earliest recorded (C.E. 1222) institutionalized use of standardized educational dress ordered by Stephen Langton, archbishop of Canterbury. The contemporary tree of our school clothing debate has its roots planted deeply in British soil. Though the British educational system is fundamentally different, the common symbol of the uniformed school lad/lass is etched in our minds as an English icon. The school uniform in England has a long tradition in the universities and primary/secondary schools that the population is compelled to attend. There are several reasons associated with the use of the school uniform in England, reasons that are still with us today, reasons that provide the contours of the contemporary debate over educational dress.

In order to keep the flamboyancy of societal fashion *outside* the ivory tower, thereby hoping to enforce an adoption of institutional values via mandated clothing, Cambridge University, which had been enforcing various forms of standardized dress since the thirteenth century, required long scholastic robes and a skull cap (a modified *cappa clausa*) for undergraduates, with a different cap for graduate students. Over time, the dress codes at Cambridge became more specific, attempting to preempt societal influence and control and define what was acceptable. Continuous student resistance to "acceptable school attire" was commonplace, and, according to historians, by the sixteenth century, students typically wore what they wanted to wear.

While school uniforms were also used as a marker of status, the history complicates this fact. What would ultimately become the model for school uniforms among English schoolchildren, for private and parochial schooling worldwide, and for a growing proportion of American public school students is rooted in the clothing worn by children at Christ's Hospital in the sixteenth century. These were cassock-like cloaks and were designed to emphasize the *lower status* of these children. This interesting historical fact, that uniforms were used to distinguish the *lower* classes from everyone else in British society, though contrary to reigning assumptions, is important for our understanding of the contemporary reality of school uniform discourse in America. Uniforms, a mode of educational clothing, were used in Britain as a marker of social status—first of the lowest classes (orphaned children) and later as a symbol of elite education (a badge signifying class status).

Another related use of school uniforms in England was as an instrument for indoctrinating the masses and inculcating the herd instinct among the majority of English citizens: the working class. As a rigid system of education mirrored an equally rigid occupational hierarchy, uniforms attempted to accomplish two things. First, they engineered a powerful tonic against individuality and expression by flattening student body distinctions as well as creating distinctions *within* schools (teachers vs. students)—mirroring the relations faced at work. Second, as certain schools were for a certain class of children, the iconography of uniforms (e.g., logos, badges) shaped distinction *between* schools—encouraging inter- and intra-class conflict in the pursuance of social mobility.

Overall, standardized school dress requirements are linked to a semiotics of legitimacy and authority, a reservoir of institutional socio-educational values, and a method of social and cultural control over cohorts of students moving through the system. Those without a school uniform would feel left out, and divergence from the uniform was akin to divergence from the institutional values defined by the institution and therefore punishable by a variety of sanctioning procedures. As such, they were imported into the United States.

Public schooling in the United States dates back to the middle of the nineteenth century—its foundations, much further. The growth of public schooling in the United States since the 1850s has been extraordinary when compared to other industrialized nations. Public schooling arose in the United States primarily as a means of preparing and socializing the young into their adult roles: as citizens and workers. Thus, the beginnings of American public education corresponded tightly to the needs of industry and linked to the religious and moral climate of the period. Of course, public schooling was, contradictorily, not available to everyone. The elite continued to support and send their children to preparatory schools, while the poor and minorities were denied public schooling.

The American introduction to the school uniform began in the private/parochial sector—a marker of class status and tradition. For most, uniforms and Catholic schooling are synonymous, and, by extension, with educational success. By the early 1960s, half of Catholic schools had uniform policies; however, Catholic experience with uniforms has been anything but congenial. In the 1950s protests and concerns in the Catholic laity regarding the requirement of school uniforms began, raising concerns that uniforms infringe on parental rights and duties; are inherently conformists; were not cheaper for all families; and, do *not* mask distinctions—concerns echoed today. It is significant that the laity, and ultimately the church via Vatican II, were concerned with educational dress. The timbre of such concerns mirrored the public disquiet as the civil rights movement and student movements concerning free speech, the Vietnam

War, and other issues were ongoing and socially, culturally, and politically significant.

Before the 1950s, the literature concerning educational dress in American schools is sparse. This paucity of literature on the debates concerning "appropriate" school clothing or even the issues of whether clothing impedes or encourages unity and academic success is indeed curious. However, the 1960s clarified what was *not* apparent in the previous popular and scholarly work from earlier educational history: that clothing in American public schools mirrored, to a large extent, material, social, and cultural contextual realities. In material terms, the clothes that children wore to school were predicated upon their class status. Affluent children who *did* attend public schools wore clothing that bespoke their parents' positions and the ideology of individualism. Working class children primarily wore clothes designated for their station in society, while poor children and minority children who were overrepresented in the poorest rural areas of the United States wore whatever clothing they had.

It was during the 1950s and 1960s that the baby boom generation became a target market for Madison Avenue. It was a large group with disposable income, and as a result, the role of fashion, music, expression, and identity became tightly linked—what it meant to be American was changing. The notion that schools would create citizens, workers, indeed people of a *certain* type, was withering. From this cohort, notions of convention, propriety, race, class, gender, and sexuality, and, yes, student dress would be seriously challenged. There is no doubt that the battles fought in the 1960s and early 1970s concerning student rights and freedom of expression were largely influenced by the sheer size of the baby boom generation and the increasing diversity of student bodies. By 1969, the U.S. Supreme Court, in *Tinker v. Des Moines Independent School District*, interpreted dress as a protected form of expression and pronounced that students do not shed their constitutional rights at the schoolhouse gate. As the major social movements waned, one could say that the emperor had fewer clothes than before. However, the gains would be swiftly usurped.

The seventies saw Joseph Califano Jr., President Carter's Health, Education, and Welfare secretary, propose taking the U.S. government out of the business of long hair and jeans in schools; yet after Reagan's election in 1979, his proposal was reversed. Up until the early 1980s, states had been weary of enforcing dress codes because they feared losing federal funds. Federal regulations throughout the 1970s prevented recipients of aid from discriminating against any person in the application of rules of appearance. In 1981, Education Secretary Terrel H. Bell proposed canceling such federal regulations on public schools' dress codes and, ultimately, the Reagan administration did not enforce these stipulations. Government was beginning to reverse the results of the student movements of the previous two decades regarding freedoms of expression as manifested through clothing and appearance. Enter the public school uniform.

The first documented discussions regarding school uniforms as an option for public schools came from the Barry administration. Late in 1980, Washington D.C. mayor Marion Barry began discussing with his administration the possibility of a proposal of a standardized dress code for D.C.'s public schools. Prompted by recent incidents of violence in or near D.C. public schools, Barry figured that uniforms would help to remedy such situations. Not using the term "uniform," because it sounded too militaristic, he speculated that such a policy would foster school spirit, save parents money, and deter the infiltration of outsiders on campuses. Reaction spanned disbelief, sarcastic criticism, and cautious approval. It wouldn't be until 1987, after the publication of *A Nation at Risk* and the strengthening of corporate influence in schooling and educational policy, that the first heavily publicized public school uniform policy would be implemented.

The first public school to heavily publicize its uniform policy was Cherry Hill Elementary School in Baltimore, Maryland, in the fall of 1987. Cherry Hill, a predominantly black elementary school of students from lower- to middle-income families, implemented their policy as a reaction to a 1986 suburban shooting over sunglasses and hoped it would cut clothing costs and reduce social pressures for children. There are conflicting reports, but by the end of the 1987–1988 school year, some five public schools in the Baltimore area and three schools in Washington D.C. had uniforms. Prophetically signaling the uniform discourse, articles appeared in the media by December of 1987, framing the anecdotal discussion of uniforms as providing a sense of togetherness, orderliness, and safety. Officials in Baltimore hoped that uniforms would lead to higher grades, better behavior, increased self-esteem, school pride, and a sense of belonging—all central facets of the current debate. There is some evidence that other schools in the mid-1980s attempted to initiate uniform policies, but parents were against them.

The idea spread quickly. By the fall of 1988, thirty-nine elementary schools and two junior high schools in Washington D.C., as well as fifteen more Baltimore schools required uniforms. Others quickly followed (many called them "dress codes") and many more were inquiring into the process—the vast majority of these were largely urban schools serving predominately poor minority students. Also this year, New York City Mayor, Ed Koch, voiced support for a pilot school uniform program with support from then School Chancellor of NYC: Richard Green. Koch and Green began mustering public support and donations from clothing manufacturers to begin a pilot program in NYC and gave a powerful voice to the school uniform movement. The pilot program was launched in the Spring of 1989 and several influential educational leaders and organizations, including the National School Board Association and the National Education Association gave their support. By 1990 school uniform programs were also implemented in Chicago, Detroit, Los Angeles, Miami, Philadelphia, and San Fernando. These programs were a mix of voluntary policies, some close to district-wide, others isolated in individual schools, most at the elementary school level, and the vast majority were directed at poor and minority urban students. Missing from all of this was any research into the effectiveness of such policies—everything was based on anecdote and assumptions. Long Beach, California launched an unprecedented program in 1994.

The board of the Long Beach Unified School District (LBUSD) unanimously adopted a mandatory school uniform policy in *all* K–8 schools in 1994. The primary reasons given for LBUSD's policy were: (1) to combat gang wear/colors; (2) to quell student battles over designer clothing; (3) to level economic disparities;

and (4) to help students focus on learning. At the same time, Governor Pete Wilson signed a state bill allowing public schools to require students to wear uniforms and assuring uninterested parents that their children would be ensured the appropriate alternative education. Other districts were watching LBUSD's lead: Los Angeles, San Diego, New York City, Miami, El Paso, Yonkers, Tacoma, and Seattle. While private schools were loosening their dress requirements, public schools were dramatically increasing theirs. Such a policy took guts: LBUSD set aside $175,000 to defend itself against legal battles.

The idea of uniforming public school students had gone from a few isolated schools to a wide variety of schools in a number of locations across the United States. The movement was in seminal form, the issues were raised, the early anecdotal "findings" were out and entering solidly into the discourse—but the spark that truly lit the fire was just around the corner. This spark was President Bill Clinton's State of the Union speech on January 23, 1996, wherein he gave the presidential seal of approval for public school uniform policies. Immediately, Clinton instructed the Department of Education to distribute manuals to all 16,000 U.S. school districts advising them how they can legally enforce a school uniform policy. In similar speeches in Washington D.C., California, and other states crucial for his re-election, Clinton advised Americans on school uniforms, playing off of the "rash" of school shootings early in that year, and, for the first time, citing the then unpublished "effects" of the Long Beach Unified School District's foray into a district-wide uniform policy some two years earlier. By the end of that crucial year, the word was out, and a movement was solidly underway in the United States bolstered by no evidence of effectiveness.

By the end of the 1996–1997 school year, the media printed figures that half of the urban school districts in the United States had adopted school uniform policies. Over 60 percent of Miami public schools, closer to 70 percent of Cleveland's public schools, 80 percent of the schools in the Chicago area, 50 percent in the Boston area, and between 10 and 25 percent of the public schools in New York City, the largest district in the nation, claimed to have adopted policies of standardized dress. It still was largely an urban and elementary school phenomenon; yet, by 1997, more suburban, rural, and secondary schools had such policies as well. That year was capped off with the creation of the Land's End school uniform division aimed to capitalize on the movement. In March of 1998, the New York City Board of Education voted and passed a resolution to require all K–6 public school students in the system to wear school uniforms. At this point two new developments emerged in the debate about school uniforms: (1) Some schools were abandoning the policy for reasons of compliance, parental support, "fashion policing," etc; and, (2) the research was starting to emerge that warned of the inconclusiveness and possible unintended consequences of such policies.

The massacre at Columbine in 1999 provided increasing fuel for the school uniform fire. By the end of 2000, 35 of the 50 U.S. states had schools with uniform policies. According to a 2000 school safety study, the CDC found that uniforms were required in about 20 percent of public and Roman Catholic elementary and middle schools and 10 percent of high schools. The events of September 11, 2001, also changed Americans' perceptions of American institutions and seemed to do three things relevant to the discussion at hand: (1) continued the path of limited freedoms and privacy rights; (2) raised both increased suspicions as well as bolstered Americans' faith in government; and (3) exponentially elevated the already irrational culture of fear in the United States to unprecedented heights. All play into the debate over school clothing, and the number of public school students required to wear uniforms is still increasing amidst academic and public concern.

Those who oppose mandatory school uniform policies use several arguments. First, they are concerned that schools and boards should not dictate what children should wear. Second, parents (and some educators) also have concerns that such policies undermine students' rights of free speech and expression. Third, there is often an undercurrent of concern that uniforms are distractive from the larger issues facing public education in the twenty-first century. Fourth, there has been much concern over the lack of granting opt-outs for those parents opposed to the policies. Fifth, there is concern that teachers have enough to do without policing dress code and uniform violations. Finally, and others argue that ultimately, mandating a school uniform policy is akin to charging a fee for public education, and that, they argue, is against everything that American public education is to stand for.

Paramount to this history is the role of the courts. Four key mandatory uniform code cases have been ruled on, and, in all cases, the uniform policy has been upheld. Three of these cases utilized primarily noneducational precedents and steered clear of utilizing free speech cases like *Tinker*. In general, students have been more successful in challenging dress codes than mandatory school uniform policies. So far, the courts do seem willing to allow the school uniform movement a chance to improve our schools, stating that more restriction is constitutional. One thing is certain in all of this—the debate and controversy over school clothing, educational dress codes, and school uniform policies is not going away any time soon. It is a battleground that will continue to wage its divisive and distractive war amidst misinformation and politics.

Further Reading: Bernstein, R. P., 1995, *Dress codes: Meanings and messages in American culture*, Boulder, CO: Westview Press; Brunsma, D. L., 2004, *What the school uniform movement tells us about American education: A symbolic crusade*, Lanham, MD: Rowman & Littlefield Education; Brunsma, D. L., ed., 2006, *School uniforms: A decade of research and debate*, Lanham, MD: Rowman & Littlefield Education; Brunsma, D. L., & Rockquemore, K. A., 1998, Effects of student uniforms on attendance, behavior problems, substance use, and academic achievement, *Journal of Educational Research*, 92(1), 53–62; Davidson, A., & Rae, J., 1990, *Blazers, badges and boaters: A pictorial history of the school uniform*, London: Scope International.

David L. Brunsma

COMMERCIALIZATION OF SCHOOLS

School commercialism typically refers to business involvement in public schooling. School commercialism involves advertising to children in schools, sponsored educational materials, sales of particular products in schools (sometimes through the use of exclusive contracts), electronic marketing in schools, for-profit provision of educational services such as tutoring, the management of entire schools for profit (often done by Educational Management Organizations (EMOs) like Edison Schools), and voucher schemes that allow public tax money to pay for private educational provision. Charter schools are viewed by many as an important aspect of school commercialism. Even though most charter schools are nonprofit, most public schools that are being managed for profit are enabled through charter school laws that deregulate public schools. About half of the Edison Schools are charter schools being run for profit.

Marketing to children has seen a 150-fold increase in the last 20 years, with $15 billion in advertising targeting kids by 2004. Children between the ages of 3 and 17 by 1998 spent about $45 billion a year and influenced spending of $295 billion. By 2002 kids 12 to 19 spent $170 billion and kids under 12 influenced $500 billion in spending. There is enormous money at stake for business in terms of both capturing these dollars and creating lifelong brand impressions, associations, and identifications in malleable young minds.

Although it is less obvious than junk food billboards on hallways and buses or ads for running shoes and candy in textbooks, the sweeping federal No Child Left Behind Act facilitates school commercialism in a number of ways including by heavily funding charter school creation and forcing localities to use for-profit tutoring companies rather than their own teachers. NCLB's emphasis on frequent high-stakes standardized tests has resulted in test-publishing companies making a fortune as schools and students are punished by their schools losing funds if they perform badly. NCLB's threats to close schools that do not meet adequate yearly progress (AYP) is viewed by many as a form of backdoor privatization that is setting up schools that have suffered longstanding disinvestment to be declared as "failed." Once declared "failed," these schools will be subject to being made into for-profit entities. In fact, this declaration of school failure to justify privatization and commodification of public schooling is a trend that includes capitalizing on natural and unnatural disasters such as Hurricane Katrina, the Iraq War, and the historical production of urban ghettos. For example, after Katrina numerous right-wing think tanks and publications described as "the silver lining" of the storm privatizing the destroyed New Orleans public schools with vouchers, charters, and contracting. In fact, refusing to rebuild the schools was used to keep poor predominantly black residents from returning to their communities as business groups orchestrated their own rebuilding plan.

Up-to-date information on trends in school commercialism can be found at the Commercialism in Education Research Unit at the University of Arizona, available on-line at http://www.schoolcommercialism.org. This organization measures trends in school commercialism.

School commercialism includes modeling public schools on businesses. This is evident at every level of the public school system from classroom pedagogy that asks students to be little managers or entrepreneurs to widespread proposals for teachers to get merit pay like Wall Street traders, to the widespread expectation that teachers act entrepreneurially to write grants, to the naming of business people as educational administrators and the title "CEO" for head of school districts. Business as a model for schooling appears throughout educational policy literature as well as in the popular press. According to advocates of school privatization schools are best off when they are starved of resources and forced to compete with other schools for scarce resources. Then "just like business" the bad schools should be allowed to "fail" while the good schools should be allowed to prosper. Language of business efficiency is widely invoked in both academic and popular circles. Schools, it is said, are to be made more efficient by being treated more like businesses. This means that the quality of educational services should be measurable and quantifiable and that constant pressure for increasing quantifiable measures of "achievement" are to be pushed. The heavy emphasis on testing is largely driven by such thought. Schools "just like businesses" must compete against other schools. The market should be given a chance to "compete" with public schools that have a "monopoly" over education. Students and parents should be given "choice" to shop for educational services, and consumer dollars will strengthen good schools and punish bad.

Liberal humanist critics of treating schools like business suggest that business values as they organize teaching and learning threaten human values that can be fostered by classrooms oriented around collaborative learning rather than individualistic and competitive learning practices. Learning in this view should not be based in a high-stakes, high-pressure fashion modeled after industrial and corporate efficiency. Knowledge should not be treated like units of commodity to be deposited in children. Rather, collaboration, an orientation towards dialogue in learning, and an approach to learning based in the curiosity of the student should be fostered. Critics of the high-pressure approach point to how fear becomes the motivation for student learning and teacher performance rather than interest in meaningful, relevant, or socially transformative knowledge. Additionally, these critics of school commercialism view the incursion of advertising and marketing in the classroom as threatening the public school, where such collective values can be addressed without the values of business determining and informing the conversation. For example, the consumerism, individualism, and social Darwinism, the emphasis on exclusionary forms of competition, and the removal of knowledge from broader contexts are all thought to be fostered by the treatment of schools like the consumer culture common to societies organized and oriented by contemporary consumer capitalism.

Some advocates of school commercialism attempt to naturalize it as having always been a part of the U.S. public school experience from the business involvement in producing curriculum (*McGuffey's Readers*) to the contracting for infrastructure to even advertising in schools. However, the scale of school commercialism from the nineteenth century through most of the twentieth was miniscule relative to the rapid expansion of commercialism from the 1980s to the present. Some of the more sophisticated and theoretical analyses of school commercialism view the phenomenon in relation to broader economic, social, historical, and cultural struggles and issues. For example, scholars Alex Molnar and Joel Spring have done important work on situating school commercialism in the context of the historical rise of modern consumer culture. Others have written about how school commercialism has drastically expanded since the early 1980s in part due to the rise of "neoliberal ideology" that treats social, political, and public matters as business matters, that denigrates all things public, calls for privatization of the public sector, and calls for deregulating government controls on public goods and services like public schooling to allow for expanded market involvement. Neoliberalism is a kind of faith in markets that are viewed as always more efficient than the bureaucratic and inefficient public sector. Although at the time of its inception in the 1950s and 1960s it was widely considered a radical and off-beat view, by the 1990s, following the rise of the Reagan revolution and the fall of the Soviet Union as a symbol of an alternative system, neoliberalism's TINA thesis (there is no alternative to the market) became omnipresent in the United States; it had overtaken the culture of the United States. Within such a cultural climate privatizing and commercializing public schools began to appear commonsensical. Neoliberalism collapses the economic and the political, the social and the individual, and the public and the private.

Public institutions have a mission of furthering the public interest. Private organizations like businesses exist to accumulate profit. When public schools are treated as businesses the possibilities of profit accumulation and the framing concerns of business eclipse concerns with justice, equality, and the ways that school practices foster social goals and visions that are collectively determined by the society.

In the 1980s the neoliberal faith in business created a climate ripe for market experimentation with public schooling. Despite the struggles waged over school commercialism by the state, the private sector, teacher's unions, policy workers, teachers, scholars, and the public, the cultural and political climate created the conditions for entrepreneurs like Christopher Whittle to set his sights on making a killing from public schools. Whittle, an advertising and magazine entrepreneur, was at the forefront of school commercialism, starting Channel One, which sought to place ads in school classrooms under the guise of educating students with TV news programming. Many critics have derided the programming as lacking in educational value. He sold the enterprise and built Edison Schools, which aimed to create the largest for-profit company managing public schools.

Though long celebrated in the popular press, Edison increasingly faced a series of intertwined problems that highlighted the troubles with running public schools for profit. To impress investors with continually rising test scores, the company pressured administrators and teachers who, it was revealed, cheated to show test gains. The school counseled out students expected to lower test scores. They were accused of manipulating financial and accounting data and misrepresenting test scores and the number of schools under management. They suffered high teacher turnover and sought to avoid teachers' unions that afforded labor protections to their workers. Expected to work long overtime hours, teachers' turnover was high while the best teachers were taken out of the classroom to be used as managers.

Edison became a publicly traded company only to have their stock price plummet with the plethora of bad news and the slim likelihood of profitability.

Edison claimed that if they grew large enough, economies of scale would allow them to provide quality educational services superior to public schools at a cheaper cost and also provide for investor profit to be taken away. This has yet to be achieved, with conventional measures of quality viewing Edison as poor to mixed and costs running on par or higher than comparable public schools. Critics have pointed out that Edison's free market education plan has disproportionately relied upon getting philanthropic grants and thereby calling into question the trumpeted claims about the alleged benefits of business efficiency. Although throughout the 1990s the conservative business press had been hailing public school privatization as a ripe opportunity, by 2002, with the Edison debacle, they declared for-profit management of schools to be a poor business. This has not stopped Edison and the other EMOs from continuing to run public schools for profit. However, Edison and other companies have focused their expansion on the for-profit tutoring market that NCLB has fostered. While the promises of the company have been radically redefined from its inception, the company has failed to fulfill its promises regarding quality or costs. Nonetheless Whittle and other business executives made millions of dollars of profit that could have otherwise been invested in the education of children.

The school commercialism debates tend to focus on two central issues: educational resources and the purpose and mission of public schooling.

Contemporary defenders and advocates of school commercialism include marketing companies, businesses interested in making early "brand impressions" on youth, school administration organizations, and associations representing such industries as soft drinks. Advocates of advertising, sponsored educational materials, and sales of goods in school point out that public schools suffer from a shortage of money and resources and suggest that by allowing marketers in, they can offset some of the financial and material shortages. For example, soft drink companies such as Coca Cola and Pepsi promise cash for schools that sign on to exclusive vending contracts and bonuses for excessive consumption of beverages. Other companies such as Channel One, a news program that includes advertising, promise the installation of expensive equipment such as televisions and video recording devices on the condition that students be held as a captive audience for the programming. Advocates of commercialism typically frame such potentially lucrative endeavors as beneficial to the students, schools, and communities. Often marketing to youth is framed as "business-school partnerships." The businesses get access to potential consumers and the ability to saturate the atmosphere with ads to make powerful brand impressions. In exchange the schools get to be "partners" with the businesses.

Critics of school commercialism view such marketing to youth in school as a cynical ploy to capitalize on the unfair distribution of educational resources. Within this view, the problems of school funding need to be remedied to provide quality universal public education and should not be exploited for the benefit of those who have plenty of resources and are looking to get more. School commercialism provides meager financial benefits if any, while it has numerous deleterious effects including eroding public school as one of the few places where noncommercial values can be addressed by students. Commercialism places the authority and power of the school and the public to endorse products that may have no redeeming worth or individual or public value. Soft drinks are a case in point. Critics of commercialism point to the epidemic level of early onset type II diabetes that is being fed by the steadily rising consumption of sugar-laden soda. They point out that while the financial benefit to the schools is trivial, the social cost of a society of diabetics and the financial cost of caring for them is far more detrimental than the promise of the vendors. The public health issue raised by soft drink marketing points to how the school commercialism debates are inextricably bound to competing social visions for public schools.

Disagreements about the purpose and mission of public schooling have much to do with the view of commercialism people hold. Views on commercialism tend to correspond to political perspectives. Fiscal conservatives or neoliberals view public schooling as a market. They hold that the purpose of public schooling is to prepare workers for the economy or prepare nations to compete economically. From this perspective public schooling has a principally economic role for the individual and an economic role for the society. Because the market appears as always efficient and always better than the moribund public sector, the fiscal conservative takes a radical stance in favor of privatization of public schools. For-profit charter schools, voucher schemes, and competition-based pay for teachers appeal to the fiscal conservative because they make schooling like business. As well, standardized testing and quantification of knowledge appeal to the fiscal conservative because knowledge can be treated as units of commodity or money to be deposited in students who can then cash in that knowledge for grades and universities and jobs and commodities. Quantification and measurability appear valuable because they allow for the attempt to test continually for the increased acquisition of knowledge just like capitalism fosters the continual growth of capital at any cost. Unfortunately, such business framing of knowledge tends to decontextualize knowledge and fails to account for more complex understandings of learning that treat knowledge holistically in terms of broader understandings, relations between subjects, the social, political, and cultural implications of claims to truth, and the interests and relations of authority tied to particular interpretations.

Cultural conservatives are typified by E. D. Hirsch with his Core Knowledge scheme and William Bennett who has, like Hirsch, written numerous books about what students should know. Cultural conservatives believe in a canon of knowledge that everyone should learn. This perspective is contrary to more critical approaches to knowledge that consider knowledge in relation to power, politics, history, and ethics. Critical approaches emphasize that knowledge ought to be ruthlessly interrogated and interpreted in relation to the perspectives and interests of those who make claims to truth. For criticalists, truth is arrived at collectively, while for cultural conservatives truth is inherited from "those who know." The cultural conservatives are in a sense a variety of fundamentalists who put forward dogmatic truth. They champion the partial values and perspectives of those with power and privilege while alleging these values and perspectives as universally valuable. Within this view, difference and contestation are viewed as a problem to be eradicated. This perspective shares with fiscal conservatism the insistence on the standardized body of knowledge, the enforcement of knowledge from above, and the treatment of knowledge as commodity to be consumed by students. The overlaps between these conservative approaches can be seen in such recent projects as William Bennett's company K12, which sells on-line homeschooling and charter school curriculum. It adopts Hirsch's Core Knowledge curriculum of what every student should know and marketizes it so that the conservative and dogmatic perspective can be mass marketed for profit. Acquisition of knowledge being quantifiable and measurable satisfies the fiscal conservative obsession with treating school like business while at the same time satisfying the right-wing cultural framing of knowledge important to the cultural conservatives.

For left-wing proponents of critical, progressive, or radical schooling the problems with the right-wing approach to commercialism are that it threatens to undermine the socially and individually transformative potential of public schooling. Transformative views of public schooling ask how schools participate in enacting the future. For example, the reconstructionist views of progressive philosopher of education John Dewey asked how schools are involved in educating citizens for democratic participation, self and social governance, democratic culture, and ethical life. Contemporary transformative thinkers such as Henry Giroux, a leading figure of critical pedagogy, draw on modern and postmodern theoretical traditions to call for education to be reconfigured such that teachers are politically engaged transformative intellectuals with the task of teaching students to engage knowledge critically in relation to broader structures of power and relations of domination and oppression. The task of critical pedagogy is to expand democratic social relationships in terms of politics, economics, and culture. In this view the school process is political at the core in that knowledge and school practices are shot through with values and ideologies that are best critically analyzed by learners. For critical pedagogy knowledge cannot be canonized and treated as dogma because learning ideally ought to begin with the knowledge and experience of the learner in a particular context. Students need to learn to theorize their experiences, to act on and transform the structures of power informing their experiences. Whether the object of knowledge is a work of literature, a science lesson, a particular version of history, or an advertisement, the critical approach views them all as needing to be interpreted in relation to power and politics. While liberal critics of school commercialism might frame school commercialism as a threat to the innocent space of school culture, criticalists view advertising and commercialism as a worthwhile object of critical analysis to dissect in terms of the sorts of political and cultural pedagogies it proffers. Strategies of critical media literacy and the insights of cultural studies benefit teachers who want to give students the critical intellectual tools to understand, for example, the financial interests and industries in relation to the ideological messages, cultural values, and identity positions promoted by an advertisement.

For cultural conservatives and for liberals (both of whom tend to deny the cultural politics of the curriculum) school commercialism in the form of advertising and sponsored educational materials appears as a threat to the innocent space of school that must be kept pure for authentic learning to take place. However, liberals and cultural conservatives tend to embrace privatization initiatives if they believe they effectively deliver this allegedly neutral and universally valuable school content. Some liberals and fiscal conservatives have no problem with sponsored educational materials (like ads for Nike and M&Ms integrated as math problems in textbooks) because of the belief that students learn more effectively when they are taught about things that are relevant to their lives. This is distinct from the critical view that suggests that relevant and meaningful objects of knowledge then need to be problematized in relation to both experiences of oppression and broader structures of power informing those experiences. From a critical perspective such sponsored educational materials should be kept out of the curriculum. However, if they are found in it they ought to be critically analyzed in terms of broader relations of power.

Two less commonly discussed but important aspects of school commercialism involve the way commercialism defines individual identity and the way it relates to global politics.

As discussed above, school commercialism treats knowledge as objects to be consumed by students like commodities. As well, commercialism treats individual subjects as objects in that it makes them into the means towards the end of commercial profit. That is, commercialism makes subjects in the passive spectatorial role of consumers. Subjects who define themselves principally as consumers define their individual and social value largely through their consumption practices. They define the worth of others largely through passive and private consumption practices. Subjects in this case are educated into the identity position of objects. In an economic sense the education of subjects into objects through consumer culture extends and deepens the ways that subjects are made objects through the sale of labor power on the job market. The ideology of consumer culture works in complement with the objectification of the subject by making individuals who understand their leisure and enjoyment as passive objects. Such objectification treats people instrumentally as tools for the use of others, thereby making people unfree. School commercialism educates subjects to identify principally as consumers who maximize their human capacities through choosing from an array of predetermined objects and services but not to exercise their human capacities to imagine and enact different ways of living, of spending time, of consuming, or different ways of producing that would maximize individual and collective freedom and creativity and minimize exploitation and ecological destruction. In a political sense these commercial ways of being are at odds with habits of engaged public citizenship that view individuals as active participants who ideally should be working with others to address public problems. Culturally, commercialism reduces all cultural values to their market value. This is increasingly evident as science and mathematics are emphasized at every level by the fiscal conservatives who dominate the U.S. Department of Education while all other subjects are defunded.

Increasingly, school commercialism produced by multinational companies like oil companies, chemical companies, and food companies in the form of advertising and sponsored educational materials can be found in North American public schools. These tend to offer a view of the world that portrays the earth, work, science, leisure, and human beings as ideally under benevolent corporate management. Critics contend that such corporate curricula misrepresent social and political struggle, and they highlight the ways that these very same corporations are involved in threatening public interest in the pursuit of profit. School commercialism also appears to be going global as the World Trade Organization's General Agreement on Trade in Services (GATS) makes no distinction between public schooling and private schooling. The implications are that public schools may be forced by national governments who sign on to the WTO or other global trade agreements to allow foreign for-profit education companies to compete for provision of educational services. The public mission of the public schools in any given nation (democratic schooling for example) would lose out to the possibilities of multinational companies earning profits. Advocates of global justice staunchly oppose the uses of national sovereignty to undermine the public possibilities of public schooling.

Further Reading: Apple, M., 2001, *Educating the right way,* New York: Routledge; Boyles, D., 2005, *Schools or markets?* Mahwah, NJ: Lawrence Erlbaum; Goodman, R., & Saltman, K., 2002, *Strange love, or how we learn to stop worrying and love the market,* Lanham, MD: Rowman & Littlefield; Molnar, A., 2005, *School commercialism,* New York: Routledge; Saltman, K., 2000, *Collateral damage: Corporatizing public schools—A threat to democracy,* Lanham: MD: Rowman & Littlefield; Saltman, K., 2005, *The Edison Schools,* New York: Routledge; Saltman, K., 2007, *Capitalizing on disaster: Taking and breaking public schools,* Boulder, CO: Paradigm Publishers; Spring, J., 2001, *Educating the consumer-citizen,* Mahwah, NJ: Lawrence Erlbaum.

Kenneth J. Saltman

COMPULSORY SCHOOLING

Recognizing education (schooling) and development for what they are—compulsory programs for integrating individuals and peoples into a rapidly globalizing, market-dominated culture, imposing on them a pattern of thinking and living that otherwise has been alien to all known traditional, linguistically distinct cultures—is crucial to the formation and success of grassroots movements that seek to achieve sustainable social and ecological relationships. Following this train of thought, it becomes vital for grassroots movements that seek social and ecological sustainability to closely monitor and guide the schooling and development processes within their communities. The reason for this is simple. As the driving force behind the current epoch's rush toward modern development, or toward what Lewis Mumford has called the "megatechnic" economy, the market's growth imperative, which schooling and development promote, helps to expose it as a socially and ecologically devastating virus. As it infects human communities, this economic growth imperative launches an uncompromising assault on the symbolic and literal soil upon which more traditional cultures had created their identity as a people. As it destroys the foundations of that which had once defined them as human beings, it moves like a contagion to transform them and their progeny into agents of its future replication. For once it has sucked the life from one community and destroyed the commons that had once sustained it, the market-dominated culture, promoting growth, progress, and development, must spread to find another. The spread of the market virus (aka global economy) will only result in further undermining the sustainability of humanity's social and environmental relationships.

Though many politicians and educationists, such as those who served on the National Commission for Excellence in Education that produced the now infamous *A Nation at Risk* report, like to implicitly credit the quality of American schools for the ascendancy of U.S. economic power, it is clear that military and political domination over an expanding global system of economic imperialism fell to the United States largely by default in the aftermath of World War II. The war had left the national, industrial infrastructures of that system's other traditional powers in ruin. While prewar planners in America's Council on Foreign Relations had hoped for and predicted a German defeat of the Soviet Union that would have permitted the United States to claim total hegemony, the survival of the Soviet state and its acquired satellites offered U.S. strategists a useful foil in formulating their postwar plans. The ideology of the Cold War, from the U.S. perspective, pitted the benevolent American system of democracy and free market capitalism against the Soviet system of totalitarian socialism. American propaganda immediately exploited the internationalist flavor of the various socialist movements that emerged as early as the nineteenth century to paint the Soviet Union as an evil nation dedicated to world domination. Hence, the doctrine of the Cold War allowed the United States to cast its own plans for global hegemony as defensive in nature, never to be perceived as naked aggression.

Though hardly a military threat to U.S. power, the Marxist rhetoric exploited by the Soviets did pose, in the eyes of American planners, a very real ideological threat to their designs. This threat rested in the appeal that socialist ideals held for common people, which U.S. planners recognized as lacking in their own plans. To counter that appeal and disguise its own imperial designs behind a cloak of righteousness, President Harry Truman pronounced a global campaign to replace the old system of colonial expansion and economic imperialism with a new program of *development*, allegedly based on the concept of democratic fair dealing. This global campaign promised to lift the world's social majorities out of their undignified condition of *underdevelopment* by remolding their societies in the image of the new global, democratic capitalist masters.

THE GENOCIDAL NATURE OF DEVELOPMENT

Less than two years before Truman pronounced *development* as the rationale for expanding U.S. intervention in the affairs of other nations, the United Nations retained Rafaël Lemkin to head a committee charged with drafting a law to define, prevent, and punish the crime of genocide. It was Lemkin who had originally coined the term *genocide* in 1944, by combining the ancient Greek word for race, tribe, or nation (*genes*) with the Latin word for killing (*cide*), to refer to any policy intended to bring about the elimination of a targeted human group. Though obviously moved by the atrocities of Nazism in Germany, this original definition recognizes that outright physical acts of murder represent only one method by which to carry out policies aimed at the extermination of a people. Even so, in pursuing its activities that would lead to the creation of the Secretariat's Draft of the current Genocide Convention, Lemkin's committee significantly expanded and lent greater specificity to Lemkin's original definition. Not only would a policy qualify as genocidal if it intentionally sought the destruction of some racial, national, linguistic, religious, or political group, but also if it sought to prevent the preservation and development of that group. The committee also specified three means by which such policies could be carried out.

1. *Physical Genocide* could include the direct method of physical extermination as employed by the Nazis against numerous groups during their reign of terror, but Lemkin's committee included a number of other measures under this category:

   - Deliberately imposing conditions of life that would surely result in the slow death of a people
   - Mutilations and biological experiments not intended for curative purposes
   - Depriving a group of their means of livelihood by confiscation, curtailment of work, and the denial of housing and supplies otherwise available to other groups within the same geographic area

2. *Biological Genocide* included programs of involuntary sterilization, creating obstacles to marriage, and segregating the sexes so as to prevent procreation among the target population.

3. *Cultural Genocide,* which will come to hold the greatest significance for this article, includes all policies intended to eradicate the specific traits by which a targeted population defines itself as a culture by imposing on that population an alien national pattern.

By refusing to assign a hierarchy to these three categories of genocide, Lemkin's committee acknowledged no moral or legal distinction between physical violence and cultural violence. In fact, Lemkin used the terms *genocide* and *ethnocide* (which he also coined) interchangeably. He viewed them as synonymous.

Lemkin's committee submitted its draft to the UN's Economic and Security Council (ECOSOC) in November of 1947. From there, it was sent for review to a seven-member ad hoc committee. Given the imperial intent of development as defined in this article, it comes as no surprise that the U.S. delegate who chaired that committee would have successfully worked to eliminate the category of *cultural genocide* from what would be adopted in 1948 by the General Assembly as the Convention on Prevention and Punishment of the Crime of Genocide. What is "development," after all, if not the eradication of a culture through the imposition of an alien national pattern—the very essence of cultural genocide? Neither should it be a surprise that the United States, also in light of its imperial intent, refused to fully ratify this convention, even in its diluted form, until 1996. When the United States finally submitted its ratification with the UN in 1998, it used a perverse form of self-proclaimed, international executive privilege known as the "Sovereignty Package" to effectively exempt itself from compliance.

In order to fully understand the connections between imperialism, development, and cultural genocide it is necessary to examine the nature of the "alien national pattern" that development seeks to impose on targeted populations. Prior to that, however, it is vital to recognize that the practice of imposing an alien national pattern on targeted populations under some ruse of benevolence has always functioned as part of imperial strategies. Even the Roman Empire did not expand its sphere of domination through brute military force alone. Beginning in the sixth century B.C.E., the Romans established settlements known as *colonia*, from which the word *colonialism* is derived. The *colonia* served many functions, none more important to considerations of cultural genocide than their status as showcases of Roman culture and examples of the Roman way of life. Such examples demonstrated to the targeted native populations of the provinces—those referred to by the Romans as *barbarians* (the "underdeveloped" of the age!)—how they were expected to live. Once members of the barbarian population proved that they had satisfactorily internalized the alien, Roman national pattern, the emperor promoted the settlement to the status of *colonia civium Romanorum*, bestowing on its targets full citizen rights, and dedicated a temple to the so-called Capitoline triad: Jupiter, Juno, and Minerva, the deities venerated in the temple of "Jupiter Best and Biggest" on the Capitol in Rome.

The cultural genocide initiated under the Romanization of Europe would continue through its later "Christianization." Though Christianity became the official state religion of the Roman Empire—formally outlawing the practice of all other religions—during the reign of Theodosius I (379–395 C.E.), the Christianization of northern and Western Europe did not begin in earnest until the fifth and sixth centuries. While space prohibits a full accounting of their significance, the histories of these two processes—Romanization and Christianization—mark a crucial starting point from which to begin expanding current understandings of the contemporary patterns of cultural genocide perpetrated in the name of contemporary "development." Typically, scholars associate those patterns solely with atrocities committed by European and American governments against non-European peoples. While those associations cannot be denied, they frustrate efforts to build stronger networks of grassroots solidarity by unnecessarily putting people of European ancestry on the defensive by characterizing them as members of a victimizing class. In tracing the origins of the cultural genocide perpetrated under the banner of development back to the forces of imperial domination that destroyed the indigenous cultures of Europe, a basis is provided for strengthening possible networks of solidarity by situating those of European ancestry in a more paradoxical position—as victimizers and victims. While the nation-states under which they live have victimized peoples outside of Europe, those same nation-states took their current form through their participation in similar imperial patterns of cultural genocide against the various indigenous cultures of Europe.

The vestiges of those indigenous cultures of Europe, which survived the geno-cidal activities of Roman and Holy Roman Empires, would later be destroyed by the same alien pattern associated with development.

The Rise of the Alien National Pattern (and Genocide) in Europe

The "alien national pattern" associated with development as a strategy of empire has always been foreign to traditional human communities, including those of Europe, which happened to be the first targeted populations upon which that pattern was imposed. Two of its most alien—and alienating—features will be treated here. In the first case, persons in traditional cultures demonstrate a concern for the general welfare of other individual members of the collective group. This concern works to preserve the group's culturally determined patterns of social organization and places significant limits on the extent to which economic concerns could become a dominant force in their lives, thoughts, and behaviors. The subsistence orientation of those cultures leads them to draw from their environment only what the group requires for its collective survival. Refuting the standard claim that the tendency to "barter and truck" represents a cross-cultural constant, anthropological evidence demonstrates that trade with neighboring groups was limited and infrequent. Evidence also exists to highlight the fact that individuals within traditional societies gain status from what they contribute to the collective effort. Hence, such societies place a premium on generosity. They never learn to equate status with individual economic gain or acquisitiveness.

In market societies, where the alien national pattern of "development" has already taken root and become institutionalized as the dominant social paradigm, the situation is reversed. Rather than embedding the economy within social relations, market societies embed their social relations within the economy. Individual gain motivates productive activity. It is not essential that productive activity contribute to the welfare of the group. Individuals derive status from how much gain they derive from market activity, not from what they contribute to the welfare of others. Acquisitiveness, even when performed in the name of providing for one's own family, places the ties of friendship and kinship under tremendous strain. Even in the current age of labor-saving technologies, members of market societies are working more than ever, much to the neglect of familial and communal ties.

An early episode in the history of the imposition of the market pattern on targeted European populations occurred during the English Agrarian Revolution of the fifteenth and sixteenth centuries. During this period, the *enclosure movement* fenced off public fields and forests known as "the commons" that had been used for collective farming and fuel collection. The enclosure movement marked an important step in the destruction of the traditional cultures of Europe, for it transformed the basis of village life from a subsistence-oriented fellowship of collective service and protection to an alienating pattern of servicing the economic interests of the great proprietor class. The individual legal and property rights of the great proprietors began taking precedence over moral claims of the larger community.

This transformation of the commons (nature) into "property"—a commodity that could be privately owned, bought, and sold—accompanied industrialization's transformation of "people" into "labor." Human beings ceased to be viewed as social beings connected to one another through mutual obligations, but rather as atomist individuals whose chances for survival in "the market" depended on their ability and willingness to rent themselves and their energies, as human capital or commodities, to others to harness in the pursuit of individual profit. Displacing the motivation of subsistence with the motivation of gain or greed, the market emerged as Europe's dominant social paradigm. It redefined human nature as "red in tooth and claw" and demanded a separation of the economic sphere from the political sphere in order to effect a total subordination of the entire society to the requirements of the market. The market deems social relations themselves as impediments to its growth. Even friendship, by the end of the sixteenth century, came to be viewed by some as an unreasonable passion that caused division and great discontent. The individual pursuit of wealth, on the other hand, received much praise as a moral virtue and a civic responsibility.

The same disdain for social bonds and allegiances would later resonate in the efforts of post-WWII "development experts" to explain why indigenous and more traditional (nonmarket) societies seemed so resistant to the marketization process. People's culturally ingrained allegiances and loyalties, their community-centeredness, and their lack of individualistic motivations frustrated development workers from the beginning, as did their view of land as communal property. These customs and mores, some development specialists argued, would have to be eliminated, even though the resulting social disorganization would surely create much suffering and dislocation. Moreover, cultural genocide was recognized as necessary if the alien national pattern of marketization was to be successful in replacing the existing patterns of life that had successfully sustained the targeted populations for millennia. Such replacement called for market-dominated cultural patterns, which would promote individualistic exertion for the sake of "economic development." A similar attitude was also expressed by those who clearly benefited from the imposition of this pattern in Europe in the early seventeenth century. The nobles of the seventeenth century sought their desired "public improvements"—the then contemporarily equivalent euphemism for "development" in the post-WWII era—that profited them privately at the expense of the poor, who would have to remain satisfied in clinging to their hovels and mere habitation, if they were lucky.

It is apparent that the "rich men" of the seventeenth century faced the same problem at home as the "development" expert of the twentieth century faced abroad: how to secure continued personal exertion from the victims of social dislocation. This dilemma suggests the second of the two features of the market pattern that had always been foreign to traditional cultures; namely, *scarcity*. Traditional cultures have always organized themselves to obviate the possibility of scarcity coming to dominate their social relations. In doing so, they sought to remove envy and the fear of scarcity that might encourage individualistic economic behavior (i.e., greed—the motivating force of the market) to infect those same relations. In order to ensure continued personal exertion from isolated individuals, the market pattern declared war against such subsistence-oriented customs. This war entailed the introduction of scarcity as the defining characteristic of the human condition and, therefore, the universal condition of social life everywhere. Some designers of the policies, who intended to force people into the alien patterns of the market, crudely and brutally asserted that inducing hunger and starvation among the people represented the surest way to tame those who might demonstrate the indecency and lack of civility to resist selling themselves to the great proprietors of the age. In this view, hunger would secure the obedience and subjection of even the most perverse recalcitrants in order to harness their labor in the "satanic mills." It became the task of government to increase want among the targeted populations in order to make the physical sanction of hunger effective.

However, the state would eventually develop far more effective and subtle means than hunger for grappling with this problem of disciplining people to labor. The enclosure of the commons dislocated many thousands of Europeans from their homes and generated new levels of poverty. In England during the latter half of the sixteenth century, a law covering both "the punishment of vagabonds and the relief of the poor" prescribed the construction of *houses of correction,* to number at least one per county. A century later, workhouses were established to confine an amazing heterogeneity of persons—criminals, the insane, the unemployed, the homeless, and many of the poor. Concurrently in France, the state dictated that each city establish similar institutions based on the model of the Hôpital Général in Paris. Similar patterns emerged within the *Zuchthäusern* (workhouses) in Germany.

Originally intended to suppress beggary, the confinement of this mass of undifferentiated bodies would eventually assume a new use. In addition to confining those without work, confinement would later function as a mechanism to force them to work. The great houses of confinement became houses of correction, aimed at remedying poverty and idleness through "moral enchantment." Even as early as the seventeenth century, the logic of this alien pattern (ever so present in *A Nation at Risk*'s scapegoating of schools and its implied accusations of the American workers' general stupidity!) promulgated the view that "the origin of poverty was neither scarcity of commodities nor unemployment," but "the weakening of discipline and the relaxation of morals." The massive confinements of the sixteenth and seventeenth centuries, then, represented the first efforts on the part of the state to reform individuals in the name of rendering them useful and productive members of society. In the eighteenth and nineteenth centuries, that task would be transferred to an altogether different institution seldom associated with confinement: namely, the compulsory school.

THE STATE AND THE MARKET FUNCTION
OF COMPULSORY SCHOOLING

In a very real sense, the imposition of the hitherto alien pattern of the market on the peoples of Europe and—later—elsewhere requires a re-programming of state power. Where the power of the sovereign had once fixated itself on the repression of those internal and external forces that threatened its right to rule, the market now claimed sovereignty, transforming the state into an instrument, a machine for ensuring its security and its freedom to expand and dominate life in all of its forms and dimensions.

Domestically, the market demanded that the state secure access to isolated and docile bodies in order to subject, use, transform, and improve those bodies. This docility, predicated on viewing the body as a labor-machine, allows, then, for an increase in the utility of that body. The state would go on to develop techniques of power for exercising control over that mechanism's movements, gestures, and attitudes that would increase their utility in terms of their efficiency. Michel Foucault describes those techniques as "disciplines"—a machinery of power aimed at exploring the human body as a mechanism, breaking it down, and re-arranging it not only to advance the growth of its skills, but to render the body more obedient as it became more useful, and more useful as it became more obedient.

From Foucault, it is learned that the form of power that emerged alongside the market's transformation of the state was *disciplinary power.* This form of power met the requirements of an emerging art of government that properly disposed and arranged things to service the market's demands for growth. In order to effect the right dispositions in people, disciplinary power seeks to increase the economic utility of each individual by increasing the forces that the individual's body feeds into the market as both a worker/producer and consumer. Paradoxi-cally, disciplinary power further seeks to control the body's forces by seeking to instill political obedience (allegiance) to the state and, thereby, to the market that it serves. Whereas, as previously noted, traditional societies are marked by deep allegiances to community, these disciplinary measures seek to reinforce people's primary allegiances to the state.

From the above analysis, we can discern how the state compels people (citi-zens) to attend school for two primary reasons that go far in defining the tradi-tional role of schooling. In short, schooling conditions children for their future lives as batteries, whose primary purpose in life is to provide energy to fuel the machinery of a market-dominated culture. It also simultaneously cultivates their obedience to the state. The state accomplishes this, in part, by disguising the dis-ciplinary functions of schools that treat children as batteries behind a mask of benevolence. In order to achieve maximum efficiency, the mechanism and the supporting ideology of disciplinary power has to remain hidden. The state must prevent people from recognizing the true nature of compulsory schooling—that the state claims the right to lay hold of the bodies of children to carry out the disciplinary measures required to maximize their utility to a market-dominated culture. To blur the connections between school, state, and law, schooling was tied to the value of education and presented as a human right and an opportunity. Framed as a value and protected as a right, schooling came to fit into the logic of the market as something that could be acquired. In the vernacular of schooling, parents have learned to say that they want their children to *get* an education, or to *receive* an education. Suddenly, something that had previously been seen as a process became a thing that one could possess. Befitting the market's logic of acquisitiveness, education devolved into a commodity, and the more of it that students consumed, as evidenced by the number of diplomas and degrees received, the more student use-value grew within the market-dominated culture. Human beings, then, could be "graded" like batteries. Some are AAAs, some are AAs, some are Cs, and some are Ds. As they increase their charge through the consumption of schooling, the students/batteries clearly increase their certified use-value for the market.

The market-dominated culture, itself, played a role in this when employers began requiring educational credentials (diplomas, degrees, and certificates— testimonials to the degree to which a person's use-value had been developed) as a precondition of employment. To the degree that the market literally became people's only means for satisfying their wants and needs through the buying and selling of goods and services, these formal job requirements made compulsory school laws somewhat obsolete. Because the market itself began requiring participation in the ritual of schooling as a condition of employment, the connection between the compulsory nature of schooling, the state, and the law became less discernable. As a consequence, school could become viewed less in terms of being an institution that the state forced people to attend, and more in terms of an "opportunity" and, later, a "right" that the state granted to individuals, enabling them to meet the demands of the market.

The notion of "use-value" allowed the state to introduce the "law of scarcity" into public policy planning that would also contribute to both its own benevolent image and that of the market. While the "doctrine of original sin" provided the church with its moral imperative, one of the most fundamental laws of the market provided the state with the imperative that it needed: namely, the law of scarcity. The law of scarcity defines the human condition and social conditions everywhere. Applied to the human condition, the law of scarcity proclaims that human wants are great (if not immeasurable), while their means for satisfying those wants are scarce. Only the market can provide those means—the means for achieving secular salvation, defined as the satisfaction of wants. But in order to access those means through participation in the market, one must possess something of value to exchange on the market. One must possess something akin to grace sought by those who identified with the church. The market's equivalent of grace is *use-value* and the money it generates.

The "doctrine of original sin" taught people to understand that they were born without grace, and that without grace they could not acquire eternal salvation. The "law of scarcity" teaches people that they have been born without use-value. Without use-value, people have nothing to exchange on the market. Therefore, they have no means for satisfying their wants or achieving salvation in the secular world of a market society. In their raw-state, like any resource, people possess no use-value. Also like any resource, however, they can be subjected to disciplinary processes designed to make them useful. Again, however, the means for developing that use-value are scarce. Fortunately, or so their conscience is molded to believe, the benevolent state organizes a subsidy to support public education for cultivating people's use-value in order that they can find their own individual salvation in the market while contributing to the broader salvation that the market bestows upon the society as a whole.

COMPULSORY SCHOOLING AS CULTURAL GENOCIDE

Compulsory schooling's role in cultural genocide as it was imposed on the children of European peoples evades our immediate recognition, in part because "education" has always been presented to us as an "opportunity" and a "right," not a state-imposed obligation, the neglect of which is punishable under the law. It also evades us because much of the cultural memory of the descendents of those peoples, as testimony to their status as victims of cultural genocide, has been erased. Students in teacher education programs, if not all or most people in "developed" nations, find it difficult to conceptualize that people once found it entirely possible to sustain social order in the absence of schools. They express great fear that any semblance of social order would survive the elimination of compulsory schooling. Going to schools is as natural to them as breathing. Nevertheless, the origins and the primary function of contemporary, compulsory schooling need to be recognized as the forced integration of individuals into the market pattern. From this angle, compulsory schooling can be understood as the domestic equivalent of "development" insofar as "development" was never genuinely presented to the members of traditional peoples as an option. Development as a strategy of imperialism, like schooling, has always been a compulsory program for integrating peoples into the market pattern, and compulsory schooling is typically a constituent element of that same program.

While the cultural memory of the descendents of the traditional cultures of Europe may have suffered devastating levels of erasure under the impress of a market-dominated culture's power of assimilation, the memory of the indigenous peoples of North America remains alive and continues to struggle against those powers. Many of them still recall, and work to remind those around them, how the governments of the United States and Canada restrained the violence of physical genocide against their peoples only once they recognized that the methods of cultural genocide were both less expensive and more effective. Instead of eliminating Indians through physical extermination, the patterns of cultural genocide perpetrated by the systems of residential schools in the United States and Canada killed Indians by making them "white." Indian children were torn from their families and forcibly sent to these schools to be "civilized." Their hair was cut; they were forced to wear western clothes; and they were prohibited from speaking their indigenous languages. Congruent with the experiences of other indigenous peoples with the forces of development, the Christian church played an important role in the operation of these schools. Children there were forbidden from practicing their native religions. Instead, they were forced to attend Christian church services and to read from the Bible as part of the broader effort to eliminate their cultural identities. Most significantly, in keeping with the traditional function of compulsory schooling, the primary component of the curriculum at these schools focused on cultivating these students' appreciation for the value of work. In fact, they were frequently used as slave labor for local ranchers and farmers in the communities adjacent to the schools.

IMPLICATIONS FOR GRASSROOTS MOVEMENTS

Once they recognize that development, in the guise of an imperialistic expansion of a market-dominated cultural pattern, threatens to *dis*member people from the cultural patterns that had once formed them into a network of sustainable social and environmental relationships, even the grassroots movements in market societies can begin to reclaim the conservative character that once defined them. Grassroots hold the soil together in order to prevent erosion. For grassroots movements among the surviving more traditional and indigenous peoples on the planet, holding together the soil of their traditional cultures represents the most pressing challenge. For people adrift in market-dominated societies that want to refer to their movements as "grassroots," the task entails greater complications. They are adrift because the soil of their culture has been washed away by the flood of a long and brutal, though seldom acknowledged, history of cultural genocide by market expansion. It is difficult for these people to see themselves as other than citizens of the state, who possess rights—including especially the right to equal opportunity to participate actively and acquisitively in the economic market that dominates their lives. Most of what they refer to as grassroots movements seek to expand that opportunity to others, even to those who may not want to participate. They fail to recognize the conservative nature of what it means to be a grassroots movement. Overcoming this failure hinges on a twofold process of remembrance. On the one hand, they must remember a past that has been lost to them. Rather than accepting the market's view of change as natural or progressive, they must confront the history of their own indigenous cultures' respective dissolutions by the myriad of forces discussed here and others. On the other hand, while this first act of remembrance should not be taken to suggest some romantic return to the past, it holds vital importance for motivating the second step. The most crucial task for authentic grassroots movements in market societies requires that the participants in those movements "*remember*" themselves—putting themselves back *together* in the sense of living their way back into sustainable relationships with one another and the environment. They must recreate the soil of their own culture(s). Only once that soil has been recreated can those movements realize the truly conservative qualities of their grassroots character in the struggle to hold that soil together.

Further Reading: Churchill, W., 2004, *Kill the Indian, save the man: The genocidal impact of American Indian residential schools*, San Francisco: City Lights Books [a brilliant exposé of how the residential school movements in the United States and Canada functioned as part of an effort to eliminate the indigenous peoples of North America; a highly instructive primer in cultural genocide]; Esteva, G., and Prakash, M. S., 1998, *Grassroots postmodernism: Remaking the soil of cultures*, New York: Zed Books [a very useful account of the numerous ways in which the world's social majorities are escaping from the global monoculture of the market and regenerating their own cultural and natural spaces]; Gabbard, D., & Ross, E. W., eds., 2004, *Defending public schools: Education* *under the security state,* Westport, CT: Praeger [describes the high-stakes testing and teacher accountability schemes that are central to contemporary school reform as part of an effort to delegitimate the public control of schooling; these reforms are a trap, programmed to ensure the failure of public schools in order to transfer their control over to private corporations; once this control is established, the public will lose any voice in shaping the agenda of compulsory schooling]; Illich, I., 1971, *Deschooling society,* New York: Harper & Row [one of the first books to challenge the school's self-proclaimed ability to deliver the individual and/or society into a condition of secular salvation]; Illich, I., 1992, *In the mirror of the past: Lectures and addresses 1978–1990,* New York: M. Boyars [a seminal collection of Illich's ideas for recognizing the radical otherness of our twentieth-century mental topology and to become aware of its generative axioms that usually remain below the horizon of contemporary attention].

David Gabbard

CREATIONISM, INTELLIGENT DESIGN, AND EVOLUTION

THE CREATIONIST CRUSADE

Evolution is clearly the most controversial topic in the public school science curriculum in the United States. Among scientists, there is no significant controversy about the basic scientific issues: The earth is ancient (about 4.5 billion years old); living things have descended, with modification, from common ancestors; and natural selection, by adapting living things to their environments, is a major driving force in the history of life. As the National Academy of Sciences observes, "The scientific consensus around evolution is overwhelming." Recognizing the centrality of evolution to biology, the National Association of Biology Teachers and the National Science Teachers Association have taken a firm stand on the pedagogical necessity of teaching evolution. Teaching evolution is a matter of social controversy, however, owing to the prevalence of creationism—the rejection of a scientific explanation of the history of life in favor of a supernatural account—among the public. Not all antievolutionists are creationists, and not all creationists are fundamentalist Christians—there are creationists who identify themselves with Jewish, Islamic, Hindu, New Age, and Native American religious traditions—but the juggernaut of antievolutionist activity in the United States is propelled by Christian fundamentalism.

Creationists are not unanimous in their attitudes toward the antiquity of the earth, common ancestry, and the efficacy of natural selection. Those who reject all three are called young-earth or recent creationists; young-earth creationism is currently the dominant form of creationism in the United States. Those who reject only the latter two are usually called old-earth creationists; different forms of old-earth creationism, corresponding to different interpretations of the book of Genesis to accommodate the antiquity of the earth, include Day/Age and Gap creationism. There is not a standard term for creationists who reject only the efficacy of natural selection, perhaps reflecting their relative unimportance in the debate. The latest incarnation of creationism—intelligent design—is strategically vague in its attitudes toward the age of the earth and common ancestry, in the hope of maintaining a big tent under which creationists of all varieties are

CREATIONISM, INTELLIGENT DESIGN, AND EVOLUTION WEB SITES

Following is a sampling of organizations (and their Web sites) active in controversies over creationism, evolution, and their places in public science education. Where applicable, a relevant subsection of the Web sites is identified. All Web site addresses were operational as of November 2007.

Creationist Web Sites

Young-earth Creationist Organizations

Answers in Genesis: http://www.answersingenesis.org
Creation Research Society: http://www.creationresearch.org
Institute for Creation Research: http://www.icr.org

Old-earth Creationist Organizations

Reasons to Believe: http://www.reasons.org

Intelligent Design Organizations

The Discovery Institute's Center for Science and Culture: http://www.discovery.org/csc
Intelligent Design Network: http://www.intelligentdesignnetwork.org

Evolution Web Sites

Scientific Organizations

American Association for the Advancement of Science: http://www.aaas.org/news/
    press_room/evolution
The National Academies: http://www.nationalacademies.org/evolution/

Science Education Organizations

National Association of Biology Teachers: http://www.nabt.org/
National Science Teachers Association: http://www.nsta.org/publications/evolution.aspx

Anticreationist Organizations

National Center for Science Education: http://www.ncseweb.org
TalkOrigins Foundation: http://www.talkorigins.org

welcome to shelter; its representatives run the gamut from antiselectionist creationists to young-earth creationists, while the bulk of its public support seems to be provided by young-earth creationists.

In its traditional forms, creationism is typically based on biblical inerrantism—the belief that the Bible, as God's Word, is necessarily accurate and authoritative in matters of science and history as well as in matters of morals and doctrine. Inerrantism allows for the nonliteral interpretation of metaphorical or figurative language, and thus young-earth and old-earth creationists are able to agree on the principle of inerrantism while disagreeing on its application. Mindful of the legal failures of attempts to include creationism in the public school classroom, proponents of intelligent design sedulously disavow any commitment to the Bible, but such a commitment tends to surface nevertheless—for example, in their frequent invocation of the Gospel of John's opening verse, "In the beginning was the Word . . ." Whether avowing inerrantism or not, creationists typically express a passionate concern for the supposed moral consequences of the acceptance of evolution; the "tree of evil"—with evolution at its root and various evils, real and imagined, as its branches—is a common image in creationist literature. Creationism is primarily a moral crusade.

It is a crusade that is waged against any public exposition of evolution—in recent years, national parks, science museums, public television stations, and municipal zoos have faced challenges to their presentations of evolution—but the primary battleground is the public school system. Attempts to remove, balance, or compromise the teaching of evolution occur at every level of governance: from the individual classroom (where teachers may themselves be creationists, or may mistakenly think it fair to present creationism along with evolution, or may decide to omit evolution to avoid controversy), to the local school district, to the state government's executive or legislative branch or even—rarely, and then usually as a mere token of support—to the federal government. Such attempts are a recurring feature of American science education from the 1920s onward, in a basically sinusoidal trajectory. Whenever there is a significant improvement in the extent or quality of evolution education, a creationist backlash quickly ensues, only to meet with resistance and ultimately defeat in the courts.

FROM *SCOPES* TO *EDWARDS*

The first phase of the antievolutionist movement in the United States, beginning after the close of World War I, involved attempts to constrain or even to ban the teaching of evolution, in response to its appearance in high school textbooks around the turn of the century. Due in part to the rise of organized fundamentalism, antievolution legislation was widely proposed (in 20 states between 1921 and 1929) and sometimes enacted (in Arkansas, Florida, Mississippi, Oklahoma, and Tennessee). It was Tennessee's Butler Act, which forbade teachers in the public schools "to teach any theory that denies the story of the Divine Creation of man as taught in the Bible, and to teach instead that man has descended from a lower order of animals," under which John Thomas Scopes was prosecuted in 1925. Although Scopes's conviction was overturned on appeal, on a technicality, the trial exerted a chilling influence on science education. Under the pressure of legislation, administrative decree, and public opinion, evolution swiftly disappeared from textbooks and curricula across the country.

It was not until after the launching of Sputnik in 1957 that evolution returned to the public school science classroom. Fearing a loss of scientific superiority to the Soviet Union, the federal government funded a massive effort to improve science education, which included a strong emphasis on evolution. Particularly

This textbook contains material on evolution. Evolution is a theory, not a fact, regarding the origin of living things. This material should be approached with an open mind, studied carefully, and critically considered.

Approved by
Cobb County Board of Education
Thursday, March 28, 2002

Figure C.5   The Cobb County, Georgia, evolution warning sticker (2002–2005).

important were the biology textbooks produced by the Biological Science Curriculum Study, established in 1959 by a grant from the National Science Foundation to the education committee of the American Institute of Biological Sciences. The popular BSCS textbooks, written with the aid of biologists such as Hermann J. Muller (who complained of the inadequate treatment of evolution in biology textbooks in a famous address entitled "One Hundred Years Without Darwin Are Enough"), treated evolution as a central theme, and commercial publishers began to follow suit. Meanwhile, the Tennessee legislature repealed the Butler Act in 1967, anticipating the Supreme Court's decision in *Epperson v. Arkansas* (1968) that laws prohibiting the teaching of evolution in the public schools violate the Establishment Clause of the First Amendment.

After it was no longer possible to ban the teaching of evolution, creationists increasingly began to argue that creationism was a viable scientific alternative that deserved to be taught alongside evolution. Poised to take the lead was young-earth creationism, in the form of the creation science movement, which contended that there is scientific evidence that the earth (and the universe) are relatively young (on the order of 10,000 years), that the earth was inundated by a global flood responsible for a mass extinction and for major geological features such as the Grand Canyon, and that evolution is impossible except within undefined but narrow limits (since living things were created to reproduce "after their own kind"). Organizations such as the Creation Research Society (1963) and the Institute for Creation Research (1972) were founded, ostensibly to promote scientific research supporting creationism. Creation science remained absent from the scientific literature—but was increasingly prominent in controversies over science education.

During the second phase of the antievolution movement, science teachers, school administrators, and textbook publishers found themselves pressured to provide equal time to creation science. Creationists started to prepare their own textbooks, such as the CRS's *Biology: A Search for Order in Complexity* (1970) and the ICR's *Scientific Creationism* (1974), for use in the public schools. The movement received a boost in 1980 from Republican presidential nominee Ronald Reagan, who endorsed teaching creationism whenever evolution was taught. And legislation calling for equal time for creationism was introduced in no fewer than 27 states, successfully in both Arkansas and Louisiana in 1981. But both

A MESSAGE FROM THE ALABAMA STATE BOARD OF EDUCATION

This textbook discusses evolution, a controversial theory some scientists present as a scientific explanation for the origin of living things, such as plants, animals and humans.

No one was present when life first appeared on earth. Therefore, any statement about life's origins should be considered as theory, not fact.

The word "evolution" may refer to many types of change. Evolution describes changes that occur within a species. (White moths, for example, may "evolve" into gray moths.) This process is microevolution, which can be observed and described as fact. Evolution may also refer to the change of one living thing to another, such as reptiles into birds. This process, called macroevolution, has never been observed and should be considered a theory. Evolution also refers to the unproven belief that random, undirected forces produced a world of living things.

There are many unanswered questions about the origin of life which are not mentioned in your textbook, including:

- Why did the major groups of animals suddenly appear in the fossil record (known as the "Cambrian Explosion")?

- Why have no new major groups of living things appeared in the fossil record for a long time?

- Why do major groups of plants and animals have no transitional forms in the fossil record?

- How did you and all living things come to possess such a complete and complex set of "Instructions" for building a living body?

Study hard and keep an open mind. Someday, you may contribute to the theories of how living things appeared on earth.

Figure C.6 The Alabama evolution warning sticker (1996–2001).

laws were ruled unconstitutional, the Arkansas law by a federal district court (*McLean v. Arkansas,* 1982) and the Louisiana law ultimately by the Supreme Court (*Edwards v. Aguillard,* 1987), on the grounds that teaching creationism in the public schools violates the Establishment Clause.

INTELLIGENT DESIGN

In the wake of the decision in *Edwards,* which held that the Louisiana law impermissibly endorsed religion "by advancing the religious belief that a supernatural being created humankind," a group of creationists sought to devise a form of creationism able to survive constitutional scrutiny. A scant two years after *Edwards,* intelligent design was introduced to a wide audience in *Of Pandas and People* (1989; second edition 1993), produced by a fundamentalist organization called the Foundation for Thought and Ethics and intended for use as a supplementary biology textbook. Like its creation science predecessors, *Of Pandas and People* contended that evolution was a theory in crisis, on the common creationist assumption that (supposed) evidence against evolution is perforce evidence for creationism. Unlike them, however, it attempted to maintain a studied neutrality on the identity and nature of the designer, as well as on issues, such as the age of the earth, on which creationists differ.

During the 1990s, the intelligent design movement coalesced, with its de facto headquarters shifting from FTE to the Center for the Renewal of Science and Culture (later renamed the Center for Science and Culture), founded in 1996 as a division of the Discovery Institute, a think tank based in Seattle. At the same time, as states began to introduce state science standards, which provide guidelines for local school districts to follow in their individual science curricula, the treatment of evolution was improving, penetrating even to districts and schools where creationism was taught—the Supreme Court's decision in *Edwards* notwithstanding—or where evolution was downplayed or omitted altogether. (The importance of state science standards was cemented by the federal No Child Left Behind Act, enacted in 2002, which requires states to develop and periodically revise standards.) The stage was set for the third phase of the antievolution movement, which is going on today.

Like the creation science movement before it, the intelligent design movement claimed to favor a top-down approach, in which the scientific establishment would be convinced first, with educational reform following in due course. But like creation science before it, intelligent design was in fact aimed at the public schools. Supporters of intelligent design have attempted to have *Of Pandas and People* approved for use in Alabama and Idaho, proposed laws to require or allow the teaching of intelligent design in at least eight states, and attempted to rewrite state science standards in at least four states, including Kansas, where in 2005 the state board of education rewrote the standards to disparage the scientific status of evolution. As with a similar episode in 1999, the antievolution faction on the board lost its majority in the next election, and the rewritten standards were abandoned in 2007. Such activity at the state level was mirrored at the local level, where attempts to require or allow the teaching of intelligent design caused uproar sporadically across the country.

In the small Pennsylvania town of Dover, the result was the first legal challenge to the constitutionality of teaching intelligent design in the public schools, *Kitzmiller v. Dover*. After a summer of wrangling over evolution in biology textbooks, the Dover school board adopted a policy in October 2004 providing that "[s]tudents will be made aware of gaps/problems in Darwin's Theory and of other theories of evolution including, but not limited to, intelligent design." The board subsequently required a disclaimer to be read aloud in the classroom, according to which evolution is a "Theory...not a fact," "Gaps in the Theory exist for which there is no evidence," and intelligent design as presented in *Of Pandas and People* is a credible scientific alternative to evolution. Eleven local parents filed suit in federal district court, arguing that the policy violated the Establishment Clause. The court agreed, writing that it was "abundantly clear that the Board's ID Policy violates the Establishment Clause," adding, "In making this determination, we have addressed the seminal question of whether ID is science. We have concluded that it is not, and moreover that ID cannot uncouple itself from its creationist, and thus religious, antecedents."

THE FALLBACK STRATEGY

Like *McLean*, *Kitzmiller* was tried in a federal district court, and the decision is directly precedential only in the district. (The Dover school board chose not to appeal the decision, in part because the supporters of the policy on the school board were defeated at the polls.) Thus there is no decisive ruling at the highest judicial level that explicitly addresses the constitutionality of teaching intelligent design in the public schools so far, and it is possible that a future case will ultimately produce a decision by the Supreme Court. Even before the *Kitzmiller* verdict, however, the Center for Science and Culture was already retreating from its previous goal of requiring the teaching of intelligent design in favor of what it called "teaching the controversy"—in effect, a fallback strategy of attacking evolution without mentioning any creationist alternative. To its creationist supporters, such a strategy offers the promise of accomplishing the goal of encouraging students to acquire or retain a belief in creationism while not running afoul of the Establishment Clause. Unless there is a significant change in church/state jurisprudence, forms of the fallback strategy are likely to become increasingly prominent in the antievolution movement.

A perennially popular form of the fallback strategy involves disclaimers, whether oral or written. Between 1974 and 1984, for example, the state of Texas required textbooks to carry a disclaimer that any material on evolution included in the book is to be regarded as "theoretical rather than factually verifiable"; in 1984, the state attorney general declared that the disclaimer was unconstitutional. The state of Alabama began to require evolution disclaimers in textbooks in 1996; the original disclaimer (since revised twice) described evolution as "a controversial theory some scientists present as a scientific explanation for the origin of living things, such as plants, animals and humans." Disclaimers have been challenged in court twice. In *Freiler v. Tangipahoa* (1997), a policy requiring teachers to read a disclaimer that conveyed the message that evolution is a religious viewpoint at odds with accepting the Bible was ruled to be unconstitutional. In *Selman v. Cobb County* (2005), a textbook disclaimer describing evolution as "a theory, not a fact" was ruled to be unconstitutional, but the decision was vacated on appeal and remanded to the trial court, where a settlement was reached.

Attacking the content of textbooks is also a perennially popular form of the fallback strategy, especially in so-called adoption states, where textbooks are selected by a state agency for use throughout the state, and the publishers consequently have a strong incentive to accommodate the demands of the agency. In Texas, Educational Research Associates, founded by the husband-and-wife team of Mel and Norma Gabler, lobbied the state board of education against evolution in textbooks, succeeding in having the BSCS textbooks removed from the list of state-approved textbooks in 1969. Owing both to changes in the Texan political landscape and opposition from groups concerned with civil liberties and science education, ERA's influence waned in the 1980s. But the tradition is alive and well: while evaluating biology textbooks for adoption in 2003, the Texas board of education was inundated with testimony from creationists, complaining of supposedly mistaken and even fraudulent information in the textbooks. All 11 textbooks under consideration were adopted nevertheless.

Calling for "critical analysis" of evolution—and, significantly, *only* of evolution, or of evolution and a handful of issues that are similarly controversial, such as global warming or stem-cell research—is the latest form of the fallback strategy. Its most conspicuous venture so far was in Ohio, where in 2002, after a dispute over whether to include intelligent design in the state science standards was apparently resolved, the state board of education voted to include in the standards a requirement that students be able to "describe how scientists continue to investigate and critically analyze aspects of evolutionary theory." The requirement served as a pretext for the adoption in 2004 of a corresponding model lesson plan that, relying on a number of creationist publications, appeared to be intended to instill scientifically unwarranted doubts about evolution. Following the decision in *Kitzmiller* and the revelation that the board ignored criticisms of the lesson plan from experts at the Ohio Department of Education, the board reversed itself in 2006, voting to rescind the lesson plan and to remove the "critical analysis" requirement from the standards.

WHAT NEXT?

The United States is not the only country with controversies about evolution in the public schools: In recent years, there have been reports of such controversies from Brazil, Canada, Germany, Italy, Malaysia, the Netherlands, Poland, Russia, Serbia, Turkey, and the United Kingdom, for example. But the United States is clearly exceptional in the amount and influence of creationist activity—and of creationist belief. Comparing the levels of acceptance of evolution in the United States with those in 32 European countries and Japan, a recent report noted, "Only Turkish adults were less likely to accept the concept of evolution than American adults" (Miller et al., 2006), and plausibly attributed resistance to evolution among the American public to three factors: the acceptance of fundamentalist religious beliefs, the politicization of science, and the widespread ignorance of biology. Longitudinally, the report adds, "After 20 years of public debate, the percentage of U.S. adults accepting the idea of evolution has declined from 45% to 40% and the percentage of adults overtly rejecting evolution declined from 48% to 39%. The percentage of adults who were not sure about evolution increased from 7% in 1985 to 21% in 2005."

These attitudes appear to be reflected in the public's attitude toward the teaching of evolution in the public schools. According to a pair of recent national polls (CBS News, November 2004; *Newsweek*, December 2004), a majority—60–65 percent—favors teaching creationism along with evolution, while a large minority—37–40 percent—favors teaching creationism instead of evolution. The situation is perhaps not quite so dire as these data suggest, however; in a poll that offered respondents a wider array of choices, only 13 percent favored teaching creationism as a "scientific theory" along with evolution, and only 16 percent favored teaching creationism instead of evolution (DYG, on behalf of the People for the American Way Foundation, November 1999). Still, it seems clear that in the public there is a reservoir of creationist sentiment, which frequently splashes toward the classroom. In a recent informal survey among members of the National Science Teachers Association (March 2005), 30 percent of respondents indicated that they experienced pressure to omit or downplay evolution and related topics from their science curriculum, while 31 percent indicated that they felt pressure to include nonscientific alternatives to evolution in their science classroom.

In addition to whatever creationist sympathies there are in the public at large, reinforced by the efforts of a creationist counterestablishment, there are also systemic factors that combine to sustain creationism and inhibit evolution education. Perhaps the most important among these is the decentralized nature of the public school system in the United States. There are over 15,000 local school districts, each with a degree of autonomy over curriculum and instruction, typically governed by a school board comprised of elected members of the community usually without any special training in either science or education. Each district thus offers a chance for creationist activists—who may, of course, be elected to school boards themselves—to pressure the school board to remove, balance, or compromise the teaching of evolution. Also important is the comparative lack of attention to preparing educators to understand evolution and to teach it effectively. Especially in communities with a tradition of ignorance of, skepticism about, and hostility toward evolution, it is not surprising that teachers who are neither knowledgeable about evolution nor prepared to teach it effectively often quietly decide to avoid any possible controversy.

There are signs of hope for supporters of the teaching of evolution, however, in addition to the consistency with which courts have ruled against the constitutionality of efforts to remove, balance, or compromise the teaching of evolution. Rallied by the spate of intelligent design activity, the scientific community is increasing its public engagement and advocacy, including outreach efforts to science educators in the public schools. Academic work in the burgeoning field of science and religion is producing a renewed interest in exploring ways to reconcile faith with science, while over 10,000 members of the Christian clergy have endorsed a statement affirming the compatibility of evolution with their faith. And the increasing economic importance of the applied biological sciences, of which evolution is a central principle, is likely to be increasingly cited in defense of the teaching of evolution. Still, controversies over the teaching of evolution are clearly going to continue for the foreseeable future.

Further Reading: Alters, B. J., & Alters S. M., 2001, *Defending evolution: A guide to the evolution/creation controversy,* Sudbury, MA: Jones and Bartlett; Larson, E. J., 2003, *Trial and error: The American controversy over creation and evolution,* 3rd ed., New York: Oxford University Press; Miller, J. D., Scott, E. C., & Okamoto, S., 2006, Public acceptance of evolution, *Science 313:* 765–766; National Academy of Sciences, 1999, *Science and creationism,* 2nd ed., Washington DC: National Academies Press; Scott, E. C., 2005, *Evolution vs. creationism: An introduction,* Berkeley: University of California Press.

Glenn Branch

CRITICAL PEDAGOGY

WHAT IS CRITICAL PEDAGOGY?

Perhaps the most distinguishing element of critical pedagogy is its aim to empower people to transform their world. There is no uniform definition of critical pedagogy, as educators and theorists have transformed the concept over the years as they deployed new approaches to understanding the world and changing it.

Critical pedagogy usually refers to educational theory, teaching, and learning practices that aim to raise learners' critical consciousness regarding oppressive social conditions. Critical pedagogy focuses on the development of critical consciousness for both "personal liberation" and collective political action aimed at overcoming oppressive social conditions and to create a more egalitarian, socially just world. Pedagogy that is critical encourages students and teachers to understand the interconnected relationships among knowledge, culture, authority, ideology, and power. Understanding these relationships in turn facilitates the recognition, critique, and transformation of existing undemocratic social practices and institutional structures that produce and sustain inequalities and oppressive social relations.

Critical pedagogy is particularly concerned with reconfiguring the traditional student/teacher relationship, where the teacher is the active agent, the one who knows, and the students are the passive recipients of the teacher's knowledge. The critical classroom is envisioned as a site where new knowledge, grounded in the experiences of students and teachers alike, is produced through meaningful dialogue. In short, critical pedagogy aims to empower to students by (1) engaging them in the creation of personally meaningful understandings of the world; and (2) providing opportunities for students to learn that they have agency, that is their actions can enable social change.

Critical Theory and Critical Pedagogy

The terms critical theory, critical thinking, and critical pedagogy are sometimes conflated. In 1843, Karl Marx defined critical theory as "the self-clarification of the struggles and wishes of the age." In more recent times, critical theory has come to be treated as an umbrella term for a wide array of academic theories, but current use of the term has two distinct meanings and origins—one related to neo-Marxian social theory and the other to literary criticism. Many of the key concepts and arguments of critical pedagogy are grounded in the critical social theory tradition that began to emerge in the 1930s with the work of thinkers affiliated with the Institute for Social Research at the University of Frankfurt and others influenced by them. Known informally as the Frankfurt School, these theorists developed analyses of the changes in Western capitalist societies that had occurred since the classical theories of Marx. Frankfurt School critical theorists were oriented toward radical social change, as opposed to "traditional theory," that is theory in the positivistic, scientistic, or purely observational mode. Their emphasis on the "critical" component of theory was derived in an attempt to overcome the limits of positivism and phenomenology by returning to Kant's critical philosophy and Hegel's philosophy, with its emphasis on negation and contradiction as inherent properties of reality. The rise of Nazism and the 1930s publication of Marx's *Economic-Philosophical Manuscripts* and *The German Ideology*, as well as the theories of Max Weber and Sigmund Freud, exerted an enormous influence on Frankfurt School critical theory—which includes the work Max Horkheimer, Theodor Adorno, Walter Benjamin, Herbert Marcuse, Eric Fromm, and later Jürgen Habermas, among others. The Frankfurt School thinkers broadened the scope of Marxism beyond its dogmatic use by communist and social-democratic political parties to include issues such as how people and institutions interact and by merging philosophical and empirical problems introduced the idea that theory is a part of everyday life. Brazilian educator and key critical pedagogy theorist Paulo Freire was heavily influenced by Frankfurt School critical theory.

Critical Thinking and Critical Pedagogy

On a broad level, critical thinking and critical pedagogy share some common concerns. In *Critical Theories in Education*, Burbules and Berk note that both approaches imagine a population who to some extent are deficient in dispositions or abilities to discern inaccuracies, distortions, and falsehoods that limit freedom (although this concern is more explicit in critical pedagogy, which "sees society as fundamentally divided by relations of unequal power"). Critical pedagogues are specifically concerned with the influences knowledge and cultural formations that legitimate an unjust status quo. Fostering a critical capacity in citizens is a way of enabling them to resist such effects of power. Critical thinking authors often cite similar concerns, but in general regard them as less important than the problem of people making life choices on unsubstantiated truth claims—a problem that is conceived as nonpartisan in its nature or effects.

As critical thinking advocate Richard Paul puts it, the basic problem is irrational, illogical, and unexamined living.

Both critical thinking advocates and critical pedagogues "argue that by helping to make people more critical in thought and action, progressively minded educators can help to free learners to see the world as it is and to act accordingly; critical education can increase freedom and enlarge the scope of human possibilities." However, as Burbules and Berk point out, the critical thinking tradition primarily concerns itself with "criteria of epistemic adequacy" or the logical analysis of truth claims. To be "critical" in the critical thinking tradition means to be more "discerning in recognizing faulty arguments, hasty generalization, assertions lacking evidence, truth claims based on unreliable authority... The primary preoccupation of critical thinking is to supplant sloppy or distorted thinking with thinking based upon reliable procedures of inquiry."

Critical pedagogy, on the other hand, regards belief claims, "not primarily as propositions to be assessed for their truth content, but as parts of systems of belief and action that have aggregate effects within the power structures of society. It asks first about these systems of belief and action, who benefits?" Indeed, a crucial dimension of critical pedagogy is that certain claims, even if they might be "true" or substantiated within particular confines and assumptions, might nevertheless be partisan in their effects. Critical pedagogy is primarily concerned with social justice and the transformation of oppressive, inequitable, and undemocratic social conditions and relations.

PAULO FREIRE AND CRITICAL PEDAGOGY

Paulo Freire (1921–1997) was perhaps the most renowned educator of the twentieth century and is the central figure in the development of critical pedagogy. Freire wrote numerous books, the most influential of which, *The Pedagogy of the Oppressed*, was published in 1968. *The Pedagogy of the Oppressed* argues against the "banking concept of education" and in favor of a liberatory, dialogical pedagogy designed to raise individuals' consciousness of oppression and to in turn transform oppressive social structures through "praxis."

According to Freire, the "banking concept of education" positions students as empty vessels, and traditional education is characterized as "an act of depositing, in which the students are the depositories and the teacher is the depositor." The teacher lectures, and the students "receive, memorize, and repeat." Banking education is characterized by the following oppressive attitudes and practices:

- the teacher teaches and the students are taught;
- the teacher knows everything and the students know nothing;
- the teacher thinks and the students are thought about;
- the teacher talks and the students listen meekly;
- the teacher disciplines and the students are disciplined;
- the teacher chooses and enforces his choice, and the students comply;
- the teacher acts and the students have the illusion of acting through the action of the teacher;

- the teacher chooses the program content and the students (who are not consulted) adapt to it;
- the teacher confuses the authority of knowledge with her or his own professional authority, which she or he sets in opposition to the freedom of the students;
- the teacher is the subject of the learning process, while the pupils are mere objects.

Freire's dialogical approach to education (also known as "problem-posing education") eschews the lecture format in favor of dialogue and open communication among students and teachers. According to Freire, in this method, all teach and all learn. The dialogical approach contrasts with the banking approach, which positions the teacher as the transmitter of knowledge, a hierarchical framework that leads to domination and oppression through the silencing of students' knowledge and experiences. Using a process of collaborative dialogue, Freirean critical pedagogy engages students in critique (e.g., detailed analysis and assessment) of social realities and enables praxis—which Freire defined as the complex activity by which individuals create culture and society and become critically conscious human beings. Praxis comprises a cycle of action-reflection-action that is central to critical pedagogy. Characteristics of praxis include self-determination (as opposed to coercion), intentionality (as opposed to reaction), creativity (as opposed to homogeneity), and rationality (as opposed to chance).

Freire and his work are not without critics. Rich Gibson, for example, has critiqued his work as a cul-de-sac, a combination of old-style revolutionary socialism (wherever Freire was not) and liberal reformism (wherever Freire was). Gibson describes Freire as "a paradigm shifter, willing to enclose postmodernism, Catholicism, Marxism, and liberalism, a person far more complex than many of those who appropriate his work."

CRITICAL PEDAGOGY AND ITS CRITICS

Critical pedagogy is inclusive of a wide variety of alternative educational practices that not only challenge the status quo of teaching, learning, and schooling, but are often critical of the competing varieties of the critical pedagogy project.

It is not surprising that critical pedagogy has critics from without, as in nearly every variation it offers up challenges of one sort or the other to the traditional, "banking" approach to education. For example, public schools are primarily concerned with reproduction of the status quo as they prepare students to assimilate into the world as it is. Critical pedagogy aims to engage students in collaboratively constructing their own understandings of the world, which, at least potentially, serve as platforms for reconstructing the world and their place in it. Thus, critical pedagogy is controversial because it strikes at the very heart of what teaching and schooling is assumed to be about by the vast majority of stakeholders in public education (e.g., students, teachers, parents, local school communities, politicians, and corporations).

The very nature of critical pedagogy demands that it be continually reexamined, and some of the most scathing critiques of critical pedagogy have come from within its broad boundaries. Critical pedagogy is a label that includes educators and theorists working in traditions such as, but not limited to, Marxism and neo-Marxism (Michael Apple, Jean Anyon, Gustavo Fischman, Rich Gibson, Pauline Lipman, Peter McLaren), cultural studies (Henry A. Giroux, Pepi Leistyna), feminism (Patty Lather, Elizabeth Ellsworth), critical literacy (Ira Shor), anarchism/social ecology (David Gabbard, Matt Hern, Ivan Illich), and ecology (C. A. Bowers).

One line of self-criticism might be labeled the theory-practice gap. The few authors or practitioners who offer concrete examples of critical teaching and learning practices are contrasted with the relative many who focus on theorizing a vision of society and schooling that is intended to shape the direction of a critical pedagogy. A common criticism within the critical pedagogy community has been that authors of theoretical texts—sometimes written in abstruse, jargon-laden language—fail to engage with the problems and everyday educational contexts practitioners face. Few, if any, critical pedagogues believe that critical teaching practices can be reduced to recipes. Indeed, it is because it is the responsibility of teachers in collaboration with their students to create appropriate critical pedagogies that there is a concern that critical pedagogy theorists engage more forthrightly with the pragmatics of critical teaching.

On the other hand, some radical critical pedagogues argue that in practice critical pedagogy has been "domesticated" or diluted to the point that it has been assimilated into the mainstream. In his book *Che Guevara, Paulo Freire, and the Pedagogy of Revolution* Peter McLaren (2000) puts it this way

> Once considered by the faint-hearted guardians of the American dream as a term of opprobrium, critical pedagogy has become so completely psychologized, so liberally humanized, so technologized, and so conceptually postmodernized, that its current relationship to broader liberation struggles seems severely attenuated if not fatally terminated. The conceptual net known as critical pedagogy has been cast so wide and at times so cavalierly that it has come to be associated with anything dragged up out of the troubled and infested waters of educational practice, from classroom furniture organized in a "dialogue friendly" circle to "feel-good" curricula designed to increase students' self-image.

Lastly, the modernist assumptions of critical pedagogy—as evident in Frankfurt School thought—have opened it to criticism from the postmodernists. Postmodernism encompasses a hugely diverse set of theories, but in general is marked by a rejection of the universalizing tendencies of philosophy and totalizing systems of knowledge, meaning, or belief metanarratives. Postmodernists' major criticisms of critical pedagogy include its use of categories and definitions that are presented as self-evident (e.g., "oppression," "liberation," "humanization," "empowerment"); its assumption that there is an objective reality that can be understood in a rational way (the postmodern worldview sees one perception of reality as no more true or accurate than another); and its reliance on the metanarratives such as Marxism.

Despite the postmodernist critique, the critical pedagogical project of interrogating institutional structures that are implicated in relations of domination and oppression can, some believe, be consistent with postmodernism. For example, Henry Giroux argues in his book *Postmodernism as Border Pedagogy* that postmodernism can be viewed as equipping critical pedagogues with a new set of theoretical tools for raising questions about how narratives get constructed, what they mean, how they regulate experience, and how they presuppose particular epistemological and political world views.

In response to the postmodernist critique, some critical pedagogues counter that postmodernism provides neither a viable educational politics nor the foundation for effective radical educational practice and argue that critical pedagogy provides an alternative "politics of human resistance" that puts the challenge to capitalism firmly on the agenda of educational theory, politics, and practice.

Further Reading: Burbules, N. C., & Berk, R., 1999, Critical thinking and critical pedagogy: Relations, differences, and limits, in T. S. Popkewitz & L. Fendler (Eds.), *Critical theories in education,* New York: Routledge; Darder, A., Torres, R. D., & Baltodano, M., eds., 2002, *The critical pedagogy reader,* New York: Routledge; Freire, P., 1970, *Pedagogy of the oppressed,* New York: Continuum; Freire, P., 1995, *Pedagogy of hope: Reliving pedagogy of the oppressed,* New York: Continuum; Gadotti, M., 1994, *Reading Paulo Freire: His life and work,* Albany: State University of New York Press; Gibson, R., 2007, Paulo Freire and revolutionary pedagogy for social justice, in E. W. Ross & R. Gibson (Eds.), *Neoliberalism and education reform* (pp. 177–215), Cresskill, NJ: Hampton Press; Hill, D., McLaren, P., Cole, M., & Rikowski, G., 2002, *Marxism against postmodernism in educational theory,* Lanham, MD: Lexington Books; McLaren, P., 2000, *Che Guevara, Paulo Freire, and the pedagogy of revolution,* Lanham, MD: Rowman and Littlefield; McLaren, P., 2006, *Life in school,* 5th ed., Boston: Allyn & Bacon; Taylor, P., 1993, *The texts of Paulo Freire,* Buckingham: Open University Press.

E. Wayne Ross

CULTURALLY RELEVANT EDUCATION

We have all heard the statistics before. Students of color are rapidly becoming the majority in many schools and districts across the country. Immigrant and linguistically diverse students are filling up our public classrooms. Teachers, who are mainly white, monolingual, and middle class, increasingly face a larger number of students who do not look like them and who come from backgrounds unfamiliar to them. How do we teach these students?

Educators agree that the current school system is failing these students. However, there is disagreement over how best to educate them. Some believe that these marginalized students need to assimilate into the American culture and school system. They need to change in order to survive in today's world. Others believe that schools and teachers need to change and adapt education to the cultural backgrounds and needs of students.

Fortunately, these beliefs are not mutually exclusive. These viewpoints need not be opposed. Culturally relevant education is an approach that enables teachers to connect with their students of color while these students attain academic achievement. Through culturally relevant education, academic success is not predicated on abandoning their culture.

DEFINITION OF CULTURALLY RELEVANT EDUCATION

Culturally relevant education is a broad term that encompasses an educational philosophy, theory, and method that places culture at the heart of teaching and learning. Related approaches include culturally relevant pedagogy, culturally responsive teaching, culturally congruent instruction, engaged pedagogy, and equity pedagogy, among others. Though they slightly differ in terminology, they all share the belief that it is important to use diverse students' prior experiences, cultural knowledge, and references to make learning more meaningful and accessible to them. When we connect their personal backgrounds to what they are learning, all of our students have a greater chance of succeeding academically.

THE RISE OF CULTURALLY RELEVANT EDUCATION

Public education has historically been used to assimilate different students into mainstream dominant American society. Imagine a young child walking to school every day. When she arrives at school, she expects to interact in ways that are familiar to her. For most white middle-class children, they pass through school doors without much thought to adjusting to the environment and its expectations. However, for students whose cultural norms do not match the status quo of schools, they are expected to fit into this foreign environment. Unconsciously, these students are forced to leave their culture at the door, leaving them disenfranchised and underachieving.

Culturally relevant education calls for changes in how teachers, administrators, and institutions conduct business so that the cultural backgrounds of all students are welcomed and used to inform classroom practices and curriculum. Though these ideas of culturally relevant education may be considered transformative, they are not new. Gay's (2000) review of its beginnings shows that scholars have discussed the importance of cultural diversity in education and its positive impact on student learning since the 1970s. Already, early scholars highlighted the ethnic differences between students and teachers and discussed how to eliminate differences between the culture of ethnic minority students and schools. Others focused on teacher bias and identified traits of effective teachers with particular ethnic minority students (Kleinfield, 1975). As a result, scholars introduced "culturally appropriate ways" to capitalize on students' cultural background.

These early scholars laid the foundation for the field of cultural relevant education—as we currently name and know it. The focus on teacher role and reflection, cultural congruent communication, culturally responsive pedagogy, and curriculum continue to be reoccurring themes that shape our understanding of culturally relevant education today.

Teacher as Caring Cultural Mediator

Most scholars agree that the success of culturally relevant education rests on the teacher. Therefore, it is important that teachers critically reflect upon their cultural backgrounds and understand how factors such as race, class, and gender affect their teaching. Recognizing that their cultural lenses are clouded by biases and assumptions moves teachers from being cultural dictators in the classroom to cultural "mediators." In Ladson-Billings' (1994, p. 34) study of exemplary teachers of African American students, she described a culturally responsive teacher in a similar role as a "coach/conductor" who:

- sees herself as an artist, and teaching as an art;
- sees herself as part of a the community, and teaching as giving back to the community and encouraging students to do the same;
- believes all students can succeed;
- helps students make connection between their community, national, and global identities;
- sees teaching as "pulling knowledge out"—like "mining."

Underlying each of these characteristics is the ethic of care. A culturally relevant teacher views her profession as more than a job, but as a commitment to humanity. She feels connected and cares deeply for the souls of her students, their families, and the community. She values the home cultures that students bring to the classroom and views their backgrounds as strengths and not limitations. Students are not viewed as culturally deficit or culturally deprived, but rather rich with culture, abilities, and life circumstances. She spends time establishing relationships and getting to know her students. As Delpit (1995) states: "In order to teach, I must know you." Learning about student backgrounds helps her understand, not judge particular and different behaviors, and helps her to bridge discrepancies between home and school culture. Finally, along with caring comes high expectation of excellence from his students. A culturally relevant teacher displays tough love. He is a "warm demander," who is emotionally warm and holds high standards for all his students.

Culturally Congruent Communication

Within the last two decades, much of the literature on culturally relevant education has focused on the mismatch between home language and communication patterns and those used at school and how this disparity affects classroom dynamics. In mainstream classrooms, language and communication is largely based on white, middle class, and monolingual communication structures. Standard English, "the passive—receptive posture" or the one-way communication from teacher to student and single turn-taking tends to be the norm. This contrasts with the communication style of some ethnic groups. For example, African Americans tend to communicate with a "call and response" pattern whereby listeners verbally affirm and respond to speakers as they are talking. While African Americans are likely to "talk back," Native Hawaiian students tend to use a discourse structure in their homes called "talk story," a communal form of communication to promote solidarity where speakers recall events, share personal experiences, ramble, and joke as a means to promote a shared feeling.

Researchers also found disconnect between adult and child oral interactions that occurred at home and at school. In Shirley Brice-Heath's 1983 book *Ways with Words: Language, Life and Work in Communities and Classrooms,* she found that European American middle-class parents posed commands in the form of questions, while African American and working-class parents posed commands in a more authoritative and direct manner. For example, African American parents might state: "Go to sleep," while European American parents ask: "Why don't you go to sleep now?" Though phrased as a question, it was "code" for "Go to sleep." In the classroom, this communication mismatch can be problematic. When a European American teacher states a command in the form of a question like, "Why don't you sit down now?" to a student who is accustomed to direct commands, the student interprets that he has a choice to stand or sit. When the student decides to stand, his action is misinterpreted as defiance rather than an act of cultural miscommunication. In effect, students who do not think, behave, and express themselves in mainstream manners face greater obstacles in learning.

To a teacher unfamiliar with talking back and talk story, these communal styles of communication may be viewed as talking out of turn, undignified, illogical, or uneducated. To a teacher who expects compliance in response to a command posed as a question, she might be frustrated with the lack of classroom management. However, instead of viewing these different styles of communication as nonstandard, inferior, or a hindrance, culturally relevant education argues for teachers to be aware of these differences and their impact on classroom dynamics and relationships. Teachers must capitalize on different communication patterns and work to make their speech patterns, communication styles, and participation congruent with their students.

Culturally Responsive Teaching and Curriculum

Culturally relevant education views teaching and learning as a dynamic and joint venture between teacher and student. Knowledge is shared, subjective, and critically analyzed. The teacher's curriculum "mines" the lives and perspectives of students, utilizing their familiar worlds to teach unfamiliar concepts. For example, Ladson-Billings (1994) describes a culturally relevant lesson where one teacher discusses the bylaws and social structure of an African American church or local civic association to learn about the formation of the U.S. Constitution. In the Algebra Project, a national mathematics literacy effort aimed at helping low-income students and students of color, a look at the Washington D.C.

Metro-line map helps students build on concrete life experiences to understand integers. To teach science concepts of sustainability and service learning, Chinn (2006) immerses her students in a local Hawaiian state park to restore lo'ikalo, the flooded pond fields that produce taro.

In *Introduction to Multicultural Education*, James Banks (2007) offers a hierarchical curricular framework that incorporates multiple perspectives and diverse content into curriculum. Teachers must move beyond the "contributions approach" or the only focus on "ethnic foods, festival, and folk-dancing," so culture does not become trivialized or essentialized. They must move away from the "additive stage," which merely adds cultural content without changing the Eurocentric and mainstream structure of curriculum and results in this content being perceived as "an after-thought," Teachers must strive to include perspectives from the marginalized groups themselves and a good faith effort to include the perspective of marginalized groups can be more harmful when not represented critically and authentically.

Curriculum becomes culturally responsive when it reaches Banks' most advanced stage, the "transformative and social actions" stage, where key concepts or issues are examined from multiple viewpoints, including the students', and acted upon to make society a better place. For example, when teaching the American Revolution to a class largely composed of Filipino American students, teachers can begin by conducting an exercise to demonstrate the rebellious nature of students. Next connect learning about the stages of the American Revolution to other examples like the Philippine Revolution. Finally, teachers should encourage students to take action on an important issue in their community that needs to be revolutionized. Hence, students become creators of knowledge instead of consumers of knowledge.

UPRISE OVER CULTURALLY RELEVANT EDUCATION

The rise of culturally relevant education has not been without contention. In the era of conservatism, "back to basics," and the "standards-movement," culturally relevant education has come under attack over its necessity and practicality. Opponents of culturally relevant education argue that culturally relevant education is not rigorous or academic enough. They fear that it is so focused on culture and making students of color and poor children feel good about themselves that the academics are lost, especially in our test-driven environment. They believe that if we attend too much to students' well-being and different cultural backgrounds then we further deny marginalized students more from accessing mainstream curriculum. Some believe these students are culturally deficient and in need of becoming culturally literate with mainstream knowledge.

Proponents of culturally relevant education counter that the approach is directly intended to improve the academic performance of students who are culturally, ethnically, racially, and linguistically diverse. Their backgrounds become central to accessing mainstream content. Furthermore, proponents see value in embracing the whole child with care and high expectations. Students from groups who have been historically discriminated against experience self-denigration and low self-esteem. Therefore, proponents believe that increasing cultural pride, seeing a connection to what is being learned, and finding oneself represented in the curriculum all produce a positive outlook on oneself and an increased motivation to learn.

Nowhere do these issues of culturally relevant education become more controversial than in the role home language plays in schools. Should students be allowed to speak their home language such as Ebonics (African American Vernacular English) or Pidgin/Hawaiian English Creole (a multicultural English) in school? In 1996, this debate gained national attention when California's Oakland Public School District's Board of Education and teachers passed a resolution stating that Ebonics was not a dialect, but a language that teachers should value, learn, and integrate into the school environment to teach mainstream English language and literacy skills. The resolution was based on research that showed that children who spoke a language different other than the dominant language can best learn the mainstream language by teachers legitimizing and drawing on the home language of students. The Linguistic Society of America supported the resolution as a linguistically and pedagogical sound practice.

Though well intentioned, this resolution created divisive camps between European Americans and African Americans, and within the African American community. Some opponents to the Ebonics resolution misread its goals, believing that Ebonics was to supplant standard English, ultimately doing a disservice to students of color. African American activists like Maya Angelou and Jesse Jackson viewed this resolution as a mistake. They believed that it was an attack on African American students' potential to speak standard English and a conspiracy to keep African American children illiterate. The intent of the resolution, to improve the academic achievement of African American students, quickly became buried under media sensationalism and distortion.

The controversy over Ebonics highlights the relationship between language, culture, personal identity, and the "power of language" and "language of power" (Ladson-Billings, 1994). Skeptics of culturally relevant education ask, "Will talk-story help them on Wall Street?" Delpit (1995) believes we must encourage students to hold on to their sense of self, identity, home language, and culture, but also learn the "culture of power," the codes or rules of the dominant groups' ways of talking, ways of writing, ways of dressing, and ways of interacting. For example, this means teaching marginalized students standard English and discussing its importance, appropriateness, and need. In doing so, teachers help students learn to "code-switch" or identify appropriate times to speak home language and standard English. Students then learn to function in home culture, community, school culture, and within and across other cultural groups and the global community.

Finally, there is the issue of the feasibility and practicality of implementing culturally relevant education. "It can be a dizzying pedagogy," teachers sometimes express. Teachers might initially feel overwhelmed when thinking about what it means to be culturally congruent. Does this mean behaving one way towards a particular student and then turning around and act another way towards a different student? Culturally relevant teaching does not call for schizophrenic teaching, but first awareness of one's own preferred ways of learning, teaching, and communicating. This allows teachers to make transparent the rules and norms of the classroom to students. For example, discussing classroom norms and making the rules explicit for the need to take turns when talking creates a learning environment that is accessible to all children regardless of different cultural communication styles. Simultaneously, teachers need to be open to incorporating diverse styles of learning and communicating so as to reach all students.

The quest to acknowledge particularities should not prevent looking for universal ways of teaching students from diverse backgrounds. In synthesizing the latest research on "educational diversity," Tharp, Estrada, Dalton, & Yamauchi (2000) offers five universal principles that maximized teaching and learning for *all* students, especially students of color, language minority, and disabled students. They organized their findings into "Five Standards for Effective Pedagogy": (1) Teachers and Students Producing Together; (2) Developing Language and Literacy across the Curriculum; (3) Making Meaning: Connecting School to Students' Lives; (4) Teaching Complex Thinking; (5) Teaching through Conversation (p. 20).

ON-LINE RESOURCES ABOUT CULTURALLY RELEVANT EDUCATION

Center for Multicultural Education: http://depts.washington.edu/centerme/home.htm
Center for Research on Education, Diversity, and Excellence (CREDE): http://www.crede.ucse.edu
The Diversity Kit: http://www.alliance.brown.edu/pubs/diversity_kit/index.shtml
Rethinking Schools: http://www.rethinkingschools.org
Teaching Diverse Learners: http://www.alliance.brown.edu/tdl/
Teaching Tolerance: http://www.teachingtolerance.org

CONCLUSION

The debate over culturally relevant education will remain so long as the fundamental assumptions over the mission and goals of our schools are challenged. After all, what is the purpose of education? Is it merely to ensure that students learn a pre-defined set of facts, concepts, and principles? Or should teachers be charged with the responsibility of inspiring students to learn and developing our children into life-long learners?

Critics of culturally relevant education contend that it is impractical, unnecessary, and, ultimately, will prevent students from accessing mainstream curriculum. However, advocates of culturally relevant education do not necessarily believe that students' cultural communication styles need to be abandoned or mainstream content be sacrificed. They do not automatically oppose the content that is being taught; rather, they favor an alternative method of *how* that content should be taught. Culturally relevant education proponents not only put a premium on knowledge; they also value how that knowledge is being learned.

It is well settled that when delivering a speech, the speaker must tailor his message to the audience. The most successful speakers focus on the traits and characteristics of their audience members in order to determine the best way to connect with them, which in turn, helps them get their message across more effectively. This is not much different from the foundational elements of culturally relevant education. Under culturally relevant education, students are placed at the center. They are the focus. Teachers find the best ways to deliver their message to their particular students. With culturally relevant education, the requisite knowledge is learned and, most importantly, the learning experience is richer and will make our children better students in school and in life.

Further Reading: Chinn, P., 2006, Preparing science teachers for culturally diverse students: Developing cultural literacy through cultural immersion, cultural translators and communities of practice, *Cultural Studies of Science Education*, 1, 367–402; Delpit, L., 1995, *Other people's children: Cultural conflicts in the classroom*, New York: The New Press; Gay, G., 2000, *Culturally responsive teaching: Theory, research, and practice*, New York: Teachers College Press; Kleinfield, J., 1975, Effective teachers of Eskimo and Indian students, *School Review*, 83(2), 301–344; Ladson-Billings, G., 1994, *The dreamkeepers: Successful teachers of African American children*, San Francisco: Jossey-Bass; Tharp, R. G., Estrada, P., Dalton, S. S., & Yamauchi, L., 2000, *Teaching transformed: Achieving excellence, fairness, inclusion, and harmony*, Boulder, CO: Westview Press.

Patricia Espiritu Halagao

CURRICULUM

There is a sense in which the sum total of what is taught in school, which for the moment we can think of as the curriculum, is ignored as a debatable topic as educational theorists and practitioners worry more about how to teach, how to group, how to find and organize materials, how to assess, and how to report results for what is assumed should be taught because it is included in the textbook, the curriculum guide, or district or state directives that were issued just recently or during some long-ago period. That is, the critical examination of the actual academic content, skills, dispositions, appreciations, and ways of learning to be planned, designed, taught, and assessed in an educational setting is taken for granted, approached as unproblematic, and accepted as the conventional and commonsensical wisdom, not the object of thorough and sustained scrutiny. Books and articles that tout "best practices" of curriculum design and organization and instructional and assessment strategies help teachers and administrators to do better what presumably needs to take place in the classroom.

On the other hand, a careful examination of educational discourse and policymaking, starting from the early years of the twentieth century—contained in scholarly books and journals as well as countless articles that appear in popular newspapers and magazines—belies this sense of consensus about and lack of attention to substantive issues of curriculum. Indeed, it is not uncommon for the title of this collection or something very much like it to be referred to in headlines that highlight the contested terrain that is curriculum work, as in a recent article in the *Wall Street Journal* that announced one content area (sex education) as having become the "latest school battleground." If "culture wars" exist, as many scholars and media pundits would have us believe, they involve not just political parties, professional organizations, and national and community interest groups, but our classrooms as well.

Put simply, there exists a universe of knowledge, skills, etc., from which to select a relatively small amount to comprise a curriculum; the curriculum can be planned and organized in a variety of ways; deliberations about curriculum choices can take many different forms and involve many different stakeholders; and the results of what we plan for and do in the classroom can be assessed in a range of ways, with regard to both its educational and sociopolitical ramifications. There continues, always, somewhere to be many choices to make, and there is much contention, even if in partially stifled voices, about whether or not we are resolving curriculum questions—of content selection, for example—in the best, most effective and most equitable ways for/in a democratic society.

SELECTIONS FROM THE HISTORY OF AMERICAN CURRICULUM

1870s–1890s

- Mental discipline theory and faculty psychology (Yale Report, 1828)
- Humanistic tradition (C. W. Eliot, W. T. Harris)
- Herbartians (C. DeGarmo, F. and C. McMurry)
- Committee of Ten Report, 1893

1900s–1930s

- Child Study Movement (G. S. Hall)
- Social Efficiency and Scientific Curriculum Making (F. Bobbitt, W. W. Charters, R. Finney, D. Snedden)
- The Project Method and Activity Curriculum (L. T. Hopkins, W. H. Kilpatrick)
- NEA Commission on the Reorganization of Secondary Education, Cardinal Principles Report, 1918
- Progressive Education Association
- John Dewey (Democracy and Education and Experience and Education)
- Social Reconstructionism (T. Brameld, G. Counts, H. Rugg)

1940s–1950s

- Essentialism (Council for Basic Education, W. Bagley)
- Life Adjustment Education (C. Prosser)
- Structure of the Disciplines (J. Bruner, P. Phenix, J. Schwab)
- The Tyler Rationale and Behavioral Objectives (R. Gagne, J. Popham, R. Tyler)

1960s–1980s

- Open Education and Radical Criticism (S. Ashton-Warner, G. Dennison, J. Holt, H. Kohl, J. Kozol, A. S. Neill, C. Silberman)
- Career Education (S. P. Marland)
- Back to Basics and Academic Excellence (A Nation At Risk, M. Adler, W. Bennett, E. D. Hirsch)
- Critical and Feminist Theories (J. Anyon, M. Apple, H. Giroux, M. Greene, M. Grumet, J. Macdonald, N. Noddings, W. Pinar)
- Multiculturalism (J. Banks, G. Gay, C. Grant, C. McCarthy, S. Nieto, C. Sleeter)

1990s–2000s

All of the above... and, for example: arts-based education; "at-risk" programs; authentic assessment; brain research; character education; cognitive pluralism; computer-based education; concept-based education; constructivism; cooperative learning; critical thinking; curriculum integration; democratic schooling; distance learning; ecological education; gay-lesbian-bisexual studies; gifted education; globalization; high-stakes standardized testing; HIV/AIDS education; inclusive education; multi-age classrooms; multiple intelligences; national standards; No Child Left Behind Act; poststructuralist and postmodern theories; religion-based education and spirituality; school-university partnerships; school vouchers and charter schools; shared decision making; whole language; etc.

DIFFERENCES OF DEFINITION

Several different areas of controversy regarding curriculum can be identified, starting with its very definition. While arguments about definition can seem stodgy and irrelevant to what takes place in the classroom, in fact the way one conceives of curriculum can have a significant impact on its study and practice. The fact that there are estimated to be more than 120 definitions in the professional literature, taking us well beyond the word's Latin root of "racecourse," perhaps testifies to the importance and variance of its basic characteristics.

Thus, for example, James Popham and Eva Baker's well-known definition in *Systematic Instruction* stresses "all planned learning outcomes for which the school is responsible." Such a definition places a priority on what has been planned and what can be determined to be learned. Curriculum developers and evaluators (and scholars) would have such characteristics uppermost in their minds when studying, planning, organizing, and assessing the curriculum. But what about what occurs and is observable in classrooms that are not planned, e.g., what are often referred to as "teachable moments"? Do they have no significance with regard to student learning and what can be considered part of the curriculum that students experience? And what about those experiences that are planned (or unplanned) for which learning outcomes are not easily determined, especially in the short run, such as appreciations and more expressive ways of learning? Should they be excluded from consideration and perhaps downplayed with regard to their potential educational value?

Another definition focuses on all experiences children have under the guidance of teachers, which de-emphasizes the planned and at the same time specifies the teacher's role. Some might argue that the experiences students have in school that are not under the direct guidance of teachers should also be considered (and assessed) as part of the curriculum, for example, what occurs in playgrounds, hallways, cafeterias, and the like. Some curriculum scholars posit curriculum as the interrelated complex set of plans and experiences that students have under the guidance of the school. This definition highlights "plans" but does seem to allow for the unplanned (experiences) as well (though what exactly is meant by "interrelated" is unclear). Moreover, it does not specify the teacher as the only school participant who is involved with what can be considered the curriculum, placing the emphasis instead on what "a student undertakes." Anyone adopting such a definition, then, will give careful attention to all experiences that students have in school, which will include more than just what the teacher does in the classroom.

Another definition was offered almost 100 years ago by J. Franklin Bobbitt in his book, *The Curriculum* (1918), which is generally recognized to be the first textbook focused specifically on "curriculum." For Bobbitt, the curriculum was "*that series of things which children and youth must do and experience* by way of developing abilities to do the things well that make up the affairs of adult life; and to be in all respects what adults should do" (p. 42; emphasis in original). This definition implies a broadening of the scope beyond what takes place directly in school. At the same time, it specifically fosters the notion that the curriculum should be primarily (or exclusively) about "abilities to do things." Enhanced understandings and deeply held appreciations, for example, are apparently not included. In addition, preparing for "the affairs of adult life" is primary, rather than, for example, what children are experiencing (or reflecting about) currently in their lives or critically examining social conditions. This definition also appears to assume that there is a consensus about the things that all "children and youth must do and experience," that is, what the most important "affairs of adult life" actually are and what specifically "adults should do." All aspects of a definition have serious repercussions not only for one's view of what is (should be) taught and evaluated in school but also with regard to what researchers might emphasize in their own work in addressing the curriculum. If one accepts Bobbitt's definition, much time needs to be spent in determining the specific "things" that children and youth must learn to do in school and how they align with what adults presumably *should* do.

There are many other definitions of curriculum that could be considered. The point is that the curriculum is an applied field of inquiry whose very definition has been a "battleground" of sorts, with significant implications for the way one determines school knowledge as well as approaches to teaching, learning, and evaluation. The definition one adopts also sets parameters for the kind of research that is most meaningful, including the extent to which one attends to the hidden curriculum (i.e., institutional norms and values not openly acknowledged by school officials that are in fact immersed in classrooms and schools) and the null curriculum (i.e., subject matter and ways of learning that are not selected to be a part of school life). It can even indicate whether or not the exclusive focus of one's attention should be on the classroom or school life in general, or, perhaps, broader institutional and discursive practices, structures, images, and experiences that go beyond the school setting. Different conceptions, while in the background of debates, do lead to significant differences regarding curriculum study, development, implementation, and assessment.

THE STRUGGLE OVER THE CURRICULUM

As Herbert Kliebard (2004) makes clear, the historical struggle over the curriculum, including its definition, has involved a variety of competing interest groups. Their debates, sometimes quite heated in the scholarly writings and popular journals of the field, have focused on a number of related, crucial issues, for example the nature and effects of societal forces, the nature of learners and learning, the nature of subject matter, and the purposes of schooling.

One of the fundamental questions of curriculum deliberation, though not always explicitly articulated, involves the extent to which and how the curriculum should respond to social change. For example, throughout the past century various educators and others have expressed concerns about the lessening influence of the family and the church. Should the school be expected to play a more expansive role in children's lives, such as regarding what is taught in the classroom? Should the curriculum focus on aspects of daily life that other institutions previously could be expected to address, for example involving personal character, physical health, and domestic affairs? Likewise, concerns about economic and technical-scientific changes have convinced some educators that the curriculum should place a high priority on preparing students for work (vocational skills), for utilizing the latest technologies, and for proficiency in mathematics and science. Others have been more concerned with what they perceive to be a significant decrease in civic participation and have advocated a curriculum that places more emphasis on the active and critical engagement of social issues and problems.

Another broad issue involves the extent to which children should be involved in their own learning experiences, that is, in directly helping to plan them or at least to have their personal interests and concerns providing guidance when planned by others. Some educators have argued that active engagement with activities and materials, so that children initiate and direct (construct) their own understandings, is in fact necessary for authentic learning to take place. If so, then the curriculum would need to be organized with the learners' experiences uppermost in mind. Standardized content and a top-down design approach would be downplayed and flexibility, creativity, and direct student (and teacher) involvement would be expected.

Issues involving the nature of subject matter for schools have also been intensely addressed during the last century. For example, some have argued strongly for curriculum to follow the structures of the recognized and longstanding academic disciplines, building on the work done by recognized scholars over several centuries. Thus, children might study the discipline of history and in essence become "junior historians" at a young age. Others have argued that subject matter needs to be more broadly conceived and made more "relevant" to learners; thus, it is argued, a field like social studies that focuses on citizenship rather than the discipline of history would be more appropriate for a population of students who are not necessarily college bound. And others have suggested a more integrated approach to curriculum, with multidisciplinary content and skills being brought to bear on projects or social problems that children are studying and that may be of more personal interest to them.

Finally, the larger social purpose of schooling has always been a matter of considerable dispute. What is the primary goal that schools should aspire to? Is it extensive knowledge of the academic disciplines; critical understanding of the social and natural worlds; advanced literacy skills; development of the full range of intelligences; preparation for adult careers; advanced reasoning and problem-solving abilities; active involvement in democratic citizenship; a passion for learning and self-understanding; or some other overall aim? Indeed, to what extent should there even be predetermined goals toward which curriculum decisions should be directed? Such fundamental questions can lead to very different perspectives on what the curriculum is, what it is for, and how it should be determined.

There were at least four interest groups during the first half of the twentieth century that competed for supremacy in the determination of the curriculum (Kliebard, 2004). The first group, which held sway on curriculum matters during the late nineteenth and early twentieth centuries, was the humanists, who could be considered "the guardians of an ancient tradition tied to the power of reason and the finest elements of Western cultural heritage" (p. 23). They sought to provide all children with a common curriculum that stressed mental discipline and the powers of reasoning on the one hand and the classical traditions (including religious) and academic (university-based) disciplines on the other. Reacting to this approach were at least three groups of reformers who sought to change what schools taught and how the curriculum was organized. The developmentalists or child-centered progressives were educators who sought curriculum that was more "in harmony with the child's real interests, needs, and learning patterns" (p. 24). Some adherents, such as William Heard Kilpatrick in 1918, believed that children should not be taught directly but instead should engage in projects that essentially linked their immediate experiences and interests with worthy living. Academic content would be brought to bear when necessary for the fulfillment of "purposeful acts."

Another group consisted of social efficiency educators or scientific curriculum makers who were particularly concerned with "creating a coolly efficient, smoothly running society," which included "applying standardized techniques of industry to the business of schooling" (Kliebard, p. 24). Like Franklin Bobbitt, they sought to ascertain, with expanded testing and counseling, the expected futures of children and then differentiate the curriculum so that children would receive the kind of education that would best prepare (fit) them for their predicted life after school. In such a way, schools would be less wasteful and the curriculum could more directly link to the presumed adult roles that future citizens would occupy. Identifying precise objectives for each subject area, creating more school subjects to transmit the knowledge that was needed to live and work in an increasingly industrialized and urbanized nation, and providing different kinds of education for the different potential futures of students were important aspects of this group's agenda.

A fourth group of educators took a social meliorist or social reconstructionist approach to curriculum work, whereby they "saw the schools as a major, perhaps the principal, force for [progressive] social change and social justice" (Kliebard, p. 24). When in 1932 George Counts asked, "Dare the school build a new social order?" it wasn't a question of whether it could or not, but whether it would strive to do so. Emphasizing the political character of the curriculum choices that are made, the primary question for these educators was not whether to advocate or not, but the nature and extent of one's advocacy; not whether or not to encourage a particular social vision in the classroom, but what kind of social vision it would be. For these educators it was to be one dedicated to the elimination of poverty, inequality, and prejudice.

While other important interest groups could be mentioned, especially for the last half-century (for example, see Michael Apple's book *Educating the "Right" Way: Markets, Standards, God, and Inequality,* for a discussion of the New Right alliance consisting of neoliberals, neoconservatives, authoritarian populists, and elements of the professional managerial class), the point being made here is that groups of educators and others have long advocated for different approaches to certain fundamental issues of schooling. Their different ideas, policies, and practices relating to curriculum have in fact helped to shape the battleground that is our schools today.

WHAT KNOWLEDGE IS OF MOST WORTH TO SCHOOLS?

Issues of planning and development have been arguably the least contentious aspect of this applied field of study, but in fact here too differing approaches have served as a source of conflict. The dominant approach that was made famous by Ralph Tyler and others has been challenged by those seeking an approach to curriculum design that is based less on linearity, specificity, and observable and measurable performance than on reflective inquiry, flexibility, expressive outcomes, and democratic life.

Probably the most evident source of conflict in schools involves what should be taught to which students at what time, involving issues of scope and sequence. Here, the contentious nature of the debates appears more regularly in the popular media as well as in the work of curriculum theorists and policymakers. This may be of little surprise when one considers the fact that in the state of Florida, for example, 440 viable high school majors were recently approved for school adoption (and, college-style, for students to choose from). Obviously no school can select more than a handful to offer. Who will make these choices, using what criteria? What will make up the actual sequence of courses in each major chosen? What will comprise the content of the courses offered? From animal caretaker, business publishing, cabinetmaking, florist assistant, and eurhythmics to art and theatre, social studies, English and journalism, mathematics, and biological sciences, the options for what can be studied in school—the universe of knowledge that can be viewed as legitimate for school adoption—is made more explicit here.

The conflicts that rage over the courses to be taught as well as the character of the courses chosen can often be found in bold form in the headlines of local and national newspapers and popular periodicals. What follows are 40 representative examples from the last several years that provide an indication of the wide-ranging debates over content selection that are currently taking place:

- As AP expands, studies disagree on its value
- Panel sounds alarm on science education
- Can less equal more? Proposal to teach math students fewer concepts in greater depth has divided Maryland educators
- Yoga, hip-hop… *This* is P.E.? Updated programs are more active and varied, but new tests, finances, training, and traditions slow their adoption
- Rethinking recess: As more schools trim breaks, new research points to value of unstructured playtime
- Law tells schools to teach students about on-line safety
- Computer science fighting for time
- Driver education hits dead end
- High schools teach more kids basics in Finance 101: 14 states require money management to graduate
- Arabic, the new French? Pressure to compete globally and boost national security is driving interest in less-common languages such as Chinese and Arabic
- U.S. students need more math, not Mandarin
- Traditional social focus yielding to academics: Instead of a year to adjust to puberty, 13-year olds now given algebra and other demanding coursework
- Giving voice to teen's thoughts: Programs in Miami-Dade and Broward counties give high-schoolers the opportunity to learn through poetry slams and spoken word workshops
- Students set the rules at New York City high school
- High schoolers combine service learning projects with classroom learning
- As the evolution-creationism debate rages, Florida picks a new generation of textbooks
- Intimidation alleged on "intelligent design": Teacher cites school board pressure
- Ohio board undoes stand on evolution
- Vocational education conflict heating up
- Vocational education: "It's not your grandfather's trade school"
- Educators divided over what to learn from 9/11
- Have we forgotten civic education? Two centuries after Jefferson, social studies are lacking at public schools
- Philly schools to require African history class

- Tennessee creates official curriculum for African American history: Many schools offer the subject, but now classes will be uniform
- International studies a hard sell in U.S.
- Today's textbooks labor to be careful with Clinton scandal
- Need to celebrate Constitution Day called into question
- How can we fix the world if we can't read a map?
- Social Studies losing out to reading, math
- Teaching Thanksgiving from a different perspective
- Clauses and commas make a comeback: SAT helps return grammar to class
- Some teachers say tests stifling creativity: Drilling for exams replaces hands-on learning activities
- Facing obstacles to sex education: Maryland schools reach to parents from different cultures
- Sex-ed class becomes latest school battleground: Some parents and states object to restrictions linked to federal abstinence funds
- Education Commission of the States wants to put arts back on states' high-priority list
- Democrats in 2 southern states push bills on Bible study
- For teachers, much gray if curriculum adds gays
- Lawsuit in Massachusetts challenges use of gay-themed storybook
- School must teach back-to-basics "phonics"
- Teach the simple joys of reading

One can see from these and other examples that many of the issues discussed earlier in this chapter are embedded in our more public debates, with reference to the purpose of schooling, the nature of learners and learning, the nature of subject matter, and the relationship of schools to social change, as well as issues more directly involving, e.g., standardized testing, legislative and school board activities, the decision-making process, scholarly research, and cultural differences. Indeed, the curriculum represents the essence of what schools do—that is, what they teach, or, put more broadly, what experiences they provide for students—and so it is hardly a surprise that this is where the conflicts sometimes rage most intense. Headlines trumpet; politicians legislate; advocacy groups lobby; parents inquire or insist; and teachers and their students are left to work out the possibilities for teaching and learning in their classrooms.

As Fred Inglis (1985) suggests, at a basic level the curriculum is "another name for the officially sanctioned and world-political picture which we produce, circulate and reproduce in our society" (p. 63). It does not merely imply but actually teaches particular versions of not only what is "good" in life and what is not but also who is good and who is not. The curriculum represents a kind of battleground in which contrasting messages of who we are and what we should become, both individually and as a society, are played out. In effect, the curriculum comprises "stories we tell ourselves about ourselves" (p. 31). What "stories," then, are we telling by the arguments that we have and the choices that we make? Are they ones that emphasize democratic social relations, an expansive view of intelligence, and critical understandings of the social and natural worlds, or do they instead stress competitive individualism, "basic skills," and preparation for work? It is clear that these are truly stories that matter.

Further Reading: Bobbitt, F., 1918, *The curriculum,* Boston: Houghton Mifflin; Eisner, E. W., 2002, *The education imagination: On the design and evaluation of school programs,* Upper Saddle River, NJ: Prentice Hall; Inglis, F., 1985, *The management of ignorance: A political theory of the curriculum,* Oxford, UK: Basil Blackwell; Jackson, P. L., ed., 1992, *Handbook of research on curriculum,* New York: Macmillan; Kliebard, H., 2004, *The struggle for the American curriculum, 1893–1958,* New York: RoutledgeFalmer; Marshall, J. D., Sears, J. T., & Schubert, W. H., 2000, *Turning points in curriculum: A contemporary American memoir,* Upper Saddle River, NJ: Merrill; Ornstein, A. C., Pajak, E. F., & Ornstein, S. B., eds., 2007, *Contemporary issues in curriculum,* Boston: Pearson; Schubert, W. H., Lopez Schubert, A. L., Thomas, T. P., & Carroll, W. M., 2002, *Curriculum books: The first hundred years,* New York: Peter Lang.

Kenneth Teitelbaum

D

DESEGREGATION

For all too many, the fiftieth anniversary of *Brown v. Board of Education* in 2004 provided an opportunity to celebrate the decision as a victory for racial justice and to presume that large-scale racial inequality was an artifact of the past, of little concern to us today. Yet it is clear that segregated or near-segregated schools continue to exist, and that school resegregation has been on the rise since the 1980s.

Public school segregation has increased over the past two decades not because we have learned that desegregation failed or because Americans have turned against it. In fact, there is now more information about the benefits of integration than ever before, and public support for integrated education remains high, particularly among those who have personal experience with desegregated schools. Rather, resegregation has been primarily a result of the changing legal and political landscape, which in recent years has severely limited what school districts must—or may—do to promote racial integration in their schools.

WHY DESEGREGATION?

Why should we care about segregation? Public school segregation can have a powerfully negative impact on students, an impact that prompted the Supreme Court to declare segregated schools unconstitutional in 1954. One of the common misconceptions about desegregation is that it is simply about seating black students next to white students in a classroom. If skin color were not systematically and inextricably linked to other forms of inequality, perhaps segregation would have less educational or legal significance. But when we talk about schools that are segregated by race, we are also usually talking about schools that are segregated along other dimensions as well, including poverty and English language learner status.

Racial segregation is highly correlated with the concentration of student poverty, and the differences, by race/ethnicity, in students' exposure to poverty are striking. Nationally, about half of all black and Latino students attend schools in which three-quarters or more students are poor, while only 5 percent of white students attend such schools. No fewer than 80 percent of students in schools of extreme poverty are black or Latino. As a result, minority students in these segregated schools are isolated not only from white students, but from schools with students from middle-class families, and exposure to students with middle-class backgrounds is a predictor of academic success. Further, Latino ELL students are even more isolated from whites than their native-speaking Latino peers and, as a result, have little exposure to native English speakers who could aid their acquisition of English.

Racially isolated minority schools are also often vastly unequal to schools with higher percentages of white students in terms of other tangible resources, such as qualified, experienced teachers and college preparatory curriculum, as well as intangible resources, such as lower teacher turnover and more college-bound peers—all of which are associated with higher educational outcomes. Social science research, then, confirms that the central premise of *Brown* remains true: Racially minority segregated schools offer students an inferior education, which is likely to harm their future life opportunities, such as graduation from high school and college. While a handful of successfully segregated minority schools certainly exist across the nation, these schools represent the exception to the general trend and are typically places with stable, committed leadership and faculty that are difficult to replicate on a large scale.

Desegregation has offered an opportunity to study how interracial schools can affect the education of students. Research generally concludes that integrated schools have important benefits for students who attend these schools and for the society in which these students will one day be citizens and workers. While early studies of the effects of desegregation focused on its impact on minority students, more recent research has revealed that white students, too, benefit from racial integration. Of course, these benefits depend on how desegregation is structured and implemented within diverse schools.

Over 50 years ago, Harvard psychologist Gordon Allport suggested that one of the essential conditions to reducing prejudice was that people needed to be in contact with one another. Research in racially integrated schools confirms that, by allowing for students of different races and ethnicities to be in contact with one another, students can develop improved cross-racial understanding and experience a reduction of racial prejudice and bias.

Additionally, black and Latino students in desegregated schools have higher achievement than their peers in segregated schools, while the achievement of white students in racially diverse but majority white schools remains unaffected. Some evidence also suggests that diverse classrooms can improve the critical thinking skills of all students.

Benefits from such environments extend beyond the time spent in schools to improved life opportunities. Students in integrated schools are also more likely to graduate from high school and go on to college than their segregated peers, meaning that integrated schools result in a more highly skilled workforce. These students are also connected to social networks that give them information about and access to competitive colleges and higher-status jobs. Perhaps because of this access or the fact that students who attend integrated schools tend to be more likely to attain graduate degrees, labor market studies show that African Americans who attend integrated schools have higher salaries than their peers from segregated schools. Finally, students who attend racially diverse schools are more likely to be civically engaged after graduation and to feel comfortable working in diverse settings.

There are important benefits for communities with racially diverse schools. For example, students who graduate from integrated schools will have experience and be adept working with people of other racial/ethnic backgrounds, an important skill for the demands of the workforce in our global economy. Research also indicates that communities with extensive school desegregation have experienced declines in residential integration. Further, desegregation that encompasses most of a region can stem white flight. Communities with integrated schools tend to experience higher levels of parental involvement in and support for the schools.

It is no wonder, then, that over the years, many school districts have come to realize the value of racial and ethnic diversity and its important influence on educating our future citizens. A number of these school districts, as a result, have voluntarily enacted policies and student assignment methods designed to promote racial integration in their schools. In other words, more and more school districts are trying to create diverse learning environments not out of legal obligation, but on their own accord, as an essential part of their core educational mission. They do so in recognition of the critical role schools play in fostering racial and ethnic harmony in our increasingly heterogeneous society, and of the significance of an integrated school experience in shaping students' worldviews. Yet even these efforts may be imperiled.

THE DEVELOPMENT OF SCHOOL DESEGREGATION LAW

Most scholars and laypersons alike consider *Brown v. Board of Education* the most famous U.S. Supreme Court ruling in American history. That landmark 1954 decision was the culmination of decades of civil rights litigation and strategizing to overturn the deeply entrenched doctrine from *Plessy v. Ferguson* (1896) of "separate but equal," which had applied to 17 southern states where segregated schools were required. *Brown* held for the first time that racially segregated public schools violate the Equal Protection guarantees of the Fourteenth Amendment of the U.S. Constitution.

Although an enormous moral victory for civil rights advocates—indeed for the entire nation—*Brown* itself did not require the immediate elimination of segregation in our nation's public schools. In fact, one year later, in a follow-up decision popularly known as *Brown II,* the Supreme Court allowed racially segregated school systems to move forward in dismantling their segregative practices "with all deliberate speed"—an infamous phrase that, for many years, meant without any speed or urgency at all. What's more, *Brown II* placed the duty to supervise school desegregation squarely on local federal district courts and then provided these courts little guidance.

Thus, despite the efforts of countless black communities across the nation demanding immediate relief in the wake of the *Brown* decision—often at the risk of grave danger and violence, and mostly in the segregated South, where resistance was greatest—a full decade passed with virtually no progress in desegregating schools. By 1963, when President John F. Kennedy asked Congress to pass legislation prohibiting racial discrimination in all programs receiving federal aid (including schools), well over 98 percent of Southern black students were still attending segregated schools.

A social and cultural revolution was sweeping the country during the civil rights era, however, and by the mid-1960s and early 1970s, school desegregation too began to take hold. Congress enacted Kennedy's proposed legislation as the Civil Rights Act of 1964, which empowered the Department of Justice to initiate desegregation lawsuits independent of private plaintiffs. The act also authorized the Department of Health, Education, and Welfare to deny federal funds to segregating school districts. With these new governmental tools and allies, civil rights attorneys used the power of America's courts and television sets against recalcitrant school districts that refused to comply with the law.

During these critical years, the Supreme Court, also frustrated by the lack of progress in school desegregation, issued a number of important decisions that lent valuable support and legitimacy to the cause. For instance, in *Green v. County School Board of New Kent County* (1968), the Court expressly defined what desegregation required: the elimination of all traces of a school system's prior segregation in every facet of school operations—from student, faculty, and staff assignment to extracurricular activities, facilities, and transportation.

Three years later, the Supreme Court ruled unanimously in *Swann v. Charlotte-Mecklenburg Board of Education* (1971) that lower courts supervising the desegregation of individual school districts could order the use of transportation, or busing, to achieve desegregated student assignments. In so doing, it rejected the argument that formerly dual school systems had discharged their desegregation duties by assigning students to segregated schools that happened to correspond with segregated neighborhoods.

Shortly thereafter, the Supreme Court decided *Keyes v. School District No. 1* (1973), a case originating in Denver, Colorado, that extended school desegregation obligations to systems outside the South that had employed discriminatory policies. The *Keyes* case was also the first to order desegregation for Latino students. Federal district courts took guidance from these and other Supreme Court decisions as they ordered desegregation plans unique to the communities for which they were responsible. In response to these decisions, the federal judiciary began more actively issuing detailed desegregation orders and then monitoring the school districts' progress, or lack thereof, on a regular basis. Segregation was on the run.

JUDICIAL RETRENCHMENT

By the mid-1970s, significant changes in the Supreme Court's composition rendered its reputation as a champion of civil rights relatively short-lived. In perhaps the most significant case from this latter era, *Milliken v. Bradley* (1974), the Court dealt a serious blow to school desegregation by concluding that lower courts could not order "inter-district" desegregation remedies that encompass urban as well as suburban school districts without first showing that the suburban district or the state was liable for the segregation across district boundaries. The practical impact of the decision was the establishment of a bright line between city and suburban school systems beyond which the courts could not traverse in designing their desegregation plans: Whites who for decades had tried to flee school desegregation finally had a place to go where they could avoid it.

Just one year prior to *Milliken,* the Supreme Court had decided a case, *San Antonio Independent School District v. Rodriguez* (1973), that seriously undermined a parallel strategy of the educational equity movement. There, the Court refused to strike down a public school financing scheme that resulted in significantly lower expenditures for poor and minority children who lived in school districts with lower tax property bases in comparison to their more affluent, white neighbors who lived in the neighboring district. In so doing, the Court foreclosed an important argument that civil rights lawyers had tried to advance in both school funding and segregation cases: that public education was a "fundamental right" under the Constitution, which must be available on an equal basis. With this legal avenue shut down by *Rodriguez,* and with inter-district remedies effectively eliminated by *Milliken,* the Supreme Court's brief, forward charge on school desegregation law had officially come to a screeching halt.

Soon the executive branch of government, which had been fairly aggressive in litigation and enforcement of school desegregation cases, followed the increasingly more conservative federal courts. In the 1980s, the Reagan administration adopted a new philosophy that focused on school choice—rather than on the firm insistence of compliance with court orders requiring mandatory student assignments—to accomplish school desegregation. As a result, scores of school districts abandoned busing as a remedy and began more actively employing strategies and tools such as "magnet schools" and "controlled-choice plans" as the primary means of advancing desegregation. In general, the government's focus during this era turned away from educational equity and toward other issues, namely, an emphasis on standards-based accountability to improve student achievement.

The 1990s ushered in another phase of judicial retreat from school desegregation. Between 1991 and 1995, the Supreme Court handed down three important decisions: *Oklahoma City Board of Education v. Dowell* (1991), *Freeman v. Pitts* (1992), and *Missouri v. Jenkins* (1995). Taken together, these cases essentially invited school districts to initiate proceedings to bring their desegregation obligations to an end. They permitted federal district courts overseeing desegregation plans to declare a school system "unitary" if they determined that the system had done all that was feasible to eliminate the effects of past racial discrimination. In contrast to earlier decisions, now, according to the Supreme Court, a good faith effort to desegregate along with reasonable compliance with prior desegregation orders for a decent period of time were considered sufficient for a school district to achieve unitary status and thus have its desegregation orders permanently dissolved—even if severe racial isolation or other racial disparities remained. Advocates of school desegregation view these changes as a significant dilution of the desegregation obligations the Supreme Court had placed on school districts in the previous decades.

In the years since that trilogy of cases was decided, a large number of school systems have been declared unitary. In some instances, the school district itself sought to end federal court supervision, arguing it had met its constitutional obligations. In others, parents opposed to desegregation led the attack to relieve the school district of any continuing legal duties to desegregate, leaving the district in the awkward position of having to defend the kinds of policies that it had, ironically, resisted implementing in prior decades. Recently, in fact, a handful of federal courts have declared districts unitary even when the school district itself argued that its desegregation policies were still necessary to remedy past discrimination.

Once a school district has been declared unitary, it is no longer under a legal duty to continue any of the desegregation efforts that it had undertaken in the decades when it was under court order. The school district remains, of course, under a broad constitutional obligation—as do all districts—to avoid taking actions that intentionally create racially segregated and unequal schools. However, courts presume that the school district's actions are innocent and legal, even if they produce racially disparate results, unless there is evidence of *intentional* discrimination. The past history of segregation and desegregation is completely wiped away in the eyes of the law. These fully discretionary, "innocent and legal" policies in many instances have contributed to a disturbing phenomenon of racial resegregation in our public schools, which are more racially separate now than at any point in the past two decades.

TRENDS IN DESEGREGATION AND RESEGREGATION

As a result of the courts' guidance, there were dramatic gains in desegregation for black students in the South, a region with the most black students and the most integrated region of the country by the late 1960s due to court-ordered desegregation and federal enforcement of desegregation plans. Desegregation of black students remained stable for several decades; by 1988, 43.5 percent of southern black students were in majority white schools. During the 1990s, however, the proportion of black students in majority white schools in the region steadily declined as desegregation plans were dismantled. In 2003, only 29 percent of southern black students were in majority white schools, lower than any year since 1968.

When there was a concerted effort to desegregate black and white students in the South during the mid- to late-1960s, there was major progress, demonstrating that desegregation can and has succeeded. We are experiencing a period of steady decline in desegregation since the late 1980s and much of the success that led to several decades of desegregated schooling for millions of students in the South is being undone. Nevertheless, black and white students in the South attend schools that are considerably more integrated than before the time of *Brown*.

The judicial changes discussed above have had a major impact on the desegregation of schools at a time of racial transformation of the nation's public school enrollment. Since the end of the civil rights era, the racial composition of our nation's public school students has changed dramatically. The United States was once overwhelmingly white, but that is no longer the case. Minority students are now more than 40 percent of all U.S. public school students, nearly twice their share of students during the 1960s.

Not only are there more minority students than ever before, but the minority population is also more diverse than it was during the civil rights era, when most nonwhite students were black. Black and Latino students are now more than a third of all students in public schools. The most rapidly growing racial/ethnic group is Latinos, who have almost quadrupled in size from 1968 to 2000 to 7.7 million students. Asian enrollment, like that of Latinos, is also increasing. Meanwhile, by 2003, whites comprised only 58 percent of the public school enrollment. There were seven million fewer white public school students at the beginning of the twenty-first century than there were at the end of the 1960s. As a result of this growing diversity, nearly nine million students in 2003 attended schools with at least three racial groups of students.

U.S. public schools are more than two decades into a period of rapid resegregation. The desegregation of black students has now declined to levels not seen in three decades. Latinos, by contrast, have never experienced a time of increased integration and today are the most segregated minority group in our schools.

Remarkably, almost 2.4 million students attend schools that are 99–100 percent minority, including almost one in six of black students and one in nine Latino students. Nearly 40 percent of both black and Latino students attend intensely segregated schools (90–100 percent of students are nonwhite); yet less than 1 percent of white students attend such schools. Nearly three-fourths of black and Latino students attend predominantly minority schools.

Whites are the most racially isolated group of students in the United States. In a perfectly integrated system of schools, the racial composition of every school would mirror that of the overall U.S. enrollment. The typical white public school student, however, attends a school that is nearly 80 percent white, which is much higher than the white percentage of the overall public school enrollment (58 percent). This means that white students, on average, attend schools in which only *one in five* students are of another race, which, conversely, reduces the opportunities for students of other races to be in schools with white students. Schools with high percentages of white students are also likely to have overwhelmingly white faculties, meaning that such schools have few people of color.

Black and Latino students are also extremely isolated from students of other races, and they are particularly isolated from whites. Blacks and Latinos attend schools where two-thirds of students are also black and Latino, and over half of the students in their schools are students of their same race. Despite earlier progress in desegregation, the percentage of white students that attend schools with black students, another measure of school desegregation, has been declining since 1988. Asians are the most desegregated of all students; three-fourths of students in their schools are from other racial/ethnic groups, and only a small percentage of Asian students are in segregated minority schools.

The resegregation of blacks and Latinos is a trend seen in almost every large school district since the mid-1980s. One reason is that the public school districts in many of our nation's largest cities, which educate one-tenth of all public school students in the 26 largest districts, contain few white students—without which even the best designed desegregation plans cannot create substantial desegregation. While the largest urban districts (enrollment greater than 60,000) enroll over one-fifth of all black and Latino students, less than 1 in 40 white students attend these central city schools.

Minority students in suburban districts generally attend schools with more white students than their counterparts in central city districts, although there is substantial variation within the largest suburban districts. In over half of the suburban districts with more than 60,000 students, the typical black and Latino student attends schools that, on average, have a white majority. However, black and Latino students in these districts are more segregated from whites than in the mid-1980s. In some large suburban districts there has been drastic racial change in a short time span, and these districts are now predominantly minority like the urban districts discussed above. Countywide districts, or districts that encompass both city and suburban areas of a metro, have often been able to create stable desegregation. In rural districts there is generally less segregation since there are fewer schools for students to enroll in, although in some rural areas private schools disproportionately enroll white students while public schools remain overwhelmingly minority.

CURRENT STATUS OF THE LAW

In more recent years, a number of school districts that have been released from their formal, constitutional desegregation obligations—as well as some that had never been any legal duty to desegregate in the first place—have adopted *voluntary* measures to promote integration in their schools. These so-called "voluntary school integration" measures, in other words, are designed not by courts to be imposed on school districts, with the goal of curing historical, illegal segregation, but rather by the districts themselves, often with the support of and input from parents, students, and others in the community. They are future-oriented and intended to assist the school districts realize *Brown*'s promise and vision of equal opportunity and high-quality integrated public education for all.

Odd as it may seem, however, it may turn out that a unitary school district's voluntary consideration of race for the laudable goal of stemming resegregation and promoting integration is illegal. Despite the success and popularity of well-designed voluntary school integration plans, opponents of desegregation in a handful of communities have sued their school systems for adopting them, alleging that such efforts violate the same Constitution's Equal Protection guarantees that outlawed segregated schools 50 years ago in *Brown*. Indeed, in June 2007, the U.S. Supreme Court issued a much anticipated and sharply divided ruling in two cases challenging voluntary integration plans in Seattle and Louisville. The court struck down aspects of the student assignment plans because they were not sufficiently tailored to achieve those goals. But a majority of Justice's left the window open for school districts to take race conscious measures to promote diversity.

Even though it dramatically changed the landscape of school integration, this Supreme Court decision did not provide a clear set of rules and principles for school districts, creating some confusion about what can be done to promote integration. How communities and school districts will react to the ruling, and whether they choose to forge ahead with new ways to fulfill Brown's promise of equal, integrated public education remain open questions.

Further Reading: Boger, J. C., & Orfield, G., eds., 2005, *School resegregation: Must the South turn back?* Chapel Hill: University of North Carolina Press; Frankenberg, E., & Orfield, G., eds., 2007, *Lessons in integration: Realizing the promise of racial diversity in America's schools,* Charlottesville: University of Virginia Press; Kluger, R., 2004, *Simple justice: The history of* Brown v. Board of Education *and black America's struggle for equality,* 2nd. ed., New York: Knopf; NAACP Legal Defense Fund, June 28, 2007, Statement from the NAACP Legal Defense Fund on the Supreme Court's Rulings in Seattle and Louisville School Cases, retrieved October 15, 2007 from http://www.naacp/df.org/content.aspx?article=1181 Orfield, G., & Lee, C., 2006, *Racial transformation and the changing nature of segregation,* Cambridge, MA: The Civil Rights Project at Harvard University.

Erica Frankenberg and Chinh Q. Le

DISCIPLINE

Year after year, results of Phi Delta Kappan surveys show school discipline to be rated by educators and the larger community as one of the most important educational issues. Teachers consistently rate student discipline issues as a major impetus for leaving the profession and as a source of stress. Along with its important place as an educational issue, school discipline is one of the most controversial and hotly debated school issues of our time. Key stakeholders (parents, students, community members, educators) have personal views of school discipline that are tied to one's belief and value system, sociocultural background, and the larger societal context in which schools operate. Other factors that greatly impact school discipline include local, state, and federal legislation that require procedural safeguards, the dominant political structure at any given time, and media depictions of school events related to discipline and student behavior.

The word discipline is literally taken from the Latin root word "disciplus," meaning "to teach." Over time, school discipline has been equated with "punishment" or retribution for an unacceptable act. In exploring the historical context that has led to modern-day debates about discipline, some of the most controversial school discipline topics emerge, such as suspension and expulsion, zero tolerance policies, corporal punishment in schools, possible ethnic biases in exclusionary discipline methods and more recent work and federal legislation focused on Positive Behavioral Interventions and Supports (PBIS) as a prevention-oriented approach to school discipline.

HISTORICAL CONTEXT OF SCHOOL DISCIPLINE

School discipline and related policies have been found in schools for at least a century. Schools increasingly viewed discipline as a means of teaching obedience and compliance when industrialization occurred in the United States. Schools were viewed as institutions important in training a primarily immigrant population in the behaviors of timeliness and deference to authority. Standards for order and control of students through discipline were also viewed as important with the advent of mandatory schooling. School discipline was an avenue for containment and control of students who perhaps were not necessarily considered part of the mainstream society and would now be mandated to attend school.

It is within this context that written standards for behavior were developed, termed discipline codes of conduct. Standard written discipline policies were enacted that outlined behavioral infractions and consequences for noncompliance. These written standards for behavior have been found in schools since at least 1916.

In the years following, public opinion of schools as failing to control students who were viewed as increasingly violent prompted legislation and additional scrutiny of school discipline methods. For example, in 1978 Senator Evan Bayh chaired a subcommittee to study school violence based on public concern about student behavior and the ability of schools to maintain order. As a result, legislation based on the Safe School Report to Congress was written to commission a study about the amount and type of violence in schools. In 1978, the National Institute of Education conducted this study and had three main conclusions: (1) school violence had actually decreased in comparison to previous decades, the 1970s and 1960s, (2) despite this data, the media and larger community continued to perceive school violence as a problem, necessitating the action of school personnel to address student behavior through school discipline, and (3) school rules were more difficult to enforce when they were arbitrary and enforced by those who were considered excessively punitive. A major recommendation of this national study was the development of uniform codes for behavior for all of the nation's schools, with the intended outcome of making rules clear and consistent on a preset basis.

In roughly the same time period, the *Goss v. Lopez* case (1977) had direct implications for the ways in which school discipline was addressed. In this federal case, it was determined that suspensions could not be determined by a single administrator and that due process rights were to be provided for any student removed because of discipline. These findings were in keeping with the focus at that time to document fairness in school discipline. However, the court case was very controversial with school personnel, many of whom felt the legislation limited their ability to satisfy the larger societal priority of maintaining order and control in the classroom.

In 1980, the National School Resource Network (NSRN) developed a handbook providing recommendations for schools to follow when writing behavioral guidelines in discipline policies. Specific language that schools could use to balance the rights of the individual student with the rights of the larger community was provided.

RELEVANT LEGISLATION

The course of school discipline at the time of the NSRN report and the two decades following it (the 1980s and 1990s) was greatly affected by legislation, particularly federal legislation drawn to protect the rights of individuals with diagnosed disabilities. Indeed, a related reason for having written discipline codes of conduct was the opportunity for schools to show compliance with more substantive discipline legislation. For example, the pioneering federal education legislation in 1975, Public Law 94–142, mandated that all students with disabilities were to receive a free and appropriate education among other due process provisions. Particular to discipline, these individuals were required to receive specific due process rights when suspension (or removal from the school due to discipline) was considered.

The federal courts intervened to more clearly define these requirements pertaining to discipline. For example, *Hoenig v. Doe* (1987) specified the number of days of suspension that were considered a change of placement from the school. This legislation led to federal language related to discipline in more recent versions of Public Law 94–142, particularly the Individuals with Disabilities Education Act (1997) and more recently, the Individuals with Education Improvement Act (signed into law by President Bush in December of 2004). This more recent federal legislation requires school districts to conduct a "manifest determination hearing" if the student has reached the maximum allowed 10 days of suspension. The purpose of the hearing is to determine whether the behavior of a student in special education is related to his disability. If it is related to the student's disability, the school cannot discipline the student like others. Further, if the individual education plan (the school's specific educational goals for the student) is not appropriate, the school may not further suspend the student. Certain exclusions exist, such as when a student brings weapons or drugs to the school or, in the most recent legislation, is involved in serious bodily injury (although the courts have not yet clearly defined this meaning).

This legislation may also apply to students who are not in special education, but about whom the school is aware of behavioral concerns that are impacting learning. Significant controversy has centered on this legislation. Some have continued to argue that they are increasingly limited from maintaining order and that the law has gone too far in protecting the rights of individual students and hindering the rights of the school as a whole. Some have argued that due process rights give unruly students better protection and create more chaos and disorder in the educational process. Disability rights advocates, on the other hand, have pushed for increased due process rights for students with disabilities and have pointed to evidence that those caught in the web of suspension and expulsion are among the most powerless and disenfranchised members of the school community.

SUSPENSION, EXPULSION, AND ZERO TOLERANCE POLICIES

Arguably, among the most controversial issues in the school discipline arena are procedures that, in some form or another, remove students from the school setting for varying lengths of time. Suspension involves removal of a student from school for a set number of days following the violation of a school-defined offense. A student who receives in-school suspension is removed from the classroom but stays in the school building and may or may not be allowed to do academic work, depending on the school policy. Expulsion, on the other hand, is associated with long-term removal of a student, typically a period of one year or more. Zero tolerance procedures are an outgrowth of expulsion that became widespread in the 1990s. Under zero tolerance, certain offenses would not "be tolerated" under any circumstances and students would automatically be removed from the school if they engaged in such behaviors. Each of these related concepts will be considered separately, culminating with a discussion of implications of these procedures for ongoing educational policy debates.

Suspension is the most widely used discipline procedure in policy and practice. Empirical documentation of reliance on suspension dates to the early 1970s. School personnel have relied on and, in some cases, supported their use of suspension because of their perceived need to maintain order and to curb school violence. Alternatively, researchers and policymakers have argued that suspension tends to be used for nonviolent offenses and actually is associated with less safe schools. That suspension tends to be used repeatedly with the same students is an additional argument that it does not work. While suspension is intended to be uniformly applied based on the written discipline policies and due process procedures described above, several researchers have pointed to factors that increase the likelihood of suspension. Student academic problems, not the offense itself, were the biggest factors that predicted those who would be suspended.

Still others have questioned whether suspension is applied fairly (as well as expulsion and related zero tolerance procedures) with ethnic minority students, particularly African American males. That suspension and expulsion are disproportionately applied to ethnic minority students has been documented over the past 40 years. These results are also corroborated in other countries for students who are perceived to be ethnic minority students in the particular societal culture. In *The Color of Discipline*, authors Skiba, Michael, Nardo, and Peterson reviewed studies of ethnic disproportionate representation in discipline from 1975 to 2000. Every study included in their review showed that ethnic minority students, in particular African American males, were overrepresented in the exclusionary discipline consequences of suspension and expulsion. There have been several explanations for this phenomenon. Advocates for the use of suspension and expulsion have argued that these long-standing practices do not imply bias, as other factors besides ethnicity are plausible explanations. In the same publication, Skiba and colleagues analyzed data collected in the Midwest to rule out the most common explanations. Their findings were that ethnic disproportionality remains when factors confounded with race, such as socioeconomic status, the severity of the offense, and the statistical procedures used to analyze the data were controlled for.

In recent years, others have further explored the issue of equity in school discipline. In 2003, a joint research conference co-sponsored by the Civil Rights Project and Northeastern University's Institute on Race and Justice (IRJ) was held to explore possible links between the removal of students of color through suspension and expulsion, and dropping out of school and their entry into the juvenile justice system. Prison data parallels school drop out data in terms of who is represented. In addition, the removal of students due to suspension is associated with dropping out of school, which is also related to ending up in prison.

Much of the related debate around the issue of zero tolerance policies centers on issues of equity and justness. Zero tolerance policies have their origins in the Gun Free Schools Act of 1995, which stated that school must automatically expel students for at least one calendar year for drug or weapons offenses. Zero tolerance policies have their origins in the amount of drugs that were permitted on vessels. This concept was then directly applied to school discipline offenses.

As with other discipline policies that have occurred across the century, zero tolerance policies arose amidst a public perception that schools are not in control of student behavior. For example, in the early to mid-1990s, highly publicized school shootings led to media attention about the nature of schools and reported violence in them. The alternative side to this argument was that school violence overall at this time was actually decreasing instead of increasing, according to the Surgeon General's Report on School Violence of 2001. Indeed, schools have remained the safest places for children to be, much safer than a child's own home.

Much of the debate about zero tolerance was fueled by factors outside of schools, such as public perceptions of school safety, the political climate at the time, and media portrayals of schools. As a result, there were numerous conflicting opinions about the topic. Many policy analysts have come out against the use of zero tolerance policies, citing possible ethnic biases as one of the reasons. Likely one of the most cited works to date about zero tolerance is the written proceedings from a conference sponsored by the Harvard University Advancement and Civil Rights Project. *Opportunities Suspended: The Devastating Consequences of Zero Tolerance and School Discipline Policies* chronicled the overuse of zero tolerance policies with the most disenfranchised in schools, primarily ethnic minority students and those in poverty. The findings of the report were that minority students, particularly African Americans and Hispanics, were overrepresented in zero tolerance procedures and not as a result of committing more severe offenses. In addition, the application of zero tolerance was done in an overzealous manner and without consideration for the offense. For example, a young elementary student was expelled for bringing a butter knife to school for lunch. The media frequently publicized these incidents. Zero tolerance procedures were criticized for failing to achieve the intended outcome of making schools safer. At the same time, others counter these findings and cite their need to comply with this federal legislation and necessary for the functioning of schools.

In sum, zero tolerance procedures have been controversial. They are legislated procedures for schools to follow, receive extensive media publicity, and have arisen at a time when schools are perceived once again as lacking control, as was the case in the 1970s prior to the Safe Schools Study. As a result, they are among the most debated topics in school discipline and are core to our personal values and belief system about the rights of individual students and the rights of schools to remove students from the educational process due to behavior.

CORPORAL PUNISHMENT

Corporal punishment has been used in schools for centuries. Typically, the practice involves physical pain inflicted on a student for a school offense. There remains a great divide on this issue among parents and educators. While popular lore may consider this issue something of the past, corporal punishment is banned in only 27 states in America. The most recent data available (Office of Civil Rights in 2002) indicates that 70 percent of instances of corporal punishment occurred in five southern states.

A number of influential professional associations, such as the American Medical Association, the American Academy of Pediatrics, the National Association of Schools Psychologists, the American Psychological Association, and the American Psychiatric Association, have strongly opposed corporal punishment in schools and have advocated for its elimination. The National Coalition to Abolish Corporal Punishment in Schools and the National Center for the Study of Corporal Punishment and Alternatives have been instrumental in enacting legislation to ban corporal punishment in schools. The negative impact on the self-esteem of students and the chance of significant physical injury (as has been cited in numerous court cases) are arguments made by these groups for the elimination of this practice. In addition, opponents of corporal punishment cite the likelihood of the perpetuation of abuse as an additional reason for abandoning this practice. Continued findings that this form of punishment is more likely to be used with African American students, boys, and those who are poor is seen as further evidence that corporal punishment has no place in schools. It is further argued that schools with corporal punishment have lower achievement and higher rates of vandalism. Similar to the disproportionate representation of ethnic minorities in suspension data, these findings are not a result of these individuals committing more severe offenses. Views of corporal punishment, however, remain less tied to outcome data than one's personal background, own child-rearing practices and treatment as a child, sociocultural background, and religious allegiance. Therefore, while the debate continues, and more and more legislation is enacted on a district, state, and national level, proponents of this practice will remain likely and unchanged in the face of the increasing empirical data that is counter to its use.

ALTERNATIVES TO SUSPENSION, EXPULSION, AND PUNITIVE PROCEDURES

A significant part of the debate has been the tension between the use of punitive and exclusionary discipline procedures, such as suspension, expulsion, zero tolerance, and corporal punishment, and those who have argued that these responses do not work. In particular, researchers, policymakers, and the larger community have suggested that punitive practices associated with discipline promulgate biases that unfairly impact ethnic minority students and put those with academic problems at further risk for failure. Many who feel that suspension and expulsion do not work have had limited alternatives at their disposal until relatively recent changes in the use of prevention-oriented approaches to discipline. Most recently, special education legislation (Individuals with Disabilities Education Act of 2004) has called for the consideration of Positive Behavioral Interventions and Supports (PBIS) with those whose behavior impacts their own learning or that of others. PBIS is an approach to school discipline that is based on the prevention of behavioral problems through the direct teaching of expected behaviors on a school-wide basis. Students who continue to need additional support are then provided support on a group and individual basis. George Sugai and Robert Horner are pioneering researchers who have developed and evaluated this model. Their work has shown that discipline referrals for behavioral infractions can be greatly reduced through the direct teaching and acknowledgment of expected behaviors. In addition, they have reported improvements in school climate. In contrast, they argue that the use of punishment in isolation is actually associated with increases in undesirable behaviors, drawing on the previous work of other researchers.

PBIS is increasingly being evaluated in thousands of schools across the country, with the greatest amount of empirical study concentrated in elementary and middle schools to date, with emerging study in high schools. The premise of this model is that discipline is equated with its original word "disciplus" (or "to teach"). The tension between philosophies of discipline and the role of schools in teaching behaviors remain. According to prevention-oriented models such as PBIS, schools need to teach behaviors in order to increase instructional minutes associated with achievement. On the other hand, others argue that the role of school is strictly academic and that the teaching of behavioral or social skills is not the domain of schools Again, legislation has a strong hand in directing these issues. For example, in Illinois, public schools are now required to teach social-emotional learning standards because of the Illinois Mental Health Act of 2004.

CONCLUSION

School discipline has been a center of controversy since the inception of formal schooling. It remains one of the most salient issues in education and one that is tied to our sociocultural backgrounds and personal values and beliefs. A primary debate has been the limits by which school personnel can deliver consequence by using punitive procedures such as suspension, expulsion, and corporal punishment. The impact of school discipline on those who are most disenfranchised (e.g. ethnic minority students, those with academic problems) has been center stage throughout our struggle with this issue.

The role of discipline in schools has been greatly affected by factors outside of it, such as legislation, the political climate, and the media. History in school discipline has a way of repeating itself. In times when schools are perceived as lacking control or in chaos (whether the data supports this or not), educators have been more influenced by these external factors and have been greatly encouraged to regain order and control. Often the means have been an increased use of punishment as a major component of school discipline procedures. While this is counter to the original intentions of discipline policies advocated strongly in the late 1970s as a means of clearly describing behaviors on a prevention-basis, exclusionary discipline (through suspension and expulsion) remains the most widely used in schools.

Recent system-wide reforms, such as PBIS, have gained momentum in recent years in redefining the meaning of discipline and aligning it with the original root word, "disciplus" or "to teach." Periodic waves of community concerns about discipline appear to have followed a cyclical pattern. Examining our history in school discipline will help us to chart a future path that, hopefully, will be beneficial to the education and development of our youth. As one of the most controversial topics in education that is given top billing in education, it will be interesting to see what the next decade in school discipline inquiry and debate will bring upon us.

Further Reading: Harvard University, the Advancement Project and the Civil Rights Project, 2000, Opportunities suspended: The devastating consequences of zero tolerance and school discipline policies, retrieved October 9, 2002, from http://www.law.harvard.edu/groups/civilrights/conferences/zero/zt_report2html; Noguera, P. A., 1995, Preventing and producing violence: A critical analysis of responses to school violence, *Harvard Educational Review* 65(2): 189–212; Skiba, R. J., Michael, R. S., Nardo, A. C., & Peterson, R., 2000, The color of discipline: Sources of racial and gender disproportionality in school punishment, retrieved August 20, 2006, from http://www.indiana.edu/~safeschl/cod.pdf/minor.html; Skiba, R., & Rausch, M. K., 2006, Zero tolerance, suspension, and expulsion: Questions of equity and effectiveness, in C. M. Evertson and C. S. Weinstein (Eds.), *Handbook of classroom management: Research, practice, and contemporary issues* (pp. 1063–1092), Mahwah, NJ: Lawrence Erlbaum Associates; Wald, J., & Losen, D. J., eds., 2003, *New directions for youth development: Deconstructing the school-to-prison pipeline*, San Francisco: Jossey-Bass.

Pamela A. Fenning, Sara Golomb, and Taylor Morello

DROPOUTS

Colloquially, the term "school dropout" refers to a young person who has not completed high school. Linguistically the choice of the word "dropout" places the responsibility and onus of leaving school solely on the individual. It deludes the pathways by which students ultimately "choose" to leave school, and the structures that lead to dropout remain blameless. School dropout reflects not on the structures of the school the youth attended, on their schooling experiences, nor on their worlds and realities outside of school.

School dropout is a term that refers to a young person who does not graduate from school with a traditional diploma. These youth either leave school, by choice or by force, or are pushed out due to "rationalized policies and practices of exclusion that organize" public high schools (Fine, 1991, p. 6). In any event, the ultimate result is the same: a young person does not finish high school. Historic educational policies and practices mask the phenomenon of school dropout such that it rears itself as an outlier: a rare dysfunction of an individual failing within a system, and, like all social outcomes resulting from structural preclusion, it carries a detrimental "blame the victim" ideology. In the context of education, this ideology presents young people who drop out as failing to measure up to academic standards, and their subsequent bleak social status and life outcomes as a natural consequence of education's ethos of equal opportunity for all.

Given that the graduation rate crisis disproportionately plagues students of color and low-income and special education students; recent immigrants; lesbian, gay, bisexual, transgender/sexual, and queer/questioning youth; students with disabilities; homeless youth; youth caught in Foster care; and youth caught in the criminal and juvenile justice systems, school dropout has a disparate impact, affecting youth who are already lacking in resources, opportunities, and voice.

A *miseducation*, however we name its end results, has substantial costs. For each youth and community disenfranchised by their school system, there are staggering economic and social impacts, heavy consequences for criminal justice, costs to civic and political participation, and grave implications for health. Dropouts are more likely to receive public assistance, be unemployed, live in poverty, end up in prison and on death row, die earlier, and suffer from a wide range of chronic and acute diseases and health problems. On average, dropouts earn $9,200 less per year that high school graduates and $1 million less over their lifetime than do college graduates. Beyond dropping out, children forced out of the school system are more likely to engage in conduct harmful to the safety of themselves, their families, and communities.

THE CURRENT LANDSCAPE OF GRADUATION

Nationally, 68 percent of all students graduate from high school over the traditional four-year period; yet ethnic disparities in these graduation rates are striking. While 76.8 and 74.9 percent of Asian/Pacific Islanders and whites, respectively, graduate from high school, American Indians, Blacks, and Latinos all have graduation rates that hover right around the 50 percent margin. In some cases, Asian refugees, particularly Laotian, Cambodian, Vietnamese and Hmong, and Pacific Islander students graduate at rates similarly as bleak. Immigration and socioeconomic status are important contextual variables in the success of immigrant students. On average, males graduate at a rate 8 percent lower than their female counterparts, and graduation rates for youth attending high-poverty, racially segregated, urban schools fall between 15 and 18 percent behind their peers.

The data is just as dissimilar for the special needs population, where only 32 percent of classified "students with disabilities" graduate from high school. Low-income children and children of color are overrepresented in special education (including being labeled as having emotional or behavior problems), school disciplinary actions, and in the juvenile and criminal justice systems—all of which correlate to school dropout. Compounding these statistics is the fact that children from low-income families are twice as likely to drop out of school as children from middle-income families and are six times more likely than children from high-income households. Ninth grade is thought to be the most critical year in influencing school dropout. A silenced history exemplifies this trend: Between 1970 and 2000, the rate at which students disappeared from school between 9th and 10th grade *tripled*. And we don't even look at the leakage from 8th to 9th grade.

Data this staggering has inherent antecedents, leaving the current graduation rate crisis to illuminate a *historical* genesis of an institution that systematically fails entire groups of youth.

HISTORICAL CONTROVERSIES OF SCHOOL DROPOUT

In closely examining the history of schooling, it becomes readily apparent that school dropout is a dialectic: It is both a deliberate *and* an unintended consequence of a system structured to maintain the status quo. This becomes evident through the ways by which schools ensure the development, success, and privilege of the white, dominant classes at the expense of those on the margins. The process of schooling is a means to assimilate and acculturate on one hand, and to provide liberation, freedom, and educational, social, and economic equity on the other. Deeply contested, and holding these two antithetical meanings, school dropout can no longer remain invisible. It has seeped through the cracks: appearing in the staggeringly low graduation rates and in real dollar costs to the criminal justice and health care systems at the expense of the educationally disenfranchised. The façade of "educational opportunity" and the influence of differing ideologies seem to be the interface between these two conflicting forces.

The Muddled Roots of "School Dropout"

Several educational practices throughout the history of schooling have been discussed in relation to school dropout. Academic tracking, a practice that has been around since the post–Civil War era, has always had the greatest percentage of low-income and students of color occupying the lower academic tracks. These students are labeled and tracked into a marginal future, without the personal growth of one's own soul, aspirations, and spirit. With limited occupational and economic opportunity, being placed in a low academic track has always been a practice that serves as a precursor to school dropout.

One of the biggest misconceptions about young people who drop out is that they have no desire and motivation to learn, place little value on an education and learning, and aren't interested in school. As it turns out, and as is detailed in the following section, schools often prevent young people from enacting their desire and motivation for learning and success. In fact, history is pervasive with examples of *social movements* for education, acts that can only be explained by both individual and a collective's desire and motivation for schooling.

Underfunding, chronic overcrowding, and poor schooling conditions are also historic educational practices that contribute to school dropout. Schools and districts that serve large immigrant, low-income, and communities of color have been underfunded, overcrowded, and not well maintained. Subsequently, the quality of education achievable in these conditions pales in comparison to the educational opportunities and access to resources of their more privileged and white counterparts. Deliberate underdevelopment and a decrepit physical environment significantly shape educational limitations. For example, it has often been reported that overcrowding schools was a way to get young people to drop out. This was achieved through the practice of double-shift schooling, in which schools were filled beyond overcapacity to the extent that they needed to run several shifts of students throughout one single day. As a result, class time and total hours spent in school for each pupil decreased, and the time spent *out of school* increased. This practice, in essence, manufactured dropouts.

CONTEMPORARY CONFLICTS IN SCHOOL DROPOUT

School dropout is the end stage in a cumulative and dynamic process of educational disengagement and dispossession. The controversy and conflict surrounding who is to "blame" for dropout—the individual or the school system—are embedded into each category and represented by the range and scope of the data. The research reflects a diverse array of ideological and theoretical positions. Themes of alienation, lack of school engagement, and the nature of the school setting and culture that emerge from the literature are presented.

Causes of School Dropout

Individual Level Characteristics

Individual attributes associated with school dropout include feelings of alienation, disliking or feeling disconnected from school, decreased levels of school participation, and low educational or occupational self-expectations. Diminished academic aspirations may reflect the changing labor market and economic forces operating at higher levels of social organization. Additionally, when students feel that the locus of control for their success resides outside of themselves, they report feeling less academically inclined.

Compared to their counterparts who complete school, dropouts are less socially conforming; more likely to challenge openly their perceived injustice of the social system; less accepting of parental, school, social, and legal authority; more autonomous; more socially isolated; and less involved in their communities. For some young people, dropout may be a form of resistance or critique of the educational system. And the effect of self-esteem on school dropout is contested, with some research showing an association and others not.

Behaviors associated with dropout include disruptive conduct; truancy; absenteeism; lateness; substance use; pregnancy and parenting; mental, emotional, psychological, or behavioral difficulties; and low participation in extracurricular activities. These behaviors may be influenced by differing school environments, again pointing to the role that inequitable schools play in shaping the production of school dropout.

The foremost cause of school dropout for adolescent women is teenage pregnancy, accounting for between 30 and 40 percent of the young women who leave school, although alternative evidence demonstrates that often young women stop attending school and *then* get pregnant. Adolescent men are also affected by teen pregnancy, as they may drop out to earn money to support a child. Compared to school completers, dropouts are more likely to be substance abusers, and to have started substance abuse early; more likely to be involved in the sale of drugs; and more likely to have friends engaging in behavior deemed to be socially deviant. Mental illness and emotional disturbance also account for a significant percentage of high school dropouts—reports state that anywhere between 48 and 55 percent of young people with mental and emotional troubles fail to graduate high school.

Individual school experiences greatly impact the likelihood of graduation. Students held back in school are more than *11* times as likely to leave school as their peers, and several studies identify grade retention (being held back a grade) as the most significant predictor of school dropout. Poor academic achievement, low self-expectations, low grades, lower test scores, and course failure all contribute to school dropout. Here too, these individual factors must be viewed as manifestations of accumulating poor educational experiences. In fact, 45 percent of students report starting high school very underprepared by their earlier schooling.

Economic constraints also influence dropout. Surveys of dropouts show that having to get a job, conflicts between work and school, and having to support a family are important reasons for leaving school. However, the overwhelming majority of all dropouts report that education and graduating are important to success in life. Data indicates the strong *value* and *desire* for education, despite rhetoric on dropouts that argue the opposite.

Family Characteristics

Family characteristics associated with dropout are low levels of family support, involvement, and expectations for education achievement; low parental education attainment; single-parent homes; parenting style; few study aids available at home; less opportunity for nonschool learning; financial problems; and low socioeconomic status. Low expectations for a child's academic success by adults have been shown to increase a child's likelihood of dropping out five-fold.

And residential or school mobility are also considerably linked to school dropout. Importantly, what often appears to be lack of parental involvement in education is actual life constraints of living in poverty, having to work more than one job, employment where parents cannot take time off of work, language barriers between the family and school personnel, and/or the symbolic representation of schools as unwelcoming institutions for parents who were not successful in schools themselves.

Many adolescents, especially young women, carry the burden of caring for their family, forcing them to leave high school due to social or health needs of their loved ones. Compared to school completers, dropouts are more likely to translate for family members, help to find health care for their family, and care for the elderly and children in their families. Young men are often forced to economically sustain their families. Family stress, parental substance abuse, physical or sexual abuse of children, lack of health insurance, family health problems, having to care for a family member, or the death of a loved one can contribute to the decision (or need) to drop out.

Neighborhood and Community Characteristics

Communities with high levels of crime, violence, drug-related crime, and arson have higher rates of school dropout than communities with fewer of these problems. Some studies indicate that communal social support promotes school engagement and improves chances for school graduation among racial and ethnic minority students. Similarly, cultural norms of schools and cultural and linguistic tensions between the home and community (and often country) from which students come contribute to educational disenfranchisement, leading to school dropout.

School Characteristics

Attributes of schools and school systems significantly influence dropout rates. Poverty again plays a central role, with a school's mean socioeconomic status being the most significant independent influence on graduation rates. In addition, higher levels of segregation, more students of color, more students enrolled in special education, and location in central cities or larger districts are also associated with lower graduation rates. It is neither an accidental correlation nor coincidence that race/ethnicity, class, and level of urbanization are implicated in higher rates of school dropout.

School climate is a central component of school engagement and, therefore, school completion. Punitive school policies (standardized testing, changing academic standards without supports, tracking, unfair/stringent discipline policies, frequent use of suspensions) all affect academic engagement and success. When social support and positive relationships with adults in the school are diminished, so is a young person's connectedness to school. And school engagement and connectedness are two widely supported causes of staying in school.

School Policies

High-stakes testing, a practice whereby student advancement is determined primarily by tests, also influences dropout. Comparing states that employ high-stakes testing to those that do not shows that states using such tests hold students back at much higher rates than states that do not.

More recent studies publish findings of "school pushout"; in which school dropouts are in fact forced out of school through a variety of policies and practices, like policing, discipline, and educational-tracking measures. *School pushout* is a concept that reframes the choice to leave school as a reflection of the larger educational systems, structures, and policies that have failed youth, and that often ultimately force young people out of schools. Stemming from this phenomenon is the associated school-to-prison pipeline, a term that refers to policies and practices that ensure that when young people "misbehave" in school, they are turned over the police and juvenile justice system.

School safety and discipline policies appear to have a strong effect on dropout. Student perceptions of unfair discipline, of low teacher interest in students, and of lack of attachment to an adult in the school all predict dropout. School disciplinary contact is among the strongest predictors of school dropout. Surveys of dropouts show that being suspended often and getting expelled contribute to the decision to drop out. Propensity for being a target of school discipline actions (number of office referrals, suspensions, and expulsions) is overwhelmingly racialized: Low-income children, children of color, those in special education, and those labeled as emotionally disturbed are disproportionally impacted. Developmentally, school discipline has severe effects on a child's perception of justice, fairness, trust, capability, and self-worth and may contribute to feelings of social isolation and alienation and to engaging in high-risk behaviors.

Other school policies that have been associated with dropout include high student-to-teacher ratios, academic tracking, and a discrepancy between faculty and student demographic characteristics. Low levels of engagement to school also predict dropout. Related, a lack of sufficient programs for pregnant and parenting teens as well as comprehensive health and sex-education programs and availability of social services build barriers that make the success of particular groups of students nearly impossible. Schools that adopt such programs buffer school dropout with tremendous success.

The Controversy over Data Reporting

The issue of reporting data becomes controversial due to its *absence* and lack of any standardized, reliable, and valid data-collection formula. Until the No Child Left Behind Act (NCLB) of 2002, there was no federal mandate requiring graduation rate reporting. Before this, only some states kept graduation rate data. This law, while unearthing the chasm in public education, has also positioned itself in a way that can promulgate the crisis. This NCLB mandate provides little protection for low-performing students to not be pushed out of schools. Districts, in order to meet the incentives for improving their graduation rates and for meeting the annual yearly progress requirement, *push* lower-performing students into alternative school programs, where they are not counted as dropouts.

Also undermining any real attempt by NCLB to ensure equal educational attainment are two principles of the law. First, unlike the accountability mandates, which require test score and achievement data to be kept demographically—by income, race/ethnicity, special education status, and limited English proficiency students—and for which adequate yearly progress must be made in at least one of these historically low-performing groups, when calculating the graduation rate, states must only count the *overall* rate; they do not have to record by demographics. This allows young people on the margins to be practically ignored, and disparities in graduation rates to be silenced. Second, and also incongruent with the accountability mandates that stipulate that 100 percent of all students receive "proficient" test scores by 2014, states can establish their own formula for calculating graduation rates and their own graduation rate goals, *which can range between 50 to 100 percent*. What NCLB has effectively done is to create a loophole that ensures, if not requires, students to be pushed out of schools in order to meet the more stringent accountability mandates—to which funding and school takeover sanctions are attached. By giving federal permission for states to aspire to a mere 50 percent graduation rate *without having to record demographic data,* the federal government has given the doorway for *how to* achieve 100 percent proficiency while maintaining the historic class and racial structure of society.

In recent years, several reports have published studies that examine and develop more accurate, comprehensive, and representative methods for calculating and capturing the landscape of educational attainment. Specifically, these measures are indicators of high school graduation rates rather than of the more traditional and common statistics that measure either dropout rates or high school completion rates. (Dropout rates can be calculated in one of three ways: event dropout rates, status dropout rates, and cohort dropout rates.) Each of these different measures will produce very different results. To date, most states calculate dropout rates, a figure that is *not the equivalent* of graduation rates (those reported here).

While these newer reports calculate nearly identical statistics on high school *graduation rates,* data used here are from a formula developed by Christopher Swanson of the Urban Institute. This formula is the best proxy for current graduation rates, and the subsequent research details the most "extensive set of systematic empirical findings on public school graduation rates available to date for the nation as a whole and for each of the states" (Swanson, 2004b, p. 1). The method developed is called the Cumulative Promotion Index (CPI), and it is applied to data from the Common Core of Data (CCD), the U.S. Department of Education's database, as the measure to calculate high school graduation rates. The CCD database is the most complete source of information on all public schools and local education agencies in the United States. The CPI is a variation of cohort dropout rates in that it "approximates the probability that a student entering the 9th grade will complete high school on time [in four years] with a regular diploma. It does this by representing high school graduation as a stepwise process composed of three grade-to-grade promotion transitions (9 to 10, 10 to 11, and 11 to 12) in addition to the ultimate high school graduation event (grade 12 to diploma)" (Swanson,

2004a, p. 7). It is important to emphasize that the CPI only counts students who receive high school diplomas as graduates and not those who earn a GED or other alternative credentials, thus overrepresenting the number of people "graduating" from high school. This is in keeping with the new NCLB mandate for what constitutes a diploma. This index was created as a response to extant methods that are commonly used to determine educational attainment.

The more common statistical measures of dropout rates and high school completion rates have significant limitations. *Dropout rates,* meant to capture only the percentage of students that actually drop out of school, are based on underreported and underrepresented data, since there is no standard mechanism for reporting, coding, or accounting for students who drop out. Districts often title students who may have indeed dropped out or been pushed out as having transferred or moved or as missing. This false representation leads to an exaggerated picture of how well a school is doing. High school *completion rates* count General Educational Development (GED) graduates and students receiving alternative credentials as high school graduates. As such, data measuring high school completion differs greatly from those measuring graduation rates. Incorporating GEDs and other alternative credentials in graduation rates is problematic for two primary reasons. First, recipients of the GED or alternative certifications are not graduates of high school; therefore, their credentials cannot be attributed to the school system. Second, the economic and higher educational returns from students with a GED is not equivalent to those with a high school diploma.

The most common "graduation" and "dropout" statistics are cited from the National Center for Education Statistics (NCES), which *calculates its data as high school completion rates but reports* its data as a high school *graduation rate* of 85 percent. The NCES statistic has very low levels of national coverage and is computed using data from only 54 percent of U.S. school districts and 45 percent of the student population. Due to missing data, the 2001 NCES measure could only estimate completion rates for 34 states.

The NCES uses data from the Current Population Survey (CPS). The CPS, conducted by the U.S. Census Bureau, is a simple self-report survey conducted in noninstitutionalized settings and on people who are neither currently in school nor recently graduated. This measure surveys the general young adult population (ages 18–24), not school district information. Students may report GED attainment as high school completion, they may misrepresent their education level, and it may underrepresent low-income youth who are disproportionately dropouts. Youth in low-income communities are often harder to find and interview. The CPS also underrepresents black and Latino youth, who are incarcerated at high rates and are therefore excluded from participating in the survey because prisons are institutionalized settings. Collectively, this measure offers a much higher and nonreliable depiction of the state of high school graduation—one that masks the crisis.

CONCLUSION

The implications of how "dropout" is framed—either as an individual burden or as the fault of the institution—have drastically different consequences. For each young person disenfranchised by their school system, there is a fraying of the public belief in the common good, a threat to a collective sense of democratic belonging, substantial losses to communities, economic and social impacts, heavy consequences for criminal justice, costs to civic and political participation, and dire implications for health.

With increasing public and educational consciousness about the graduation rate crisis, many innovative and effective dropout-prevention programs are being created and implemented. With the move for schools to incorporate school-based health centers and other social service supports, young people are provided supports and resources that make their engagement and success in school possible. When schools and programs reflect the stance that schools need to support students, and not that students are deficient of success, this crisis has the ability to change.

Further Reading: Fine, M., 1991, *Framing dropouts: Notes on the politics of an urban public high school,* Albany: State University of New York Press; Mishel, L., & Roy, J., 2006, *Rethinking high school graduation rates and trends,* Washington DC: Economic Policy Institute; Orfield, G., ed., 2004, *Dropouts in America: Confronting the graduation rate crisis,* Cambridge, MA: Harvard Education Press; Skiba, R., & Knesting, K., 2001, Zero tolerance, zero evidence: An analysis of school disciplinary practice, *New Directions for Youth Development 92*: 17–43; Swanson, C., 2004a, *The real truth about low graduation rates, an evidence-based commentary,* Washington, DC: The Urban Institute; Swanson, C., 2004b, *Who graduates? Who doesn't? A statistical portrait of public high school graduation, class of 2001,* Washington, DC: The Urban Institute.

Jessica Ruglis

DRUG USE AND PREVENTION

Drug use and abuse among youth is a significant problem in the United States. Although recent data suggest a slight decrease in youth drug usage from past years, in 2003 almost a fourth (23 percent) of 12- to 17-year-olds engaged in some form of tobacco use and over one-third (34 percent) reported using alcohol. Youth behavior is often characterized by experimentation, curiosity, rebellion, insecurity, and poor self-esteem. Many of these attributes if not managed in positive ways can lead to problems such as truancy, gang-related behaviors, suicide, and drug use. For many individuals, education of students and implementation of school-based prevention programs may seem to be a proactive approach to drug use and abuse in youth. Current research suggests that if drug use is delayed during adolescence long-term adult use is often reduced or avoided. Throughout the last several decades, however, some drug-prevention efforts have had a limited impact on youth drug-taking behaviors and have cast doubts as to whether drug education and prevention has a place in the schools. Moreover, some individuals perceive that the responsibility of youth drug education and prevention should be the responsibility of parents. Others suggest that providing materials and curricula on drugs may actually increase the likelihood of drug use and abuse among children and adolescents.

DEFINITIONS RELATED TO DRUG USE

When discussing the topic of drugs there are many terms used. The word *drug* refers to any natural or artificial substance, other than food, that because of its chemical nature alters an organism's structure or function. One confusing aspect of this definition is that sometimes a drug can also be considered a food, for example, alcoholic beverages may also be considered a food. But usually, the terms *drug* or *drugs* refer to alcohol, tobacco, marijuana, over-the-counter substances used to induce a high, and illicit substances.

Drug abuse refers to the use of a substance in a manner, in amounts, or in situations that causes problems or increases the risk of problems, which may be physical, psychological, social, or occupational. *Drug addiction* is defined as frequent or daily use of a particular drug. With drug addiction a large portion of an individual's behavior is often focused on using, obtaining, or talking about the drug or associated paraphernalia. The term *drug misuse* is often associated with overuse of prescription medications or using a drug for purposes that it was not intended to be used for. For example, various chemicals such as paints or solvents may be used to obtain a high. The term *binge drinking* is used commonly in the scientific literature to indicate a level of alcohol consumption. In males, five or more drinks consumed in a row is considered a binge-drinking episode, and binge drinking in females is defined as having consumed four or more drinks in a row.

THE EFFECTS OF DRUG ABUSE IN YOUTH

Some individuals may perceive drug-abuse prevention to be ineffective or think that moderate use of drugs has little impact on the health status or academic achievement of students. This perception may have developed from the past when drugs were not as strong and potent as they are today. So-called "natural" or soft drugs like marijuana are many times more powerful than they were in the 1960s. Over the last several decades, these drugs have been modified to create higher concentrations of the active ingredients that cause a person to become "high." The introduction of new drugs such as crack cocaine or methamphetamine has rapidly increased the rate and degree of addiction in many individuals. Recently, youth have also increased usage of over-the-counter medications for the purposes of getting "high." Research has repeatedly contradicted the perception that drug use and abuse have limited effects on individuals, particularly youth. Moreover, there may be more pronounced effects on youth who use drugs than previously thought. These effects may include impaired health, increases in violence, mental health problems, and decreases in academic achievement.

There are many potential health consequences from the use and abuse of drugs. While some negative health effects experienced by the user may be generic, some health risks are dependent on the specific drug used. Usage among adolescents is particularly risky because of the potential lifelong damage that may occur during critical periods of growth and development. Potential health problems associated with drug use include impaired mental function and several

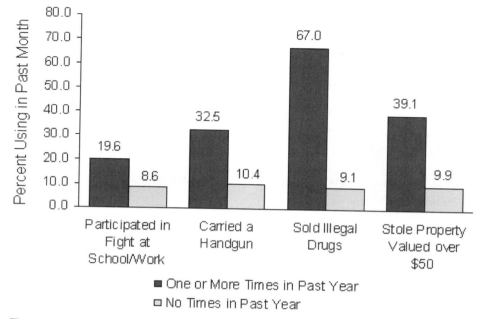

Figure D.1   Past-month Illicit Drug Use among Youths Aged 12 to 17, by Participation in Delinquent Behaviors: 2003

Source: 2002–2003 National Survey on Drug Use and Health.

medical conditions including gastrointestinal problems, malnutrition, high blood pressure, and lower resistance to disease. Drug use has also been linked to several types of cancers including esophagus, stomach, liver, pancreas, and colon. Steroid use in this population can be particularly harmful as it can impair growth, change or delay reproductive growth, and cause heart attacks and strokes. For adolescents who begin smoking at a young age it can impair respiratory function and greatly increase their increased risk of cancer in adulthood.

Drug use among youth has been linked to other risky behaviors including violence and criminal behavior. Periodically, the Substance Abuse and Mental Health Services Agency (SAMHSA) conducts the National Survey on Drug Use & Health. Recently, this study found that youths aged 12 to 17 who used an illicit drug in the past year were almost twice as likely to have engaged in a violent behavior as those who did not use an illicit drug (49.8 percent vs. 26.6 percent). In the same study, engagement in violent behavior increased with the number of drugs used in the past year: 45.6 percent of youths who used one illicit drug engaged in violent behavior compared to 61.9 percent of youths who used three or more illicit drugs.

Drug use can also dramatically impact the social and mental health status of youth. While adolescence is already a period of time where personal changes and insecurity cause significant fluctuation in mood, drug use can exacerbate feelings of depression and isolation. In SAMHSA's 2002–2003 National Survey on Drug Use and Health, an estimated 9 percent of adolescents aged 12 to 17 (approximately 2.2 million adolescents) had experienced at least one major depressive episode during the past year. Adolescents who had experienced a major depressive episode in the past year were more than twice as likely to have used illicit drugs in the past month compared to their peers who had not experienced a major depressive episode in the past year (21.2 percent vs. 9.6 percent). These findings are troublesome considering the fact that depression has been linked to other self-destructive behaviors in adolescents such as suicide. Moreover, treatment for depression in youth is often not available or the signs of use go unrecognized by parents, teachers, or others. For example, in adolescents aged 12 to 17 who experienced at least one major depressive episode during the past year, only 40.3 percent reported having received treatment for depression during the past year.

Academic performance has gained significant attention due to the increased accountability placed on schools and the competitive nature of college admissions and the job market. Numerous studies have shown how drinking alcohol and the use of other drugs impact the academic achievement of college students and adolescents. Drug use can impede academic progress in many ways. For example, use of marijuana may weaken mental ability and influence the capacity to learn. Marijuana use has been found to impair memory and concentration and can impact the ability to solve complex problems and store new information in the brain.

According to the 2002–2003 National Survey on Drug Use and Health an estimated 70.4 percent of students aged 12 to 17 reported that they had an A or B grade average in their last semester or grading period, while 29.6 percent had a C average or less. In the same study, students who did not use alcohol in the past month (72.5 percent) were more likely to have an A or B grade average than those who drank alcohol but did not binge (67.1 percent) or those who binged in the past month (57.7 percent). Students who did not use marijuana in the past month (72.2 percent) were more likely to have an A or B grade average than those who used marijuana on one to four days in the past month (58.0 percent) or those using marijuana on five or more days in the past month (44.9 percent). It is important to note that academic achievement of youth is not only impeded by the use of alcohol and illicit drugs, but also by use of tobacco. Secondary school students who used tobacco are also more likely to have lower level of academic achievement.

RISK FACTORS

All youth are potentially at risk for drug use and abuse. Several risk factors are associated with drug use, although it is often difficult to determine if these risk factors are precursors for drug use or are actually caused by drug use and abuse behaviors. For example, could a student who is depressed drink alcohol to self-medicate or could the student's symptoms be due to the depressive effects of alcohol or a result of problems caused or exacerbated by alcohol use? The National Institute on Drug Abuse (NIDA) has identified both possible risk and protective factors for youth drug use. Students at highest risk are those with low expectations for education, low school achievement, school truancy and

Table D.1 Potential Drug Use Risk and Prevention Factors

Risk Factor	Domain	Protective Factor
Early aggressive behavior	Individual	Self-control
Lack of parental supervision	Family	Parental monitoring
Substance abuse	Peer	Academic competence
Drug availability	School	Anti-drug use policies
Poverty	Community	Strong neighborhood attachment

Source: National Institute on Drug Abuse. *Preventing Youth Drug Abuse among Youth and Adolescents. A Research Guide for Parents, Educators, and Community Leaders.* 2nd ed. Available at http://www.nida.nih.gov/Prevention/Prevopen.html.

misconduct records, low resistance to peer influence, peer use of substances, lack of belief that use is harmful, and lack of parental support. Other groups at risk include youth from families who use drugs; youth who are physically challenged; and gay and lesbian youth.

Availability of drugs has also been associated with use and abuse. According to the 2002–2003 National Drug Use and Health Survey, approximately one in six youths (16.1 percent) reported that he or she had been approached by someone selling drugs in the past month. Those youths who had been approached by someone selling drugs reported a much higher rate of past-month use of an illicit drug (35.0 percent) than those who had not been approached (6.7 percent). In the same study, slightly more than half of youths aged 12 to 17 indicated that it would be fairly or very easy to obtain marijuana if they wanted some (53.6 percent).

PROTECTIVE FACTORS

A number of factors appear to deter youth drug use and abuse. Youth often learn many of their behaviors from members of their own family; therefore, when parents model anti-drug-use behaviors children often will adopt similar beliefs and practices. This modeling is most influential when coupled with parental monitoring and a strong bond between parent and child. For example, in the 1997–1998 National Survey on Drug Use and Health Survey, adolescents surveyed indicated that those who would talk to a parent about a serious problem were less likely to report past-year marijuana use than those who would not (11 vs. 30 percent). Further, 62 percent of those adolescents who thought that their parents would be "not at all upset" if they tried marijuana used this drug during the last year. Other potential protective factors include having friends who do not use drugs, having a high self-esteem, and school connectedness.

HISTORY OF SCHOOL-BASED DRUG-PREVENTION PROGRAMS

Over the last several decades drug-abuse prevention has taken many directions. As drug use increased, particularly by middle-class youth in the late 1970s, concerned parents attempted to change social norms by confronting various environmental influences they perceived as threatening to their children. During this period most drug-prevention programs focused on dissemination of knowledge regarding the dangers of drugs. At the same time, parent and community groups challenged governmental lack of interest and action and the entertainment industry's perceived acceptance of recreational use of drugs. These groups criticized the media for its glamorization of drugs, in particular use of marijuana (Cheech and Chong's *Up in Smoke* album, the Doobie Brothers band, and so on). Efforts by these grassroots groups were key in identifying inconsistent messages about the acceptability of drug use present in many sectors of the community.

In the 1980s, the social influence model was predominant in drug-prevention efforts. As a result of the concern regarding inconsistent messages and the increasing involvement by community and parent groups in preventing drug use, task forces, community partnerships, and coalitions formed with the goal of developing a consistent and comprehensive no-use message given to children. Most of these efforts focused on decision making, social skills, and stress management. When recalling past efforts using this methodology, one of the most memorable media campaigns was the image of an egg in a frying pan with the caption "This Is Your Brain on Drugs." Many early programs commonly employed scare tactics and warned young people about the dangers of drugs. Some early programs showcased samples or various drugs look-alikes or drug paraphernalia used to administer them without specific education on the various effects of each drug.

Also during this time, drug-prevention programs were designed for and implemented in the school setting, with structured curricula being the prime intervention. For some individuals, the implementation of school-based drug-prevention programs was controversial due to the perception that drug education should be the primary responsibility of parents. Moreover, some parents expressed concern that educating youth about drugs may actually make them more curious about experimentation and use. School administrators and teachers cited concerns over the loss of class time for academic material, lack of expertise in teaching the prevention curricula, and the potential cost of implementation of the prevention program.

Later prevention strategies incorporated efforts directed towards domains outside of the schools such as families, peer groups, the community, environmental modification, and drug-related policies. It became evident that prevention efforts needed to be comprehensive, with interventions being developed for multiple settings and targeting various groups. These efforts were consistent with the public health model, where the individual, environment, and agent (drug) were independently and collectively addressed in the prevention efforts. Recognition of youth drug use and abuse as a public health problem became a catalyst for drug-abuse prevention efforts taking on greater significance at the state level, where commonly coordinators were brought on board to administer the prevention efforts within each state.

As efforts increased during the 1990s to implement youth drug-prevention programs that were intuitive and often desirable, there was a steady increase in the recognition of the importance of crafting particular strategies that were deemed effective in reducing and preventing youth drug use and abuse. Specifically, it became more and more important that youth-targeted programs become based on these key strategic elements and result in positive changes in youth, families, and communities rather than programs simply providing any information obtainable, disseminated by anyone, for any duration. This shift may have been a result of the failed efforts of large-scale drug-prevention campaign in the 1980s such as the previously mentioned "This Is Your Brain on Drugs" media message or the widely publicized slogan endorsed by former first lady Nancy Regan, "Just Say No."

As it became more and more apparent that funding for youth drug-prevention programs was being utilized on poorly designed programs, funding from philanthropic organizations began to be awarded with restrictions requiring programs to include key strategic elements or have shown some merit in smaller-scale interventions. Policies were adopted at the federal, state, and local level. For example, interventions provided under the federal government's Safe and Drug Free School program began to require that funded programs were to be based on established scientific standards and interventions that have been shown to be effective in drug prevention in youth. To establish these standards various federal agencies and private sector organization began to establish procedures for identifying and creating effective drug-prevention programs. Groups and organizations such as the Department of Education's National Diffusion Network, the Department of Justice's Office of Juvenile Justice and Delinquency Prevention, the National Institute on Drug Abuse, and the Center for Substance Abuse Prevention's (CSAP's) National Registry of Effective Prevention Programs have all worked to develop such standards.

CURRENT DRUG-PREVENTION PROGRAMS

Drug-abuse-prevention programs have evolved to address the complexities of both risk and protective factors as well as various settings and groups. Current youth-centered drug-prevention programs, although perceived as controversial by some individuals, employ a wide variety of strategies depending on the target population. The current scope of these programs has broadened to include increasing knowledge about drugs, reducing use, delaying the onset of first use, reducing abuse, and minimizing harm from the use. There has also been promising new research on the importance of family-based drug-prevention programs. In 2003, NIDA identified several fundamental principles that are considered best practices when designing and implementing programs to decrease drug use and abuse among children. These key recommendations include:

- Prevention programs should enhance protective factors and reverse or reduce risk factors;
- Prevention programs should target all forms of drug abuse, including use of tobacco, alcohol, marijuana, and inhalants;
- Prevention programs aimed at young people should be age-specific, developmentally appropriate, and culturally sensitive; and they should be

long-term with repeat interventions to reinforce prevention goals originally presented early in a school career;

- Prevention programs should include a component that equips parents or caregivers to reinforce family anti-drug norms;
- Family-focused prevention programs have a greater impact than those that target parents only or children only; and
- Prevention programs should be adapted to address specific drug-abuse problems in the local community.

In addition to these recommendations, prevention programs can also be described by their target audience. According to NIDA, potential interventions can be categorized as universal, selective, and indicated. Universal programs are designed for the general population, such as students in a school setting. Selective programs are designed to address specific risk factors or subsets of a given population, such as those who have poor grades or have parents who have substance abuse problems. Indicated programs target those who may have already used or experimented with drugs but who do not meet diagnostic criteria for addiction.

Although these recommendations are designed to improve the effectiveness of youth drug-prevention programs, some individuals remain unsupportive and skeptical of school-based and various other prevention programs due to the fact that many existing programs have been shown to be ineffective at changing or preventing drug use. For example, the most widely utilized school-based drug-prevention program is Project DARE (Drug Abuse Resistance Education). This program was created by members of law enforcement and used specially trained officers to teach drug education curriculum in the schools. Since its creation, 50 percent of school districts in the United States have used this curriculum. Numerous studies found the DARE program to be ineffective in producing a long-term reduction in youth substance abuse. Even a published report issued by the Office of the Surgeon General has deemed this program as ineffective, yet this program continues to be implemented because of its wide popularity. To help avoid the implementation of ineffective youth drug-prevention programs, several federal agencies such as the U.S. Department of Education, SAMHSA, and the U.S. Department of Justice have begun to compile databases of programs that have either been found to be effective or have shown promise in reducing youth drug use and abuse. These compilations of program can be useful for parents, teachers, and school systems when selecting youth drug-prevention programs.

SUMMARY

Drug use and abuse is a significant problem among youth. Many of the behaviors that lead to adult drug use behaviors are developed through use and experimentation during adolescence. Although some individuals may perceive drug use to be relatively harmless, drug use and abuse can have a significant impact on an individual in both the long and the short term. These effects can lead to impaired health, social and emotional problems, increases in violent and criminal behaviors, and lower level of academic achievement. Over the last several decades there have been significant changes in the methods and programs implemented to reduce youth drug use and abuse. Initially, programs focused solely on the acquisition of knowledge. Early prevention efforts were also not drug specific and often focused on using scare tactics or broader issues such as decision making or stress management. Today, much of the youth drug use and abuse-prevention efforts are occurring at the school level. For some individuals, this approach may seem to be controversial due to the perceptions that drug-prevention efforts should be maintained by parents, participation in drug education may actually make youth more curious about drug use, and drug education and prevention efforts are neither effective nor cost effective. To address many of these obstacles, recommendations and frameworks have been created to help agencies, communities, and schools design and implement more scientific and effective youth-targeted drug-prevention programs. Future drug-prevention efforts will continue to focus on tailoring programs toward more specific audiences and settings, addressing risk and protective factors, and involving family and community members in the dissemination and participation in these prevention efforts.

Further Reading: Canadian Center on Substance Abuse, Drug Trends in the United States and Europe, retrieved January 13, 2007, from http://www.unodc.org/youthnet/youth net_youth_drugs_trends_drug_trends_eur_us.html; Center for Substance Abuse Prevention (CSAP), Model Programs, retrieved from http://www.samhsa.gov/centers/csap/modelprograms; Ennett, S., Tobler, N., Ringwalt, C., & Flewelling, R., 1994, How effective is drug abuse resistance education? A meta-analysis of project DARE outcome evaluations, *American Journal of Public Health 84*(9), 1394–1401; Goldberg, R., 2006, *Clashing views in drugs and society,* 7th ed., Dubuque, IA: McGraw-Hill; National Institute on Drug Abuse, Monitoring our future, National results of adolescent drug use, Key findings, 2005, retrieved from http://monitoringthefuture.org/pubs/monographs/over view2005.pdf; National Institute on Drug Abuse, Preventing youth drug abuse among youth and adolescents, A research guide for parents, educators, and community leaders, 2nd ed, retrieved from http://www.nida.nih.gov/Prevention/Prevopen.html; SAMHSA, Office of Applied Health Studies, National survey on drug use and health 2002 and 2003, retrieved January 13, 2007, from http://www.oas.samhsa.gov/NHSDA/2k3NSDUH/appg.htm#tabg.15; U.S. Department of Education (DED), Exemplary and promising: Safe, disciplined, and drug-free schools programs, retrieved from http://www.ed.gov/admins/lead/safety/exemplary01/report_pg9.html?exp = 0.U.S.; Department of Justice (DOJ), Promising strategies, retrieved from http://www.ojp.usdoj.gov/docs/psrsa.pdf.

Amy Thompson

EARLY CHILDHOOD EDUCATION

Early childhood education (ECE) is a controversial and contested field. Since the Progressive Era, debate has existed over what role federal, state, and local government agencies should play in providing families and their young children with access to ECE programs. Within the field itself, there are disputes over issues such as what type of care should be provided to children and their families; what type of training should early childhood educators possess; and what type of instruction should take place and at what age.

Even with a majority of mothers within the United States in the workforce and numerous scientific studies demonstrating the importance of the early years of a child's life on later development and academic performance, society has yet to accept the idea that access to high-quality ECE programs should be a basic right for all children. A key reason for this is the patriarchal norms that dominate the American psyche. In general, society still defines the role of the mother as the primary caregiver of the child, and thus it is her responsibility to ensure that the child is cared for and ready to enter elementary school. Ideally, the mother is married and has husband who is able to support her and her child. While these images have been contested across numerous fronts, the nuclear family is still a key construct in federal policy and used by many who oppose an expanding role of government into early childhood education.

A DEFINITION OF EARLY CHILDHOOD EDUCATION

The National Association for the Education of Young Children (NAEYC), the largest professional organization for early childhood educators, defines the early childhood years as those from birth through third grade, and thus this field of practice balances between systems of compulsory and noncompulsory schooling. This entry focuses on early childhood programs that serve children from birth through age five, including kindergarten.

THE STATUS OF EARLY CHILDHOOD EDUCATION WITHIN THE UNITED STATES

For children from birth through age five, early childhood services are offered through a patchwork system of care that includes public and private nonprofit agencies, religious organizations, corporations, for-profit enterprises, family child care providers, and public schools. Programs serve a range of ages, offers various types of services, and instill a range of curricula. For the most part, the early childhood community represents a fractured group of practitioners who are loosely coupled by licensure requirements that emphasize health, safety, and teacher/staff issues rather than academic expectations or curricula.

Government Support

While the debate over the role of government support for ECE continues, federal, state, and local governments do provide some funding for early childhood services and programs. As of 2007, federal support for ECE exists through three funding sources: providing funding for child care services as an incentive to mothers who receive public assistance and are trying to enter the labor force, providing funding for or access to services such as Head Start to children whom governmental agencies deem to be at risk due to factors such as poverty, language status, developmental delays, psychological issues, or a combination of these factors, and providing financial support to families and corporations through tax credits.

The passage of the Personal Responsibility and Work Opportunity Reconciliation Act (PRWORA) in 1996 altered previous federal social services by mandating recipients to achieve particular goals and reducing the length of time they could receive support, which increased the need for early childhood services for these families. For instance, the Temporary Assistance for Needy Families block grant, replaced programs such as Aid to Families with Dependent Children (AFDC), provides states with funds that they are to use to assist families in taking care of their children at home, and provides childcare for parents so that they can participate in job training. The Child Care and Development block grant provides funds to states to subsidize the child care expenses of low-income working parents, parents who are receiving training for work, and/or parents in school.

The most well known federally funded early childhood program is Head Start, which operates through the Department of Health and Human Services (DHHS). The DHHS directly funds local grantees to provide Head Start programs to promote children's school readiness by enhancing their social and cognitive development. Head Start grantees are to offer children and their families' educational, health, nutritional, social, and other services.

Finally, the federal government offers two types of tax credits: (1) the dependent care tax credit for families who use out-of-home ECE services (which began as the child care tax deduction in 1954 and converted to a child care tax credit in 1972) and (2) tax credits for employers who establish or provide access for their employees to child care services (which began in 1962).

At the state and local level, funding is more eclectic. The availability of programs and services that extend beyond federal funding depends on the individual state or local community. Some state governments supplement these federal funds, create their own programs for targeted populations, and encourage local participation in the process, while others do not.

The most common form of state involvement in ECE is kindergarten, and the fastest-growing program area among the states is prekindergarten (PreK) for four- and sometimes three-year-olds. As of 2006, only 14 states require children to attend kindergarten, 29 of the remaining 36 require school districts to offer kindergarten, and the remaining 7 states do not require school districts to offer any type of kindergarten. Forty states offer some form of PreK funding to local school districts and community organizations, and three states, Oklahoma, Georgia, and Florida offer all four-year-old children in their states access to prekindergarten, typically referred to as universal prekindergarten (UPK). Many states, such as New York, Illinois, and Massachusetts, are taking steps towards UPK.

Making the Case for Further Government Support of ECE

Those who support the expansion of federal, state, and local early childhood services typically make their case through two interconnected lines of reasoning. The first frames ECE as an investment. The second sees ECE as a necessary step to ready children for the increasing demands of elementary school.

The investment argument emerges from a collection of longitudinal studies that examine the effects of specific early childhood programs on a child's life. This research demonstrates that children who participate in high-quality early childhood programs are less likely as students to be retained or to require special education service and are more likely to graduate from high school. As adults, these children are more likely to be employed and not require social services and are less likely to be incarcerated (e.g., Reynolds, Ou, & Topitzes's [2004] analysis of the effects of the Chicago Parent Child Centers). As a result, every dollar that is invested in high-quality ECE programs will save taxpayers from having to spend additional monies on supplemental education and/or social services for that child through her lifetime.

The readiness argument, which follows a similar line of reasoning as the investment argument, states that in order to have students ready for the increasing demands of elementary school, government agencies need to provide families with access to high-quality early education services to ensure that their children are ready to learn.

Making the Case for Less Government Support of ECE

Those who oppose expanding the role of government also frame their argument through two lines of reasoning. The first, which takes a libertarian approach, contends that the government should limit its social responsibilities in taking care of children, except in the direst consequences, and allow the market to deem the need and role of ECE (e.g., the Cato Institute). The second, which takes a more conservative approach, argues that the government should implement policies that encourage family members to stay home and care for their children, such as tax credits for stay-at-home family members or incentives for corporations to encourage part-time employment.

EARLY CHILDHOOD EDUCATION

The following is a sample of organizations active in the debates surrounding early childhood education. Links to information about state early childhood education programs and family participation in such programs are provided.

Professional and Research Organizations that Support ECE

National Association for the Education of Young Children: http://www.naeyc.org
National Institute for Early Education Research: http://www.nieer.org
Pre-K Now: http://www.preknow.org
Foundation for Child Development: http://www.fcd-us.org
Association for Childhood Education International: http://www.acei.org

Organizations that Oppose the Expansion of ECE

The Cato Institute: http://www.cato.org
The Reason Foundation: http://www.reason.org
Concerned Women for America: http://www.cwfa.org

Statistics on Family Participation in ECE Programs

National Center for Education Statistics: http://nces.ed.gov

Information about State Early Childhood Programs and Kindergarten

Education Commission of the States: http://www.ecs.org

EARLY CHILDHOOD EDUCATION FROM THE PROGRESSIVE ERA THROUGH TODAY

As the Progressive Era took shape, ECE emerged along two streams of care: the kindergarten movement and the day nursery movement. Within these two movements, issues of gender, class, and cultural affiliation not only affected the goals of each program but also which children and their families had access to these care and education services.

Kindergarten

The U.S. kindergarten movement began in 1854 when Margarethe Meyer Schurz founded the first kindergarten in Watertown, WI. These early kindergartens were supplemental programs that were designed to foster a child's growth and development and to provide mothers with a break from their children. (See Beatty [1995] for a detailed history of the development of kindergarten in the United States.)

Public kindergarten emerged in the 1870s through the work of individuals such as Susan Blow in St. Louis and spread across numerous urban cities. As these programs became part of education systems across the United States, stakeholders implemented them to achieve many goals—all of which framed kindergarten as a necessary and not supplemental service. For instance, some supporters saw these programs as a form of "child rescue," others saw it as means to Americanize the influx of immigrants that were arriving in this country, and many viewed these programs as form of preparation for elementary school. These programs steadily grew because education and community stakeholders began to see more children as being unprepared for elementary school, and thus, this construct of the deficient child infuses itself within the need for an expansion of early childhood services.

The idea of children following a normal developmental path emerged out of the work of child psychologists such as G. Stanley Hall, who began his child study experiments in Pauline Shaw's charity kindergartens in Boston. Hall's studies led him as well as many others psychologists to question what type of experiences should be taking place in kindergarten as well as in the home to prepare children for a successful life.

Day Nurseries

Prior to kindergarten or elementary school entry, the dominant understanding of children's early childhood experiences was that their mothers were to raise them in their homes. The day nursery movement emerged as an intervention for mothers who had to seek employment to take care of their families so that they would not have to institutionalize their children. These nurseries emerged as the philanthropic projects of wealthy women who wanted to assist working poor and immigrant mothers in getting back on their feet so that they could take their rightful place in the home. Day nurseries emphasized patriotism and hygiene as part of their instruction and only sought governmental assistance for regulatory purposes to improve nursery program conditions. Even though these programs had less than appealing reputations, the need for their services far outstripped their availability. In most instances, particularly in the South, rural areas, and for African American families, kith and kin provided the majority of care for these families. Ironically, many of these working mothers struggled to find care for their own children while working for wealthier families as the caretakers of their children. (See Michel [1999] for a detailed history of the day nursery movement and the positioning of mothers and women in general within this and other debates over the role of government in child rearing and education.)

Nursery Schools

Academically, the increased interest in understanding child development by the work of theorists and researchers such as Hall, Gesell, Freud, Piaget, and others led to the growing child-study movement among universities. For instance, the Laura Spelman Rockefeller Memorial Foundation awarded significant sums of money to several colleges and universities to establish child study institutes. The institutes' lab schools began the nursery school movement, and middle-class families became attracted to the notion that science can enhance their child's development. Furthermore, this scientific emphasis on child development extended the view of ECE beyond the traditional academic notion of cognitive development that dominates elementary education. Early education included the child's social, emotional, physical, and cognitive development. This expanded view of learning caused conflict between early childhood educators and their elementary school colleagues as these programs became part of the elementary school environment.

The Federal Government Becomes Part of Early Childhood Education

The onset of the Great Depression resulted in a collapse of the day nursery movement for working mothers, and a majority of the ECE programs that remained were supplemental nursery programs used by middle-class families. In 1933, the Federal Emergency Relief Administration (FERA) changed this by starting a federally funded nursery school program as a means of employing schoolteachers and school staff. The custodial care of children was a secondary goal. The program was incorporated into the WPA in 1934 when FERA was terminated.

As the Great Depression ended and World War II began, the funding for this program dwindled. However, the need for female labor to support the war industry led to the Lanham Act, which funded over 3,000 child care centers to care for children whose mothers worked in defense-related industries.

When the Depression and the war ended, federal support for these custodial programs subsided and mothers were to return home to care for their children. However, the kindergarten movement had come to be seen by education stakeholders as a much-needed vehicle for preparing children for school. Kindergarten survived these two national crises, and by the 1940s it became a permanent fixture of many school systems across the United States.

Project Head Start

For the next 20 years, the federal government abstained from funding ECE programs until the implementation of Project Head Start in 1965. This project emerged from the Economic Opportunity Act and the Elementary and Secondary Education Act (ESEA) as a part of the Johnson Administration's War on Poverty.

This legislation shifted the role of the federal government in developing ECE and K–12 policy within the United States. Federal policymakers created legislation that defined the role of the federal government in ECE as a provider of intervention services that could alter the academic trajectory of particular populations of children. These policies identified the root cause of academic failure, which leads to economic failure, in the child's home environment. By identifying educational attainment as the means by which this cycle of poverty can be broken, policymakers defined the central role of ECE as readying students for school. ECE became a tool for intervention.

As soon as the federal government took on these roles in ECE and K–12 education, controversy arose. For instance, the Nixon administration responded to Johnson's Great Society education policies by creating the National Institute of Education, which investigated the return that society received for its investment in education. Furthermore, Nixon vetoed the Comprehensive Child Development Act of 1971, which was to expand the federal government's funding of child care and education while creating a framework for child services. Additionally, studies such as the Westinghouse Learning House's evaluation of Head Start in 1969 suggested that any gains in the IQs of students who participated in the program quickly faded, which raised concerns over the effectiveness of these government-funded programs.

Researchers responded to these critiques of Head Start by arguing that while increases in IQ might not be sustainable, students who participated in such programs were more successful academically and socially as they continued through school than those students who did not receive these services. These longitudinal studies, which examined a range of early childhood programs outside of Head Start, spawned the investment argument, which is outlined in the above.

This argument shifts the premise for funding ECE programs slightly. Rather than break the cycle of poverty for others, funding programs will save taxpayers money. Thus, this argument for ECE deemphasizes assisting families to be able to take care of their children at home, and rather, it contends that experts in ECE can design and implement programs that prepare the child, and in some cases the family, for success in compulsory schooling and later life.

Standards for Early Childhood Education

The emphasis on student performance that emerged during the Reagan administration put pressure on early childhood educators to align their practices with K–12 education. While such pressure on ECE programs has been around since the 1920s, particularly for kindergarten programs (see Beatty, 1995), organizations such as NAEYC began to produce position statements and documents that defined what empirical research identified to be appropriate teaching, learning, and assessment experiences for young children.

While these empirically based responses did deflect the pressures of accountability for children until later in their academic careers, recent federal and state standards-based accountability reforms have caused education stakeholders to again scrutinize what types of experiences students are having prior to their entry to elementary school. For instance, policymakers and early childhood stakeholders are debating the role of early learning standards, readiness assessments, and literacy and math instruction in early childhood programs.

Additional reforms that stakeholders are considering to improve children's preparation for elementary schooling include requiring student participation in full-day kindergarten programs, expanding prekindergarten services, improving the quality of early childhood programs, increasing training requirements for ECE teachers, and aligning early childhood programs across the field as well as with the K–12 education system. (See Cryer & Clifford [2003] for current discussions surrounding ECE policy.)

Whatever policies emerge, the recent history of education reform demonstrates that these reforms will be linked to increased accountability expectations, making the expansion of the field dependent on the ability of ECE programs to improve student performance.

An added question that is somewhat unique to ECE is who should be providing these services. For-profit centers have a long history in ECE and provide care for a significant population of children and their families. These providers include national and international companies (e.g., the Australian-based publicly traded for-profit child care corporation ABC Learning, which is the world's largest provider of childcare services and operates over 1,100 centers in the United States). Additionally, nonprofit and church-based centers provide a large portion of infant and toddler care for families. Thus, expanding or reforming early childhood services involves numerous stakeholders, and simply adding programs to the nation's public schools or implementing unfunded mandates has the ability to upset many who support as well as provide care for young children and their families.

SUMMARY

ECE has a long and unique history within the United States. Those who support the field have framed its need in numerous ways. Current advocates argue that ECE is a necessity for families in which the primary caregiver works outside the home, is a smart investment of public resources, or is a basic right for all children. Those who oppose its expansion contend that the government agencies should not be involved in child rearing, should not pay for additional social services, or should implement policies that encourage families to stay at home and take care of their children. Either way, the battle over ECE boils down to how stakeholders perceive the role of government agencies in financing the care and education of young children, and thus the debate will continue as long as there are children and families who need or desire out-of-home care.

Further Reading: Beatty, B., 1995, *Preschool education in America: The culture of young children from the colonial era to the present*, New Haven, CT: Yale University Press; Cryer, D., & Clifford, R. M., eds., 2003, *Early education and care in the USA*, Baltimore, MD: Paul H. Brookes Publishing Co.; Michel, S., 1999, *Children's interests/mothers'* *rights: The shaping of America's child care policy,* New Haven, CT: Yale University Press; Reynolds, A. J., Ou, S., & Topitzes, J., 2004, Paths of effects of early childhood intervention on educational attainment and delinquency: A confirmatory analysis of the Chicago child-parent centers, *Child Development,* 75(5), 1299–1328; Siegel, C., 2000, *What's wrong with day care? Freeing parents to raise their own children,* New York: Teachers College Press.

Christopher P. Brown

E-LEARNING

The digital revolution is transforming culture, communication, and commerce, but nowhere is faith in technology's power more clearly demonstrated than in the classroom.

E-learning is about much more than just plugging in a classroom computer. Some advocates predict that computers and modems will replace pencils and books, and others believe that brick-and-mortar schools (and all but elite universities) will soon be obsolete. E-learning has been defined as becoming literate in new mechanisms for communication: computer networks, multimedia, content portals, search engines, electronic libraries, distance learning, and web-enabled classrooms. E-learning is characterized by speed, technological transformation, and mediated human interactions, but virtual learning environments are not new. Institutionally sponsored distance education (correspondence courses) was in place as early as 1873 in the United States.

Many technology advocates believe e-learning will revolutionize the traditional classroom by augmenting textbooks with on-line resources; making lectures interactive and multimedia based; and extending discussions beyond the classroom walls via new communication platforms. Education beyond the classroom is also being transformed, with web-based tutoring, parental access to real-time student evaluation systems (rather than report cards), and student access to coursework from multiple locations. Advocates argue that e-learning represents a powerful convergence of technological opportunity and economic necessity, which makes it the basis of intimate contact between schools and private, entrepreneurial businesses, such as the technology companies whose hardware and software make e-learning possible.

The conventional wisdom in educational policy circles has been that children need to be introduced to computers early and that technology should be a strong presence in their school lives. In 1994, when the Clinton administration promised to connect every school to the Internet, only one in three schools and just 3 percent of classrooms were wired. Now, according to the National Center for Educational Statistics, 95 percent of schools and 63 percent of all classrooms had Internet access—a project that has cost $100 billion according to some estimates. Fourth-graders are now building their own Web sites, a suburban Chicago school district has purchased Palm Pilots for all their high school students, and virtual schools have been in operation for years, with students as young as five years old. The rationale most often proffered for e-learning is that it can more effectively develop knowledge workers with high-tech skills who are necessary to sustain the growth of the "new economy."

Recent polls indicate that most Americans believe PCs and the Internet are benign or beneficial. They certainly aren't afraid of technology and seem to believe the conventional wisdom that early exposure to technology is a good thing. More than 95 percent of parents of middle school and high school students recently surveyed see educational technology playing an important role in their children's education. A recent Kaiser Family Foundation study showed children six and under spend an average of two hours a day using screen media, about the same amount of time they spend playing outside, and well over the amount they spend reading or being read to (39 minutes).

The public, however, is somewhat conflicted about the impact of technology as they also blame it for accelerating already-frantic lifestyles or creating more problems than it solves. This was evident at the Wired Culture Forum, held in Toronto, when over 400 high school students raised serious questions about the rate at which technology is taking over their lives—their growing dependence on machines, the isolating nature of the Internet, and how technology threatens their privacy and ability to relate to others. A growing number of technology skeptics argue that the digital revolution has produced a variety of deleterious effects, such as disconnecting people from nature, their communities, and one another.

The generally laissez faire approach to technology adoption in education and other parts of our culture has produced a disturbing lack of critical thinking about technology's impact. Critics point to the fact that warning messages of environmental and child-advocacy groups about the negative impact of the automobile and television were largely ignored for decades. The public's lack of questioning about technology has been compared to the early euphoria over the automobile. The benefits are personally experienced, but the downside is more diffused. It took decades before people started to balance the advantages of individual mobility and convenience provided by cars, with the collective impact of smog and unsustainable development patterns.

E-LEARNING AND CHILDREN: A HARMFUL MIX?

The most remarkable fact about the rise of e-learning in K–12 and higher education, however, is the speculative nature of the effort. There is little or no evidence to support the beneficial claims of proponents of e-learning for children. The Alliance for Childhood (http://www.allianceforchildhood.net/) argues that the use of computers in education has had no proven positive effects on children and may even be physically, intellectually, and socially harmful, especially for kids under the age of 11. The report *Fool's Gold: A Critical Look at Computers and Childhood* grew out of the founding gathering of the U.S. branch of the Alliance for Childhood—an international effort of educators, physicians, and others concerned about the plight of children today and who believe that by working together in broad-based partnerships of individuals and organizations the lives of children can be improved. The alliance argues that the benefits of computers for preschool and elementary students are vastly overstated and the costs—in terms of money spent, loss of creative, hands-on educational opportunities, and damage to children's emotional health—are not accurately reported.

Do Computers Motivate Children to Learn Faster and Better?

The *Fool's Gold* report claims that 30 years of research on educational technology has produced just one clear link between computers and children's learning: "Drill-and-practice programs appear to improve test scores modestly—though not as much or as cheaply as one-on-one tutoring—on some standardized tests in narrow skill areas." Furthermore, Larry Cuban, a Stanford University education professor and former president of the American Educational Research Association, is quoted in the report saying that "there is no clear, commanding body of evidence that students' sustained use of multimedia machines, the Internet, word processing, spreadsheets, and other popular applications has any impact on academic achievement." When it comes to intellectual growth, the Alliance for Childhood argues that what is good for adults and older students is often inappropriate for youngsters. Rather than relying on information technologies, for example, face-to-face conversation with more competent language users is the one constant in studies of how children become expert speakers, listeners, and writers.

Cuban describes the strong support of technology advocates and educational policymakers for investment in "hard" (e.g., wiring and machines) and "soft" (e.g., technical support and professional development) infrastructure for schools in the face of so little evidence as "irrational exuberance." Moreover, while the alliance acknowledges that for children with certain disabilities technology offers clear benefits, for the majority of children computers pose (or contribute to) health hazards and serious developmental problems, such as repetitive stress injuries, eyestrain, obesity, and social isolation. More generally, the rapid technology changes of our era have accelerated our daily lives and caused the development of what James Gleick—in his book *Faster: The Acceleration of Just About Everything*—calls "hurry-sickness."

Must Five-Year-Olds Be Trained on Computers to Get the High-Paying Jobs?

A major part of the argument for placing computers in classrooms has essentially been a vocational one: Students should learn computer skills needed in the modern workplace. The need for "technological literacy" has become a myth that masks the fact that it is credentials, like a college degree, not computer-related skills that one needs to get a high-paying job in today's economy. Technology critics such as Cuban argue that the focus of education should be on developing morally responsible citizens and helping children, especially those who are labeled "at risk," gain the necessary skills and knowledge to earn those highly important credentials. The emphasis on technology is diverting us from the urgent social and educational needs of low-income children. As Massachusetts Institute of Technology professor Sherry Turkle, a clinical psychologist and author of *The*

Second Self: Computers and the Human Spirit, has asked: "Are we using computer technology not because it teaches best but because we have lost the political will to fund education adequately?"

There is strong evidence that major investments in areas such as expanded preschool and adult literacy education, reducing class size, and ensuring that teachers are qualified and well paid help children to avoid academic failure and produce more high school graduates who pursue higher education.

Do Computers Really "Connect" Children to the World?

The Alliance for Childhood claims that what computers actually connect children to are trivial games, inappropriate adult content, and aggressive advertising. The "distance" education technology promotes is the opposite of what all children need—close relationships with caring adults. The *Fool's Gold* report states, "Research shows that strengthening bonds between teachers, students, and families is a powerful remedy for troubled students and struggling schools. Overemphasizing technology can weaken those bonds. The National Science Board reported in 1998 that prolonged exposure to computing environments may create 'individuals incapable of dealing with the messiness of reality, the needs of community building, and the demands of personal commitments.'"

The bottom line for the Alliance for Childhood is that rather than placing our faith in technology to solve the problems of education, we should look more deeply into the needs of children.

Tech Tonic, a follow-up report to *Fool's Gold,* proposes seven reforms in education and family life that are aimed at freeing children from a passive attachment to screen-based entertainment and teach them about their "technological heritage" in a new way, rooted in the study and practice of technology "as social ethics in action" and in a renewed respect for nature. The seven reforms:

- Make human relationships and a commitment to strong communities a top priority at home and school
- Color childhood green to refocus education on children's relationships with the rest of the living world
- Foster creativity every day, with time for the arts and play
- Put community-based research and action at the heart of the science and technology curriculum
- Declare one day a week an electronic entertainment-free zone
- End marketing aimed at children
- Shift spending from unproven high-tech products in the classroom to children's unmet basic needs

Few would disagree with their conclusion that "the renewal of education requires personal attention to students from good teachers and active parents, strongly supported by their communities." We have yet to see the development of K–12 educational policy that attends to the full range of children's real world, low-tech needs.

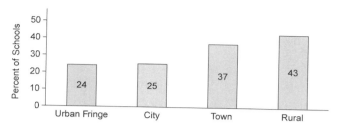

Figure E.1 Online Course Offerings.

ON-LINE DISTANCE LEARNING AND VIRTUAL SCHOOLS

The impact of e-learning, in the form of on-line distance education, on K–12 schools (and higher education) has been dramatic. A 2007 survey by the Sloan Foundation reports that almost two-thirds of public school districts are now offering on-line courses, and of those over 60 percent anticipate that on-line enrollment will increase significantly in the next two years. In the 2005–2006 school year, over 700,000 students were taking on-line courses in K–12 schools (compared to 40,000 in 2002). A 2006 survey of 2,200 colleges and universities found that nearly 3.2 million students took at least one on-line course in the fall of 2005, up from 2.3 million the previous year. Michigan recently became the first state to require high school students to participate in an "on-line learning experience." And 39 states now provide some form of professional development to educators over the Internet.

Virtual schools are in operation in 23 states. A number of states, such as Florida, Kentucky, and Illinois, have funded and established statewide virtual schools designed to meet the needs of large numbers of students. Virtual schools are primarily at the high school level; however, the number of enrolling middle school and elementary school students are growing. The Florida Virtual School, founded in 1997, now enrolls more than 45,000 students in grades 6 to 12.

There are currently 170 cyber charter schools (e.g., on-line schools that are publicly funded independent of public school systems) serving nearly 100,000 students. With the recent proliferation of virtual schools, there are new policy concerns regarding cyber-school funding, monitoring, and accountability. Critics of cyber charter schools, including teachers' unions and school boards' advocates in some states, have complained about questionable spending by some of those schools. Critics also argue that cyber schools are cheaper to run and ought to receive substantially less funding than brick-and-mortar schools. But advocates argue that costs for virtual charter schools are different and not necessarily lower, and as in regular schools teacher salaries make up the bulk of their budgets.

Distance learning proponents argue that on-line learning is more convenient and flexible for students; that students receive speedier feedback on assignments and get more personal attention; that students have more control over their learning experiences; that on-line learning enhances information technology

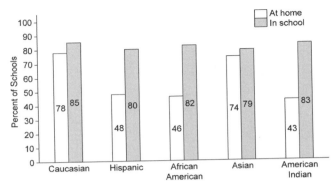

Figure E.2 Computers at Home and School.

skills and fosters new ways of constructing knowledge; and that it is quicker and more efficient. The availability of on-line learning in small rural school districts is seen as particularly important in order to provide students with a variety of course choices and, in some cases, the basic curriculum courses. In 2005, rural public schools were more likely than other localities to provide students with access to on-line distance learning for courses that would not be available otherwise.

As for the nature and quality of on-line education, it varies widely. Courses may be delivered fully on-line; as a hybrid blend of on-line and face-to-face delivery; or Web-enhanced, that is, essentially face-to-face with a small portion of the course material delivered via the Web-based technology. In some classes students merely read lecture notes and answer questions via e-mail. Other classes are more elaborate, with interactive CDs, downloadable videos, chat rooms, weblogs, wikis, and regularly scheduled sessions.

Distance education advocates point to a study by Thomas Russell as evidence that distance learning is at least the equivalent of traditional education in terms of narrowly defined outcomes. Russell's report, "The No Significant Difference Phenomenon" (2001), is a comparative research annotated bibliography on technology for distance education that examines the findings of 355 studies on various forms of distance learning—correspondence courses, televised classes, and Internet-based courses. Russell concludes that based on test scores and grades there is little difference between traditional and distance learning. Critics, on the other hand, argue that distance learning can never replace the classroom and the social experience that is a key part of life in schools.

The conflict between on-line education advocates and critics is at least in part based on contradictory conceptions of education. Is education merely a form of information-transfer ("banking" as Paulo Freire labeled it) or is education fundamentally about a relationship among people? Can computer-mediated interaction substitute for the human interaction/experience that is at the heart of learning? David Noble, a professor at York University in Toronto and author of *Digital Diploma Mills*, believes on-line higher education is being driven by profit, not educational, motives. Noble argues that the trend towards distance learning in higher education as implemented in North American universities today "is a battle between students and professors on one side, and university administrations and companies with 'educational products' to sell on the other. It is not a progressive trend towards a new era at all, but a regressive trend, towards the rather old era of mass-production, standardization and purely commercial interests."

Noble sees on-line learning as an exact parallel to the correspondence courses of the 1890s, where the main challenge was how to turn a profit and there was no economic incentive to improve instruction. Elite universities like Columbia and the University of Chicago lent their names to correspondence programs promoted as a chance for the average person to get an elite education. The problem, according to Noble, was that even the better programs had to compete with cheaper fly-by-night operations and, in an effort to cut costs, universities ended up paying readers—often graduate students—a piece rate to grade students' work. "The economics of correspondence learning was to put all your money into hype and promotion," according to Noble in a *Washington Post* article published last year, "You get a high rate of sign up. Students pay tuition up front, and instructors are paid a piece rate." The result was that quality suffered, and students (and then universities) got wise and abandoned correspondence learning.

On-line learning is a key element in the trend toward commercialization of education (which includes vouchers as well as charter schools and the for-profit educational management organizations running them). High-tech corporations are eager to partner with educational institutions because they see a large undeveloped market in a $200 billion a year industry and desire the instant integrity that university and school partnerships can offer to their educational products. Only 20 percent of schools districts with on-line programs deliver them directly to students. The vast majority of schools district rely on external providers—either postsecondary institutions (47 percent) or independent vendors (32 percent)—for fully on-line courses.

Recent business acquisitions confirm the commercialization trend in on-line K–12 education. In January 2007, the Apollo Group Inc., which owns the for-profit University of Phoenix (the largest private university in the United States and first to offer on-line courses) moved into the business of secondary education with its purchase of Insight Schools, which runs public, on-line high schools. Shortly afterward, Kaplan Inc. became the second higher-education company to move into the business of running virtual high schools. The company, which is owned by the Washington Post Company, acquired Sagemont Virtual, which runs a school called the University of Miami Online High School and a company that develops on-line high school courses.

Distance learning promises (perhaps vainly) to give cash-strapped education institutions the opportunity to peddle on-line versions of courses to new markets and potentially even turn a profit—squeezing more surplus value from faculty, the intellectual and creative sources of courses. On-line education also threatens to intensify the work of teachers and university faculty and undercut academic freedom. Faculty work harder and longer for on-line courses than for traditional classes without increased compensation.

Educational managers are also using technology to deprive educators of their intellectual property rights by claiming copyright over their course material. When an educator prepares a class Web page or an on-line course these are legally works for hire. This means that they are the property of the school or university, and the university can modify and distribute them as it sees fit, with or without the permission of the educator who created the page or course. Educators are deskilled and students short-changed when on-line courses are constructed by teachers for a flat fee and then administered by technicians and student work graded by graduate students.

Just as it does for culture, commerce, and communication, the digital revolution harbors great changes, both good and ill, for education. We cannot, however, expect that a laissez faire approach to technology adoption in education will necessarily produce positive educational experiences. Instead we must be aware of the potential downside of e-learning and demand wise use of technology for the collective good. Clearly the potential benefits of e-learning for learners and teachers are great, but what are the trade-offs? How do we employ technology for appropriate educational ends, as opposed to quick-fix pedagogical or budgetary ends? These are questions that should compel us to consider what role we want for technology in our lives and what might be missing in our schools and communities in a machine-dominated age. As learning technologies become more sophisticated so too must our critical assessments of their impact on our lives.

Further Reading: Alliance for Childhood, 2000, *Fool's gold: A critical look at computers and childhood,* College Park, MD: Alliance for Childhood; Alliance for Childhood, 2004 *Tech tonic,* College Park, MD: Alliance for Childhood; Noble, D., 2003, *Digital diploma mills,* New York: Monthly Review Press; Picciano, A. G., & Seaman J., 2007, *K–12 Online Learning: A survey of U.S. school district administrators,* Needham, MA: Sloan Foundation; Russell, T. L., 2001, *The no significant difference phenomenon,* Montgomery, AL: International Distance Education Certification Center, retrieved from http://www.nosignificantdifference.org/; Turkle, S., 1984, *The second self: Computers and the human spirit,* New York: Simon and Schuster.

E. Wayne Ross

ENGLISH LANGUAGE LEARNERS

Schools in the United States have responded differently at different times to the reality, challenge, and opportunity afforded by the presence of immigrant students and other English language learners (ELs). While many ELs are first- or second-generation immigrants, others may be Native Americans, Puerto Ricans, or Native Hawaiians. Regardless, those who work in public schools and the general public have thought about EL students typically in terms of how they present a challenge to the system. The challenge has involved how to most efficiently teach them English while at the same time making sure they are able to meet the demands of the curriculum appropriate to their age and grade level. As will become clear, the twin demands of simultaneously learning English and working at grade level are enormously difficult to achieve both for students and for the institutions serving them.

Current estimates place the total number of foreign-born in the United States at around 35 million, or 12 percent of the total population. Fifteen million, or 20 percent, of all U.S. school-aged children have immigrant parents and many, if not most, of these students are ELs. These young people, however, are very likely to live in poverty and less likely to complete high school, and their failure to complete secondary schooling—at times referred to as "push-outs" as opposed to dropouts—is related to the ways that English language instruction is structured, delivered, and conceptualized by school personnel, policymakers, and the general public. As such, English as a second-language instruction has huge implications for the educational system as a whole.

The way that English language instruction is conceptualized is also connected to how ELs themselves are positioned within popular discourses of nationhood. At present, they are lumped into the larger category of immigrants, which is currently the subject of a frenzied shouting match. Within this unpleasant interaction, descriptive statistics about immigrants and ELs produce anxiety and even panic. The fact that foreign-born students are more than twice as likely to drop out of school as native-born students is one of these numbers. Another is the fact that there are now almost 40 million "Latinos" residing in the United States, over half of whom are of foreign birth. Close to 20 percent of the school-aged population is made up of immigrant children or the children of immigrants. These children of immigrants constitute 10 million of those enrolled in schools, and their number will increase to 26 million by the year 2030. In other words, a growing percentage of ELs in the future will be born in the United States, they will be citizens of this country, and they will constitute the future work force. As such, responding to this reality is of vital interest to all educators, and indeed, to the nation as a whole.

DEMAGOGUERY CONCERNING IMMIGRANTS

Of course, the anxiety concerning immigrants and their effects on the nation are nothing new. In fact, it should be pointed out that immigrants constituted a larger overall percentage of the population at the turn of the last century than they do currently. At that time, the English language was never in any danger of being replaced, U.S. culture was not negatively impacted, and U.S. institutions were not threatened. The presence of large numbers of non-English-speaking residents, however, has always attracted attention in the United States. Language becomes an issue whenever the majority feels threatened politically, socially, or economically.

At present, immigrants are attracting more negative attention than ever from the media, policymakers, and the public. In fact, the lines between foreigners, terrorists, and immigrants—regardless of their legal status and particularly those of Mexican origin—have been purposely blurred. Precipitating events include the terrorist attacks of 9/11 on New York and Washington D.C., the U.S. government's war on terror, and nativist reaction to growing immigrant communities.

This larger context influences decisions such as to deport high school graduates raised almost entirely in the United States. It also shapes the kind of thinking that blames English language learners for low local and state test scores.

Pierre Bourdieu in *Practical Reason* calls the development of these ways of thinking about immigrants and ELs "the obviousness of ordinary experience." He goes on to explain that this obviousness or common wisdom is not neutral, natural, or without political consequences. There are those who benefit from these ways of thinking and those who are excluded, marginalized, and scapegoated. Immigrants, and by extension, many EL students, are presented as illegitimate, illegal, criminal, undesirable, and unwanted. The recurring politicization and scapegoating of immigrants reflects a public anxious about its national identity. ELs have always found themselves squarely within this controversy.

Groups with political and economic power are positioned to shape and influence the kinds of educational opportunities the state provides for children. Those groups without political power are pressured and compelled to assimilate in both the realms of language and culture. In the following section, we provide evidence for our line of reasoning.

FOUR COMMUNITIES AND THEIR EXPERIENCES IN U.S. SCHOOLS

From its beginning as a nation, the United States had a wide variety of languages spoken within its borders. At that time, linguistic diversity was not seen as a detriment to the country. However, this changed as these populations— earliest among them the German-speaking enclaves in Pennsylvania—and the country grew in size. Benjamin Franklin, specifically, was concerned about what he considered to be the inability of the German populations to assimilate to the prevailing American cultural ideals. Initial suspicion resulted in efforts to insert the English language into the German communities through schooling. German parents, however, successfully resisted what they considered to be a heavy-handed attempt to marginalize the German language by passing their own protective legislation.

The rural areas of the United States contained large numbers of German speakers, and many of their schools provided instruction solely in German. The laws of the day did not mandate the use of any given language in American schools, and, in fact, by the mid-1800s any hint of requiring English in the schools often provoked a political backlash. Specifically, German communities in Ohio fought successfully to use the German language for instruction. German, in this case, was intended as an addition to English, not as a substitute. The German population, then, over time, gained political and economic power, and they wielded it effectively in order to secure educational opportunities for their communities.

This community established a network of German-language schools throughout the German triangle between Milwaukee, St. Louis, and Cincinnati. These schools flourished up until the outbreak of WWI when anti-German sentiment instigated legislation that specifically targeted and banned the use of German in the schools. The use of both oral and printed German was criminalized, and the use of German in the schools, a legacy extending back to the founding of the country, was almost entirely eliminated.

Some ethnolinguistic communities were not able to attain the same kinds of political power as German-Americans to determine the scope of their educational opportunities. Indigenous populations, for example, were subjected to extreme forces of linguistic imperialism, and the result has been language death for many of these groups. One mechanism that accelerated this process was the use of boarding schools, which were put in place by the Bureau of Indian Affairs, an agency of the federal government. Children were often forcibly removed from their homes and communities, and use of their languages was prohibited. In fact, they were punished for the use of any language other than English. As a result of this treatment, generations of Native Americans experienced massive school failure. Further, it has been estimated that only 11 percent of the languages currently spoken by indigenous peoples in North America are being taught to children. Policies of forced assimilation and language extermination speak to the lack of legitimacy, both politically and economically, afforded Native American populations within the greater American society.

Another example of language policy levied against a specific population is the case of Puerto Rico. Similar to Native America policies, the language policies enacted in Puerto Rico emerged from within a context of American colonialism. Initially, English was installed as the language of instruction in lieu of Spanish. Local response was that of defiance, which led to a 50-year period of revolving language legislation. Of interest in this case is that with each subsequent shift in policy, the civic action and the political power wielded by the citizens of Puerto Rico led to an increased level of Spanish use in the classroom. What's more, the vacillation between mandates for the use of English and Spanish helped instill a fierce nationalism in the people of Puerto Rico, who used the issue of language as a political vehicle through which they could resist the forces of American imperialism.

An example of a community utilizing its legitimate status toward educational ends can be seen in New Mexico. In 1850, Spanish speakers were the largest language group in the territory. In 1910, in pursuance of statehood, New Mexico was required by Congress to make English the language of instruction and also a requirement for holding state offices and positions. Despite this requirement, the citizenry of New Mexico ratified a constitution that included provisions protecting language rights for Spanish speakers. Specifically, the educational regulations included in the constitutions provided that teachers were to learn English and Spanish and protected the educational rights of Spanish-speaking students. Effectively, New Mexico succeeded in making Spanish equal to English through their constitutional provisions.

LANGUAGE LEGISLATION IN THE TWENTIETH CENTURY

Interestingly, compulsory schooling was not firmly established in the United States until the end of the 1880s. Up until that time schools needed to actively recruit students, and they targeted immigrants and their children, particularly those of European backgrounds. These students and their families were attracted by the offer of instruction in their native languages. This is one reason why German-language schooling was so widespread up until anti-German hysteria broke out around WWI. The WWI period was a watershed moment in the United States for the history of teaching ELs.

During that period, the great Americanization campaign raged until the end of WWI. The campaign was designed to protect the United States from "ignorant, incendiary foreigners" but after the war, it lost momentum. The campaign's goals had been to push immigrants to seek citizenship, pressure them to learn English, and compel them to adopt unquestioning reverence for American institutions. Because of widespread failure, these goals were later transformed to that of denying admission to future waves of immigration, a mindset that appears to have reemerged in the last decade. Immigrants were considered incorrigible and unassimilable after WWI; ironically, this conclusion is far from the modern myth of enthusiastic immigrant response to nativistic pressure to learn English and deny their cultural heritage.

From 1929 until 1941, an immigration hiatus, accompanied by an era of arrests, deportations, and massive oppression of immigrants, lasted until the labor shortages caused by WWII. At that time, the United States and Mexico negotiated a binational treaty that came to be known as the Bracero (farmhand) Program. This program, punctuated by economic downturns and periodic harassing and deporting of foreigners, lasted until 1964. Hundreds of thousands of Mexican workers entered the United States both legally and illegally during this period until Congress passed the Civil Rights Act in 1964, and then Congress completely overhauled the Nationality and Immigration Act in 1965. These changes resulted in the abolition of the Bracero Program. What is important about these legislative landmarks is that they were accompanied by both growing numbers of English learners in the schools and a growing dissatisfaction with their academic progress. For many, this lack of progress was due to these students' lack of English proficiency.

This explanation for the unsatisfactory school progress of large numbers of "language minority" students, particularly in the Southwest, drove passage of the Bilingual Education Act in 1968. The Bilingual Education Act, or Title VII of the Elementary and Secondary Education Act, provided federal funding for school districts to aid in the development of educational programs serving language minority students. This act made seed funding available to school districts that wanted to provide some native-language instruction to their students. It did not require native-language instruction, but the fact that the federal government was making funds available was a sea change in thought concerning the education of English learners. The encouragement and use of languages other than English in U.S. schools was something that, except in isolated cases, had not occurred since the onset of WWI, a period of almost 50 years.

The issue of equitable education for nonnative English speakers did not truly come to a head until the landmark decision of *Lau v. Nichols* (1974). Essentially, the Court determined that school districts had to make special efforts to make instruction comprehensible to English learners. Failure to do so was considered the withholding of educational opportunities and thus was a violation of the Civil Rights Act of 1964. As important as *Lau v. Nichols* was, the decision did not prescribe how educators were required to implement instruction. Educational administrators were provided with more guidance concerning how to best meet the needs of ELs with the *Castañeda v. Pickard* (1981) decision. Programs designed for ELs now needed to adhere to quality controls centered on theory, practice, and results. Programs had to be based on sound educational theory, and schools were required to hire qualified personnel. They also had to monitor student progress while they were enrolled in the program. A number of recent developments have occurred that prescribe English-only language assistance and limit the amount of time students have access to even this service.

CURRENT ERA

The present time may be viewed in the future as a moment when raw ethnic politics came to dominate instructional decision making for ELs in the form of citizen- (corporate-?) sponsored ballot initiatives. These initiatives, known as Proposition 227 in California, Proposition 203 in Arizona, Question 2 in Massachusetts, and Proposition 31 in Colorado, have either banned or sought to ban bilingual education. These referenda passed in California, Arizona, and Massachusetts but failed in Colorado. Their effects on student performance are now being debated, with antibilingual education advocates claiming higher levels of student learning and those in favor of bilingual education claiming that student learning has been curtailed. With the failure of Colorado's initiative and increasing dissatisfaction with EL student performance in the other states, it may be that attempts to impose instructional approaches via the electorate have been exhausted. What is clear is that the learning gap between ELs and mainstream students has not yet been closed.

CONCLUSION

Special language services for ELs have always been plagued by the damned if you do and damned if you don't syndrome. If students do well in terms of their English learning, they are mainstreamed into general education classes where they are no longer considered ELs. If they do poorly and continue to need special language assistance, the instructional services they receive are deemed to be failures because of their lack of progress.

The syndrome is reflective of mainstream thinking of ELs as it places them in an impossible situation. They are blamed for not knowing English or for coming to school without the necessary linguistic and social capital to properly benefit from the programs offered. Further, the programs themselves fail to deliver what the students need in terms of language and cultural knowledge. At this point, students' failure is certified by the school system and made official because of low rates of literacy, low academic achievement, and high dropout rates. These results are characteristic of colonizing practices. They reflect a dominating group's views vis-a-vis the colonized, the conquered, or the enslaved. These results are not characteristic of the kind of outcomes one finds for groups that are able to design instructional opportunities for their own communities.

Current efforts to legislate rather than create instructional and programmatic solutions to the achievement gap reflect mainstream assumptions of ELs, their families, and their communities. These assumptions include the belief that ELs must be forced to learn English, that they don't value education, and, also, the unsubstantiated view that they aren't willing to work hard to profit from their schooling. These legislative efforts illustrate our original contention that most ELs and their associated communities have been marginalized and excluded from the political and economic arenas. In other words, neoconservative re-engineering of educational policy has eliminated minority voices almost entirely from most influential decision bodies.

Further Reading: Bourdieu, P., 1998, *Practical reason,* Stanford, CA: Stanford University Press; Heath, S. B., 1981, English in our language heritage, in C. A. Ferguson & S. B. Heath (Eds.), *Language in the USA* (pp. 6–20), Cambridge: Cambridge University Press; Larsen, L. J., 2004, *The foreign-born population in the United States: 2003,* in U.S. Census Bureau: U.S. Department of Commerce, retrieved March 29, 2006, from http://www.census.gov/population/www/socdemo/foreign/cps2003.html; National Center for Education Statistics, 2005, *Highlights from the 2003 international adult literacy and lifeskills survey (all),* Washington, DC: U.S. Department of Education; National Education Association of the United States, 1966, *The invisible minority,* Washington DC: Department of Rural Education, National Education Association; Schmid, C. L., 2001, *The politics of language,* New York: Oxford University Press; Tienda, M., & Mitchell, F., 2006, *Multiple origins, uncertain destinies,* Washington DC: National Academies Press.

Robert T. Jiménez and Brian C. Rose

EVALUATION

The genesis of educational evaluation is generally understood to be in the stipulations of the 1965 Elementary and Secondary Education Act (ESEA). Part of Lyndon Johnson's War on Poverty, the ESEA provides federal assistance to schools, communities, and children in need. With current funding of about $9.5 billion annually, the ESEA continues to be the single largest source of federal funding to K–12 schools. Through its many title programs, and especially Title I, ESEA has been a major force in focusing how and what is taught in schools, as well as the ways those activities are evaluated.

Educational evaluation is itself a diverse sub-area within evaluation as a discipline and a profession. Educational evaluation may focus on the value, merit, worth, or effectiveness of programs, curriculum, teachers, student learning, schools, and school systems.

THE EIGHT-YEAR STUDY

While the passage of ESEA marks the beginning of the formalization of educational evaluation, one prior event, the Eight-Year Study, also played an important role in educational evaluation, although it is more often associated with developments in curriculum theory and design. The Eight-Year Study involved 30 high schools dispersed throughout the United States serving diverse communities. Each school developed its own curriculum suited to its community and each was released from government regulations as well as the need for students to take college entrance examinations. With dissension early in the project about how its success should be evaluated, a young Ralph Tyler was brought on board to direct the evaluation, which was funded by the Rockefeller Foundation. Out of the Eight-Year Study came what is now known as the Tyler Rationale, the commonsense idea that what students were supposed to learn should determine what happened in classrooms and how evaluation should be done. The basic questions of the Tyler rationale are now famous:

1. What educational purposes should the school seek to attain?
2. What educational experiences can be provided that are likely to attain these purposes?
3. How can these educational experiences be effectively organized?
4. How can we determine whether these purposes are being attained?

The first three questions point most particularly to curricular and instructional intentions and plans, and the fourth is the stepping-off point for evaluation.

Tyler's evaluation team devised many curriculum-specific tests, helped to build the capacity for each school to devise its own measures of context-specific activities and objectives, identified a role for learners in evaluation, and developed data records to serve intended purposes (including descriptive student report cards). All of these developments resonate with conceptual developments in evaluation from the 1970s to the present. The notion of opportunity to learn is related to the curriculum sensitivity of measures; the widespread focus on organizational evaluation capacity building resonates with the Tylerian commitment to helping schools help themselves in judging the quality and value of their work; democratic and empowerment approaches, indeed all stakeholder based approaches, resonate with the learners' active participation in evaluation; and the naturalistic approaches to evaluation resonate with the use of behavioral descriptive data.

The Eight-Year Study ended in 1941 and was published in five volumes in 1942, an event that was overshadowed by its unfortunate coincidence with U.S. troops taking an active role in World War II. Nonetheless, Ralph Tyler and the Eight-Year Study evaluation staff provided a foundation, whether always recognized or not, for future education evaluators.

THE ELEMENTARY AND SECONDARY EDUCATION ACT

When ESEA was passed in 1965, the requirement that the expenditure of public funds be accounted for thrust educators into a new and unfamiliar role. Educational researchers and educational psychologists stepped in to fill the need for evaluation created by ESEA. But the efforts of practitioners and researchers alike were generally considered to be only minimally successful at providing the kind of evaluative information envisioned. The compensatory programs supported by ESEA were complex and embedded in the complex organization of schooling.

Since the federal politicians, especially ESEA architect Robert Kennedy, were primarily interested in accountability, evaluation requirements for ESEA, especially for Title I—the largest compensatory program—emphasized uniform procedures and comparable data at the state and national levels, a direction many evaluators found misdirected. During this period, the advances in educational evaluation were, at least in part, over and against the federal approach to evaluating especially Title I programs, primarily a focus on student achievement (expressed as normal curve equivalents). Evaluators like Elliot Eisner, Robert Stake, Egon Guba, Lee Cronbach, and others challenged the idea that evaluations of schools and education should be narrowly focused on student achievement. Education, they suggested, was more complex and nuanced, and a broader range of criteria and evidence were necessary for judging educational programs.

The tension between meeting federally mandated reporting requirements and local needs for evaluative information was a significant part of the debate. School districts did the minimum to meet the federal reporting guidelines, but at the same time often looked for guidance in how to sincerely evaluate what was happening in local schools. While school districts may have needed only one person to meet the reporting mandate, a broader local interest lead to the creation of evaluation departments in many, and certainly all of the large, school districts.

The late 1960s and into the 1980s were the gold rush days of educational evaluation. During this time, models of evaluation proliferated, and truly exciting intellectual work was being done, especially in education. Borrowing not only from traditional social science approaches to inquiry, educational evaluators mined other disciplines for strategies. Judicial approaches, auditing, systems design, connoisseurship, investigative strategies, case studies, and ethnography found their way into the literature on educational evaluation. In the late 1970s, a number of professional education associations joined together to create standards for evaluating educational programs, which direct both evaluators and consumers of evaluators to insure that evaluations are useful, feasible, conform to professional senses of propriety, and are accurately done.

THE NATIONAL ASSESSMENT OF EDUCATIONAL PROGRESS

The National Assessment of Educational Progress (or NAEP), sometimes referred to as the nation's report card, was also created at about the same time as the authorization of ESEA, building on and systematizing a much longer history of efforts to use educational statistics to improve and expand public education. Francis Keppel, the U.S. Commissioner of Education from 1962 to 1965 and a former dean of the Harvard School of Education, lamented the lack of information about the academic achievement of American students.

Under the direction of Ralph Tyler (Tyler's intellectual legacy in evaluation is huge, as noted by his continued involvement in pivotal events in educational evaluation), NAEP developed as a system to test a sample of students on a range of test items, rather than the simple testing of all students with the same test items. And, to allay fears that NAEP would be used to coerce local and state educational authorities, the results were initially released for four regions only. NAEP has continued to develop, early on largely with the use of private funding from the Carnegie Corporation, and the early fears of superintendents and professional associations (such as the National Council for Teachers of English) turn out to be well founded. State level NAEP scores are indeed now available. This shift in the use of NAEP occurred during the Reagan administration with then Secretary of Education Terrel Bell's infamous wall chart. With a desire to compare states' educational performance, indicators available for all states were needed, and NAEP filled that bill. Southern states, such as Arkansas, under then governor Bill Clinton, applauded the use such comparisons that would encourage competition, a presumed condition for improvement.

During these halcyon years in educational evaluation, much evaluation was publicly funded, primarily by the U.S. Department of Education, but also by other federal agencies such as the National Science Foundation in addition to many foundations such as Carnegie, Rockefeller, Ford, and Weyerhaeuser. Discussions of how best to judge if education and schooling are good contributed to a lively national debate about what counts as good education and schooling.

For example, the small number of meta-evaluations conducted during this time focused primarily on whether the evaluation was fair and in the public interest. Two good examples are the meta-evaluation of Follow-Through (that thoroughly criticized Alice Rivlin's planned variation experiment as an evaluation method that did not do justice to the unique contributions of follow-through models in local communities) and the meta-evaluation of Push-Excel, Jesse Jackson's inspirational youth program that was undone by Charles Murray's (co-author with Richard Herrnstein of *Bell Curve: Intelligence and Class Structure in American Life*) evaluation, which failed to consider the program on its own terms in the context of local communities.

ACCREDITATION

One form of educational evaluation that has been in place since the 1960s is accreditation, the process of self-study and visitation by a team of peers that is common in professional education and post-secondary institutions. Abraham Flexner's report on the quality of medical schools created the process that is now commonly used by accrediting bodies. While accreditation has been critical for post-secondary and professional programs, it has never been a serious form of educational evaluation for elementary and secondary schools.

THE NEW NEOLIBERAL ERA AND EDUCATIONAL EVALUATION

The recent reauthorization of ESEA, now called No Child Left Behind, reinforces the need for evaluation. But unlike the more general expectation for evaluation that typified the original ESEA evaluation mandate, NCLB is decidedly more prescriptive about how education should be evaluated, largely because it includes sanctions for failure to perform. While earlier versions of ESEA focused on student performance, there were vague standards and no threats for failing to show progress. NCLB invokes the particular construct of "annual yearly progress" (AYP), and continued funding from the federal government is now dependent on each school making "continuous and substantial progress" toward academic proficiency by *all* subgroups of students. Sanctions for poor performance changed the equation. Not making AYP can result in districts paying to bus children to other schools, being required to provide supplemental and remedial services outside the regular school day, or restructuring of schools (for example, new staff or schools run by educational management organizations).

While the 1965 authorization of ESEA opened new frontiers and contributed significantly to the discipline of evaluation, NCLB has narrowed the scope of evaluation. Few federal funds are now spent on educational evaluation, and the burden of evaluation has been shifted to the state and local levels through student testing. NCLB mandates what counts as evaluation (acceptable indicators, what counts as progress, consequences for lack of progress) but provides no funding to carry out the mandate. George W. Bush declared that with the reauthorization of NCLB, "America's schools will be on a new path of reform, and a new path of results." No one would disagree. Teaching has become less professional, more mechanical and test driven; business and profits for the test-publishing and scoring companies have increased markedly, even though the testing is often misdirected or misused (such as using norm-referenced tests for criterion-referenced purposes); and schools chase unattainable goals (like AYP) out of fear.

The current narrow evaluation focus of NCLB (standardized tests for evaluating student learning and schools) evolved as a result of changes in political values. The current public and governmental neoliberalist sentiment (an ideology shared by Republicans and Democrats) has had major implications for government policies beginning in the 1970s but increasingly prominent since 1980.

Concerns about a crisis in American schools are formulated around constructs such as international competitiveness and work productivity. In other words, our schools are meant to serve the interests of the economy. *A Nation at Risk,* published in 1983, was the clarion call for educational reform: "The educational foundations of our society are presently being eroded by a rising tide of mediocrity that threatens our very future as a nation and a people. . . . We have, in effect been committing an act of unthinking, unilateral educational disarmament."

Although it took a few years, in 1989 President Bush and the state governors called an education summit in Charlottesville. That summit established six broad educational goals to be reached by the year 2000. President Clinton signed Goals 2000 into law in 1994. Goals three and four were related specifically to academic achievement and thus set the stage for both what educational evaluation should focus on and how.

In 1990, the federally funded procedures for moving the country toward accomplishment of these goals were established. The National Education Goals

Panel (NEGP) and the National Council on Education Standards and Testing (NCEST) were created and charged with answering a number of questions: What is the subject matter to be addressed? What types of assessments should be used? What standards of performance should be set?

In 1996, a national education summit was attended by 40 state governors and more than 45 business leaders. They supported efforts to set clear academic standards in the core subject areas at the state and local levels, and the business leaders pledged to consider the existence of state standards when locating facilities. Another summit followed in 1999 and focused on three key challenges facing U.S. schools—improving educator quality, helping all students reach high standards, and strengthening accountability—and agreed to specify how each of their states would address these challenges. And a final summit occurred in 2001, when governors and business leaders met at the IBM Conference Center in Palisades, New York, to provide guidance to states in creating and using tests, including the development of a national testing plan. The culminating event to this series of events beginning in the early 1980s was the passage of NCLB.

The heavy hand of business interests and market metaphors in establishing what schools should do and how we should evaluate what they are doing is evident in the role business leaders have played in the education summits. The infrastructure that supports this perspective is broad and deep. The Business Roundtable, an association of chief executive officers of U.S. corporations, and the even more focused Business Coalition for Education Reform, a coalition of 13 business associations, are political supporters and active players in narrowing evaluation of education to the use of standardized achievement tests.

Simultaneous with the passage of NCLB, the U.S. Department of Education funds less evaluation partly because of a much-narrowed definition of what the government now considers good evaluation and partly because the U.S. Department of Education sees itself as the judge of educational evaluation and research, rather than its sponsor. Educational evaluation that is currently funded by the U.S. Department of Education is overwhelmingly contracted out to large research firms such as Mathematica Policy Research, Abt & Associates, Westat, RMC Research Corporation, MDRC, American Institutes for Research, and the like.

The U.S. Department of Education recognizes four kinds of program evaluation: (1) continuous improvement (employing market research techniques), (2) program performance data (use of performance based data management systems), (3) descriptive studies of program implementation (use of passive, descriptive techniques like surveys, self-reports, and case studies), and (4) rigorous field trials of specific interventions (field trials with randomized assignment). It is this last sort of evaluation that is the pièce de résistance, what are referred to as the "new generation of rigorous evaluations." It is this evaluation approach that permits entry to the What Works Clearinghouse (WWC) of the US. Department of Education's Institute of Education Sciences (IES), and thus an intervention, practice, or curriculum earns the governmental imprimatur of an "evidence based best practice."

Evaluations must preferably be randomized clinical trials, perhaps quasi-experimental or regression discontinuity designs. Few if any educational evaluations have been of this sort; indeed much of the work since the 1960s has been directed to creating different evaluation methods and models of evaluative inquiry (not just borrowed psychological research methods) that answer evaluative questions. Questions about feasibility, practicability, needs, costs, intended and unintended outcomes, ethics, and justifiability—essential questions in all evaluation—are not the focus.

The demand to accept randomized clinical trials (RCT) as the gold standard in evaluation has been forcefully championed and forcefully resisted—for example, the American Evaluation Association (AEA) responded to the U.S. Department of Education's call for feedback on this policy. AEA's response challenges the notion that causation is knowable only when using RCTs, and declares that RCTs are sometimes unethical in educational contexts and that there are many other evaluation methodologies that are adequate, appropriate, and rigorous. A group of current and past AEA members responded with a "not-AEA" position defending the primacy of RCTs.

Educational evaluation has evolved and will continue to evolve. In its early days educational evaluation bore the mark of progressivism. Education and its evaluation were supported by public funding and defined as a public good, in the interest of all. Evaluation reflected these values (including efficiency, social justice, and democracy) and was financially supported with public funds. In the 1980s the values of progressivism gave way to the emerging values of neoliberalism. All evaluation requires the specification of the good-making qualities of what is being evaluated. And these good-making qualities are socially constructed; therefore the dominant approach to education evaluation reflects the current sociopolitical zeitgeist. In the current state of neoliberalism and neoconservatism, the evaluation of education increasingly reflects those values, including commodification, privatization, and Judeo-Christian morality. The practice of evaluation (like many social practices) is a reflection of the values, beliefs, and preferences of the time.

Further Reading: Aikin, W. M., 1942, *The story of the Eight Year Study,* New York: Harper and Brothers, retrieved February 13, 2007, from http://www.8yearstudy.org; Joint Committee on Standards for Educational Evaluation, 1994, *The program evaluation standards,* 2nd ed. Newbury Park, CA: Sage Publications; Jones, L. V., & Olkin, I., eds., 2004, *The nation's report card: Evolution and perspectives,* Bloomington, IN: Phi Delta Kappa Educational Foundation; Mathison, S., & Ross, E. W., eds., 2004, *Defending public schools: The nature and limits of standards based educational reform and testing,* Westport, CT: Greenwood Press.

Sandra Mathison

FINANCE

Education finance has a long history of substantial conflict. Since the inception of the common school more than a century ago, battles have waged over the level of funding a school district receives, whether additional resources are effective, or determining the best mix of resources to improve student achievement. Such contentious fiscal issues evolve from values deeply embedded in U.S. ideology—efficiency, liberty, and equality. These three values are dynamic and often in conflict with one another. Tracing the historical debate over the importance of the values of efficiency, liberty, and equality provides insight into the controversies embedded in the evolution of education finance as a field.

CONTROVERSIES IN EDUCATION FINANCE: FROM PAST TO PRESENT

U.S. education history can be characterized as a nineteenth-century effort at constructing a scaffold for public schooling; the twentieth century, or at least the latter half of it, as a quest to ensure access to the system; and an emerging twenty-first-century challenge to render the system more effective. No doubt, such a brief summary fails to appreciate the alterations in policy and practice that have occurred during the financing of America's schools. Nevertheless, it captures the evolution of school finance as a field. The progression of education finance from the fringes of policymakers' concern to a more central role is not without debate. One can best appreciate controversies that have helped shape the field of education finance by examining their genesis during past periods.

Equality I: Access

The principle challenge facing education policymakers in the nineteenth century and early twentieth century was fashioning a system of common schooling that could contribute to and sustain a democracy. Against the backdrop of a society transitioning from an agrarian way of life to an industrialized economy, waves of immigrants in need of employment, housing, and schooling sought the American dream. The primary means for achieving this goal was education—the great equalizer.

This era was dominated by those who strove to promote democratic ideals through the implementation of a system of financial mandates and incentives to influence expansion of the education system. State and federal grants concentrated on inducements for local districts to construct public schools, staff them, extend the range of grades and services offered, and share costs between local and state sources. By the conclusion of the nineteenth and beginning of the twentieth centuries, under the leadership of Ellwood Patterson Cubberley, Paul R. Mort, and George D. Strayer, distribution formulas were developed that combined revenue from local property taxes with state subsidies and established financial incentives for localities to extend education offerings. State statutes mandating the formation of schools had their intended effects—by the early 1900s, 80 percent of the nation's school-age children were enrolled.

In the decades following the end of World War II, it became evident to policymakers and educators alike that the original system of common schools, however well intended, had bypassed or shortchanged important populations. Disadvantaged racial and ethnic minorities, those with disabilities, the indigent immigrant who spoke limited English, and students who resided in property-poor locations became major targets for school improvement.

Inequalities in the availability of resources to provide various student groups access to equitable education sparked decades of litigation and legislation. Commencing with the post–World War II civil rights movement, assessments of the equality of educational opportunity among racial and other groups in the United States were mandated. Judicial and legislative steps were taken, allowing a wider portion of the population to gain access to public schools. *Brown v. Board of Education* (1954) struck racially segregated schools. *Lau v. Nichols* (1974) facilitated provision of services to limited English proficient students. Disabled students were included in public schools by courts and then by Congress with the Education for All Handicapped Children Act (1976). The 1978 Higher Education Act's Title VI extended these issues of equity to include parity of resources and services based on gender. In *Plyler v. Doe* (1980), courts extended the rights of a public education to illegal immigrant students.

Beginning in the 1960s, education finance theorists provided the conceptual foundation to support efforts aimed at achieving greater equity in revenue generation and distribution. Thanks particularly to the pioneering efforts of Arthur Wise, John E. Coons, William H. Clune, and Stephen Sugarman, legal arguments were constructed applying the U.S. Constitution's Fourteenth Amendment Equal Protection Clause to intrastate finance distribution disparities. A result of their efforts was what today is known as the Principle of Fiscal Neutrality, specifying that a link between local or household wealth and quality of a child's schooling is unacceptable. Formation of this idea enabled the education finance equal protection crusade to proceed.

The quest for fiscal equity sustained a major setback with the Texas Supreme Court's decision in *San Antonio v. Rodriguez* (1973). Here the Court rejected arguments that education was a fundamental right under the U.S. Constitution. Plaintiff's failure to prevail in *Rodriguez* redirected the equal protection crusade to a state-by-state endeavor.

From the decade of the 1970s emerged watershed equity lawsuits challenging the state constitutionality of school funding arrangements. In New Jersey, the judicial system's decision in *Robinson v. Cahill* (1973) eventually undid the state's school funding structure, which failed to apportion funds equally between school districts. Similarly, the California Supreme Court declared the state's funding disparities across schools districts in violation of the state constitution in *Serrano v. Priest* (1976).

Defendants in early equal protection cases attempted to capitalize upon skepticism that "dollars did not make scholars." This line of reasoning stemmed from the 1966 release of the Coleman Report, also known as "Equality of Educational Opportunity." The federal report was commissioned in an effort to understand the influence of variations in resources on student achievement. Among the conclusions of this landmark publication was that school resources were less important than a student's social and economic circumstances.

Findings of the Coleman Report sparked a debate about the influence of fiscal resources on student achievement, a controversy that remains problematic. Defendants in court cases continue, sometimes persuasively, to argue that dollars may be a necessary threshold for operating schools, but beyond this, it is difficult to determine a minimum spending level as it is not only money that characterizes a good school.

Equality II: Adequacy

Whereas the challenge of equitable distribution and generation of school revenue has not, and likely will not, soon disappear as a concern, it may be overtaken by adequacy. The concept of adequacy is gaining in both legal and judicial application and thus may represent the newest stage in the contentious evolution of education finance.

The legal assaults of the last three decades were mostly intended to ensure the equity of statewide per pupil revenue levels, be they adequate or inadequate. Increasingly, legislative and legal scrutiny has broadened, as evidenced in the Kentucky Supreme Court's 1989 decision in *Rose v. Council for Better Education, Inc.* In this legal battle, Kentucky's entire education system was declared unconstitutional and the general assembly was directed to ensure that every child had access to an adequate education. The court defined "adequate" to be a level of knowledge and skills that enabled students to participate fully in contemporary civic, economic, and cultural affairs.

The evolving concept of educational "adequacy" builds upon prior components of equity, shifting from the prior era's emphasis on educational inputs to a concentration on student outcomes. Adequacy entails specifying resource levels minimally necessary to produce desired outcomes. However, few satisfying answers exist to the question of how much fiscal revenue is adequate or what standards compromise desired outcomes. While different conceptualizations of adequacy have been introduced by contemporary decision makers, be it a judge, education and finance expert, or elected official, the determination of a legally fit definition has yet to be found.

Efficiency I: Operation

In the early 1900s, common schools were woefully unprepared to teach the large number of enrollees caused by rapid increases in immigrant populations. Operational inefficiencies plagued schools as they grappled with problems such as shortages of classrooms and teachers. During this time period of rapid industrialization, the nation was deeply entrenched in harnessing and promoting practices that increased productivity in a wide array of industries. Thus it was natural that the American public turned its eye to education, demanding that schools be organized and operated in a businesslike fashion.

A priority of educational leaders was to remediate educational inefficiencies in the operations of schooling. To achieve this goal, Frederick Taylor's new industrial management system, known as "scientific management" or "Taylorism," was applied to education. The principle concept of Taylorism, operating more efficiently while minimizing costs, rapidly spread throughout education systems. School leaders' attention was turned away from the instructional facets of schooling and focused instead on eradicating inefficiencies by translating education, including classroom learning and instruction, into financial terms. Educators also sought to maximize the utilization of school facilities by adopting the Gary Plan. Known as the platoon school, the Gary Plan utilized a departmentalized system permitting students to move from room to room, concepts that were commonplace in factories but novel for schools.

Legitimate criticisms were raised of schools modeled after factories relentlessly pursuing a businesslike efficiency. Educational reformers, such as John Dewey, characterized schools as repressive institutions promoting rote routines that failed to endorse exploration and student growth. To be sure, countless education decisions were made not on instructional grounds but rather on motivations of cost minimization and output maximization.

The next major expression of Taylorism was the school district consolidation movement. Launched in the 1920s, this initiative to reduce the number of schools and school districts has had lasting and dramatic effects. In 1920, the United States had 127,000 local school districts. By the turn of the twenty-first century, this number had been reduced to 14,000, a nine-fold reduction in a three-quarter-century span. More importantly, the number of schoolchildren expanded greatly during the same period. The result was the contemporary condition wherein 25 percent of America's school-age children attend school in only 1 percent of the nation's school districts. Fifty percent of all students attend school in only 5 percent of America's school districts. The school districts consolidation movement is responsible for the dominance of the nation's mega-school districts and its current reliance on large schools.

Efficiency II: Performance

Renewed interest in educational efficiency gained a foothold in the adequacy movement. The concept of using adequacy as the baseline from which to determine the level of resources distributed per pupil finds its origins in the major reordering of national education priorities in the 1980s. Declining productivity, unmatched federal government deficits, unprecedented reversals in foreign indebtedness, and growing personal debt are examples of dismal economic conditions of the early 1980s that contributed to a growing unease about the quality and productivity of the nation's schools.

The uncertainty about whether Americans were getting the most value from educational dollars became a national worry, fueled in part by the National Commission on Excellence in Education's 1983 release of *A Nation at Risk: The Imperative for Educational Reform*. This influential report generated an awareness of the decrease in productivity of American public schools and spotlighted the decline of excellence in education. The essential message from the report was unsettling—the nation's previously unchallenged position as an economic and technological leader is at risk. The commission observed that worldwide economic competition had overtaken the United States during the postindustrial age, identifying education as the primary contributing factor.

The release of *A Nation at Risk* triggered a sustained period of public concern and policymaker attention to higher levels of performance in public schools. Twenty years after *A Nation at Risk,* the education policy arena persists in engaging massive reforms directed at enhancing student performance. State and local educational leaders' efforts continue to develop an onslaught of learning standards, curriculum guidelines, subject matter benchmarks, and academic performance targets directed at increasing student performance and productivity from a beleaguered education system.

Policymakers and educators' gravitation toward an outcome-oriented notion of education forged with revenue matters was reinforced with the 2001 passage of the federal No Child Left Behind Act (NCLB). Enactment of NCLB signaled an intensification of efforts to improve student outcomes with mandated requirements such as high-stakes testing and school accountability programs linked with statewide learning standards.

While the American electorate heavily endorses the purposes for which NCLB stands, the act has become a source of intense controversy as school districts claim that they lack fiscal capacity to meet the federal requirements. Furthermore, educators and policymakers are deeply divided over using standardized examinations to measure adequate yearly progress towards state learning standards. Mounting pressure for higher student performance and a prospect of higher stakes for failure are key contributors to the debate over providing an adequate opportunity.

Attempting to define an "adequate" opportunity to learn and thereafter to translate such a definition into the reality of school finance has ignited legislative and legal warfare. Beginning in the 1990s, enactment in virtually every state of learning objectives and curriculum standards provided a reference point for plaintiffs arguing that funding was inadequate overall. Coupling learning standards with performance tests, particularly high-stakes tests, under the mantle of accountability programs offers a ripe opportunity to attach consequences for low and high performance of students, teachers, and schools.

Accountability systems are utilized to varying degrees in every state, with some states, such as Florida, measuring not only performance but also academic return on public dollars investment. Since 1989, the constitutionality of funding mechanisms in 39 states had been challenged on adequacy grounds. In 2005 alone, high-court decisions were handed down in eight states, including Kansas and Texas, with a decision rendered in South Carolina that has national implications regarding state funding mechanisms.

It is against this political and judicial backdrop that modern policymakers seek added information regarding the costs of offering services geared toward elevated performance expectations. A variety of adequacy cost study approaches are employed to estimate the amount of money actually needed to make available all the educational services required to provide each child an opportunity to meet applicable state education standards.

Many of the adequacy cost-modeling methods tread on conceptually unstable ground. The evolving concept of fiscal adequacy requires researchers to ascertain far more elusive relationships between education inputs, processes, and outcomes than is currently feasible with present-day methodology and information. In spite of what have often proven to be biased and unreliable estimates, adequacy cost studies have proliferated. According to ACCESS, a project of the Campaign for Fiscal Equity, Inc., a total of 58 cost studies had been conducted in 39 states as of October 2006.

The growing number of state court decisions, paired with the current policy environment that values educational accountability, suggest that the national adequacy debate will continue to thrive. Ensuring that sufficient resources are available for all students to meet federal and state-specified learning standards is a laudable policy objective. However, the concept of adequacy is evolving and no one yet knows with any degree of certainty how much money it takes for a student to meet set state-derived learning standards. While the query is significant, there is a regrettable lack of analytic capacity to construct credible answers to questions about adequacy.

Liberty: Choice

Liberty and the associated freedom to choose among alternatives is a fundamental notion deeply rooted in American culture. When applied to schooling, liberty is often a controversial idea, one with which the United States continues to wrestle through courts and elective processes.

Contemporary liberty debates primarily involve the notion of family liberty. Liberty proponents contend that parents have the right to direct their child's education. Often the idea of family liberty in the education process is expressed as school choice. This most often refers to the right of the parents to choose where their child attends school; a choice between various public schools or between public schools and private schools. Interest in school choice has predictably intensified with NCLB's accountability movement. Under the guidelines of NCLB, parents have the choice of enrolling their children in a school out of their zoning district if the school in which they are zoned fails to make adequate yearly progress in student achievement.

A variety of proposals involving school choice have emerged as the public's dissatisfaction with the public school system has increased. One proposal provoking intense controversy is providing parents with a financial grant known as a voucher. The 1965 publication of Milton Friedman's voucher proposal helped school choice gain purchase in the U.S. policy system. Scholars used Freidman's ideas to develop and articulate the first notions of family choice in the modern era.

Momentum for the voucher movement increased with the Ohio lawsuit, *Zelman v. Simmons-Harris* (2002). *Zelman* resulted in the U.S. Supreme Court's decision to pronounce that publicly funded tuition vouchers used at religious schools are not in violation of the U.S. Constitution. From this seminal judicial ruling it was expected the voucher movement would expand dramatically. Nonetheless, due to judicial and political obstacles, voucher programs currently operate in only a handful of states.

The future of vouchers as a school choice option may rest in changes taking place in the adequacy movement. Lawyers are working on initiatives to ask judges in adequacy cases to give vouchers to students, rather than more money to public schools, until the school system is brought into compliance.

Another proposal for expanding parental liberty that is more palatable among policymakers and the public is the establishment of charter schools. Charter schools are public schools, approved by a government entity, operating outside of the traditional system of public-school governance. Most are nonprofit, but a growing proportion of charter schools are operated by for-profit educational management organizations. Despite recent studies indicating overall achievement for charter school attendees is not significantly greater than their traditional school counterparts, the number of charter schools is growing at a rapid pace. The Center for Education Reform reports that as of September 2006, there are approximately 4,000 operating charter schools across the nation, a 13 percent increase from the previous year.

Other options capturing a surprising amount of attention in the school choice wars include magnet schools, homeschooling, and education tax credits.

While magnet schools' original purpose was intended to be a solution to school integration, the present day concept of a magnet school is thematic. Magnet school themes, such as foreign language, performing arts, or science, typically attract students from throughout a school district who are admitted by meeting district-determined qualifications and/or by a lottery system.

Homeschooling is a fast-growing movement that finds its origins in parents seeking religious freedom. Today, parental concerns ranging from increases in school violence to curriculum inclusion of liberal values motivate a wide range of parents to turn to homeschooling. The exact number of children schooled at home is not known. Estimates indicate the number is small but growing. The most recent survey by the Department of Education (2001) estimated that 850,000 students are homeschooled, or 1.7 percent of K–12 students nationwide.

Education tax credits for school expenses are an emerging preference in the school choice movement. Education tax credits have various mechanisms that operate as a tuition subsidy for schools. Most commonly, parents who choose to send their children to private schools are eligible to claim a tax credit by directly subtracting a proportion of private schooling expenses from their tax liability. Education tax credit programs have been successfully enacted in six states, four of which failed previous efforts to implement a voucher system. A strong political advantage of education tax credits over vouchers is that they sidestep the issue of directing public money away from public schools to private schools.

Some educational theorists contend that adding choice, or liberty, to public schooling will create the requisite environment from which a competitive market will emerge, competition that will force public schools be more effective. The largest fiscal concern opponents of school choice raise is that privatization of education drains funds from traditional public schools. The financial implications of expanding the concept of liberty in the school system add to the complexity of determining if and how additional liberty should be legislated into the U.S. schooling system.

SUMMARY

Prodded by public policy developments, societal movements, economic fluctuations, and judicial decisions, the field of education finance is playing a more central role in schooling than ever before. Having forged a link between schooling outcomes and revenue matters, school finance is no longer considered independent of instructional practice and student achievement. Dramatic legal and legislative decisions have occurred to fortify school finance's purpose not as secondary to instruction and learning, but rather as an operative precondition.

The transition from prior policy preoccupation with per-pupil spending equity to a new predisposition toward resource sufficiency and system efficiency has not always been smooth. From every vantage point, be it social, political, economic, or legal, school finance is a controversial topic. Much tension exists within the process of generating and appropriating school funds, tension created by balancing values encapsulated in the core of the American experience—efficiency, equality, and liberty. Differing interpretations of these values is a sustained contention in the field of education finance that shows no signs of diminishing.

Further Reading: Callahan, R., 1962, *Education and the cult of efficiency: A study of the social forces that have shaped the administration of the public schools,* Chicago: University of Chicago Press; Cubberley, E. P., 1906, *School funds and their apportionment,* New York: Teachers College Press; Huerta, L., & d'Entremont, C., in press, Education tax credits in a post-Zelman era: Legal, political and policy alternatives to vouchers? *Education Policy* 21(1), 73–109; Peterson, Paul E., ed., 2006, *Choice and competition in American education,* Lanham, Maryland: Rowman and Littlefield Publishers, Inc.

James W. Guthrie and Christina Hart

FOREIGN LANGUAGE EDUCATION

A distinction is commonly made between second and foreign languages. *Second languages,* e.g., English for a Spanish-speaking migrant worker in the United States or French for the child of an Arabic-speaking immigrant to France, are those learned (or not) by immigrants or other residents that are used as a medium of wider communication in their new environment. *Foreign languages,* e.g., Chinese, German, or Arabic for native speakers of English or French in Canada, and English, French, or Japanese for native speakers of Spanish in Mexico, are those that are not languages of wider communication in the surrounding society and are studied at school or learned some other way.

WHY LANGUAGES SHOULD MATTER IN SCHOOLS

Geopolitical forces make both second and foreign language education of considerable importance in the twenty-first century. To begin with, with the sad exception of those living in more than usually repressive states, the advent of better and cheaper systems of transportation means that people move about a lot more than they did 50 years ago. Frequently, the movement is for positive reasons and voluntary, e.g., for higher education, marriage, tourism, and employment opportunities. All too often, however, the reasons are negative and the movement involuntary, as when individuals or large groups are forced to flee the ravages of war, drought, famine, disease, abject poverty, or ethnic, religious, and political persecution. In all the former cases save tourism, functional L2 proficiency is a must, and even for the tourist, it can help. In the latter cases, the vast majority of migrants have to learn one or more new languages if they are to survive, let alone do well, in their new surroundings.

Even for those not on the move, languages, and so-called "standard" dialects, are increasingly important. Many ethnolinguistic minorities need proficiency in the language(s) or dialect(s) of the dominant social, economic, and political group(s) for access to education, social services, and economic or political power. Other powerful forces for change—globalization, mass media, ever wider access to computers, the Internet, and other new technologies, occupation by a conquering army, and in many cases, naked cultural imperialism—whether welcomed or resisted, bring with them exposure to, and in many, a desire to communicate in, one or more foreign languages, especially those of the era's economic and military superpowers, currently, English and Chinese.

Against this backdrop, it is not surprising that the teaching of foreign languages in schools is such an important topic in so many countries, and in some cases, as we shall see, such a controversial one, especially with regard to when foreign languages should be introduced and how they should be taught. If anything is surprising, it is that languages are not considered *more* important in some countries, particularly English-speaking ones.

DO LANGUAGES IN SCHOOLS MATTER IN PRACTICE?

In practice, the importance attributed to second and foreign language education in schools varies greatly. In many European countries, a foreign language is compulsory in elementary school, and secondary school students often learn two or more. In the People's Republic of China, English is a compulsory subject in all primary schools, and over 200 million children are studying the language. In the United States, conversely, while foreign languages were recognized as part of the "core" curriculum in the *Goals 2000: Educate America Act,* a 1997 survey by the Center for Applied Linguistics (CAL) in Washington, D.C., found that only about one-third of elementary schools (just a quarter of public elementary schools) offered a foreign language, usually Spanish, and only 24,000 of roughly 54 million elementary or secondary school children were studying Chinese (27 percent of the elementary schools offering foreign language instruction taught French, down from 41 percent a decade earlier). English-speaking countries in general, notably the United States, the UK, and Australia, tend to ascribe less importance to foreign languages, perhaps on the tenuous, not to mention arrogant, assumption that "everyone (else) will learn English." But while many anglophones remain devoutly monolingual, the pattern is different in officially bilingual (English and French) Canada, and in countries in Africa and South Asia where English is an official language, even though not most inhabitants' native language.

Since 2000, the numbers studying Chinese and other less commonly taught languages (LCTLs), especially Arabic, in the United States have increased rapidly at both high school and university level, in part due to the sudden injection, post-9/11, of federal funding into so-called "critical languages," i.e., those considered critical for U.S. national security. The number of students studying Chinese in public secondary schools, for example, is estimated to have risen to about 50,000 in 2006, and the College Board recently began offering an Advanced Placement test in Mandarin. The figures are still tiny, however, compared with those for English and Chinese as foreign languages in many other countries, and the overall status of foreign languages in U.S. schools is still low. The 2002 Digest of Education Statistics found only 44 percent of high school students in the United States studying a foreign language. Of those, 69 percent were taking Spanish and 18 percent French. Less than 1 percent was studying a LCTL. Even these disappointing figures overestimate U.S. interest in foreign languages. Many of those studying Spanish are the children of Latino immigrants happy to find a class made easy for them by the language skills they acquired in the home as young children. Others attend Spanish bilingual or immersion programs because of their lack of adequate English skills, i.e., use language programs originally intended for English-speaking learners of Spanish to access education through their native language. Moreover, Spanish is arguably no longer a foreign language at all in many parts of the country.

Considerable lip service is paid to the importance of foreign languages by American politicians, including some, like the younger Bush, not renowned for their own language skills. Maintenance of immigrants' heritage languages, a potentially vast linguistic resource for the country, is ill-served, however, by "English-only" legislation at the state level, by the minimal number of bilingual programs in most heritage languages, and by the passage of the same federal politicians' regressive No Child Left Behind (NCLB) legislation—or as it might be referred to more appropriately, No Child Left Bilingual. Under NCLB, schools face financial sanctions if students' average mathematics and reading scores fail to meet specified minimum standards. "Luxury" subjects like music and foreign languages are typically among the first to be cut by principals and school districts fighting to avoid penalties.

The relative neglect of foreign languages in K–12 education in the United States is even worse than the numbers above might suggest. Eighty percent of elementary school programs offering a language (usually Spanish) aim merely to provide an introduction to the language and culture, and only 20 percent something more than that. In the 1997 CAL survey, only 22 percent of secondary schoolteachers reported using the foreign language in the classroom most of the time. In many cases, foreign language teachers' own command of the language is inadequate. The same problem was identified in Australia in a 1993 survey of elementary schoolteachers of Japanese, the majority of whom reported being unable to conduct a whole lesson in the language they were teaching. Compounding the problem, roughly 80 percent of secondary school and only 20 percent of elementary school foreign language teachers in the United States are trained as such, and average class size is increasing, a particularly problematic factor for language teaching, where student talking-time is at a premium.

WHEN SHOULD FOREIGN LANGUAGES BE INTRODUCED?

There is overwhelming evidence to the effect that, like the hare and the tortoise, older children and adults progress faster through the early stages of learning a foreign or a second language, but (assuming sufficient time, motivation, and opportunity to learn) young children eventually overtake them and do better in the long run. Research shows, in fact, that age of first exposure to a new language is the single best predictor of eventual proficiency (followed by language aptitude). Researchers disagree as to the underlying cause or causes of the age effect, however. Some believe the advantage for children to result from time on task: Younger starters do better because they study longer. Others think changes in the brain's plasticity are implicated, that there are one or more so-called "critical periods" for language learning. Native-like pronunciation, the second group believe, is impossible unless learning begins well before puberty, and unlikely if not much earlier, probably before age six. They maintain that native-like grammatical accuracy and native-like knowledge of vocabulary and collocations (knowing that snakes slither, not slide, a disease is cured, not mended, someone has a gleam, not a flash, in their eye, etc.) are only possible among learners who start a language before the mid-teens. Given the right kind of exposure, these researchers believe, younger learners can learn foreign or second languages implicitly and potentially reach very high levels of proficiency, the same way they learn their native languages (successfully), whereas adolescents and adults have lost that ability and have to rely increasingly on explicit learning, instead, which is why they often fail, sometimes quite badly. The "critical periods" hypothesis (CPH) is still controversial, however.

Regardless of whether the CPH turns out to be correct, the data on age differences suggest that if high levels of proficiency in a foreign language are important in the long run, either to an individual, a family, or to society as a whole, an early start will be an advantage. This does not mean that high levels cannot be achieved by those who begin learning later, of course, just that the task they face is likely to be harder. However, starting young will not help much if the way languages are traditionally taught continues the same and is not modified for younger learners.

HOW SHOULD FOREIGN LANGUAGES BE TAUGHT?

At both elementary and secondary levels, the typical pattern in school systems around the world is for languages to be taught for three to five hours a week—far less than is required for children to obtain worthwhile functional ability. Distressingly often, moreover, they are treated as a school subject like any other, with the focus on language as object, as if children learn languages the same way they learn mathematics or geography, as opposed to the way they really learn them, by using them and hearing and seeing them used, communicatively. In the United States, only 8 percent of schools offer immersion programs, in which other subjects, like mathematics or history, are taught through the medium of another language, a system proven both popular and efficacious in many countries, notably by French immersion programs for English speakers in Canada. Further compounding the problem, many children who have studied a language at elementary school are then placed in classes with age peers once they reach secondary level, even if the latter are complete beginners.

In some countries, however, the picture is gradually changing. Mostly due to the consensus on age differences, and in some case, due also to acceptance by education policymakers of the research evidence in support of some version of a CPH, several countries have recently lowered the age at which children in state schools start learning a foreign language, e.g., from 11 to 8 for English as a foreign language in Spain. Private bilingual or immersion kindergarten and elementary schools are springing up in many parts of the world, partly for the same reasons. The hope is often that the earlier start will improve on what have often been rather poor levels of achievement in the past. The problem is that young school-age children require something different from the traditional teacher-fronted, chalk and talk, grammar rules and decontextualized drilling approaches to language teaching suffered by so many generations of adult learners (most of whom do poorly), especially if they are to take advantage of any supposed implicit learning ability.

Depending on just how young the children are, to the extent possible, it will typically be far more beneficial to recreate at school the conditions under which they successfully learned their native language at home. That can mean playing in, and learning other subjects through, the new language, not learning *about* it, as is typically the case, again, with all too many classes for adults. Much theory and research in the field of second language acquisition suggests that, certainly for young children, and for many adolescents and adults, too, languages are acquired best when they are experienced in the classroom as the *medium* of instruction, not as the *object* of instruction. Therefore, lowering the starting age for foreign language education will probably achieve very little unless it is accompanied by changes in the ways languages are taught, with bilingual and, especially, immersion models clearly favored.

Needless to say, such changes are neither easy nor cheap to accomplish, for bilingual or immersion programs require teachers who are able to conduct whole lessons in the target language, and who can also teach other subjects, such as mathematics, science, physical education, theater, or art, *through* the language. They also require subject-matter materials written in the language concerned. Potentially as important as lowering the starting age, therefore, some research on foreign language education in Quebec schools has shown that intensive instruction over a shorter period can be more effective than long, thin "drip feed" courses of, say, three hours a week spread over many years.

Even for older school students, those in secondary or high school and college, there is increasing support for more communicatively oriented approaches to foreign language learning, teaching, and testing. Grammar-focused or drill-and-kill courses tend to present artificial-sounding, decontextualized language models and to decrease student motivation to the point that many drop languages altogether. Such approaches fail to show students how the target language is really used and deny them opportunities for rich, stimulating input from which to learn it. More and more second language acquisition research has shown that not just young children, but older learners, too, acquire much of a language through experiencing it used communicatively, and by using it with others, however poorly at first, perhaps working with the teacher and interacting with other classmates as they collaborate on problem solving in small groups. Realistic, meaningful, attention-holding samples of the language provide better input for acquisition. Communicative interaction from the very early stages, with errors regarded as an inevitable by-product of early attempts to communicate, not as something to be avoided or "corrected" as soon as they occur, improves motivation and stimulates attention. Students talk to learn, and learn by doing, as they work collaboratively on intellectually stimulating problem-solving tasks. Instead of learning about a language in preparation for using it to communicate some day, they learn by communicating from the get-go.

SUMMARY

Second and foreign languages have probably never been as important for so many people and for as many reasons as they are now in the early years of the twenty-first century. As a result, while the United States, the UK, and Australia lag behind in some respects, foreign languages have become a high priority in school systems in most industrialized countries, with English and, increasingly in many countries, Chinese, the two most widely taught. One indication of the importance attached to foreign language capacity at both the individual and the national level is the trend towards earlier introduction of a compulsory foreign language in elementary school in many state school systems, with another language often added in secondary school. An early start is also supported by research showing that younger learners may start slower, but, given sufficient opportunity, ultimately achieve higher levels of proficiency. An earlier start, alone, however, is no guarantee of better results. The way languages are taught needs to change, especially, but not only, for younger students. Far less overt attention needs to be paid to grammatical accuracy and error correction in the early stages, which can easily reduce motivation and is largely misplaced, in any case, and greatly increased emphasis given to opportunities for creative language use in intellectually stimulating communicative lessons, where what children say is valued and validated as much or more than how they say it.

Further Reading: Baker, C., 2006, *Foundations of bilingual education and bilingualism*, 4th ed., Clevedon: Multilingual Matters; Doughty, C. J., & Long, M. H., 2003, September, Optimal psycholinguistic environments for distance foreign language learning, *Language Learning and Technology, 7*(3), 50–80, retrieved from http://llt.msu.edu; Hyltenstam, K., & Abrahamsson, N., 2003, Maturational constraints in second language acquisition, in C. J. Doughty, & M. H. Long (Eds.), *Handbook of second language acquisition* (pp. 539–588), Oxford: Blackwell; Lightbown, P. M., & Spada, N., 2006, *How languages are learned*, New York: Oxford University Press; Long, M. H., & Doughty, C. J., eds., in press, *Handbook of second and foreign language teaching*, Oxford: Blackwell; Rhodes, N. C., & Branaman, L. E., 1999, *Foreign language instruction in the United States: A national survey of elementary and secondary schools*, Washington, DC: Center for Applied Linguistics.

Michael H. Long

FOUNDATIONS AND SCHOOLS

Foundations' involvement in K–12 education in the United States has a long history, from foundation efforts to help establish universal education in the latter parts of the nineteenth century to more recent programs to reform or even transform school systems. Throughout, foundations have played many different roles and employed various strategies in an attempt to make their contributions have lasting impact. School issues, however, have often involved political and institutional dimensions that have complicated, limited, and even derailed many foundation endeavors. Nevertheless, at times foundations have played key roles in shaping crucial aspects of our nation's education system. Our understanding of modern school systems is necessarily incomplete without considering their impact.

HISTORICAL BACKGROUND

From the era following the Civil War to the end of World War II, seven major foundations devoted significant efforts to public schooling: the Peabody

Education Fund, the John Slater Fund, Rockefeller's General Education Board, the Russell Sage Foundation, the Jeanes Fund, the Phelps-Stokes Fund, and the Rosenwald Fund. Most of these foundations focused their efforts on expanding and developing the education system in the South and, nationally, for blacks. Strategically, these foundations gradually moved beyond filling social needs unmet by the state (the "foundations-as-charity" model) to strategies of conditional giving that stimulated government and citizen support ("partial succor" strategy) and provided funds to expand administrative capacity ("outsider within" strategy). These efforts helped to develop public school systems in the South though, in interaction with changing racial politics, they ultimately had mixed impacts on the equality of education between blacks and whites. Access for blacks and poor whites increased but often via segregated schools.

By the middle of the twentieth century, a comprehensive public school system had been largely established and foundation goals shifted from increasing access to promoting improvement and innovation within the existing system. Because funding and management of school systems now lay largely in the hands of governments, the success of foundation efforts required political support. Some foundations funded research and innovation efforts and relied on the federal government to take such initiatives to scale (the "research-development-diffusion-implementation" strategy). One example was the Rockefeller-funded General Education Board, which attempted, with relatively little success, to develop and promote a national high school curriculum. Such efforts proved to be difficult as successful diffusion required governmental cooperation, and the political nature of the issues often derailed cooperation.

The publication of A Nation at Risk report in 1983 brought further changes in the political and fiscal environment of education. In the context of increased international competition, the report framed public education as a national crisis, and businesses and foundations were called upon to play a more central role in helping to reform the nation's public school system. In this context, foundations began to take critical stances toward the government's role in the provision of public education. This focus on education reform has continued and has recently been accompanied by a change in the landscape of foundations involved in elementary and secondary education. Older foundations such as Ford, Carnegie, and Rockefeller are ceding prominence to newer foundations such as the Gates and Walton foundations. These newer actors have tended to adopt "catalyzing" strategies that attempt to mobilize new sets of actors that can pressure for systemic transformations, with the goal of stimulating waves of change in deeply institutionalized public school systems.

CURRENT SCENE

Since the 1980s, foundations have paid greater attention to K–12 education. Based on a sample of grants from large foundations, the Foundation Grants Index (created by the Foundation Center) estimates that grants given specifically for elementary and secondary education rose from approximately 3 percent of total foundation grants in 1980 to 3.5 percent in 1989, and then to

4.5 percent in 1998. Over this time, foundations have also become more directly involved in school reform efforts. Major initiatives by prominent donors such as the Annenberg and Gates foundations have increased the visibility of such efforts. According to Jay Greene (see Hess, 2005), as of 2002 the annual total of private giving to K–12 education was approximately $1.5 to $2 billion. Although impressive, this sum is dwarfed by the $427 billion of public money spent on elementary and secondary schools each year.

The current philanthropic landscape in the K–12 education sector is characterized by geographical concentration among both the foundations and the recipients. In particular, the largest donors and major recipients of grants for K–12 education cluster in a few major U.S. cities and states (i.e., large cities in New York, California, Texas, Illinois, Washington, Pennsylvania, etc.) While many of the prominent foundations give nationally, others focus almost exclusively on their home regions—for instance, the Lilly Foundation concentrates its educational giving in Indiana, and the Albertson Foundation similarly focuses on Idaho. Numerous smaller, community foundations are also active in K–12 education, though the total sums of their grants and their geographic distribution are not well documented by Foundation Center data.

Table F.1 Top 20 U.S. Foundations Awarding Grants for Elementary and Secondary Education in 2001

Foundation Name	State	Dollar Amount	No. of Grants
1. Lilly Endowment Inc.	IN	$152,820,849	68
2. Bill & Melinda Gates Foundation	WA	135,411,411	124
3. The Annenberg Foundation	PA	64,551,230	69
4. Walton Family Foundation, Inc.	AR	29,269,938	152
5. J. A. & Kathryn Albertson Foundation, Inc.	ID	24,902,326	111
6. The Ford Foundation	NY	23,731,489	106
7. Wallace-Reader's Digest Funds	NY	21,305,000	89
8. Carnegie Corporation of New York	NY	20,757,000	24
9. J. Bulow Campbell Foundation	GA	16,000,000	9
10. The Brown Foundation, Inc.	TX	15,802,082	56
11. John S. and James L. Knight Foundation	FL	14,275,300	37
12. The Packard Humanities Institute	CA	13,280,388	29
13. Bank of America Foundation, Inc.	NC	12,530,482	94
14. Oberkotter Foundation	PA	11,975,856	61
15. Chicago Annenberg Challenge Foundation	IL	11,331,874	74
16. The New York Community Trust	NY	10,961,059	178
17. Barr Foundation	MA	10,891,563	27
18. The Pew Charitable Trusts	PA	10,827,000	10
19. Charles Stewart Mott Foundation	MI	10,711,089	53
20. The Goizueta Foundation	GA	10,407,800	27

Source: The Foundation Center (www.fdncenter.org/fc_stats)

In terms of purpose, Foundation Center data for 2001 suggest that the area of school reform attracts approximately 22 percent of funding and is dominated by large grants from large foundations. Additional purposes include direct grants to schools and school systems as well as support for teacher education, special education, reading initiatives, private school endowments, scholarships, and various other school programming.

FOUNDATION IMPACT—THEORIES OF CHANGE AND IMPLEMENTATION

To understand how foundations attempt to create impact in schools and school reform, given the limited size of their grants relative to public spending, it is useful to consider general theories of change about educational reform that inform both philanthropy and public policy. These are summarized in Table F.2.

Foundations' strategies toward school reform have tended to be based—either explicitly or implicitly—on these theories of change, and ultimately, a foundation's theory of change must be relatively accurate if its initiatives are to have a chance at impacting in the desired ways. Foundations are, however, not exclusively tied

Table F.2   General Theories of Change Underlying Contemporary Education Reform Efforts

Theory of Change	Recent Examples
1. Change will follow from extra resources and increased flexibility	• The Lilly Endowment's Marion County Public and Private School Initiatives • J. A. and Kathryn Albertson Foundation
2. Change requires the provision of expertise, technical assistance, and social support from outside the school system	• The Annenberg Challenge • The Bill and Melinda Gates Foundation • The Broad Foundation's support for governance and school leadership
3. Change requires greater centralization, enhanced control, and explicit standards (i.e., "standards-based reform")	• The No Child Left Behind Act (signed into law in 2002): Key features include the annual testing of students, requirements for schools to achieve "adequate yearly progress" regarding student proficiency levels, and increased accountability for schools.
4. Change will follow from market-like systems of choice, driven by the preferences and judgments of parents and students as consumers of educational services	• Walton Family Foundation
5. Change requires reshaping current political alignments in school systems	• Alliances between foundations and mayors or superintendents • The Bill and Melinda Gates Foundation • Philadelphia Annenberg Challenge

to single strategies, but employ different variations and combinations. Within the Annenberg Challenge, for example, the Chicago project was controlled by a consortium outside the school system that was sometimes at odds with school district leadership, particularly after a strong move toward recentralization engineered by Mayor Daley. In Philadelphia, by contrast, the Annenberg Challenge mobilized an alliance of nonprofit organizations and philanthropists with school district leadership. In many cases, greater experience with educational giving has pushed foundations to pay more attention to local educational politics. Thus, in advancing its program of small high schools, the Bill and Melinda Gates Foundation has come to require strong commitments from—and trust in—school superintendents.

Both philanthropic experience and public policy research suggest that foundations need to focus not only on the design of their initiatives but also on the process of implementation. In this regard, foundations are in a position similar to that of government agencies attempting to implement public policies adopted and funded at one level of government but requiring cooperation from other levels and actors to produce results. In both instances, the funding entity is an outsider that is attempting to leverage change without provoking hostility among the insiders whose cooperation is necessary for successful implementation. Foundation efforts to promote systemic educational reform may be resisted by teachers and administrators who wish to maintain professional autonomy, by local interests that wish to maintain control of their neighborhood school, by parents and students who prefer traditional pedagogies, etc. The difficulty of striking a balance between reform and cooperation complicates implementation, as does the challenge of forging cooperative agreements among multiple parties (including nonprofits, school districts, teacher unions, individual schools, etc.). In Pressman and Wildavsky's (1984) influential study of a federal economic development grant to the city of Oakland, for instance, they make the arithmetic point that, even if there is an 80 percent probability that any single agreement needed for successful implementation is made, the probability of final agreement falls below 50 percent as soon as four agreements are needed.

In addition to the politics of implementation, foundations often find that their impact is contingent on the design of the implementation process. Brian Rowan et al. (2004) suggest that a clear specification of the initiative and provisions for an adequate infrastructure for implementation increase the chances that school reform initiatives will be successfully implemented. Furthermore, the initiative is unlikely to be successfully implemented if it is at cross purposes with those responsible for implementing it. If, for instance, teachers see the initiative as conflicting with their views on instructional purposes, they are unlikely to faithfully implement it or may alter it for their own purposes.

MAJOR INITIATIVES

Given the complexities of design and implementation, foundations' initiatives face significant challenges in creating impact in the complex political and social systems of schools. Nevertheless, a number of foundations have undertaken major initiatives in K–12 education in recent years. These include the Annenberg Challenge (comprehensive school reform), particular initiatives by the Bill and Melinda Gates Foundation (small high schools), and the Walton Family Foundation (school choice).

The Annenberg Challenge was launched in December 1993 with a $500 million "Challenge to the Nation" from Ambassador Walter H. Annenberg. At the time, it was the largest gift to public education in U.S. history. The Annenberg Challenge provided grants ranging from $10 to $53 million to nine major urban areas—Boston, Chicago, Detroit, Houston, Los Angeles, New York City, Philadelphia, the San Francisco Bay Area, and South Florida. Following a "partial succor" strategy, these grants were contingent upon various matching amounts provided by other nonprofits, businesses, foundations, universities, etc. The remainder of the gift was given as special opportunity grants to other cities, to establish a national rural challenge, to enhance arts education, and to support various related institutes and projects. For each of the nine major sites, a local planning group of education, foundation, community, and business leaders designed and administered the funds to the local public schools. The Annenberg Foundation gave great discretion to these entities in determining how to use and implement the funds, so long as the attention was dedicated toward improving the public school system. Not surprisingly, the success of the Annenberg Challenge has varied greatly from city to city depending not only on the strategies used but also on the local political and school context. Though the Annenberg Challenge has left various important legacies, such as increased nonprofit capacity and the creation of networks of schools, there is general consensus that the Challenge did not lead to large-scale systemic improvement in those public school systems.

The Bill and Melinda Gates Foundation's small high schools initiative is driven by the goals of increasing high school graduation rates and preparing more students for college, particularly disadvantaged students. To achieve this, the Gates Foundation sees small high schools as a more effective context in which to provide the relevance, rigor, and relationships (the 3 Rs) that they view as necessary for success in high school, college, and the workforce. Upon launching their formal education program in 2000, the Gates Foundation has provided large grants to help create small, innovative high schools and to transform certain large, underperforming districts into collections of smaller learning communities. In their grant making, the Gates Foundation has employed a modified "innovation and diffusion" strategy that involves the grantees directly in the research and development of the small high schools. The Gates Foundation also attempts to continuously monitor, evaluate, and refine their initiatives, while simultaneously focusing on mobilizing advocacy groups and shaping political alliances.

In contrast to many of the other large foundations' initiatives, the Walton Family Foundation has focused its reform efforts on promoting school choice through their support of private school scholarships, vouchers, and charter schools. By fostering choice, the foundation attempts to improve the public school system through competition. In particular, it has provided thousands of scholarships to help disadvantaged children exit low-performing public schools to attend private schools. The Children's Scholarship Fund is one of the major organizations the Walton Foundation has helped establish to provide such scholarships.

These initiatives by no means exhaust the many recent foundation efforts in the realm of elementary and secondary education. They do, however, provide a brief overview of some initiatives that have captured significant attention and involved large sums of money. They also illustrate some of the varied approaches that contemporary foundations are utilizing in their continued attempts to improve America's education system.

Further Reading: Clemens, E. S., & Lee, L. C., 2008, Catalysts for change? Foundations and school reform, 1950–2005 in H. K. Anheier & D. C. Hammack, eds. *Roles and contributions of American foundations*, Washington, DC: Brookings Institutions; Finn Jr., C. E., & Kanstoroom, M., 2000, Afterword: Lessons from the Annenberg Challenge, in *Can philanthropy fix our schools? Appraising Walter Annenberg's $500 million gift to public education*, Washington DC: Thomas B. Fordham Foundation Hess, F. M., ed., 2005, *The best of intentions: How philanthropy is reshaping the landscape of K-12 education*, Cambridge, MA: Harvard Education Press; Pressman, J. L., & Wildavsky, A., 1984 (1973), *Implementation: How great expectations in Washington are dashed in Oakland; Or, why it's amazing that federal programs work at all, this being a saga of the economic development administration as told by two sympathetic observers who seek to build morals on a foundation of ruined hopes*, 3rd ed., Berkeley and Los Angeles: University of California Press; Walters, P. B., & Bowman, E., 2007, Foundations and the making of public education in the United States, 1865–1950 Washington DC: Aspen Foundation.

Linda C. Lee and Elisabeth S. Clemens

G

GED (GENERAL EDUCATIONAL DEVELOPMENT) CREDENTIAL

The General Educational Development (GED) credential is widely perceived as an alternative to a high school diploma, though it is questionable whether the GED credential is widely recognized as equivalent to a high school diploma. Three interrelated themes of controversy surround the GED credential: the GED exam, the use of the GED in American education, and the value of the GED credential.

The GED is offered throughout the United States and its territories and Canada and is sponsored by the GED Testing Service of the higher-education lobbyist group the American Council on Education (ACE). Many are surprised to learn that the GED is not a public-run institution, but rather, like the SAT, is a privately run exam corroborated by private and public institutions. Thus, colleges, employers, and the military have no civic requirement to accept or support GED earners, nor are they compelled by anything beyond public perception to view the GED as an equivalent to the high school diploma.

A series of five parts, testing proficiency in mathematics, reading, science, social science, and writing, the GED is administered by official GED testing sites that are overseen by provincial, state, or territorial governments. Each year, the exam is administered by the ACE to a set of graduating high school seniors in order to establish the passing score. In order to pass the GED exam, the GED candidate must meet or achieve a higher score than the top 60 percent of high school diploma earners on each of the five parts. In the United States in 2005, 680,874 people took at least one GED test; 587,689 people completed the battery of tests; and 423,714 passed the battery of tests, earning a GED credential.

In the United States, one in seven secondary school completion credentials is a GED. In cities like New York City, this number has grown in the past ten years to be one in four. Individuals from a wide range of socioeconomic backgrounds and who identify across diverse racial and ethnic categories earn the GED credential. The credential is earned by more men than women, and is earned by men and women of many ages, although between the years of 1975 and 2000, the percentage of youth GED earners aged 19 and younger grew by 11 percent, while the percentage of GED earners aged 25 and older declined by 8 percent. In the United States in 2005, of the GED earners who reported their age, 45 percent were aged 16 to 19; 26 percent were aged 20 to 24; and 30 percent were aged 25 and older.

THE GED EXAM

The first GED exams were developed in the 1940s to accommodate returning WWII veterans whose secondary schooling was interrupted by military duty. Colleges and universities used the GED exam, based on the Iowa Test of Educational Development, as the major tool for evaluating the 2.2 million veterans who entered higher education under the GI bill. Throughout the years immediately following, the GED quickly became an exam for civilians rather than veterans. While established as an exam for adults, the rise in social capital and market value of a high school degree coupled with increasingly higher regimentation in secondary schooling has contributed to the growing population of teenagers who opt out of a traditional high school diploma for a GED. In its over 60-year history, over 15.2 million people have earned the credential.

Over the years, the exam has seen many revisions, the most historic occurring in 2002. The ACE revised the exam to reflect contemporary issues of citizenship and include a more extensive written essay component. Two concerns that educators raised around the revisions centered around the potential leaning toward patriotism of the exam material and how an extensive written essay might exclude speakers of first languages other than English and international candidates from earning a GED. Impressions that the 2002 version would be more difficult to pass than the 2001 version generated a massive wave of GED takers in 2001 and a reported drop in takers in 2002.

Perhaps more controversial were the two new, but largely under-wraps, developments put forth by the ACE that accompanied the revision: corporate involvement in the development of the exam and changes in reporting emphasis.

Corporate representatives largely informed the 2002 revision in order to reconnect the qualifications of GED earners with the needs of corporate employers. The new GED exam was developed with the help of a committee featuring representatives from businesses and organizations such as Taco Bell, Safeway, Motorola, and the National Alliance of Businesses, at least in part because of a history of employer complaints about the quality of GED holders. An analysis of this corporate involvement put forth by the Collective of Researchers on Educational Disappointment and Desire (CREDD) contends that the 2002 revision of the GED seeks to align GED earners to low-wage jobs rather than higher education.

In addition, the 2002 revision included a change in the ACE's reporting practices around the GED. The General Educational Development Testing Service of the American Council on Education shifted the focus of their annual statistical reports from a focus on "Who Took the GED Tests?" to "Who Passed the GED Tests?"

THE USE OF THE GED IN AMERICAN EDUCATION

Historically, the GED has been seen as synonymous with a high school diploma. It has been so strongly viewed and valued as an equal alternative that it was not until over 50 years after the GED's inception that GED earners were differentiated from high school diploma earners in U.S. census data. Though this change took place in 1998, GED earners are most often still calculated as high school graduates in statistics of local, state, and federal education systems and agencies. For instance, the 1998 *Education at a Glance* report put forth by the Organization of Economic Co-operation and Development (OECD) puts the United States in the bottom third of 24 industrialized countries in secondary school completion, whereas if the GED is included, the United States would be among the top half, where most Americans would expect to place. The subsequent shock that rippled through U.S. popular media in response to the report demonstrates the GED contribution to a myth of declining dropout rates and a superior American education system. The GED is used to mask dismal secondary school completion numbers not only at the international and national scales, but also at the school level. Federal mandates such as No Child Left Behind (NCLB) and state accountability (such as the state-mandated exit exams required in over 20 states such as Alaska, New York, Florida, Louisiana, Texas, and New Mexico and, as of 2006, four new states including California and Arizona) put a new kind of pressure on schools to achieve high test scores at any cost. Under NCLB and state administered high-stakes standardized testing (and in some cases, offerings of financial bonuses to administrative individuals who achieve utmost compliance with these mandates) schools benefit by siphoning out academically weak and/or disruptive students. Schools also benefit by the widespread practice of removing students who are pushed out or leave school for GED programs from school rosters, but not counting them as "dropouts." Because of the lopsided enforcement of NCLB, schools are held more highly accountable to success in standardized tests than success in student retention and reducing dropout rates.

CREDD's research in New York City reveals the ways in which this pressure is expressed by both school personnel and by students. A surprising number of current and pushed-out students that participated in CREDD's Gateways and Get-aways study reported being advised of the GED option by school personnel as early as the seventh and eighth grades, up to two years before ever setting foot in high school. This, combined with students' sensing that "school is not for me" as early as the fifth grade, has exacerbated the general school cultural belief that students who will not perform well on standardized tests should not be in school.

Struggling students, seeing state graduation exams like the New York Regents around the corner, make an early exit for the GED, mistakenly believing that they are merely swapping one set of tests for another, without having to sit through four or more years of high school. CREDD's research also reveals that this is a largely uniformed or misinformed decision, as many GED-seeking youth reported that they had no prior knowledge of the rules pertaining to age and length of time out of high school that delay youths' eligibility for the exam, or the months and sometimes years of preparation required that may delay youths' passing of this rigorous exam. Further, in the climate of standardized testing described above, and in a school culture of ever-shrinking genuine alternatives to an exit-exam based curriculum, for many students it is a forced decision, a nondecision to get out of a schooling situation in which they have been systematically excluded from success.

In these ways, a controversy in the use of the GED can be understood as an overuse or abuse of the GED option as a cover for pushing out unwanted students. Recent immigrant students who are speakers of languages other than English are often dissuaded from enrolling in high school and pushed toward GED programs. These common, yet covert practices concretize the de facto reliance on the GED as a last alternative to contemporary schooling, effectively getting school leaders off the hooks of figuring out ways to honor all students' rights to attend school until the age of 21; to develop and implement meaningful curricula, pedagogies, and assessments; and to reassess the purpose of schooling.

THE VALUE OF THE GED CREDENTIAL

Across most of the literature around the GED, the most contentious controversy is connected to the value of the credential. The discordant analyses that mark the credential as "meaningful," "meaningless," "valuable," "depleted," and as representing an education or just another piece of paper spur from a range of academic and journalistic disciplines and as a whole point to the GED as a contested degree, likely due at least in part to its status as the last alternative standing in many school systems, as described above. Nearly all of the reports analyze the value of the GED from a higher-education value or a market-value perspective. From these perspectives, the value of the GED is questionable, or better, *complicated*.

Over 66 percent of those who seek their GED cite access to higher education as their major motivator. However GED earners who enter associate's degree programs are half as likely as high school diploma earners to complete their degrees, and only 2–8 percent of GED earners who seek bachelor's degrees attain them, as compared to 20 percent of high school diploma earners. The 1992 National Adult Literacy Survey (NALS) indicates that GED earners are equal or more achieved than high school diploma earners in terms of literacy and cognition, so the fewer numbers of GED earners who complete their higher education goals can be understood as an issue of the value of the GED credential as diminished in comparison to the high school diploma. In many ways, it appears that the difference in values of these credentials in higher education has to do with socialization and the ways in which those who complete high school are more cogently socialized for a college classroom that mirrors secondary schooling. Obvious perhaps, this aspect of socialization is important to make transparent in any analysis or process that seeks to determine the purposes of secondary and higher education.

Similarly, GED earners do not experience the same rates of success in the U.S. labor market. Much of the literature does not support the GED as a distinguishing factor in getting a job. Employment rates are much higher for high school diploma holders than for GED recipients. Men with GEDs have higher job-turnover rates than men who have "dropped out," and actually do not work as often. This is not true for women who have GEDs. Overall, high school diploma earners work more and have lower job turnovers than GED earners. While GED earners' yearly wages are 8 percent higher than those of dropouts, they are 9–12 percent lower than high school diploma earners' wages.

The ACE's decision to include employer perspectives on the 2002 revision of the GED exam was due in part to employers' complaints about the work habits or the socialization of GED earners. Informing both the material covered and preparation practices for the GED exam has been a way for corporations to access and mold a future generation of workers, socializing them to meet corporate needs.

In many ways, the value of the GED is rooted in public perception. For instance, in 1992, the army stopped accepting recruits with GEDs, citing that GED earners' attrition rates were double those of high school diploma earners and almost indiscernible from rates of high school dropouts. However, the current unpopular, multifront, "no end in sight" war has invited a recruitment crises for the U.S. military, and youth report that "help in getting a GED" is a part of the propositions of military recruiters.

Because the value of the GED is linked to public perception, the value is vulnerable to racist and misogynist attitudes. The 1992 NALS study established the strikingly similar literacies of GED earners and high school diploma earners *across the board,* but that employers continue to stereotype GED holders based on race, and further that white men have greater access to both higher-paying jobs and higher-quality GED preparation programs than do white women, black men and women, and Latina/o men and women. Thus, the GED will probably work as an equivalent to the high school diploma for white young men, but probably will not work as an equivalent to the high school diploma for white young women and young women and men of color.

That the higher educational value and market value are so susceptible to admissions officers' and employers' subjectivities is highly problematic. As part of the Gateways and Get-aways project, CREDD surveyed 50 of the 2006 U.S. News and World Report's Top 100 Colleges and learned that while most but not all did not specifically exclude GED earners from applying, it was overwhelmingly rare for a GED earner to be admitted. CREDD also surveyed 100 employers, many appearing on the 2006 Fortune 500 Best Companies to Work For list, others common employers cited as ideal employers by young people. While GED earners were hired, it was difficult for human resources representatives of these companies to provide instances of GED earners in leadership positions.

The higher educational value and market value approaches fail to answer a crucial question: Why are so many young people and adults flocking to a seemingly depleted credential? Because these approaches to the valuation of the GED are limited by their exclusion of youth and adult GED earners' voices and experiences, they miss the main component of the value of the GED credential entirely. By moving to a frame that considers the *lived* value of the GED, a whole series of otherwise unseen explanations unfolds. CREDD's research has that the value of the GED is not only in it as a *gateway* to higher employment and higher education, but also is in being a *get-away* from dehumanizing high schools. The Gateways and Get-aways study had revealed the ways in which the GED holds a lived value for GED earners in bringing them a sense of accomplishment and completion, an educational setting decidedly unlike school, a way to move on in life, and most importantly, a way to get away from a school setting that is "eating (them) alive."

CONCLUSION

The GED can be read as cultural artifact, as political, as acquiescent, as subversive, as cover-up and at the same time as a magnifying lens for what is and isn't working in secondary schooling. In these ways, it is a powerful public space, and as other public spaces are, is vulnerable to the privatized, corporatized, militarized political economies that seek to streamline, anaesthetize, and close down genuine, satisfying, sustainable options for youth and disenfranchised communities. The use(s) and value(s) of the GED are supremely tenuous, yet hold profound implications for the purposes of schooling and learning when in nexus with the lived value of the GED.

It is important to read the controversies surrounding the GED not as condemnation, but as evidence of the way in which the GED is a powerful yet punished alternative to the high school diploma. It is important to read a student's jettisoning from school toward the GED exam as a critique of schooling. Finally, it is important to read the overuse and abuse of the GED option in secondary schooling as the canary in the mine, indicating the need for multiple paths to secondary school completion, not just one exit to the mine.

Further Reading: Boesel, D., Alsalam, N., & Smith, T., 1998. *Educational and labor market performance of GED recipients,* Washington DC: U.S. Dept. of Education, Office of Educational Research and Improvement, National Library of Education; General Education Testing Service, 2006, *Who passed the GED tests? 2005 statistical report.* Washington, DC: GED Testing Service, American Council on Education; Quinn, L., 2002, *An institutional history of the GED,* Milwaukee: University of Wisconsin-Milwaukee, Employment and Training Institute; Rivera-Batiz, F., 1995, Vocational education, the general equivalency diploma, and urban and minority populations, *Education & Urban Society,*

27(3), 313. Smith, T. 2003, Who values the GED? An examination of the paradox under-lying the demand for the General Educational Development credential, *Teachers College Record* 185(3), 375–415.

Eve Tuck

GENDER

The persistence of "gender turf battles" in the battleground of the schools has two main features. On the one hand, they often tend to obscure and divert attention from class and race pressures and inequalities that, if properly addressed, would take care of many problems falsely masquerading as gender issues. On the other hand, gender inequalities are real. The identification of and the struggles against their perpetuation have illuminated much about the ways gender has constructed schooling, and schooling gender, over the years.

As a central issue for our homes, our workplaces, and our culture, gender equity is a perfect example of concerns that both occupy and extend beyond classrooms and schools. Women have made major inroads into almost every previously male-dominated career and now make up half of the country's workforce. Yet they still earn little more than two-thirds of every male-earned dollar and are responsible for the bulk of housework and child care, even when they work full-time. The "double day," the persistence of sexual harassment and domestic violence, and the dominant cultural stereotypes of "the feminine" all show us that over 25 years after the failed passage of the ERA, women are still "the second sex." While these are problems and barriers for white middle-class women, they are worse for working-class women and women of color.

These contradictory patterns may also be seen in schools. In 1972, the same year that Congress narrowly failed to approve the Equal Rights Amendment, Title IX, mandating equal treatment of girls and boys in all school programs, was passed. Ever since, girls have been in shop classes and boys in domestic science courses; and, perhaps more importantly, women's teams have flourished in many sports. Many credit women's sports for producing several generations of young women with increased abilities, ambitions, and self-confidence both on and off the field. Yet gender (and racial and sexual) stereotyping in the classroom, the curriculum, and the school community remains an issue with many facets. While formal equalities have been set up by Title IX and other legislation, the working dynamics of gender and other societal inequalities are harder to change.

Schools are part and parcel of society. Since schools both reflect and contribute to the social construction of gender and other cultural norms, and because gender relations are such a central dynamic of all societal relations, it is useful to sort out the debates about gender issues in terms of wider political and ideological orientations. The conservative viewpoint emphasizes the maintenance of women's important traditional roles in the family and the community and calls for classrooms that stress discipline, character building, and academic achievement for all children. Liberal-progressives focus on the need for schools to promote gender equality as a central feature of a democratic and student-centered educational philosophy. "Women-centered" approaches look at the qualities of caring, connectedness, and concern for each other, central values of the private sphere missing from most classrooms. Finally, a social reconstructionist view emphasizes gender as a key aspect of multifaceted patterns of societal inequalities and suggests how schools and classrooms can promote practices leading towards a broader agenda of social change.

CONSERVATIVE VIEWS

Conservatives believe that schools should be focused on academics, not the promotion of a victim mentality, particularly in girls and minority group students. They argue that feminists and other critics offer nothing in the way of improving individual student progress and indeed offer rhetorical excuses in the place of the hard work that is needed for all children to succeed. The aim of the educational system should be to produce well-educated women (and men) and to support them in whatever career choices they may make, even if they choose to stay home or pursue traditional jobs and careers such as nursing and teaching. Who else will be our nurses and our teachers and who will stay home with our children? Girls and young women should be allowed, even encouraged, to adopt the values, attitudes, and training that will enhance their essential roles as homemakers, wives, and mothers. These roles are invaluable—they provide a critical service to American families and to American society.

The main business of schools should be academic achievement. American students are behind in basic skills, and more and more high school and college graduates lack exposure to the great works of Western literature, history, and philosophy. Workers need thorough training in the skills needed to compete in an increasingly internationalized workforce, and our leaders need a firm grounding in the classics of Western civilization. Instead of steady progress in these directions, building on the strengths of the past while looking towards a more prosperous and unified future, schools have fallen victim to a series of foolish gender and culture wars. The result: a watered-down curriculum in the name of "multiculturalism" and "gender equity" and the substitution of a social agenda and "self-esteem building" for the much-needed inculcation of basic skills.

LIBERAL-PROGRESSIVE VIEWS

Liberal progressive views focus on the need for equality between genders and on the removal of the barriers to individual success in our schools and elsewhere. All Americans have equal social, political, and educational rights, and public institutions have a broad responsibility to guarantee those rights to all. Schools and workplaces should be places where individuals are encouraged and rewarded to do their best, regardless of racial, ethnic, disability, age, or gender differences. The past has bequeathed a legacy of discrimination and inequality, which laws, public policies, and educational systems have often reflected and perpetuated. Schools must become places where all students, boys and girls, are helped to do their best, where they are treated above all as individuals, and where the discriminatory practices of the past have no place. In a fully gender-equal society, neither women nor men would be hindered by sex-role stereotyping from pursuing a life that draws on their individual talents and leads to personal satisfaction and fulfillment. American society can only benefit from encouraging all its members to fully explore a range of options and choices, away from the traditional limitations of gender.

Unfortunately, in spite of the passage of Title IX, school practices have tended to exacerbate these gender differences rather than challenge them. Thus teachers emphasize differences in the ways that they treat their students. Elementary schoolteachers give boys much more attention than they give girls, of both positive and negative kinds. Boys are praised for initiative and imagination, girls for obedience and conformity. Teachers usually discourage cross-gender play, partly for fear that the girls will get hurt. As for the curriculum, literature texts include many more male heroes than females, and the social studies curriculum emphasizes male exploits over female lives and experiences.

In the upper grades, these patterns persist. Girls are still expected to do better in reading and languages, boys in math and science. The curriculum is often still gender biased as well, with few female authors in English and few female topics in social studies and history classes. In spite of Title IX, many schools and school systems emphasize boys' sports at girls' expense. Female (and gay and lesbian) students are often victims of harassment, although many schools are now instituting sexual harassment policies and LGBT clubs. Finally, at all levels of schooling, women are still the teachers and men are the administrators. The vast majority of elementary school teachers are women, and high school teachers tend to be split along gender lines by subject, with women more common in English and men in math, science, and social studies. The leadership of most school systems is still predominantly male.

Along with including women's lives in the curriculum, liberal-progressives advocate programs to bring women and girls up to speed in math and science, so that they may take advantage of new and lucrative career options. There should be more women administrators to be role models for teachers and for students. Title IX must be stringently enforced, as athletics is a primary setting for the growth in self-esteem needed for women to compete on an equal basis with men. Classrooms organized in these ways will produce both men and women able to take advantage of the full range of opportunities in our society.

"WOMEN-CENTERED" VIEWS

In American society, as in almost all others, women and men have always inhabited different spheres of activity and different frames of reference. Women have been responsible for the private sphere of home, family, and relationships, men for the public sphere of work, politics, and public affairs. Moreover, women's inferior place in society and their long association with mothering and child rearing has rendered them universally vulnerable to male dominance in all aspects of our life: from economic and political hegemony, to domestic violence, to the manipulative controls over our bodies in the form of restricted access to birth control, media exploitation, and pornography.

These dynamics have profoundly shaped the educational system. Children are socialized in schools into the knowledge, skills, and attitudes that they will need to succeed in our society—a society where male traits and activities predominate. Thus competition and individual achievement take precedence over cooperation and interconnections in the ways that educational practices are organized and students rewarded. The curriculum is similarly male-centered—topics in literature and social studies emphasize male exploits in the public sphere. Teachers, who are primarily women because their particular qualities of nurturance well fit them to work with children, are prevented from responding to the interests of all their students, particularly girls, by this overwhelmingly male bias. Female students are also victims of sexual harassment and male bullying in classrooms and playgrounds.

In the short run, because of the differences between the ways girls and boys learn and the biases towards boys in many classrooms, it is a good idea in certain circumstances to institute single-sex classrooms and schools. Girls learn more math and science in settings where they are not being forced to compete with boys; some boys learn more with the firmer discipline and absence of feminine distractions signaled in all-boys classrooms.

In the long run, however, the curriculum content, learning styles, and above all, the relational values associated with women and their activities and experiences in the world should form a basis for rethinking the educational system. The lives of women represent a new world of knowledge and creativity, from the whole range of literary and artistic achievements, to a rich and complex history, to different perspectives on a number of issues. These values are missing not only from schools, but from all public institutions, to their great harm. Starting in schools, we can use the qualities and values associated with women to build a more humane society.

To conclude, while liberal feminists want to remove the barriers from women entering into the public sphere, women-centered feminists want to bring to the public sphere, and to the schools, a badly needed emphasis on the *connections* among people needed for democracies to thrive. Diversity can only be valued if all members of the community are fully heard and learn to care for one another.

SOCIAL RECONSTRUCTIONIST VIEWS

The most important challenge teachers face today is to reach children in terms of this basic understanding: that all children have gender, race, cultural, and class positions, that they live in cultural contexts, and that these contexts are shaped by societal dynamics of power and privilege. Teachers ought to engage with the whole child, build democratic classroom communities based on the perspectives the children offer, and confront societal inequalities to help their pupils envision a more just and equitable society. In this perspective, as Judith Warner indicates, gender is but one dimension of the multiple societal inequalities enacted and reproduced in schools.

Liberal and progressive educators focus too much on individual children and teachers. They downplay gender differences, think the problem is mainly about stereotypes, and ignore the sex-based power arrangements on which gender difference and inequality rest. "Women-centered" theorists are concerned with women's oppression and gender difference in ways that liberals are not, but they ignore differences based on race, class, and culture. Diversities of race, class, *and* gender must be addressed in the classroom and connected to issues in the wider community.

At no time in American history has there been such a gap between the rich and the poor. It is low wages, rather than feminism, that take women away from home and children and threaten our so-called "family values." In the educational arena, we face disintegrating public schools in many communities and a loss of public money and support for public education. Community, state, and federal funding for schools is notoriously inadequate, often due to property tax and other inequities. Yet the people blamed are often women, such as poor women of color who have too many children, working mothers who spend too little time with their children, and women teachers who don't know how to teach.

Schools, indeed, are places where such prejudices are nurtured. Teachers, themselves derided in the public consciousness, are encouraged to see many children as primed for failure; boys who act up are cast as future gang members, girls as future teenage mothers. Through tracking systems and other practices, schools reinforce rather than challenge long-standing social class, race, and gender hierarchies. Such scapegoating conceals the fact that it is not the children's or teachers' fault that schools are falling apart. The educational status quo ignores the societal context that explains the persistence and growth of societal inequalities and blames the hardest-hit victims of poor schooling for their educational failures.

Differences of gender, race, class, and culture should be understood as bases for the strength and vitality of any culture and any community. Yet in our schools today, they represent differential positions in societal hierarchies of inequality. They are used as excuses for why children don't do well and form the bases for hierarchies within the school, whether in terms of the tracking system or the grounds for popularity on the playground. Thus schools reinforce inequalities and provide excuses for them, through an individualized rhetoric of competition and achievement. The organization of many school subjects reflects and reinforces these societal status hierarchies of gender, race, and class. In the case of mathematics, for example, women and members of racial minority groups are still routinely assumed to be incapable of and uninterested in the kind of advanced work that is a prerequisite for many prestigious occupations. All students should have access to all types of subjects. (For example, introductory algebra, a gateway subject for advanced math, is offered not offered in working-class and poor middle schools to any students.) Both inside and outside the classroom, teachers should help their students understand how gender structures kids' lives in all areas of school.

Children reflect and reproduce the gender and racial/cultural roles they learn through family, school, and the culture at large. Schools must confront such issues as the toleration of sexual harassment and homophobia, the valorization of traditional masculinities and femininities in the guise of football and cheerleading, and all the ways gender and other stereotypes structure school life. Indeed, a power analysis of these dynamics could be central to the curriculum. How do gender differences provide a template and a justification for other forms of inequality? How do race and gender stereotypes intersect, so that white girls' passivity is set against the supposed aggressiveness of black girls and all boys? By forcing all kids to face such expectations as they negotiate their identities, such prejudices limit all children's potential.

Schools and teachers must begin to "center" children in all curriculum, pedagogies, and school cultures. Teachers, students, and administrators can work for reforms such as "detracking" and heterogeneous grouping, as well as setting up committees devoted to multiracial and antihomophobia training and other initiatives. They can also begin to reach out to parents and citizens in the wider community, who can then begin to see the schools as centers for community building and renewal.

THE CENTRALITY OF GENDER IN EDUCATIONAL SETTINGS

If we began looking at schooling through the lenses of gender awareness, coupled with attentiveness to race, ethnic, and cultural factors as well, we could see schools in a completely different way. Sexist assumptions and practices, enforced by gender differences and gender expectations, shape the ways we think about our schools, our teachers, and our children in schools, and some of these assumptions need to change.

As a prime example of a needed change in thinking, what would happen to our ideas and hopes about schools and classrooms if we understood the multiple implications of the fact that most teachers are women, and that furthermore the *idea* of the teacher in our society is that she is a woman? (About 80 percent of our elementary teachers are women, about 50 percent of high school teachers are women, and the majority of school administrators are men.) In the first place, we could begin to see why teachers are poorly paid and devalued by most people. After all, teaching is a women's profession, like nursing, and of course, mothering. Many people believe, without even realizing that they hold this belief, that teaching is easy and comes naturally to women because of their inborn capacities for caretaking and nurturance. Therefore, the training that they need is minimal, and the pay they deserve is the same. College professors, who are of course teachers as well (and are mostly male), are respected on the other hand mainly for what they know, not how well they convey it. In other words, good teachers are either experts in their field who know their subject matter, which is what males who dominate the upper grades and colleges are noted for, or kindly nurturers, which is what women who dominate the younger grades are noted for. The idea of pedagogy as a demanding intellectual activity is absent from educational discourses.

What are some results of this kind of thinking on our teachers and our schools? How could some peoples' sexism and lack of understanding of how demanding teaching is, intellectually as well as socially and psychologically, actually affect educational policy? Consider the following:

- In many schools, the curriculum and even the pedagogies are not determined by the teachers, but by districts and curriculum coordinators. Teachers are not presumed to be knowledgeable and skilled enough to plan curriculum on their own. It is questionable whether this kind of contempt would be visited on a profession dominated by or even participated in by men.
- Schools today are utterly dominated by NCLB testing programs; and increasingly teachers must take teacher tests to be certified. Passing these tests has become a substitute for undertaking formal teacher education programs, so that people with little or no classroom training in education whatsoever enter the classroom—and, frustrated, often leave after one or two years.
- Teachers are the least well paid of any professional group, and none of the current reform initiatives is addressing this issue.

Perhaps most harmful, if teachers were supported and respected for the work they do, there might be more attention given to the actual challenges they face in schools. The shocking conditions in urban schools might come into view: the persisting patterns of segregation (both between and within schools), sharply unequal funding, burgeoning class sizes, and inferior materials and equipment. Indeed, this emphasis on testing as the main facet of today's "education reform" initiatives might lead one to think that education reform is not about what schools really need; it is about blaming children themselves and their largely female teachers for the failures in our schools. The result of these kinds of prejudices and policies is that teachers are not given the support and the training they need to function as thoughtful and autonomous experts in helping all their students learn. To see teachers as "transformative intellectuals," as the educator Henry Giroux puts it, is to imagine how they can bring the necessary combination of intellectual rigor, culturally relevant knowledge, and personal sensitivity to all their pupils.

Inside the classroom teachers need to be aware of and knowledgeable about their own and their students' gender and cultural identities and assumptions. This includes a keen and informed understanding of their own race and gender positions and the likelihood that, as middle-class professionals, they inhabit a privileged status in relation to many of their students. Social reconstructionist teachers challenge societal inequalities reflected in their classrooms and make sure the curriculum contains explicit references to inequality and resistance. In classrooms where social and cultural differences are not swept under the table, but in fact are confronted and dealt with, crises of disagreement or misunderstandings form part of ongoing journeys of exploration with their students. It is difficult to teach in this way, but much more difficult and costly to teach as if sexism, racism, and other forms of prejudice and unequal treatment did not exist. In spite of today's barriers and obstacles, of racism and elitism as well as sexism, it is in the classrooms of individual teachers, helped by allies in their schools and communities, that our best hopes lie for resolving "gender turf battles" and building democracy.

Further Reading: *Feminist teacher,* Sarah Doyle Women's Center, Box 1829, Brown University, Providence, RI 02912, retrieved November 22, 2006, from http://www.uwec.edu/wmns/Feminist Teacher/; Raised by women, *Rethinking schools,* retrieved November 22, 2006, from http://www.rethinkingschools.org/; Sadker, D., & Sadker, M., 1994, *Failing at fairness: How America's schools cheat girls,* New York: Scribners; Schniedewind, N., & Davidson, E., 2006, *Open minds to equality: A sourcebook of learning activities to affirm diversity and promote equity,* 3rd ed., Boston: Allyn and Bacon; Woyshner, C., & Gelfond, H. S., eds., 1998, *Minding women: reshaping the educational realm,* Cambridge, MA: Harvard Educational Review.

Frances A. Maher

GIFTED AND TALENTED EDUCATION

The field of gifted and talented education is relatively new, with the need for such programs heightened after the launching of Sputnik. After losing this space war, U.S. decision makers, in a reactionary fashion, began to devote more attention and resources to students who might be able to place the United States first in various global competitions. It has been asserted or argued that gifted students, often defined as those in the top 3 to 5 percent on an intelligence or achievement test, are in the best position to keep the United States competitive. Despite this assertion, gifted education, like all of education, is ripe with controversy. As James Gallagher has noted, America has a love-hate relationship with gifted education. During competitions and times of global challenge, Americans love gifted education; at other times, gifted education is devalued and disparaged, as will be discussed later.

There are three key concerns and controversies surrounding the field of gifted education: (1) terminology and definition issues; (2) service and programming issues; and (3) diversity issues. All three issues are longstanding, with seemingly little possibility for change in the near future. That is to say, not all of these concerns and controversies are easily resolvable; however, there are some possibilities for addressing them.

TERMINOLOGY AND DEFINITIONS: GIFTED, TALENTED, OR BOTH?

Three terms are often used to refer to students who perform higher than others of their age, experience, and environment, and who need more challenge than what is provided by the general education curriculum—gifted, talented, or gifted and talented. The terms tend to be interpreted differently among educators and laypersons, with each interpretation carrying controversy. In general, students who are viewed as gifted are those with high IQ and/or achievement scores. They score in the top 3 to 5 percent on achievement and/or intelligence tests (roughly an IQ of 130 or higher and achievement score at or above the 95th percentile).

These students are considered intelligent and highly able. Others prefer the term talented; talented students are viewed as creative and/or excel in the visual and performing arts. They may not have high IQs, achievement scores, or grades. Students' work or performance (e.g., painting, singing, photography, acting, and dancing) is often evaluated by experts to identify talented students.

Since its beginning, the term gifted has sparked controversy. Some opponents contend that the term and field are elitist because the term gifted, like intelligence, is connoted with genetic endowment. From this perspective, the argument goes that gifted students inherit their skills and abilities; thus, there is little that the environment (including education) can do to change one's destiny or genetic makeup.

A related concern is that the field is viewed as elitist. Some argue that gifted students are offered a higher quality public education than other students, and that since gifted education is a part of public schools students should not receive special benefits (e.g., different curriculum, more challenging books, more field trips) or entitlements that are unavailable to all public school students. If more funds and resources are devoted to gifted (and talented) students in public schools, this is viewed as fundamentally inequitable. Further, the argument goes that gifted education gives more to those who already have a lot and who will be successful on their own. This "Matthew Effect" viewpoint troubles advocates seeking equity, especially when schools are funded by public dollars.

Less controversial is the term talented, which is less often viewed as elitist. This term seems to be more palatable, as talent speaks less to genetics and more to environment. Talent is viewed as environmental and dynamic—exposure and opportunity can improve creativity as well as skills and accomplishments in the visual and performing arts. Further, hard work and effort can improve one's talent or skills and performance.

A compromise has been the term gifted and talented, which embraces those students with high IQ scores, high achievement scores, high grades, high creativity, and/or strong skills in the visual and performing arts. Using the two terms simultaneously implies that students with these varying gifts or talents are valuable, that one skill is not superior to another.

Robert Sternberg has published several works indicating that few scholars and laypersons can agree upon the definition of intelligent or gifted. He has identified over 100 definitions of intelligence. Several definitions (and theories) of gifted and talented have been proposed by the U.S. Department of Education (six definitions since 1970), Joseph Renzulli, Robert Sternberg, Howard Gardner, Albert Tannenbaum, Lewis Terman, and others. Ongoing discussions and debates include: Which type of gift and/or talent should we identify and serve? Who is gifted and/or talented? How can these gifts and talents be assessed? What are the best delivery and programming options?

A final issue is identification; too often, schools rely extensively or solely on one test to identify, label, place, and serve gifted and talented students. While the federal government and professional organizations have highlighted that such a practice is indefensible or unjustifiable, and although they call for multidimensional assessment approaches, this practice of relying on one test score in gifted and talented education persists. Stated another way, high-stakes testing is prevalent in the process of labeling and placement.

SERVICES AND PROGRAMS FOR GIFTED AND TALENTED STUDENTS

Once students have been identified as gifted and/or talented, educators wrestle with how best to serve them. Questions regarding services and programs are most controversial regarding ability grouping, tracking, and acceleration. That is, to what extent is gifted and talented education a form of ability grouping or tracking? How much are students harmed by ability grouping and tracking? Likewise, is acceleration a viable option for meeting the needs of gifted and talented students?

Generally, ability grouping and tracking have been criticized for limiting the college and career opportunities of students in lower track groups and classes, while privileging those in higher track groups and classes. On this note, some scholars maintain that gifted and talented education is a form of ability grouping or tracking that is riddled with inequities. Those in higher track classes and groups have the added benefit of receiving educational experiences that increase their future options and their chances for succeeding in life. Given, again, that gifted and talented education is publicly funded, it is argued that such programs are inequitable. Opponents offer data indicating that students in lower-ability groups are confronted with lower expectations, lower quality curriculum, and fewer resources. It is further argued that once placed in a low group, it is virtually impossible to move to a higher group, or from a vocational track to an academic or college preparation track. This inability to move from one group or track to another is delimiting for students.

Conversely, advocates of gifted and talented education often avoid the confounding effect of equating ability grouping and tracking with gifted and talented education. Instead, they propose that gifted students need to be appropriately challenged, and that these students often benefit from being grouped with peers who are like them emotionally, cognitively (intellectually), and academically. In such settings, it is maintained that peer pressure decreases and achievement rises. Advocates who do not equate gifted and talented education with ability grouping and tracking often compare gifted and talented education with special education—giftedness is an exceptionality, and gifted and talented education is designed to meet students' exceptional or unique needs. From this view, charges of elitism are unwarranted.

In 1993, the U.S. Department of Education offered a definition that differed radically from previous definitions:

> Children and youth with outstanding talent perform or show the potential for performing at remarkably high levels of accomplishment when compared with others of their age, experience, or environment. These children and youth exhibit high performance capacity in intellectual, creative, and/or artistic areas, and unusual leadership capacity, or excel in specific academic fields. They require services or activities not ordinarily

provided by the schools. Outstanding talents are present in children and youth from all cultural groups, across all economic strata, and in all areas of human endeavor.

Noticeably, the term gifted is absent and has been replaced by talented. Also included in the definition is the notion of potential, the recognition that gifts and talents are difficult to develop without opportunity and exposure. The definition addresses the concept of relativity—comparisons must be justifiable; for instance, comparing low-income students to high-income students, comparing minority students to majority students, is not defensible. Asking them to compete for slots or gifted and talented placement is unfair. Finally, the definition boldly states that no group has a monopoly on gifts and talents; gifts and talents exist in low-income and diverse groups.

No theory of gifted and talented, or even intelligence, seems to prevail. Notwithstanding theories and models by Thurstone, Guilford, Wechsler, Binet, and others, contemporary theories by Howard Gardner, Robert Sternberg, and Joseph Renzulli seem to be in competition, with little consensus on the horizon.

Another contentious topic is acceleration. Often, concerns about acceleration surround issues of social-emotional development. Are students hurt in any way, especially socially-emotionally, when they are placed in classes with older students? In *A Nation Deceived,* James Borland warned against emotional, impulsive, and uninformed assertions about acceleration and, instead, documented that acceleration benefits gifted and talented students when their needs and development— social emotional, cognitive, and academic—are considered in the decision-making process and addressed when teaching students.

DEVELOPING TALENT IN STUDENTS LIVING IN POVERTY

Data from several reports indicate that students who live in poverty seldom participate in gifted and talented classes, including AP classes. The majority of students in such classes come from families of high income and high education. This underrepresentation of low-income or low-socioeconomic status students adds fuel to the fire regarding issues of equity. Recognizing that students living in poverty can be and are gifted and talented, some scholars have developed talent development programs. As with the newest federal definition of gifted and talented presented earlier, these programs acknowledge that lack of opportunity, experience, and exposure pose limits on students; thus, given high-quality educational experiences, these students will rise to the challenge. Such additional opportunities hold much promise for overcoming backgrounds that stifle their intelligence, achievement, and creativity.

DIVERSITY: EQUITY VERSUS EXCELLENCE OR EQUITY AND EXCELLENCE?

A controversial issue is the underrepresentation of black students in gifted education. At no time in the history of gifted education has national data indicated parity for black students. Specifically, in 2002, black students comprised approximately 17 percent of the school population nationally, but less than 9 percent of those identified as gifted. Reports indicate that underrepresentation often ranges from an average of 50 percent to 70 percent. At the high school level, blacks are also poorly represented in AP classes and among those who take the AP exam. White students take AP examinations at nearly six times the rate of Latino students and more than 13 times the rate of African American students. There is a clear need to desegregate gifted and talented education. Mindful of the loss of talent among diverse and low-income students, Congress passed legislation (i.e., the Javits Act of 1988) with the primary goal of supporting efforts to identify and serve diverse and low-income students.

Debates persist regarding changes that can be made to improve the quality of programs and services for gifted and talented black and other culturally diverse students. This discussion comes in the form of debates regarding excellence versus equity, with some works arguing that the two cannot coexist or that they are, somehow, mutually exclusive. Our belief is that excellence and equity can and must coexist.

Most recommendations regarding the identification and assessment of culturally diverse gifted students stress the need to find more reliable and valid ways to recruit them. These alternatives include less-biased or culturally sensitive instruments (e.g., nonverbal tests), multidimensional assessment strategies, and more inclusive philosophies, definitions, and theories of giftedness. While most explanations point to testing issues, the principle barrier to the recruitment and retention of diverse students in gifted education is the deficit orientation that prevails in society and its educational institutions. Deficit thinking impacts gifted education in several ways:

1. Testing and assessment issues. Tests are used extensively, sometimes exclusively, to identify and assess students. Despite concerns regarding bias and fairness, test scores play a dominant role in identification and placement decisions. Over 90 percent of school districts use these test scores. This heavy reliance on test scores for placement decisions keeps gifted programs racially segregated. While traditional intelligence tests may be effective at identifying and assessing white students, they have been less effective with diverse and low-income students. This raises the question of why we continue to use these tests so exclusively and extensively.

2. Eurocentric definitions and theories. There are many definitions and theories of giftedness and/or intelligence, and there is little agreement regarding how to effectively and equitably define "intelligent" or "gifted." Most states continue to define giftedness in limited ways, based on their experiences and views of middle-class whites. IQ-driven and test-driven definitions effectively identify this one group of students but neglect to identify or capture the strengths of students who: (a) perform poorly on paper-and-pencil tasks conducted in artificial settings; (b) perform poorly on culturally loaded and linguistically loaded tests; (c) have different learning and/or cognitive styles;

3. Static policies and practices. Procedural and policy issues also contribute to underrepresentation. Educators consistently under refer diverse students for gifted education screening and services. When teacher referral is the first (or only) recruitment step, gifted black students are likely to be underrepresented.

4. Lack of multicultural preparation among educators. Too few preservice teachers are provided multicultural educational experiences; they are seldom taught how to develop multicultural curriculum and instruction, and too few have internships and practicum in urban settings, etc. That is, too many college students graduate with a colorblind or ethnocentric curriculum that fails to prepare them to work with culturally diverse students. Not surprising, they misunderstand and misinterpret cultural differences among such students relative to learning styles, communication styles, and behavioral styles.

5. Inadequate teacher preparation in gifted education. Nationally, most schools struggle with the low representation of blacks who choose to become teachers. In 1999, the senior author surveyed culturally diverse teachers about their decisions to enter the field of gifted education, general education, or special education. Many teachers reported having little exposure to gifted education in their teacher preparation programs, and most teachers, including those who held degrees in special education, lacked any formal preparation in gifted education. This lack of preparation in recognizing the many different characteristics of gifted students, a lack of understanding of the social, emotional, and psychological needs of gifted students, and a lack of attention to underachievement among gifted students, obstructs teachers' knowledge, skills, and dispositions to make fair and equitable referrals. Again, findings indicate that teachers who lack preparation in gifted education are ineffective at identifying gifted students. Such under prepared teachers may hold stereotypes and misperceptions that undercut their ability to recognize strengths in students who behave differently from their biased expectations.

6. Inadequate communication with black families and communities. When a deficit orientation exists in their minds, school personnel may not communicate with black families about gifted education services, AP courses, and other opportunities (e.g., summer enrichment programs). Parents and caregivers who feel rejected and unappreciated are less likely to involve themselves in school settings.

7. Black students' decisions not to participate in gifted and talented education. Perhaps the worst consequence of deficit thinking is its impact on the social-emotional and psychological development of black students. Too many gifted black students internalize deficit thinking orientations. They question their own abilities and then sabotage their own achievement. For example, some black students adopt the role of class clown or athlete to hide their academic abilities and achievements, and they may refuse to participate in AP classes, academic clubs, and/or gifted education

programs. These students may also give in to negative peer pressures, such as associating academic achievement with "acting white."

SUMMARY

All of education, including gifted and talented education, faces challenges as it seeks to appropriately educate students. Concerns include (a) charges of elitism, (b) different views on terminology, definitions, theories, testing and assessment, services, and programs, (c) problems of under identifying students in poverty, and (d) problems regarding minority student underrepresentation, particularly black students. Despite some attempts to address these longstanding and ongoing debates, problems persist.

Further Reading: Ford, D. Y., 1996, *Reversing underachievement among gifted Black students: Promising practices and programs,* New York: Teachers College Press; Ford, D. Y., & Harris III, J. J., 1999, *Multicultural gifted education,* New York: Teachers College Press; Kozol, J., 2006, *The shame of the nation: The restoration of apartheid schooling in America,* New York: Crown; Suskind, R., 1998, *A hope in the unseen: An American odyssey from the inner city to the Ivy league,* New York: Broadway; U.S. Department of Education, 1993, *National excellence: A case for developing America's talent,* Washington, DC: Author.

Donna Y. Ford and Gilman W. Whiting

GLOBAL EDUCATION

Global education is a curriculum field that emerged in the 1960s with a heritage that derives from academic disciplines, curriculum practice, and sociopolitical phenomenon. As curriculum it has ebbed and flowed in various places around the world over the past four decades, though it has received increasing attention in the most recent decade sparked by interest in and concerns about globalization. Throughout its relatively brief history as a curriculum area, certain themes have coursed through its development, namely connectivity, identity, controversy, and urgency. These themes are highlighted in three approximate stages: Awareness and Interdependence (1960–1980), Diversity, Culture, and Controversy (1980–2000), and Urgency and Contested Visions (2000–present).

ORIGINS

Academic

Global education traces its origins to three broad areas—academic, curricular, and sociopolitical. While global education is not a recognized academic field of study, its heritage is rooted in many disciplines, including foreign policy/international relations, world history, geography, and anthropology. These academic roots are all similar in their focus on connectivity among phenomenon rather than seeing events, people, places, and patterns in isolation. Political scientists with an interest in the relations of nation-states often pursue comparative politics as a means of understanding interstate relations, rather than domestic politics whose unit of analysis is the nation. World history, a subfield of history that has had difficulty gaining a foothold in the academy, works from the premise that social phenomena and intellectual developments in one part of the world shape events in distant civilizations and are thereby connected. While history has been a field that values specialization and precise focus, world historians have favored connectivity and interaction as their founding presumption. Geographers, in a similar light, are predisposed to researching the specific in reference to the universal. While there are geographic anomalies throughout the world, such as the white cliffs of Dover and the fjords of Norway, the differences of Earth's landscape is more of kind than of type. The study of human culture, or anthropology, emerged as a separate discipline out of history in the nineteenth century. Most anthropological study in the latter half of the twentieth century onward has emphasized the fundamental similarity of cultural groups in meeting the basic human needs of the group, despite apparent variability.

Curriculum

While global education involves knowledge from these disciplines and even resembles them at times, it is unique in its purposes. Global education is principally aimed at (1) developing awareness about and appreciation for people who are culturally different, (2) recognizing the interdependent nature of life on the planet, (3) acknowledging challenges related to social injustice and environmental degradation, and (4) committing to thoughtful social engagement on some of these myriad issues. Unlike a disciplinary perspective that aims to educate young people in a way of knowing through a specific set of facts or tools, global education's goal is to produce social changes beyond itself rather than being an end unto itself. Further, unlike most academic disciplines, global education does not employ nation-states as the primary unit of analysis. Rather, it explores diverse relations that people, social groups, and supranational bodies like the United Nations have between and among themselves, irrespective of nations. Though global education does not ignore the importance of the nation-state, it also does not presume its sanctity, overtly challenging what otherwise appears natural to most disciplines.

The origins of this problem-based, social agency view of curriculum can be traced to educational progressivism associated with the early twentieth century. Social progressives such as John Dewey, George Counts, Boyd Bode, and Harold Rugg, for example, viewed the school as a means of transforming society and curriculum as the engine for that change. These curriculum leaders had somewhat different views about how to achieve the ends of social change, be it through child-centered curriculum or a more directive approach to teaching problems on the horizon, but their motivation to use education as a means beyond being simply educated in the traditional sense was clear. Ideally, schools would become incubators of social change rather than institutional-like organizations aimed at supplying workers for their productivity and efficiency. Teachers and students, in such a conception, would be intellectually engaged in the problems of the day and engage in action to address these problems. While there have been pockets of this type of progressive education over time and in some places, this idea of the school as an engine for social change has never been a central focus of education in the United States.

Sociopolitical

The emergence of global education in the 1960s is not coincidental. This was a period of massive social upheaval around the world as formal colonialism mainly ceased, people organized for empowerment through various social movements, and a growing consciousness of the holistic quality of life on Earth developed. Some of this awareness was precipitated by the iconic image of Earth from space, a seemingly lonely planet floating in the void of eternity. For the first time in human history, people could see in Earth-rise the singularity and relatedness of our existence on this fragile planet. This sense of connection was also evident in the struggle for power as liberation movements in one part of the world echoed in others. The civil rights movement in the United States, for example, took cues from India's casting off of more than a century of British rule. The end of legal segregation in the United States was echoed in the anti-apartheid movement of South Africa. The rise of feminism in Nordic and Western European countries resonated throughout the world. Efforts by indigenous people in North American to gain legal recognition shaped discourse for native populations elsewhere. It was a time of social change and upheaval, and global education was one example of how these changes affected the curriculum of schools.

The 1960s was also a period of international upheaval, with the proliferation of nuclear weapons globally, the proxy war in Southeast Asia between the United States and the U.S.S.R., principally in Vietnam, along with the increased bipolarization and related struggles for power in Latin America, Africa, and Asia. Given this context, the Cold War was a prominent sociopolitical force in the origins of global education. As international affairs began to affect domestic life, as in the anxious autumn days in the southeastern United States during the Cuban Missile Crisis of 1962, there was a growing sense in the United States that schools should be more than simply bomb shelters or places to propagandize anticommunist sentiments (though they were used towards those ends). Rather, global education arose from an earnest desire to teach about the points of contention in the Cold War, the use of propaganda on all sides of this divide, and the importance of avoiding annihilation through the build-down and eventual denuclearization of nations through peaceful negotiations.

AWARENESS AND INTERDEPENDENCE (1960–1980)

The first period of global education is characterized by growing awareness that the planet is a fragile place that required stewardship if humankind was to survive. R. Buckminster Fuller's publication of *Operating Manual for Spaceship Earth* in 1963 juxtaposed the fragility of Earth's limited resources with the limitless want of people. He likens the planet to a mechanical system that, if not properly maintained, would surely fail to operate. This seminal work, though widely criticized, developed into an intellectual hallmark and a springboard for further discourse about planetary awareness.

This nondisciplinary work had disciplinary implications in the academy. A new generation of scholars who grew up in the tumultuous 1960s was emerging. One of their primary challenges was to the nature of higher education that rigidly adhered to disciplines and failed to engage students in *relevant* studies. This shift towards relevancy, however unrealized it may have been, did shape the creation of cross-disciplinary courses, programs, and departments. Hybridization was the result as studies such as history and earth science became environmental history and sociology and psychology morphed into social psychology. The move towards relevancy also spawned discourses that largely shook off their disciplinary roots, as women's studies, peace studies, ethnic/area group studies, and sexual identity studies became increasingly prominent.

The notion that knowledge and being were more connected than modern discourses up to the early twentieth century had fully recognized also took shape in K–12 education. Experimentation with knowledge constructs occurred, particularly in social studies curriculum, as life, issues, and problem-based curriculum made significant inroads into schools. Global education was very much a part of this turn. In November 1968, *Social Education,* the national professional journal for social studies teachers, published a special issue entitled *International Education for the Twenty-first Century.* This was a collection of articles from disciplinary scholars in fields such as social psychology, economics, geography, political science, and international relations who attempted to outline the rationale for and development of an international education curriculum. This journal represents the first collection of global education scholarship in one forum, and arguably, the birth of the field. Parenthetically, it is important to note that the term "international" was and continues to be used synonymously with "global." There is an important distinction, however, between these terms, which was alluded to previously: While international presumes the nation-state as the central unit of analysis, global recognizes the nation as significant but does not privilege it in light of the many other means of communication, interaction, and border crossing that exist.

Global education in this formative era was concerned with the Cold War. Much of foreign policy and international relations studies was centered on the relationship between the United States and the U.S.S.R. and their many satellites. Global education was offered in response to, though simultaneous with, curricula such as the once-mandatory course in Florida, *Americanism versus Capitalism,* wherein the course objectives required students to study communism such that they would recognize the supposed superiority of the American way of life. Similar notions, perhaps less overtly, have and continue to be a mainstay of American history and government courses, though the anticommunism theme has less saliency today. In contrast with such curriculum, global education aimed to explore the nature of economic and political difference through a comparative framework, hoping to engage students in earnest consideration of different ways of organizing society. Global education aimed to demonstrate that even though societies organized in different manners, we remained inter-dependent, or one world, despite these differences. The Cold War notwithstand-ing, the United States and the U.S.S.R., and by implication the rest of the world, were dependent on each other for peace, if not a total peace and if only through an anxiety-ridden deterrence policy of mutually assured destruction.

Global education had a degree of relativity built into its curricular outlook, to the extent that it was needed to have a fair, full, and free interplay of ideas about the nature of human life and its interdependent character. A manifesta-tion of global education in this period was the now infamous federally funded course, Man: A Course of Study (or MACOS). The National Science Foundation funded this course from 1964–1975, and it aimed to use disciplinary method-ologies in secondary schools so that students could engage in analytic com-parisons of societies and their own. One of those groups, the Inuit people of Northern Canada, to whom the study referred as "Eskimos" [sic], allowed such comparisons. MACOS aimed to give students a set of comparative models for thinking about the world while fostering an appreciation of human diversity. A wave of popular press and scholarly reports in the mid-1970s contended that MACOS encouraged students to be morally relativistic about divorce, senilicide, murder, female infanticide, and cannibalism. Despite empirical evidence to the contrary, MACOS was not funded and ended rather abruptly. In terms of global education, it foreshadowed the very controversial nature of such curriculum that would become its undoing in the next era.

DIVERSITY, CULTURE, AND CONTROVERSY (1980–2000)

Global education, as if to turn away from the systemic difficulties associated with pressing for world peace, developed a smaller focus in the second era: peo-ple. Coupled with increasing attention to diversity within multiculturalism, global education took a sociological and anthropological turn. Courses of study such as world geography, world literature, global cultures, and multicultural studies were increasingly in evidence in K–12 schools during this era. The central focus of many of these courses was a parade and pageantry of difference. Some have referred to such curriculum as the *foods, festivals, and fairs approach,* as culture was presented to students in celebratory and reified ways. Whereas the earlier era of global edu-cation emphasized the world as a whole, its systemic nature, and our stewardship of it as peace-makers and ecologically aware beings, the middle era downsized this focus to look at people in communities and as members of social groups.

Diversity discourses carried the day in schools rather than global education. While many viewed global education as too broad, incomprehensible, far away, and politically untenable, they took refuge in multiculturalism that celebrated differences within a national context. Most multiculturalism, even to the current day, presumes diversity remains bound by the nation-state. This is due in part to the development of multiculturalism around issues of social justice and towards antidiscriminatory education. As education was almost entirely a matter bound by nations, to redress the social inequities of education systems required a focus on the nation by definition.

Global education employed diversity in a similar vein, though it moved the conversation towards a consideration of global others, however complicated a focus that may be. A few sociopolitical phenomena guided this focus, as society and schools in the United States increasingly dealt with immigration from Latin America, specifically Mexico, refugees from Cambodia, Haiti, and elsewhere, and tensions within the United States and Western Europe around demographic changes. As technology capital led a period of economic expansion among Western and some Asian countries such as Japan, the North/South gap of living standards grew. This difference created an increase in immigration to economically developed societies, or a south to north flow of people. Tensions arose in this period, and remain today, around the cultural identity of immigrants. In the United States, this new group of immigrants from Pacific Rim countries and Latin America sought to maintain a strong ethnic identity through cultural ways and language.

Schools, to varying degrees, accommodated these changes in various ways. Multicultural education was increasingly evident, particularly as textbook companies began to ride the wave of identity. Teaching English as a Second Language (or TESOL) and bilingual education grew programmatically across the country, as schools needed to serve an increasingly polyglot population. Global relief efforts were also increasingly evident in schools, evidenced by the surge of interest about famine in East Africa in the mid-1980s sparked by the *We Are the World* music video and related MTV attention to this crisis. The teaching of world languages in U.S. secondary schools more than doubled in the period 1982–2000, courses that were for some students the only contact they would have with a culture outside the nation.

Increased attention to diversity, in global education, per se, and in other aligned studies such as world languages, multiculturalism, and world literature led to an aggressive backlash against "other" discourses by educational conservatives, mainly at the state and local level. Many of these groups, such as the Fordham Foundation and Eagle Forum, provided financial support. In 1979, the U.S. Department of Education created a Task Force on Global Education to support its development, but by 1986, support waned. The Denver office of the U.S. Department of Education published a report entitled "Blowing the Whistle on 'Global Education,'" accusing the field of being anti-American, one-sided, relativistic/nihilistic with regard to moral issues, and obsessed with promoting a redistributive economic world order. There were many state challenges to global education that undid much of the curriculum policy achieved in the initial era. By the mid-1990s, global education seemed to be just another passing fad in education relegated to minor curriculum status.

URGENCY AND CONTESTED VISIONS (2000–PRESENT)

The current era is characterized by a growing sense of urgency for something like global education and a cacophony of contested visions about what that something should be. Thomas Friedman's widely read books about globalization, *The Lexus and the Olive Tree* (1999) and *The World is Flat* (2005), along with an array of academic publications that reached a wide audience, created a palpable energy about global discourses. Friedman's basic thesis is that the world has irrevocably changed in a way that has decentered nation-states and centered technology sectors and corporate capital who can effectively morph to survive in this new, flat world. This intellectual climate coupled with the events of September 11, 2001, and subsequent wars in Afghanistan and Iraq provided a gravity and impetus for renewed urgency about world affairs. Additional developments added to this attention, such as definitive scientific evidence of global warming, increasing evidence of a beleaguered ocean system that threatens much of aquatic life in the near term, numerous studies documenting an unprecedented period of mass extinction among nonhuman animals presently, and catastrophic natural disasters including hurricanes and tsunamis that destroyed flood prone regions and their inhabitants. The interest in global education, which had languished for over a decade, was rekindled out of a sense of urgency for some, desperation for others.

Yet this third era of globalization promises to be much more diffuse and contested than the previous ones. Where the period 1960 to 2000 involved a relatively small group of people interested in and dedicated to expanding global education, in the current period, a much wider audience has become engaged in those efforts. Global education projects are no longer largely the domain of scholars in education, as academics across academe have taken an interest. Colleges and universities increasingly fund and develop a variety of global programs, from student exchanges to launching universities in other countries to developing research networks among various countries. One would be hard-pressed to find a four-year college or institution that does not include a world, international, or global focus as part of its core mission. And the same can be said of many high schools as they increasingly get on the global bandwagon.

The contested visions of global education that are beginning to emerge can be roughly categorized into five clusters: neoliberal, cosmopolitan, disciplinary, critical, and social justice. The neoliberal argument for global education follows closely with Thomas Friedman's critique, that an economically interconnected world that is hypercompetitive requires entrepreneurial skills, business acumen, and an adroitness to change rapidly among the next generation. The National Center on Education and Economy, for example, released a report in 2006 entitled "Tough Choices, Tough Times: The report of the new commission on the skills of the American workforce." This report epitomizes the global education advocated by neoliberals, or an education that is internationally benchmarked, is equal to leading economic countries, and affords students the knowledge and skills to be internationally competitive. The cosmopolitan notion of a global education is also outwardly oriented, though focused on the ethics of such interactions. Cosmopolitan global education emphasizes the commonality of all people, rather than focusing on particular identities, and seeks to explore and develop the many ways in which people are more alike than dissimilar.

A disciplinary global education is one that values knowing the world but within an academic framework that allows it to be comprehensible. World historians, for example, advocate knowing about the world's history of interconnection so that actions taken are grounded in a thoroughgoing examination of our shared past. Geographers and those in international relations, similarly, advocate knowing the world but are largely dismissive of the notion that such knowing can occur beyond the boundaries of well-honed, disciplinary way of knowing. Critical perspectives, and they range in kinds from those related to gender, deep ecology, and neo-Marxist, are highly suspect and critical of globalization. As to global education, their notion is one that aims to critique the base economic and power moves that are at work in globalization. For the various critical perspectives, a global education must be suspect of the very phenomenon that gave rise to its urgency, globalization, and must engage in a strident critique of its means, objects, and aims.

Civic global education is one that is also of a critical nature, but does not see the global system as inherently unworkable. Rather, civic global educators aim to push the global community in the direction of creating structures for global citizens to be part of a larger civic than their localities and nations. This aim is perhaps best illustrated by the move to adjudicate the most heinous human rights violations through supranational bodies like the newly founded International Criminal Court. The recently integrated European Union is a model for civic global education advocates, as it has numerous supranational bodies that work in, through, and with nations of Europe to achieve a broader notion both of a European identity and a global civic ideal. The urgency of the current era of global education is apparent as it manifests in multiple areas and at various levels of curriculum, becomes cross-fertilized by other areas of discourse, and is increasingly viewed as contested terrain. Predicting the future of the next era of global education is impossible. Yet based on a curricular history that consistently reflects and mirrors wider social concerns of the day, we can be reasonably certain of an interplay between significant global events and phenomena in the world to come and the curriculum era that awaits.

Further Reading: Bigelow, B., & Peterson, B., 2002, Rethinking globalization: Teaching for justice in an unjust world. Milwaukee: Rethinking Schools Press; Gaudelli, W., 2003, *World class: Teaching and learning in global times,* Mahwah, NJ: Erlbaum Associates; Hanvey, R. G., 1976, *An attainable global perspective,* New York: Center for War/Peace Studies; Heilman, E., 2006, Critical, liberal, and poststructural challenges for global education, in A. Segall, E. Heilman, & C. Cherryholmes (Eds.), *Social studies the next generation: Researching in the postmodern,* New York: Peter Lang; Merryfield, M. M., 2001, Moving the center of global education: From imperial world views that divide the world to double consciousness, contrapuntal pedagogy, hybridity, and cross-cultural competence, in W. B. Stanley (Ed.), *Critical issues in social studies research for the 21st century,* Greenwich, CT: Information Age Publishing; Pike, G., & Selby, D., 1999, *In the global classroom: Volumes 1 & 2,* Toronto: Pippen Publishing.

William Gaudelli

GOVERNMENT ROLE IN SCHOOLING

At the beginning of the twentieth century, the role of government in schooling was to provide free public schools for children. So it was at the fin de siècle.

What, then, changed? In 1900, schools were almost entirely the creatures of local governments. States played little role in their financing and operations, and the federal government was wholly absent. Come 2000, the role of local governments in schooling had ebbed while the role of state governments and the federal government had grown. Expressed as dollars, in 1900, local governments provided more than 80 percent of school funds; state governments contributed the rest. The federal government contributed none. By 2000, localities provided 43 percent of school funds, states 48 percent, and the federal government 9 percent.

These funding figures exhibit the growth of state influence over the schools. To cite just a few examples: State governments set high school graduation requirements, operate student learning testing and assessment programs, and dictate the certification requirements for teachers.

However, these numbers obscure arguably the most profound transformation in the government role in schooling, which is the dramatic rise in the power of the federal government to influence school operations. During the twentieth century, the federal government went from having no role whatsoever to playing some part in virtually every aspect of schooling. Policies and actions of the federal government have affected schools' curricula and school policies toward minority (racial, language) and handicapped children, provided school lunches, funded cultural and arts programs and drug and alcohol abuse deterrence programs, and more. Furthermore, the growth of state education agencies and their development into highly professionalized entities was spurred, largely, by the federal government. Increasingly, the roles of state and local governments have been sculpted by actions of the federal government. As will be seen, the growth of the federal government's role in schooling has come through two means: federal court decisions and federal grants-in-aid policies.

GOVERNMENT ROLE IN SCHOOLING ENTERING THE TWENTIETH CENTURY

Government's role as the provider of free education developed in fits and starts since the earliest settlement of North America. Though many children were educated by their parents or in private academies, some early localities and colonies did provide schools. In 1642 the Massachusetts Colonial Court decreed that due to the "great neglect of many parents and masters, in training up their children in learning and labor, and other employments, which may be profitable to the commonwealth," that we the court "do hereby order and decree, that in every town, the chosen men appointed to manage the prudential affairs . . . shall henceforth stand charged with the redress of this evil." The leaders of the towns could be fined and punished if they failed to remedy illiteracy among children, who were thought ignorant of "the principles of religion and the capital laws of this country."

The establishment of public schools was encouraged by the land management policies of the earliest federal governments of America. For example, the Northwest Ordinance of 1785 provided for the sale of Western lands by the federal government. As a condition of sale, it required that "[t]here shall be reserved the lot N. 16, of every township, for the maintenance of public schools within the said township." During the nineteenth century, the growth of government-sponsored schools accelerated. Many local governments, often nudged by states and zealous educators, established simple schools that would provide rudimentary educational skills training, such as reading and writing. Progress, though, was uneven, particularly in rural and low-income communities, where limited tax bases and the agrarian way of life inhibited the development of modern schools.

GOVERNMENT PROVISION BUT NOT COMPULSION

Private schools have existed since the European settlers arrived in North America. While all levels of government have recognized a community interest in the education of children, this has not meant that government has an absolute power to compel student attendance to government-funded or "public" schools. This limited power was stated forcefully by the Supreme Court in *Pierce v. Society of Sisters of the Holy Names of Jesus and Mary* (268 U.S. 510 [1925]) when it struck down an Oregon law that required parents to send their children to a public school. The Court declared,

> We think it entirely plain that the Act of 1922 unreasonably interferes with the liberty of parents and guardians to direct the upbringing and education of children . . . under their control. As often heretofore pointed out, rights guaranteed by the Constitution may not be abridged by legislation which has no reasonable relation to some purpose within the competency of the state. The fundamental theory of liberty upon which all governments in this Union repose excludes any general power of the state to standardize its children by forcing them to accept instruction from public teachers only. The child is not the mere creature of the state; those who nurture him and direct his destiny have the right, coupled with the high duty, to recognize and prepare him for additional obligations.

Throughout the twentieth century, this antagonism between the professed interests of communities in schooling children and the rights of parents over their children has recurred. Frequently, these disputes have been litigated and judges have had to rule on nettlesome issues, such as the right of parents to homeschool their children.

HOW THE FEDERAL GOVERNMENT ASSUMED A ROLE IN SCHOOLING

In its enumeration of the powers of the federal government, the U.S. Constitution makes no mention of schooling or education. Moreover, the Tenth Amendment of the Constitution declares: "The powers not delegated to the United States [government] by the Constitution, nor prohibited by it to the states, are reserved to the states respectively, or to the people," How, then, was the federal government able to assume a role in schooling? In great part, the vehicle has been grants-in-aid. Put succinctly, a grant-in-aid is an offer of funding by the federal government to states or localities. In exchange for the funds, the recipient of the grant must expend it on the purposes stipulated by the grant and obey the grant's mandates (i.e., "conditions of aid"). Thus, grants-in-aid, have provided the primary means through which the federal government has leapt over the federalism divide, which purported to separate governing responsibilities between the federal and state governments, and assumed a role in schooling.

The Growth of the Federal Role in Schooling, 1917–1958

In a pattern that was to be repeated during the twentieth century, the establishment of the first major federal education policy was spurred by a crisis. As the federal government began to draft men to fight in World War I, it found that 25 percent of them were illiterate. President Woodrow Wilson, a Ph.D. and former university president, found this troubling and favored education legislation to remedy this problem. He believed that the modern industrial economy and military needed workers and soldiers who were literate and skilled in industrial trades. Thus, one month before the United States formally entered World War I, President Wilson signed the Smith-Hughes Vocational Act (P.L. 64–347) on February 23, 1917.

The Smith-Hughes Act appropriated money "to be paid to the respective states for the purpose of co-operating with the states in paying the salaries of teachers, supervisors, and directors of agricultural subjects, and teachers of trade, home economics, and industrial subjects, and in the preparation of teachers of agricultural, trade, industrial, and home economics subjects." The act established the surprisingly powerful Federal Board for Vocational Education, which was empowered to set the requisite qualifications for an individual to be hired as a vocational education teacher. The board also could withhold federal funds from schools that violated federal education standards of what constituted appropriate agricultural, home economic, vocational, and industrial educational curricula. The statute mandated that states set up state vocational education boards that would work with the federal board.

Over this breakthrough, however, the federal government's role changed little over the next three decades. During the Great Depression, agencies such as the Public Works Administration, the Civilian Conservation Corps, and the National Youth Administration provided emergency funding to cash-strapped schools. In 1934, emergency aid reached approximately $2 to $3 million per month. By 1940, PWA had helped local and state authorities build 12,704 schools with 59,615 classrooms. This brief expansion of the federal role in schooling, though, contracted once the Great Depression passed.

Between 1946 and 1958, the federal role suddenly spurted. On June 4, 1946, the School Lunch Act (P.L. 79–396, 60 Stat. 231) was signed into law by President Harry S Truman. The law declared it "to be the policy of Congress . . . to safeguard the health and well-being of the Nation's children and to encourage the consumption of nutritious agricultural commodities and other foods, through grants-in-aid." The school lunch program required schools to provide low-cost or free lunches to children; in exchange, schools receive cash subsidies and food from the Department of Agriculture.

Impact aid (P.L. 81–815; 64 Stat. 967 and P.L. 81–874; 64 Stat. 1100) was enacted into law four years later (September 23, 1950, and September 30, 1950). This policy grew out of a 1940 program to fund infrastructure projects (sewers, recreational facilities, etc.) in areas where the federal government had a large presence (e.g., military installations, federal agencies, etc.) Mobilization for World War II created a huge growth in the size of the federal workforce. Military facilities occupied large swaths of land, which removed them from state and local tax rolls. (States and localities may not tax the federal government.) In time, the presence of these facilities and workers brought forth children who needed schooling. Impact aid was devised to reimburse these federally affected areas. Each year, communities provide the federal government with data on costs (e.g., educational costs) and receive reimbursement based upon a formula.

The launch of the Sputnik satellite by the Soviet Union on October 4, 1957, set off a media and political firestorm in the United States. While President Eisenhower downplayed the significance of the event, many inside and outside of Congress whipped up a frenzy. Senator Lyndon B. Johnson made especially fantastic claims. Control of space, he told the press, would make for control of the world, as the Soviets would have the power to control the weather and raise and lower the levels of the oceans. The schools were blamed for this situation. Prominent persons, such as former President Herbert Hoover and Senator Henry Jackson (D-WA), claimed that Soviet schools were producing far more brainpower than American schools. In the name of national defense, many said, more federal education aid was needed. Less than a year later, the National Defense Education Act (NDEA, P.L. 85–864; 72 Stat. 1580) became law on September 2, 1958. Much of the NDEA benefited colleges, showering them with funds for research grants for technical training and advanced studies. Public high schools also benefited. Secondary schools were given funds to identify "able" students who should be encouraged to apply for federal scholarships for collegiate study in foreign languages, mathematics, and science.

Despite this growth in the federal role, many attempts to expand it further failed. Between 1935 and 1950, dozens of bills were introduced into Congress to provide general aid to public schools. Some of the bills would have raised teachers' salaries; others would have provided grants and low-interest loans to districts that needed to build bigger and more modern schools. In a hint of things to come, a number of bills were introduced that would have provided federal monies to create a floor in per pupil spending. This latter proposal would have helped poor school districts, where property values were low, leaving schools grossly underfunded. All of the proposals to increase and equalize school funding stalled in Congress, blocked by members who saw little sense or propriety in an expansion of the federal role in schooling.

The Federal Government's Promotion of Equity in Schooling, 1954–1975

For much of its existence, the federal government did little to expand access to schooling for special needs and nonwhite children. On occasion, the U.S. Congress provided aid. For example, in 1864, the federal government helped found the Columbian Institution for the Deaf, Dumb, and Blind, which later became Gallaudet University. The federal government also aided in the development of schools for nonwhites. Subsequent to treaties signed with American Indian tribes, the federal government funded and operated schools on Indian reservations. The federal government aided blacks by chartering Howard University in 1867 (Chap. CLXII; 39 Stat. 438). At the close of the Civil War, the federal government also forced confederate states to rewrite their constitutions to include provisions to require states to provide schooling for all children. (Previously, many black children and those in isolated rural areas lacked access to schooling.) Between 1954 and 1975, however, the federal government moved to the fore in expanding access to schooling.

The federal government's first major effort at ensuring equity in education came in the form of a Supreme Court decision. The case, *Oliver Brown et al. v. Board of Education of Topeka et al.* (347 U.S. 483), popularly known as *Brown v. Board of Education*, came on May 17, 1954. The Court noted that education was "perhaps the most important function of state and local governments." That said, it denied that states and localities could require children to attend racially segregated schools. Separate schooling was "inherently unequal," said the Court, and violated the Fourteenth Amendment's due process clause. States must, the Court declared, make schooling "available to all on equal terms." The upshot of the Brown case was the gradual demolition of states' racially segregated schooling. The Brown decision and those federal court decisions that followed it led to the federal policy of busing children to achieve racial desegregation. This policy was largely abandoned after 1980.

In the wake of America's "discovery of poverty" and rising violence in urban areas, the federal government greatly expanded its role in schooling and its funding of schooling through the enactment of the Elementary and Secondary Education Act of 1965 (ESEA, P.L. 89–10; 79 Stat. 27) on April 11, 1965. The act lifted the federal contribution to school funding to over 8 percent of total school funding. The ESEA provided funds for a number of school programs, the largest of which was Title I (also known as Chapter I). This program provided funds for schools to expend on compensatory education programs for nonwhite and poor children. The ESEA also provided funds to help state education agencies professionalize their operations. Over time, ESEA funds and mandates helped build state agencies into formidable educational administration agencies.

The federal government further expanded its role as promoter of equity in schooling with the enactment of the Bilingual Education Act of 1968 (P.L. 90–247; 81 Stat.783, 816) on January 2, 1968, and the Education for All Handicapped Children Act of 1975 (P.L. 94–142; 89 Stat. 773) on November 29, 1975. Both of these acts established programs to helps public schools to better teach under served children. The former act provided funds for instruction in English and foreign languages. The latter act forbade school systems from excluding children with mental or physical handicaps from schools and provided funds for programs to help school these children.

Finally, the federal government expanded its role further still when it forbade states from denying schooling to the children of illegal immigrants. When the state of Texas enacted a statute to deny children of illegal immigrants the right to attend school, the Supreme Court struck it down. In *Plyler v. Doe* (457 U.S. 202 [1982]), the Court stated that although these children did not have a fundamental right to schooling, the law did deny the children the equal protection under the law guaranteed by the Fourteenth Amendment to the Constitution because it erected "unreasonable obstacles to advancement on the basis of individual merit."

The Proliferation and Diversification of the Federal Government's Role in Schooling, 1976–1999

Over the next quarter of a century, the federal role in schooling became more diversified. The Office of Education was replaced by the Department of Education on October 17, 1979 (P.L. 96–88; 93 Stat. 668). This upgrading of federal administration solidified the federal government role in a number of areas, including compensatory education, bilingual education, vocational education, and educational research. New grants-in-aid programs proliferated; come the end of the century, the federal government funded school programs in arts education, physical fitness, school technology, anti-drug and alcohol dependency classes, character education courses, and more.

During this period, criticism arose over the efficacy of federal programs, such as Title I of the ESEA. In response, the federal government began creating policies to increase student learning as measured by tests. Congress enacted Goals 2000 (P.L. 103–227; 108 Stat. 125) on March 31, 1994, and amended the ESEA's Title I grants-in-aid program via the Improving America's Schools Act of 1994 (P.L. 103–382; 108 Stat 3518) on October 20, 1994, and the No Child Left Behind Act of 2002 (P.L. 107–110; 115 Stat. 1425) on January 2, 2002. Under the new Title I, the conditions of aid required states and localities to experiment with school choice or voucher programs. Funds were provided for the development of privately operated but open-to-all-children charter schools. The new Title I also required local school districts to permit students attending underperforming schools to choose the public school they attended. As a further condition of aid, these policies required states to develop accountability systems consisting of academic standards and tests that would be used to hold schools accountable for student learning.

CONCLUSION

States and localities provide the vast majority of funds for public schools. It is these two levels of government that have the greatest power to prescribe schools' curricula, set the compensation and standards for the licensure of teachers and administrators, and oversee day-to-day school operations. Nevertheless, as the federal government has assumed a larger and larger role, more and more of what states do occurs within a context set by the federal government. Through court decisions and grants-in-aid programs, the federal government, despite its modest contribution to school funding, has taken a broad and significant role in the public schools.

Further Reading: Angus, D. L., & Mirel, J. E., 1999. *The failed promise of the American high school, 1895–1995,* New York: Teachers College Press; Howell, W. G., 2005, *Besieged: School boards and the future of education politics,* Washington: Brookings Institution Press; Kosar, K. R., 2005, *Failing grades: The federal politics of education standards,* Boulder, CO: Lynne Rienner Publishers; National Center for Education Statistics, 2006, *Digest of education statistics, 2005,* Washington: NCES; The No Child Left Behind Act of 2002 retrieved January 4, 2006, from http://www.ed.gov/policy/elsec/leg/esea02/index.html.

Kevin R. Kosar

GRADING POLICIES

Four school policies impose procedural barriers to the implementation of standards-based reforms, and there are specific strategies for correcting them. These policies all relate to grading and reporting practices; that is, how students' learning progress is summarized and communicated to parents, students, and others. Despite their importance, grading and reporting are seldom mentioned in discussions of curriculum or assessment reform. Nevertheless, they exert powerful influence and can prevent even modest success in any standards-based reform initiative.

POLICY 1: GRADING "ON THE CURVE"

Grading and reporting must be done in reference to specific learning criteria, rather than in reference to normative criteria or "on the curve." This means that students must be graded in terms of what they have learned and are able to do, *not* in terms of their relative standing among classmates. Using the normal distribution curve as a basis for assigning grades ensures consistent grade distributions from one teacher to the next. Consequently, every teachers' classes have approximately the same percent of As, Bs, Cs, etc. But the consequences of this practice are overwhelmingly negative. Strong evidence shows that it's detrimental to the relationships among students and to the relationships between teachers and students.

Grading "on the curve" makes learning a highly competitive activity in which students compete against one another for the few scarce rewards (high grades) distributed by the teacher. Under these conditions, students readily see that helping others become successful threatens their own chances for success. High grades are attained not through excellence in performance, but by doing better than one's classmates. As a result, learning becomes a game of winners and losers, and because the number of rewards is kept arbitrarily small, most students are forced to be losers.

Perhaps most important, grading "on the curve" communicates nothing about what students have learned or are able to do. Rather, it tells only a student's relative standing among classmates, based on what are often ill-defined criteria. Students who receive the high grades might actually have performed very poorly in terms of the established learning standards, but simply less poorly than their classmates. Differences between grades, therefore, are difficult to interpret at best and meaningless at worst.

If the purpose of grading is to reflect what students have learned and are able to do, then grading "on the curve" falls far short. Furthermore, modern research has shown that the seemingly direct relationship between aptitude or intelligence and school achievement depends on instructional conditions, *not* a normal distribution curve. When the instructional quality is high and well matched to students' learning needs, the magnitude of this relationship diminishes drastically and approaches zero. Moreover, the fairness and equity of grading "on the curve" is a myth.

Solution

In any educational setting where the central purpose is to have students learn, grading and reporting should always be done in reference to specific learning criteria. Because normative criteria or "grading on the curve" tell nothing about what students have learned or are able to do, they provide an inadequate description of student learning. Plus, they promote unhealthy competition, destroy perseverance and other motivational traits, and are generally unfair to students. At all levels of education, therefore, teachers should identify what they want their students to learn, what evidence best reflects that learning, and what criteria they will use to judge that evidence. In other words, they should clarify their standards and base their grading criteria on those standards. Grades based on specific learning criteria and standards have direct meaning and serve well the communication purposes for which they are intended.

POLICY 2: SELECTING THE CLASS VALEDICTORIAN

Although most teachers today understand the negative consequences of grading "on the curve" and have abandoned the practice, many fail to recognize other common school policies that yield similar negative consequences. One of the most prevalent is the selection of a class valedictorian. There is nothing wrong, of course, with recognizing excellence in academic performance. But in selecting the class valedictorian, most schools operate under the traditional premise that there should be *only one*. This commonly results in severe and sometimes bitter competition among high-achieving students to be that "one." Early in their high school careers, top students figure out the selection procedures and then, often with the help of their parents, find ingenious ways to improve their standing in comparison to classmates. Again, to gain that honor a student must not simply excel; he or she must outdo the other students in the class. And sometimes the difference among these top achieving students is as little as one-thousandth of a decimal point in a weighted grade point average.

Solution

An increasing number of high schools have resolved this problem by moving away from the policy of having just one valedictorian and, instead, name multiple valedictorians. This is similar to what colleges and universities do in naming graduates cum laude, magna cum laude and summa cum laude. West Springfield High School in Fairfax County, Virginia, for example, typically graduates 15 to 25 valedictorians every year. Each of these students has an exemplary academic record that includes earning the highest grade possible in numerous honors and Advanced Placement classes. Instead of trying to distinguish among these exceptional students, the faculty at West Springfield High School decided that all should be named valedictorians. In other words, rather than creating additional, arbitrary criteria in order to discriminate among these high achieving students (considering, for example, their academic record from middle school or even elementary school), they decided to recognize the excellent performance of the entire group. And because the faculty at West Springfield High School believes their purpose as teachers is not to *select* talent, but rather to *develop* talent, they take great pride in these results. All of the valedictorians are named at the graduation ceremony, and one student, selected by his or her fellow valedictorians, makes a major presentation.

Some might object to a policy that allows multiple valedictorians, arguing that colleges and universities demand such selection and often grant special scholarships to students who attain that singular distinction. But current evidence indicates this is not the case. In processing admission applications and making decisions about scholarships, college and universities are far more interested in the rigor of the curriculum students have experienced. In fact, an index composed of the number of Advanced Placement courses taken, the highest level of math studied, and total number of courses completed has been shown to be a much stronger predictor of college success than standardized test scores, grade point average, or class rank. The rigor of the academic program experienced by the valedictorians from West Springfield High School has helped them gain admission and win scholarships to many of the most selective colleges and universities in the nation.

Recognizing excellence in academic performance is a vital aspect in any learning community. But such recognition need not be based on arbitrary criteria and deleterious competition. Instead, it can and should be based on clear models of excellence that exemplify our highest standards and goals for students and for ourselves. If many students meet these high standards of excellence, all the better.

POLICY 3: USING GRADES AS A FORM OF PUNISHMENT

Although educators would undoubtedly prefer that motivation to learn be entirely intrinsic, the existence of grades and other reporting methods are important factors in determining how much effort students put forth. Studies show that most students view high grades as positive recognition of their success, and some work hard to avoid the consequences of low grades.

At the same time, no studies support the use of low grades as punishments. Instead of prompting greater effort, low grades more often cause students to withdraw from learning. To protect their self-images, many regard the low grade as irrelevant and meaningless. Other students may blame themselves for the low grade, but feel helpless to make any improvement.

Sadly, some teachers consider grades their "weapon of last resort." In their view, students who do not comply with their requests must suffer the consequences of the greatest punishment a teacher can bestow: a failing grade. Such practices have no educational value and, in the long run, adversely affect students, teachers, and the relationship they share.

Solution

Rather than attempting to punish students with a low grade in the hope it will prompt greater effort in the future, teachers can better motivate students by considering their work as incomplete and then requiring additional effort. Recognizing this, some schools have initiated grading policies that eliminate the use of failing grades altogether. Teachers at Beachwood Middle School in Beachwood, Ohio, for example, record students' grades as A, B, C, or I (Incomplete). Students who receive an I grade are required to do additional work in order to bring their performance up to an acceptable level. This policy is based on the belief that students perform at a failure level or submit failing work largely because teachers accept it. If teachers no longer accept substandard work, however, they reason that students will not submit it and, with appropriate support, will continue to work until their performance is satisfactory.

Beachwood Middle School teachers believe strongly that giving a failing grade to students who have not performed well, despite their ability to do so, offers them an easy way out. If, on the other hand, teachers insist that all assignments designed to demonstrate learning be completed and done well, then students will choose to do their work in a timely fashion and at a satisfactory level of quality. The guiding maxim of the teachers at Beachwood Middle School is "If it's not done well, then it's not done!"

Implementing such a grading policy requires additional funding for the necessary support mechanisms, of course. Students who receive an I grade at Beachwood, for example, are required to attend afterschool make-up sessions or special Saturday school programs staffed by teachers, volunteer parents, and older students. Those who are unable or unwilling to do the make-up work during the school year must attend required summer school sessions designed to help them bring their performance up to an acceptable level. Although these support mechanisms demand commitment and additional funding, schools implementing such programs generally find them to be highly successful. Many also discover that in the long run, they actually save money. Because this regular and ongoing support helps students remedy their learning difficulties before they become major problems, less time and fewer resources need to be spent in major remediation efforts later on.

At all levels of education, we need to think seriously about the use of failing grades. Although honesty must prevail in assessments and evaluations of student learning, we also must consider the negative consequences of assigning failing grades to students' work or level of performance. Especially in the early years of school, the negative consequences of failing grades are quite serious and far outweigh any benefits. Even in upper grades, the fear of failure is a questionable motivation device. Better and more effective alternatives to failing grades need to be found, especially in a standards-based system. The use of Is or incomplete grades present one meaningful alternative, especially if the necessary policies and resources are put in place to support those students who need additional assistance.

POLICY 4: USING ZEROS IN GRADING

Another related grading policy that hinders the implementation of standards-based reforms is the use of zeros. Many teachers assign zeros to students' work that is missed, neglected, or turned in late. That zero, however, seldom reflects what a student has learned or is able to do. Instead, zeros are assigned to punish students for not displaying appropriate effort or demonstrating adequate responsibility. Obviously, if the grade is to represent how well students have learned or mastered established learning standards, then the practice of assigning zeros clearly misses the mark.

The impact of assigning zeros is intensified if combined with the practice of averaging to attain a student's overall course grade. Students readily see that receiving a single zero leaves them little chance for success because such an extreme score so drastically skews the average. That is why, for example, in scoring Olympic events like gymnastics, diving, or ice-skating, the highest and lowest scores of judges are always eliminated. If they were not, one judge could control the entire competition simply by giving extreme scores.

Some teachers defend the practice of assigning zeros by arguing that they cannot give students credit for work that is incomplete or not turned in—and that's certainly true. But there are far better ways to motivate and encourage students to complete assignments in a timely manner than through the use of zeros, especially considering the overwhelmingly negative effects.

Solution

Students must learn to accept responsibility for their actions and should be held accountable for their work. Nevertheless, no evidence shows that assigning zeros helps teach students these lessons. Unless we are willing to admit that we use grades to show evidence of students' lack of effort or inappropriate responsibility, then alternatives to the practice of assigning zeros must be found.

One alternative approach is to assign an I or "Incomplete" grade with explicit requirements for completing the work, as described above. Students who do not complete their work or do not turn it in on time, for example, might be required to attend afterschool study sessions and/or special Saturday classes until their work is completed to a satisfactory level. In other words, they are not "let off the hook" with a zero. Instead, students learn that they have certain responsibilities in school and that their actions have specific consequences. Not completing assigned work on time means that you must attend special afterschool sessions to complete the work. Implementing such a policy may require additional funding and support. Still, the payoffs are likely to be great. Not only is it more beneficial to students than simply assigning a zero, it's also fairer. In addition, it helps make the grade a more accurate reflection of what students have learned.

SUMMARY

While grading will always involve professional judgment, making those judgments requires careful thought and continuous reflection on the purpose. If grades are to represent information about the adequacy of students' performance with respect to clear learning standards, then the evidence used in determining grades must denote what students have learned and are able to do. To allow other factors to influence students' grades misrepresents their learning attainments.

Grading requires careful planning, thoughtful judgment, a clear focus on purpose, excellent communication skills, and an overriding concern for students. Such qualities are necessary to ensure grading policies and practices that provide high quality information on student learning in any standards-based learning environment.

Further Reading: Guskey, T. R., 2002, *How's my kid doing? A parents' guide to grades, marks, and report cards,* San Francisco: Jossey-Bass; Guskey, T. R., ed., 1996, *Communicating student learning. 1996 yearbook of the association for supervision and curriculum development,* Alexandria, VA: Association for Supervision and Curriculum Development; Guskey, T. R., & Bailey, J. M., 2001, *Developing grading and reporting systems for student learning,* Thousand Oaks, CA: Corwin Press; Guskey, T. R., & Marzano, R. J., 2002, *Grading and reporting student learning—Professional development inquiry kit,* Alexandria, VA: Association for Supervision and Curriculum Development.

Thomas R. Guskey

HEAD START

Head Start is a comprehensive program serving low-income families with young children. Since its inception in 1965, Head Start (HS) has served more than 23 million young children and their families.

HEAD START HISTORY

In 1964 the Head Start Planning Team recommended that HS begin as a comprehensive program that would include health, dental, educational, social, and parent involvement services. Head Start was established on the basis of two assumptions: comprehensive early childhood services could positively affect the social competence of young children; and low-income children, whose home environments could not provide the stimulating environments of their middle class peers, would benefit greatly from such early childhood services. The planning team recommended a pilot program of 50,000 children so researchers could measure children's performance and undertake longitudinal studies on the benefits of the program. The team estimated that it would cost $1,000 per child to provide comprehensive services. Concerned over the costs of such a large-scale pilot program, the federal government funded the initial HS summer program at $180 for each of the 561,000 children served. (Zigler & Muenchow, 1992).

Head Start's first summer program in 1965 served 561,000 in 2,400 communities. Participation rose to 733,000 children in the second year of the summer-based program in 1966. In 1971 the program was converted from a summer program to a school-year program. However the overwhelming support that HS had enjoyed during its first stage waned so that by 1971 the number of children served had dropped to 397,000. The slowdown in funding was, in part, a reaction to the conclusions of the Westinghouse Study, the first major evaluation study of HS that was released in 1969. The study found that elementary aged children who attended HS did not score higher on standardized tests than their peers. This challenged the notion that HS would eradicate school failure and subsequently poverty. The Westinghouse Study's results, paired with the changing political climate, which focused less on social programs, had a significant impact on HS's history.

From 1969–1978 (see Table H.1), HS funding remained relatively flat and there was little growth in the program. Federal performance standards were developed during this time as well as a national Child Development Associate (CDA) credential for HS teachers. Head Start added disability services and mandated that at least 10 percent of the enrollment include young children with disabilities. In 1978 Congress increased the HS budget by 33 percent, increasing the number of HS children served by 43,000. Training and technical support services were developed to assist local grantees (Zigler & Muenchow, 1992).

In the 1990s the HS budget increased to provide services for an additional 180,000 children. Another program, Early Head Start, was begun. Early Head Start is a program for expectant families or parents with infants and toddlers. Grantees provide services through both home- and center-based programs. In response to welfare reform, Head Start legislation mandated that grantees develop or partner with child care programs to provide full-day services to HS families.

The increased funding for HS was coupled with increased expectations of grantees and program staff. A child assessment system was developed and implemented, and half of the HS teachers were required by 2003 to obtain a two-year degree in early childhood education or child development. More intensive monitoring of local programs was implemented, resulting in some grantees losing their HS program funding.

Several studies were released or begun during the 1990s. Begun in 1997, the Head Start Family and Child Care Experiences Survey (FACES) described, assessed, and evaluated the programs, children, and families enrolled in 40 HS

Table H.1 Head Start Budget and Number of Children Served

Year	Budget	Enrollment
1965	96,400,000	561,000
1970	325,700,000	477,400
1975	403,900,000	349,000
1980	735,000,000	376,300
1985	1,075,059,000	452,080
1990	1,552,000,000	540,930
1995	3,534,128,000	750,696
2000	5,267,000,000	857,664
2005	6,843,114,000	906,993

programs. The Head Start Impact Study focuses on two questions: What impact does HS have on children's development (particularly school readiness), and under what circumstances and for which children and their families does HS have the greatest impact? The Early Head Start Research and Evaluation Project assessed children and families who were randomly assigned to 17 Early Head Start programs (home-based, center-based, or combined center- and home-based programs) or a control group. Findings from these three studies include that children attending HS had significant developmental gains (particularly for African American and Latino children); families had greater access to health and dental care; specific preschool curricula positively impacted children's outcomes; and children who attended two years of HS had greater gains than children who attended the program for one year. However, HS children scored below the national average on developmental assessments regardless of how long they were enrolled in the program.

HEAD START TODAY

In 2005 1,604 local grantees served 906,993 children in HS programs at an average cost of $7,287 per child. The children are a diverse ethnic and racial population: 35 percent are Caucasian, 31 percent are African American, 24 percent are Latino, and 4 percent are Native American. The majority are 3- and 4-year-olds: 52 percent are 4-year-olds, 34 percent are 3-year-olds, 10 percent are under 3 years of age, and 4 percent are 5 year olds.

Head Start Eligibility Guidelines

Over 90 percent of families qualifying for HS do so based upon their income. HS uses the federal poverty income rate to determine eligibility for the program. In 2004, the federal poverty rate income for a family of four was $22,000. Families with young children with disabilities may apply for HS regardless of their incomes since HS regulations mandate that young children with disabilities comprise 10 percent of the enrolled population (in 2005, 12.5 percent of children enrolled in HS have a diagnosed disability).

Head Start does not provide services to all eligible families. Current estimates are that 60 percent of income eligible families with preschoolers and 10 percent of income eligible families with children under three years old are served.

Family Structure and Income

Since the inception of the Personal and Responsibility Act, or welfare reform, most HS parents are in the paid workforce: 75 percent are working, 18 percent receive public assistance, and 7 percent are enrolled in school or some other activity. Traditionally HS has served more single parent families than two parent families. The percentage of single parent families is higher than two parent families, and two parent families are more likely to have a full time parent in the workforce.

Head Start Services

There are three models of HS services: home-based (a home-based teacher conducts regularly scheduled home visits); center-based (child attends an infant/toddler or three- and-four-year-old program); or a combination of both home visits and a center-based component. Over 90 percent of the children served attend center-based services. Currently 49,000 children are enrolled in the home-based program.

HS programs provide dental, physical, mental health, social, nutritional, and educational services to families enrolled in the program. Children receive annual health and dental screening, and Head Start helps coordinate any required follow-up treatment or care. Center-based programs provide meals and educational activities to the children enrolled in the program. Head Start family support personnel work directly with individual families to assist them in accessing educational and training opportunities, employment, housing, physical and mental health services, and other community resources.

Parent Involvement

Head Start has a long-rooted commitment to working with parents and children. In 2005 890,000 parents volunteered in their child's classroom. A two-generational model provides services to parents/caregivers and children. Partnerships with adult literacy and English as a Second Language program are features found in many HS programs. Since the inception of welfare reform, Head Start grantees are increasingly offering full day services or partnering with child development centers in the community to provide full day services for working parents.

Head Start Staff

Head Start staff are racially and culturally diverse and include program directors, coordinators, classroom teachers, classroom aides, family support personnel, home visitors, and bus drivers. Twenty-nine percent of HS staff are fluent in two languages, and 27 percent of staff members are parents of children who are currently or were formerly enrolled in the program (Hamm & Ewen, 2005). In 2005 69 percent of HS teachers had at least a two-year degree in early childhood education. Recent legislation mandates that 50 percent of Head Start teachers obtain a bachelor's degree by 2008.

Head Start Governing Structure and Funding

Head Start is organized as a federal-local agency partnership operating under the auspices of the Administration for Children and Families, Department of Health and Human Services. It is funded through a Head Start Reauthorization Act that is passed by Congress every four years. The federal government provides 80 percent of program funding to local grantees, and the grantee contributes a 20 percent match. In addition to funding, which amounted to $6.8 billion in FY 2006, the act includes new policies and directives that, over time, have helped shape the current form and operations of the HS program.

Head Start agencies (or grantees) submit a grant proposal every three years to the regional HS office that includes a service plan based upon the needs of the community. This plan must comply with the Head Start Performance Standards, which are divided into three major components: early childhood development and health services (implementation of a curriculum and assessment system to prepare children for kindergarten and providing health, dental, and nutrition services); family and community partnerships (parent and community involvement on governing boards and daily operation of the program); and program management/operation (programs comply with HS procedures and mandates that are evaluated with on-site visits). Depending on the funding available, grantees may request additional funding for increasing enrollment, specialized services, or teacher salaries.

Every three years each HS grantee undergoes a peer review, an intensive on-site evaluation of the program operation that includes classroom observations, examination of records and operating procedures, and interviews with parents and community members. The peer review team includes the use of the Program Review Instrument for Systems Monitoring of Head Start and Early Head Start Grantees (PRISM), designed to assess program compliance in the following areas of service: health, environment, disabilities, mental health, family and community, transportation, education and early childhood development, fiscal management, and program design and management. If the peer review team reports that a grantee is out of compliance with HS standards, the grantee will be required to make the necessary changes. In some cases, grantees lose their funding and the HS grant in the area is open to applications from other agencies.

Head Start grantees are governed by a policy council and board of directors with the authority to make decisions regarding the operating budget, personnel, and program operation. Federal policy stipulates that HS parents comprise 51 percent of the policy council membership, and the remaining 49 percent are community members. Members of the board of directors represent the community and have the expertise to insure that HS funds and operation are in compliance with federal policies and standards.

ONGOING ISSUES

One of the ongoing issues facing HS is funding constraints; only a fraction of the income-eligible families are enrolled in the program. In 1965, during its first summer program, Head Start served over 500,000 children; after that time enrollment dropped dramatically. It was not until the early 1990s that HS enrolled the same number of children as it did in 1965. Another result of the budget is that HS teachers, 50 percent of whom are required to obtain a bachelor's degree by 2008, earn $26,500 per year compared to the average public school salary of $42,000. Teacher turnover is 18 percent, and most teachers report that salary is one of the major reasons for changing jobs. In the proposed HS bill, there is no additional funding for HS teacher salaries.

The quality of HS classrooms varies greatly, and there is concern about this disparity and how to improve the quality of services for all children and families. There are increased measures to monitor program quality and provide grantees with training and technical assistance to improve services. In addition, proposed legislation would implement procedures to defund poorly performing grantees and open the bid to other community programs.

With the enactment of the No Child Left Behind Act of 2001 there is increased pressure for program accountability including measuring children's performance. The new HS assessment system, the National Reporting System (NRS) implemented in 2003, assesses all preschool children at the beginning (430,000 four- and five-year-old children in fall 2003) and end of the program year in the areas of mathematics and literacy. Like the testing results from other studies, NRS findings are that HS children made gains in these areas but scored lower than the national norm. Since the assessment began, questions about the reliability and validity of the test have been raised including a letter of concern from 100 early childhood educators and psychologists indicating that test scores predict 25 percent or less of the variance in children's academic performance in kindergarten and first grade (Hill, 2003). Because of these concerns, the proposed Head bill requires that the National Academy of Sciences review and revise the National Reporting System.

Further Reading: Ceglowski, D., 1998, *Inside a Head Start center: Developing policies from practice,* New York: Teachers College Press; Hamm, K., & Ewen, D., 2005, Still going strong: Head Start children, families, staff, and programs in 2004, retrieved January 5, 2007, from http://www.clasp.org/publications/headstart_brief_6.pdf; Hill, W., 2003, The National Reporting System: What is it and how will it work? *Head Start Bulletin,* 76; National Head Start Association, n.d., *Head Start basics,* retrieved January 5, 2007, from http://www.nhsa.org/download/advocacy/HSBasics.pdf; U.S. Department of Health and Human Services, 2005, Head Start impact study: First year findings, retrieved January 5, 2007, from http://www.acf.hhs.gov/programs/opre/hs/impact_study/reports/firstyr_sum_title.html; U.S. Department of Health and Human Services, 2006, FACES 2003 research brief: Children's outcomes and program quality in Head Start, retrieved January 5, 2007, from http:www.acf.hss.gov/programs/opre/hs/faces/reports/research_2003/research_2003_title.html; U.S. Department of Health and Human Services, 2006, Head Start program fact sheet, retrieved January 5, 2007, from htttp://www.acf.hss.gov/programs/hsb/research/2006.html; Zigler, E., & Muenchow, S., 1992, *Head Start: The inside story of America's most successful educational experiment,* New York: Basic Books.

Deborah Ceglowski and Janet Ceglowski

HOMELESS CHILDREN AND SCHOOLS

As the waters of hurricanes Katrina and Rita receded from Gulf Coast cities in the fall of 2005, America and the world witnessed evidence of the persistent social and economic inequality in the United States despite the nation's record gains in productivity and wealth during the last two decades. Homeless children and youth are emblematic of this duality in American society, and it is important to focus on the growing population of homeless children in the United States and the challenges to educating them.

In the past 15 years, homelessness has increased dramatically across the United States. An estimated 800,000 people are homeless on any given night, and overall, between 2.3 and 3.5 million Americans—roughly 1 percent of the U.S. population—experience homelessness during a given year. Historically the majority of homeless people were white, single, middle-aged men. However, in recent decades, families of women and children have become a sizable segment of the U.S. homeless population. Children and adolescents are almost half of the homeless population. Forty-four percent of homeless individuals are members of homeless families, and they are disproportionately from racial and ethnic minority backgrounds.

HOMELESSNESS AND POVERTY

The relationship between poverty and homelessness is clear. Poverty is the result of the interaction between structural forces, tragic circumstances, and sometimes, bad choices. However, structural forces such as the restructuring of the U.S. economy, especially the disappearance of manufacturing jobs; an inadequate minimum wage; inadequate affordable housing, public transportation, and child care; and the growing holes in the social safety net are key factors contributing to the growth of poverty in twenty-first-century America. Although the United States has one of the highest per capita Gross National Products (GNP) in the world, the United States also has higher levels of poverty than most developed countries. As of 2005, over 37 million Americans lived in poverty. Children account for 25 percent of the total U.S. population, but 35 percent of the population of poor Americans. Additionally, America's child poverty rate is significantly higher than that of the majority of other Western industrialized nations.

Homeless citizens in central cities account for over 70 percent of the total homeless population in the United States. The links between urban poverty and homelessness rest on two economic trends. First, the transformation of the inner city labor market for poorly educated workers has resulted in growing income inequality. Skilled jobs that paid living wages and benefits have been relocated either to the suburbs, the Sunbelt, or overseas. Urban job growth has been largely in the tertiary sector (finance and information sectors). Poorly educated inner city residents typically do not have the credentials and skills to compete for such jobs. The lack of skills and education among the poor, especially in inner cities, and the changing labor market contribute to the economic marginalization of millions of Americans.

The second trend is the diminishing stock of affordable housing in urban centers where many poor people live. Urban renewal in many American cities led to the destruction of affordable housing as older, less expensive housing was destroyed and few suitable replacements were built. Although low-income housing is generally located in central cities, there is still a significant shortage of affordable housing in the metropolitan regions. Inadequate federal housing policy for the poor and the lack of affordable housing are key contributing factors to homelessness. This situation was exacerbated by the devastation of homes by hurricanes Katrina and Rita. An estimated 302,000 housing units were lost, the vast majority of which were affordable to low-income families.

HOW MANY HOMELESS STUDENTS?

Counting the number of homeless persons in the United States historically has been challenging. For example, estimates of the number of homeless children reflect only children from families that passed through public or private agencies serving the homeless. The estimates do not account for homeless students who are doubled up with relatives or friends or are living in hidden places. Enumerations of homeless children rarely include homeless youth.

Homeless youth should not be confused with homeless children who are members of homeless families. A homeless youth is as an individual who is not less than 16 or more than 21 years of age for whom it is not possible to live in a safe environment with a relative and who has no other safe alternative. Homeless youth often are "family-less" because they ran away from their homes (or institutional placements), usually because of conflicts with parents (or guardians); they were forced from or locked out of their homes by their parents or step-parents; they feel they no longer have a home to which they can safely return because of irreconcilable differences with their parents; or they lost track of their family's location. A significant proportion of homeless youth flee from sexual or physical abuse, high levels of familial conflict, or virulent intolerance of their homosexuality.

The best estimates indicate that, at any given time, between 300,000 and 500,000 young people are living out of the home in unstable and unsupervised environments. The difficulty in estimating the actual size of the population of homeless youth, like homeless children and adults, lies in the challenge of accurately counting people who are transitory and, in the case of youth, who are relatively secretive about their lives.

EDUCATIONAL CHALLENGES OF HOMELESS YOUTH

Arguably, homeless children and youth continue to be the most at risk for school failure of any identifiable student population. Like other low-income students, homeless youth suffer disproportionately from the effects of hunger, disease, and family crises that undermine achievement and learning. Children whose families are in crisis are less able to learn in school; children with no safe place to sleep, wash, or relax are less able to learn in school. Poor nutrition is a serious threat to their school performance. School districts themselves rarely provide medical and dental care, clothing, job referrals, housing, or other social services to homeless children and their families. Therefore, students who do not otherwise receive these services are at a marked disadvantage relative to their peers.

Homeless students face economic deprivation, family loss or separation, insecurity, social and emotional instability, and, in general, upheaval in their lives. Those who are enrolled in schools may receive some services, depending upon which school district they attend. But many homeless children and youth are not enrolled in school. Homeless parents who do not enroll their children in school may be embarrassed about their living situation or too exhausted from trying to meet daily needs for food and shelter to navigate what seems to be an impenetrable school bureaucracy. Some parents feel forced to keep their children out of school because of their lack of access to laundry or bathing facilities. Many homeless children refuse to attend school for fear of taunts from other students, lack of clean clothing and school supplies, or their inability to perform well.

Nevertheless, most homeless children attend school. They are enrolled in traditional classrooms or in special programs that serve as transitions to regular classrooms. The proportion of homeless youth who attend school is far lower. A variety of barriers prevent homeless youth from continuing their educations. These include the effects of living on the streets, work schedule conflicts, substance abuse, health problems, extreme poverty, developmental lags, and emotional and psychological problems. Schools are rarely equipped to accommodate adolescents without homes or families.

Once homeless children are in school, their problems in obtaining an appropriate education often continue. Homeless families are highly mobile. Each change of residence may involve a change in school. Teaching largely transitory and impoverished students poses numerous challenges, and teachers rarely have the necessary expertise to address the complexity of homeless students' needs. Among the problems that teachers confront is the gap in skills and knowledge that many homeless students possess due to their low rate of past school attendance. In addition, homeless children typically face all of the educational difficulties faced by other youngsters from low-income families. They frequently come to school unprepared and/or exhibit behaviors that are not socially acceptable in the school setting.

Homeless students may find the traditional classroom curriculum and learning activities irrelevant because they are so detached from students' lived experiences. The way schools are organized for instruction assumes continuity. High student mobility also makes it more difficult for schools to provide meaningful services. When children move from school to school, continuity of instruction is virtually impossible. If children remain in a school for only a short period of time, it is difficult to provide any educational services of lasting value, or to begin to repair the damage done by the combination of their prior spotty attendance, instructional instability, and the conditions of living in poverty.

Students with disabilities are an identifiable homeless subpopulation with particularly acute and often unmet needs. Even the stipulations within special education statutes designed to bring services to eligible students do not overcome the formidable barriers providing appropriate education to homeless student with disabilities. For example, by the time a referral has been made, eligibility has been determined, and a placement can be provided, homeless students may well have moved to another school. Children with limited English proficiency who require bilingual services, students with academic problems who require remedial services, gifted student who are eligible for special programs, and children who are undocumented immigrants frequently fail to obtain the special services they need and to which the law entitles them.

THE STEWART B. MCKINNEY HOMELESS ASSISTANCE ACT

The U.S. Congress recognized the threat to school success posed by homelessness when it passed the first comprehensive legislation to aid homeless students. The 1987 Stewart B. McKinney Homeless Assistance Act, its subsequent Amendments in 1990 and 1994, and more recently, the reauthorized 2001 McKinney-Vento Homeless Assistance Act provided considerable protection for the educational needs of homeless children and youth by removing many formal barriers to schooling faced by this population of students. Individual states receive funds from the McKinney Act and then channel grant monies to local educational authorities that provide services to these youngsters.

The 2001 McKinney-Vento Homeless Assistance Act was reauthorized as a part of the No Child Left Behind legislation. McKinney-Vento clarifies definitions and standards for determining eligibility and helping homeless children obtain an education. Currently, it is the only federal guideline for the education of homeless children. The central provisions of the McKinney Act and its amendments are:

- Equal access to public school education. The act requires states not only to provide appropriate education but also to ensure that local school districts do not create a separate education system for homeless children.
- Preschool. States are required to ensure that homeless preschoolers have equal access to the same public preschool programs that housed children enjoy.
- Removal of barriers to access. Educational authorities must remove barriers to enrollment and attendance. Typically these include immunization requirements, guardianship requirements, lack of transportation, birth certificates, school records, or other documentation.
- Choice of school placement. Homeless children may attend their school of origin (the last school in which the child was enrolled) or transfer into any school in the attendance area in which the child is currently living.
- Equal access to school programs and services. Educational authorities must ensure that homeless students and preschoolers have the same access to special education or gifted education as their housed peers.
- Direct services. The 1990 amendments permit schools to use McKinney funds to provide before- and afterschool programs, tutoring programs, referrals for medical and mental health services, preschool programs, parent education, counseling, social work services, transportation, and other services that may not otherwise be provided by public schools.
- Interagency coordination and communication. School systems are required to coordinate their efforts among state social services agencies and other relevant programs and service providers (including programs for preschoolers and runaway youth) in order to improve the provision of comprehensive service.

STATUS OF EDUCATION FOR HOMELESS STUDENTS

States and local school districts have improved their services to homeless students during the past 20 years. With few exceptions, states have reviewed and revised their laws, regulations, and policies to remove obstacles to the education of homeless children and youth. There is a high level of success in identifying and eliminating the barriers once posed by policies on residency and school records. Enrollment barriers related to immunization and guardianship records persist and are not so easily modified. Yet, even with improved access through removal of residency barriers, homeless students in different districts within the same state often have uneven access to educational services. State policies that exempt homeless students from enrollment requirements do not eliminate barriers unless schools and districts are aware of and enforce these policies; unfortunately, many do not.

There remain discernible subgroups whose educational and social needs are particularly striking and require special attention that is typically not provided in most schools. Among these subgroups are independent youth, gifted and talented children, students with learning or physical disabilities, and children of undocumented immigrants.

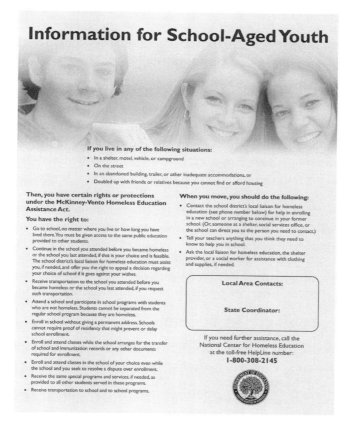

Figure H.1   Information for School-Aged Youth, *National Center for Homeless Education.*

Successful Approaches to Educating Homeless Students

Once homeless students arrive in schools and receive the various services they need as a prelude to learning (these can include nutrition, clothing, shelter, diagnostic assessments, counseling, transportation, and medical and dental care), they require rigorous curricula engagingly taught by qualified instructors. Indeed, this is what all students require. In addition, homeless students require a host of ongoing services. Successful approaches to educating homeless children include the following:

> Address family needs. Homeless students whose families receive social services are better able to succeed in school.
>
> Coordination and collaboration in service delivery. A coordinated, collaborative approach across programs, institutions, and other service providers seems to be especially important when dealing with homeless students and their families.
>
> Implementation. State and local educational authorities must remove all barriers to implementation of the McKinney-Vento Act so that all homeless children between the ages of 3 and 21 obtain the educational opportunities to which they are entitled by law. Although there have been noteworthy improvements in the removal of barriers to the education of homeless children and youth, serious implementation problems persist.
>
> Attention to homeless youth. Independent homeless youth require flexibility in school procedures in the areas of admissions criteria, attendance policies, course offerings, and class assignments. School officials must attempt to accommodate independent homeless youth's job requirements, the absence of places suitable for them to do homework, and other related problems they face. They also require emotional support, access to community resources and services such as special education and transportation.
>
> Parental involvement and support. Parental involvement and support are essential for homeless children. Although parents of homeless students may recognize the importance of education, they often are too preoccupied with securing their family's needs to effectively advocate for their children's educational needs. Services to parents that include information on the importance of involvement as well as strategies that they can employ despite their own educational limitations can facilitate their effective involvement in their children's education.

LOOKING TOWARD THE FUTURE

The aftermath of 2005, hurricanes Katrina and Rita illustrated how the problem of homelessness itself is inextricably connected to the larger issue of poverty in America. Until the sources of social, political, and economic inequality that create poverty and homelessness are addressed, homeless families and their children will be found within sight of the skyscrapers, museums, and luxury apartments of major cities, and homeless students will be a presence in American schools. Adequately educating homeless children cannot be delayed until poverty is addressed. McKinney-Vento requires public schools to educate homeless students. Whether schools can or should provide high quality, equitable education to homeless students without also providing the same to other children in poverty remains an unanswered moral and practical dilemma beyond the scope of this chapter. However, recognition that the phenomena of poverty and homelessness are linked may be helpful for policymakers and educators charged with the responsibility of educating homeless children and youth in America's schools.

Further Reading: Burt, M., 2001, *What will it take to end homelessness?* Washington, DC: Urban Institute; Cunningham, M., & Henry, M., 2007, *Homelessness counts,* Washington, DC: National alliance to end homelessness; Iceland, J., 2006, *Poverty in America: A handbook,* Los Angeles: University of California Press; Mickelson, R., 2000, *Children on the streets of the Americas: Globalization, homeless, and education in the United States, Brazil, and Cuba,* New York: Routledge; Newman, R., 1999, *Educating homeless children,* New York: Garland; Nuñez, R., 2004, *A shelter is not a home... Or is it?* New York: White Tiger Press.

Roslyn Arlin Mickelson and Rajni Shankar-Brown

HOMESCHOOLING

The contemporary homeschool movement in the United States began in the late 1960s and has since steadily gained momentum, numerically, politically, and socially. Differences in policies regulating the registration and tracking of students being homeschooled vary across the states, and the desire of many families to protect their privacy makes it difficult to obtain precise figures. Estimates place the numbers of homeschooled students in the mid-1980s at between 200,000 and 300,000, and demographers currently believe the number to be approximately 1.35 million. This represents a 450 percent increase over approximately 20 years' time and suggests that the homeschool population is growing 10 times as fast as that of students in public school.

As the homeschool movement has grown, key research has been conducted about parental motivation for homeschooling and the socialization and academic achievement of homeschooled children. At the same time, criticism has been leveled at proponents of the homeschool movement by those who see it as a threat to public education and social cohesiveness.

THE GROWTH OF THE HOMESCHOOL MOVEMENT

Although homeschooling occurred prior to the widespread legalization of its practice, it was considered a rare and isolated phenomenon, an unthinkable practice for the majority of Americans. Those who did engage in it were often considered deviants and were frequently persecuted by public school and law enforcement officials. Sociologist James S. Coleman's (1990) recollection of his first encounter with the idea of homeschooling, in the late 1940s, illustrates this point:

> I worked one summer while still in high school, as a counselor in a summer camp. Exploring one day, I found in the woods near a cliff,

which overlooked the Ohio River, a beautiful house built entirely of cedar wood. A more idyllic, rustic setting would have been difficult to imagine. But the house was vacant. When I inquired about it, I learned the owner was an artist who had lived in the house with his wife and children. The family had left, moving to another state, because of a conflict with the state law: He and his wife wanted to educate their children at home, but the state law required them to send their children to school, either a public school or a state-approved private school. The family, strong in its convictions, left the house and moved to a state in which home-based education in lieu of school attendance was legal.

I was unprepared for this experience. I had attended small-town public schools in rural Ohio which approximated the "common school" that was Horace Mann's ideal. I scarcely knew of private schools, and certainly not of education at home. True, some of the farmers grumbled about having to send their able-bodied sons to high school during planting or harvest when they were needed, but even they fully accepted the principle of the public school. (pp. x–xi)

Through the first three-quarters of the twentieth century, homeschooling was illegal in most states. The few states that permitted it did so primarily because of geographically isolated populations of children without access to public schools. As the numbers of American families choosing to homeschool their children

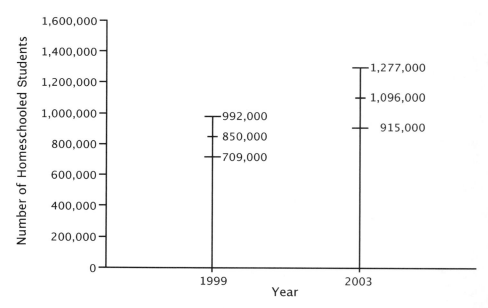

Figure H.2 Estimated Number and 95 Percent Confidence Interval for Number of Homeschooled Students, Ages 5 through 17 in Kindergarten through 12th Grade: 1999 and 2003.
Source: National Center for Educational Statistics http://nces.ed.gov/pubs2004/2004115.pdf.

grew, especially during the 1980s, they also engaged in effective lobbying efforts that resulted in legislative changes, and by 1993 homeschooling had become legal in every state. Three reasons have been suggested for this. First, home-school parents faced a relatively simple political task because they focused on educational policy and not broader issues of public policy. Second, their desire for less state intrusion required little, if any, state fiscal support and appealed to budget conscious lawmakers. Third, the relatively small size of the homeschooled population made it difficult to oppose or justify stringent regulations on the grounds that it posed an overriding threat to public education. And, if opponents drew too much attention to the growth of the homeschool movement, it could backfire and instead raise more questions about why public schools had fallen out of favor with a growing number of parents in the public sector.

Five phases summarize the development of the home education movement from 1970 to 1990: contention, confrontation, cooperation, consolidation, and compartmentalization. The contention and confrontation phases, which occurred from 1970 through the early 1980s, were periods of legal combativeness and court challenges during which parents and school districts battled over compulsory attendance laws. The cooperation phase started in the early to mid-1980s and marked the beginning of the implementation of policies allowing homeschooled children to benefit from public school facilities and programs. Despite the beginning of cooperation, there was still much contention and disagreement between homeschoolers and public school districts. The consolidation phase took place in the late 1980s and was characterized by numerical growth, networking, legislative lobbying, and public acceptance. The compartmentalization phase, which emerged in the 1990s as a result of a diminished need for a united front among homeschoolers as they succeeded in legitimizing their practice, showed signs of ideological division and dissent among various homeschool factions.

The growth, visibility, influence, and arguably the ideological direction of the homeschool movement have been strongly influenced by two organizations that were founded to promote its legitimacy. In 1983, Michael Farris and Mike Smith, two attorneys who were also homeschooling parents, began the Home School Legal Defense Association (HSLDA) as a nonprofit organization to fight for the legal rights of homeschooling families. The HSLDA identifies itself as a Christian organization, although it is careful to say that its mission is to protect the rights of all homeschoolers, regardless of religious persuasion. It limits support to parents engaged in *private* homeschooling, and will not accept as members parents whose children are in public or charter school independent study programs. The HSLDA has also formed close ties with conservative politicians and activists whom many would identify as being members of the "Religious Right" or Christian conservative persuasion.

The organization has grown over the years and now employs 9 attorneys and over 50 staff members. It is also closely aligned with Patrick Henry College in Leesburg, Virginia, which was founded in 2000 as an independent Christian college to prepare and develop students, especially those who have been home-schooled, to forward the HSLDA worldview and its political agenda. Michael

Farris served as its first president, and he is currently its chancellor. He also serves as general counsel to the HSLDA.

In 1990, Brian D. Ray, a former college professor and homeschool parent, founded the National Home Education Research Institute (NHERI), a nonprofit organization to conduct and collect research about homeschooling. Although NHERI does not publicly adopt the overtly Christian stance of the HSLDA, its research agenda is clearly one that is intended to provide research that supports and forwards the cause of homeschooling. Among its goals are working with legislators on Capitol Hill and at the state and local level "on issues related to parental rights, the freedom we have to teach our children at home, and homeschoolers coordinating with local school officials." Ray has written numerous articles about homeschooling, virtually all of which promote it as superior to public schooling, both socially and academically.

As a result of the relatively high profile of these organizations inside and outside of the homeschool community, as well as their aggressive promotion of homeschooling in the popular media, homeschooling is being favorably portrayed in circles where less than 20 years ago it was often maligned. Much of its popular portrayal is due to studies and reports that consistently seem to suggest that homeschools are academically superior to public schools.

AN OVERVIEW OF THE RESEARCH RELATED TO HOMESCHOOLING

Homeschooling has been the subject of research for the past several decades; however, homeschooling is difficult to study and the research is limited. Samples in quantitative studies tend to be small in size, nonrandom, and difficult to generalize from. Many people who homeschooled early in the movement feared exposure or persecution and actively eschewed contact with anyone who wanted to examine their methods or motives. Even after legalization and widespread acceptance, homeschoolers have been reluctant to provide information about themselves to traditional researchers, feeling they might have ulterior motives that would compromise their privacy or misrepresent their views.

Parental Motivations for Homeschooling

Early researchers of the contemporary homeschool movement suggested it was initiated by "pedagogues," parents who wanted to remove their children from traditional public and private schools because they believed that the curriculum and teaching methods being promulgated inhibited their children's development and learning. These parents felt schools were overly bureaucratic and depersonalized their children's education. Some parents thought the schools were just inept at preparing students. Another group soon joined the pedagogues in their desire to control their children's education. They were called "ideologues" and described as parents who were religiously motivated and wanted to protect their children from secular humanism and other antireligious forces they believed were being promoted in public schools. The ideologues were also portrayed as wanting to forge closer bonds with their children, and the family relationship was seen as central. Later researchers have suggested that the pedagogue/ideologue dichotomy was somewhat simplistic and incomplete, and that it is now thought to be an outdated identification scheme.

Some research studies undertaken during the mid- and late 1980s indicated that Christian parents identified politically as a part of the conservative right became more vocal and active in lobbying for homeschooling. Other studies suggested that there was a middle ground, and that parents' motivations were more multi-dimensional and complex, even mainstream. The reasons cited range from libertarian perspectives with parents not wanting involvement with the government, to unsatisfactory experiences parents had in school as children, to fear about student safety and a desire to protect children from negative peer influences.

The Socialization of Homeschooled Children

Much of the criticism of the homeschool movement has been grounded on the premise that children who don't attend school will suffer adverse effects in terms of their abilities to communicate and interact with others, both adults and peers. Not surprisingly, groups that tend to support traditional education, such as teachers' unions, warn that homeschooled children will have difficulty getting along with others, or with eventually leaving the home environment in "real life." Homeschoolers vehemently disagree, contending that schools and school-yards are inherently bad models for positive socialization and relationships.

A review of this research suggests that children are not kept at home in isolation from others and society. Parents report that their children participate in organized athletics, attend music and dance lessons, have part-time paid jobs, do volunteer work, belong to clubs and participate in hobby groups outside of home and visit cultural and educational institutions such as museums and concerts. In addition, fewer than 3 percent of fourth-graders who are home-schooled watch more than three hours of television a day, as compared with 38 percent of fourth-graders who attend school.

The research about how content homeschooled students are with the frequency and quality of contact with their peers outside of home is inconclusive. Older children report missing friends at school events such as dances and games and feel behind about "what's in style," leading to the conclusion that they feel socially isolated. In a later study, homeschooled middle school age children reported satisfaction and no sense of isolation.

A handful of studies have examined the question of how well homeschooled students are learning rules for appropriate social behavior and forming positive attitudes about themselves. This research suggests they are successful and faring no worse than their school attending peers. It is important to note, however, that neither the numbers of studies nor the sample sizes are particularly large, and that social adjustment and attitude formation is a complex area, so inferences must be made with these considerations in mind.

Now that two generations of students have been homeschooled, studies are beginning to focus on how well they do in their post-homeschooling lives. A small group of families who homeschooled their children in Hawaii demonstrate that they all attended college, many attaining graduate degrees, and that they all were working or parenting (or both) and contributing to society. In a survey of more than 230 homeschool graduates, 69 percent had gone on to post-secondary education while 31 percent were employed, figures that closely mirror those of traditional high school graduates. Homeschoolers attending a small private college scored highest among the groups on two-thirds of the indicators, many in areas related to leadership.

Academic Performance of Homeschooled Students

There have been numerous studies of the academic performance and achievement of homeschooled students. In general, research suggests that homeschooled students do at least as well or better academically than their peers in public school. In all but a few studies, students taught at home consistently scored higher than the average public school student. In one of the largest studies of homeschooled students' academic performance, homeschooled students had above average achievement in all academic areas.

The growing body of research seems to suggest that homeschooled children are well adjusted and are achieving academically at least as well as their peers being educated in public schools. Sampling methods and sizes are a problem, however, and there are questions of how much of the research has been conducted and promoted by people with an interest in portraying homeschooling in a positive light. Most of the data that have been collected and analyzed were obtained from families who were willing to share this information, and it is possible that those with less than optimal outcomes might be reluctant to share them. And while most states have procedures for monitoring homeschooled children's progress, they vary considerably and aren't widely reported, making any sort of independent verification difficult.

Social Critics and Future Trends in Homeschooling

As the homeschooling movement has gained acceptance and is portrayed in a positive light by the popular media, it has come under criticism from scholars and educators who feel that it poses a threat to public education by removing social capital (both in the removal of students and concerned parents to support schools), and by undermining the democratizing effects that shared experiences can impart on students. The two most vocal critics have been Michael Apple and Chris Lubienski. They see the embracing of homeschooling as an ominous trend toward pursuit of private interests and a move away from support for public education and local communities.

A major trend in the homeschooling movement is the proliferation of on-line and virtual schools. Parents currently may choose from over 30 virtual schools available on the Internet, representing both Christian and secular perspectives. Many states have on-line charter schools that cater to homeschoolers (with some accepting out-of-state students who pay tuition), making it possible for students from one state to "be homeschooled" in another state. And there is mounting evidence of homeschooling gaining in popularity in other countries, such as Canada, Norway, the Netherlands, Japan, and South Africa. It is possible, therefore, that American students of the future could remain at home and receive their education from a virtual school in another country, potentially changing the very definition of homeschooling.

Further Reading: Apple, M. W., 2000, The cultural politics of home schooling, *Peabody Journal of Education, 75*(1&2), 256–271; Beilick, S., Chandler, K., & Broughman, S. P., 2001, *Homeschooling in the United States: 1999,* Washington DC: U.S. Department of Education, National Center for Educational Statistics; Coleman, J. S., 1990, Choice, community, and future schools, in W. H. Clune & J. F. Witte (Eds.), *Choice and control in American education,* Bristol, PA: The Falmer Press; Green, C. L., & Hoover-Dempsey, K. V., 2007, Why do parents homeschool? A systematic examination of parental involvement, *Education and Urban Society, 39*(2), 264–285; Knowles, J. G., Marlow, S. E., & Muchmore, J. A., 1992, From pedagogy to ideology: Origins and phases of home education in the United States, *American Journal of Education, 100,* 195–235; Lubienski, C. 2000, Whither the common good? A critique of home schooling, *Peabody Journal of Education, 75*(1&2), 207–232; Mayberry, M., Knowles, J. G., Ray, B., & Marlow, S., 1995, *Homeschooling: Parents as educators,* Thousand Oaks, CA: Corwin Press; Ray, B. D., 1990, *A nationwide study of home education: Family characteristics, legal matters, and student achievement,* Salem, OR: National Home Education Research Institute; Stevens, M. L., 2001, *Kingdom of children: Culture and controversy in the home-schooling movement,* Princeton: Princeton University Press.

Stacey B. Roberts

HOMEWORK

Homework is a source of friction between home and school more often than any other teaching activity. Parents protest that assignments are ineffective, too long or too short, too hard or too easy, or poorly described. Teachers complain about a lack of support from parents and administrators, poor training in how to construct good assignments, and insufficient time to prepare effective assignments. Students object to the time homework takes from their leisure activities, if they understand the value of the exercise at all.

A DEFINITION OF HOMEWORK

Homework can be defined as tasks assigned to students by schoolteachers that are intended to be carried out during nonschool hours. This definition excludes (a) in-school or out-of-school guided study (e.g., test preparation classes) or tutoring; (b) home study courses delivered through the mail, television, on audio or video cassette, or over the Internet; and (c) extracurricular activities such as sports teams and clubs.

THE EFFECTS OF HOMEWORK

Educators have suggested a long list of both positive and negative consequences of homework. The positive effects of homework typically begin with its immediate effects on achievement and learning. Proponents of homework argue that it increases the time students spend on academic tasks. As such, the benefits of increased instructional time should accrue to students who do homework: (a) better retention of factual knowledge; (b) increased understanding of material, and; (c) enrichment of the core curriculum. Proponents also suggest that the long-term academic benefits of homework include (a) promoting better critical thinking and information processing skills, (b) encouraging students to learn during their leisure time, (c) improving students' attitudes toward school, and (d) teaching students' study habits and skills. Homework also may help students develop positive personal attributes that extend beyond academic pursuits. Homework, proponents argue, can promote greater self-discipline and self-direction, better time organization, and more independent problem solving. Finally, homework may have positive effects on home life. Parents may become familiar with and perhaps take part in the schooling process. Students become aware of the connection between home and school.

Although proponents of homework argue that it can improve students' attitudes toward school, opponents counter that attitudes may be influenced negatively. They argue that by spending more time on school learning children may become satiated, or overexposed, to academic tasks, thus reducing achievement motivation. Also, homework can lead to general physical and emotional fatigue. Assignments can interfere with sleep or replace other valued activities that teach important life skills. Further, involving parents in the homework process can interfere with learning. Sometimes parents pressure students to complete homework assignments or to do them with unrealistic rigor. Parents may create confusion if they are unfamiliar with the material presented in homework or if their approach to learning differs from that used in school. In addition, parental involvement, or the involvement of others such as siblings, can sometimes go beyond simple tutoring or assistance and become cheating. Homework may lead some students to receive inappropriate help from others. Finally, opponents of homework argue that it can increase differences between high- and low-achieving students. They suggest that high achievers from well-to-do homes are more likely to have greater parental support for homework, quiet, well-lit places in which to do assignments, and better resources to help complete assignments successfully.

THE AMERICAN PUBLIC'S ATTITUDE TOWARD HOMEWORK

Throughout the twentieth century, public opinion about homework wavered between support and opposition. Homework controversies roughly have followed a 30-year cycle, with public outcries for more homework or less homework occurring about 15 years apart. Further complicating matters, at any moment during the past century arguments and evidence both for and against homework simultaneously could be found in both the popular and the educational literature. However, at different times the proponents and opponents of homework have alternately held sway.

Early in the twentieth century, homework was believed to be an important means for disciplining children's minds. The mind was viewed as a muscle.

Memorization, most often of material like multiplication tables, names, and dates, not only led to knowledge acquisition, but was also believed to be good mental exercise. Because memorization could be accomplished easily at home, homework was a key schooling strategy.

By the 1940s a reaction against homework set in. Developing problem-solving ability, as opposed to learning through drill, became a central task of education. The use of homework to enhance memorization skills was called into question. Greater emphasis was placed on developing student initiative and interest in learning. Further, the life-adjustment movement viewed home study as an intrusion on students' time to pursue other important at-home activities.

The trend toward less homework was reversed in the late 1950s after the Soviet Union launched the Sputnik satellite. Americans became concerned that a lack of rigor in the educational system was leaving children unprepared to face a complex technological future and to compete against its ideological adversaries. Homework was viewed as a means for accelerating the pace of knowledge acquisition.

By the mid-1960s, homework came to be seen as a symptom of too much pressure being placed on children. Contemporary learning theories were again invoked that questioned the value of most approaches to homework.

In the 1980s, homework came back into favor, as it was viewed as a defense against the rising international economic threat to American society, exemplified by the booming economies of Southeast Asia. The push for more homework continued into the 1990s, fueled by educators and parents who felt it could help meet increasingly rigorous state-mandated academic standards.

As the century turned, another backlash against homework set in. Media accounts often pitted parents who felt their children were overburdened with homework against educators pressed to improve achievement test scores.

Interestingly, while the battle over homework raged in the popular press and among education pundits, there was historical evidence that practices regarding the amount of homework teachers assigned had changed little in the last half of the twentieth century. Gill and Schlossman (2003) looked at national surveys reporting time spent on homework and found little evidence of change from the 1950s onward, except perhaps among the youngest students, age six to eight, who experienced a jump in assigned homework at the very end of the century.

FACTORS AFFECTING THE UTILITY OF HOMEWORK

Given the complexity of homework assignments it is not surprising that it has been the source of much controversy. Indeed, both positive and negative consequences of homework can occur and can even occur simultaneously. For instance, homework could improve study habits at the same time that it denies access to other leisure-time activities.

Whether homework has positive or negative effects, or both, and in what combinations, can be influenced by many things. Such influences include differences in (a) student characteristics, such as age or grade level, ability, motivation, and study habits, (b) home circumstances, such as family economics and the number of siblings, and (c) subject matter, such as reading, math, or science. For example, the same assignment may be more or less effective depending on the developmental level of the child and/or the resources available in the home. One child may find reading assignments helpful but math assignments confusing while another dislikes reading but enjoys math problems. Factors that might influence successful homework completion might also include whether an appropriate setting for study is available, be that the home or an afterschool program, whether other activities leave ample time for study, and whether other people can provide positive assistance, if it is needed.

Educators and parents suggest that the way teachers introduce homework assignments in class can vary and that this can influence its effects. For example, homework may be more effective if teachers provide the materials (or know that the material is available in the home) needed to complete homework successfully. Similarly, homework may be more effective if teachers suggest helpful approaches to carrying out the assignment and show how the assignment is linked to what is going on in class.

After assignments are returned to class, teachers can use different strategies to make the relevance of assignments to the curriculum clear to students. Strategies may include giving different kinds of feedback (e.g., written comments, grades), providing rewards for completion or accuracy, testing on homework content, and using homework in classroom lessons. That is, homework may be more or less effective depending on the strategy used.

WHAT THE RESEARCH SAYS

The Causal Effect of Homework on Achievement

The best way to answer the question "Does homework cause better achievement" is to conduct studies that compare the achievement of students who were purposively assigned homework with students who were purposively assigned no homework. When doing these studies, students in the two groups need to be as similar as possible, on average, so that difference in achievement between the groups can be attributed to homework. To most closely accomplish this ideal test of homework's effects, the experiment would need to use a chance or random procedure, called random assignment, to determine which students do homework and which do not.

We found six studies comparing homework and no-homework conditions. Of the six studies, four used random assignment. The two studies that did not use random assignment tried to make the students comprising the homework and no-homework conditions as similar as possible, on average, by statistical control or by matching students in one group with a similar student in the other group (and eliminating students who did not have a good match). Students from grades 3 through 5 and 9 through 12 took part in the studies. The topics of homework varied from math to vocabulary to history to social studies.

All results involving unit tests revealed that the students doing homework did better than the students doing no homework. These studies suggested that the average student (50th percentile) doing homework had a higher unit test score than 73 percent of students not doing homework.

Factors that Influence the Association between Homework and Achievement

We also found 32 studies that contained correlations between the amount of time a student spent on homework and some measure of achievement. Although these studies do not permit causal inferences, they can be used to look for possible influences on the relationship between homework and achievement.

Measures of Achievement

One analysis compared average correlations involving class grades with average correlations involving standardized achievement tests. The relationship between homework and achievement was statistically significant for both grades and achievement test scores. The absolute difference between the two average correlations was quite small and probably not practically very important.

Subject Areas

Another analysis compared correlations looking at reading achievement with correlations looking at mathematics achievement. Homework was statistically related to both reading and math achievement. However, the average correlation between time on homework and math achievement was statistically stronger than the one for reading. But again, the absolute difference between the average correlations was quite small and probably not practically important.

Grade Levels

The strength of the average correlation between time spent on homework and achievement was noticeably different depending on the grade level of the students. The relationship was significantly higher and more positive for secondary school students (grades 7 through 12) than for elementary school students (grades kindergarten through 6), for whom the relationship was close to non-existent.

There are several possible explanations for why the relationship between homework and achievement is so weak for young children. First, younger children are less able than older children or adolescents to ignore irrelevant information or stimulation in their environment. Therefore, the distractions present in a younger student's home would make studying there less effective for them than for older students. Second, younger students have less developed study habits. This lessens the amount of improvement in achievement that might be expected from homework given to them. For example, research shows that older students allot more time to harder items compared with easier ones than do younger students. Older students are also more likely to use self-testing strategies to monitor how much of the material they had learned. Third, evidence suggests that teachers in early grades may assign homework more often to young students to help them develop management of time—a skill rarely measured on standardized achievement tests or graded in class. Studies also provide some evidence that young students who are struggling in school take more time to complete homework assignments. Thus, it may be that in earlier grades homework is being used for purposes other than improving immediate achievement outcomes.

Amount of Homework

Studies reported between 1977 and 1986 provide data on students' levels of achievement for different amounts of time spent on homework. Thus, the idea could be explored that homework might have a positive effect on achievement up to a point, but when time spent on homework passed this point it either resulted in no more improvement or started to have negative effects. These studies again suggest that the relationship differed based on the student's grade level. For junior high students the positive association with achievement appears for even the most minimal amount of time on homework (less than one hour) and grows more positive until students spend between one and two hours on homework a night. But two or more hours of homework a night is associated with no better achievement. For high school students the positive relation between homework time and achievement does not appear until at least one hour of homework per week is reported. Then achievement continues to climb unabated until students spend two hours of homework each night. However, for high school students, spending more than two hours a night on homework is associated with no better achievement. Only one study was available for elementary school students, grades one through six, making it unwise to draw any conclusions for elementary school students based on a single study.

Parent Involvement

Patall, Cooper, and Robinson (2007) found evidence that training parents to be involved in their child's homework can result in (a) higher rates of homework completion, (b) fewer homework problems, and (c) possibly improved academic performance among elementary school children. Students in middle school revealed no effects of parent training or involvement. Training targeted at high school parents and students is yet to be tested. Also, it is important to bear in mind that the training employed in these experimental studies (a) included relatively weak forms of training and (b) lasted for short durations. Thus, it should come as no surprise that parent training had its greatest impact on the outcomes that are most sensitive—homework completion rates and frequency of problems—and for students for whom involvement of parents would be easiest to provide effectively—elementary school students.

Children with Learning Disabilities

Studies involving students with learning disabilities indicate there is no reason to believe that the generally positive effects of homework for students without disabilities would not also accrue to students with learning disabilities. Clearly, however, the ingredients of successful homework assignments are different for the two types of students. A consistent theme in the literature is that completing homework assignments is more difficult for students with learning disabilities. This is not just because the same material might be more challenging, but also because learning disabilities are often accompanied by other deficits in attention, memory, or organizational skills that influence the success of homework. This suggests that homework assignments for students with learning disabilities should be short and should focus on reinforcement of material already learned, rather than the introduction of new material. It should also be closely monitored by teachers and parents.

Assignment Characteristics

Studies examining practice and preparation of homework provide a convincing pattern favoring assignments that contain distributed practice rather than massed practice. That is, assignments that allow the student to distribute his or her study of any particular topic over several study sessions are more effective than assignments that focus only on material covered in class that day. It also appears that interspersing easy and hard problems throughout an assignment can improve its effectiveness, as well as the student's perception of its difficulty and enjoyableness. Finally, individualization of assignments by difficulty may have little effect on students' ultimate achievement. However, preparing assignments that take into account students' learning styles (e.g., preferences for the context in which it is completed) may be more effective.

The research on other variations in assignments is less conclusive, most often because there is simply not much of it. There is a small amount of evidence hinting that more frequent and shorter assignments are no more effective than less frequent longer ones. Also, group assignments can be effective, depending on the content involved, but these should be structured along the lines of successful cooperative learning strategies and used most often with older students.

Research on variations in teacher feedback strategies reveals that feedback of some sort may improve the effectiveness of homework assignments. However, the research does not favor one feedback strategy over another. Finally, there is sound evidence that providing incentives for completion of homework to students who have learning disabilities proves beneficial.

SUMMARY

Homework has been a controversial teaching strategy for over a century. While attitudes toward homework have been debated in the American media on a regular basis, teachers' homework practices have varied little over the past half century. Proponents and opponents offer long lists of positive and negative effects of homework. Any and all of these effects can happen, alone and in combination. The effects of homework assignments will depend on the students involved, the home circumstances, and the preparation and use of homework by the teacher.

Studies that have experimentally tested for the effects of homework found positive and statistically significant results. Generally speaking then, it seems reasonable to conclude that doing homework can cause improved academic achievement. However, the positive effect of homework on achievement for young students may be limited. Homework for young children can improve scores on unit tests, but correlational studies suggest the homework-achievement link for young children on broader measures of achievement appears to be weak, in fact, bordering on trivial. For high school students, on the other hand, the effect of homework can be impressive. But again, even for older students, too much of a good thing may not be so good at all. Correlational evidence suggests that high school students doing more than about two hours of homework a night achieve no better than those doing about two hours. Finally, the benefits of homework for students with learning disabilities can be positive, but its success may lie in (a) teacher preparation and planning; (b) assignments that are appropriate to the skill, attention span, and motivation of students; and (c) successful involvement of parents.

Further Reading: Cooper, H., 2007, *The battle over homework: Common ground for administrators, teachers and parents,* Thousand Oaks, CA: Corwin; Cooper, H., Robinson, J. C., & Patall, E. A., 2007, Does homework improve academic achievement? A synthesis of research, 1987–2003, *Review of Educational Research, 76,* 1–62; Cooper, H., & Valentine, J. C., eds., 2001, Homework. A special issue of *Educational Psychologist 36*; Gill, B., & Schlossman, S., 2003, A nation at rest: The American way of homework, *Educational Evaluation and Policy Analysis, 25,* 319–337; Patall, E. A., Cooper, H., & Robinson, J. C., 2006, *Parent involvement in homework: A research synthesis,* Manuscript submitted for publication.

Harris Cooper and Erika A. Patall

HUMAN DEVELOPMENT

THE CULTURAL PSYCHOLOGY OF THE RIGHT AND ITS CHALLENGE TO EDUCATION

There is a back-and-forth quality to the advancement of human societies. A general reflection on history suggests that periods of regression and progress alternate in the spiral flow of civilization. On a smaller, perhaps less dramatic scale, we see a similar pattern in the evolution of society from generation to generation.

Whether the political system is traditional and autocratic, or a variation on the modern and democratic state, progressive ideas lap forward and then pull back, creating a moving line of popular consensus about the basic values and tone of society. These cultural oscillations generate explanations from the perspective of science and technology, economics, political theory, and other disciplines.

A common example of this pattern is discussion on the sexual and counter-cultural revolutions of the radical years characterized as the 1960s. From the point of view of some disciplines, we might see the role of the birth control pill as the catalyst, while economists may argue that the sheer size of the baby boom generation, and their resultant economic clout, was the significant factor in fomenting these changes. Further yet, social scientists could say the draft and the Vietnam War were fundamental to the upheaval of the 1960s.

In more recent history, the rise of the Religious Right in U.S. politics and culture has invited similar speculation from the disciplines. Have the rise of corporations and their deliberate program of channeling money into politics provided the impetus for the movement's success? Alternatively, could it be that we have a demographic standoff between rural and urban America?

If we take the Religious Right at its word, their central motivation and key narrative provide another rationale, which is to resist big government, protecting individual freedom, as well as traditional Christian values, in an era of relativism and secularity.

While these lines of argument have a contribution to make to our understanding, here, however, our purpose is to take a less-traveled, more subjective path into the motivations of the Right, as well as those who oppose them.

The strict boundaries of disciplinary traditions have their limitations and as such, leave the psychology of experience inadequately examined. How could advances in human knowledge dispose the present times to be the most brutal in human history? Why are so many citizens of a democratic state, such as the United States, antigovernment, when the people create those governments? Why are voters on the Right restrictive of the civil liberties of others and determined to limit them on narrow, sectarian religious grounds?

By examining the cultural psychology underlying the confrontational politics we now face one can attempt an explanation of that point of view. There are hazards to this approach, given the abuses of "psychohistory" and other applications of psychoanalysis to social phenomena, but unless we do a deep psychological or symbolic interpretation of historical events, certain questions will be left unasked and unanswered.

To respond by simply reverting to breakthroughs in technology or new economic forms is to forget the connection between cultural psychology and the sociopolitical and economic climate in cities and towns, homes and classrooms. In this process, however, we are attempting to understand the single-minded hostility of the Right to contemporary education as manifested particularly in the public schools and by the leadership of the education profession, including those in higher education.

Whether for better or for worse, human beings, when so motivated, are capable of moving the course of history in spite of material factors. Somewhere in our psychology there are resources and motivations that can only be explained on their own terms: the language of symbol and meaning.

THE SPIRAL OF HUMAN DEVELOPMENT

Despite attempts at popularization, such as Gail Sheehy's *Passages,* and a history that goes back at least as far as the writings of Rousseau, theories of life-span human development are not a part of general awareness.

Thanks to the pressures of child rearing and conducting K–12 education, society has some appreciation of the stages of childhood and adolescence as revealed in the developmentalist work of Piaget, Erikson, Friedenberg, and others. There is a tacit consensus, however, that these ages and stages end in adolescence and are succeeded by a long, seamless path of adulthood.

In theories of psychological development, such as Jung's, the unfolding of the psyche takes form in the ego's emergence and refinement from birth. This process is characterized by the experience of differentiation, that is, by awareness on the part of the individual of the categories with which he or she is identified and those from which he or she is separated.

Along with the acquisition of language, the sorting or differentiating process goes forward from infancy. For example, a child accepts himself as being a white, Protestant, Republican, Texan, American male athlete and he sets his identity apart from other ethnicities, religions, political parties, nationalities, and so on.

This either/or quality of thought and experience also invites a simplified worldview of binaries. We are familiar with the discomfort young people typically experience with shades of gray in meaning, relativity in thought and value, and open-ended process as opposed to closure. We also understand that it is normal for the adolescent to yearn for a black-and-white matrix through which to categorize and understand the world. Those who teach undergraduates become quite familiar with the characteristics of this worldview; however, what we are less aware of are the echoes of this simplified view in adulthood.

One of the major misconceptions of contemporary commonsense is that upon entering adulthood, one reaches a level of understanding that is beyond the need of fundamental renewal and transformation. Adults, by virtue of their age, not their behavior or ideas, are "mature" and "grown up." In the popular mind, this uninterrupted stage of adulthood is broken at most by a midlife crisis for which accessible remedies, such as divorce and Botox, are found.

Since our tradition is to presume that the personality is mature as one moves into his or her twenties, there is little ongoing commentary on the impact of egoistic, differentiating thought among adults in society. Further aggravating this presumption of maturity and completeness is the attachment the ego has for declaring its wholeness and supremacy by identifying with a set of traits, real or imagined.

As Erik Erikson and others have pointed out, there is a basic mechanism of stage development at play here. At each level of consciousness, we cling to the concepts of that age and resist deconstructing our identity, even those who are in pursuit of higher-order experience.

Following the theories of Jung and Erikson, among others, we can claim that for those who have reached fulfillment of the ego and its differentiating techniques, this penchant for stasis is doubly strong. This is because the developed ego is by definition the key instrument of will. Will is therefore turned to the purpose of elevating the ego to an unassailable status of centrality in the psychological life of the individual, and with this elevation come characteristic problems.

As suggested above, the ego-oriented personality looks for black-and-white analyses and closure in addressing the world, and at this stage of development, the individual still needs categories such as "white, Protestant, male…" to set himself apart. The ego is ultimately solitary, having relations with others only in terms of how these others serve the purposes of the egoistic individual. Eventually, at a point in the path of healthy maturation, this differentiating attitude of the ego becomes counterproductive, stalling further development.

From an egoistic point of view, selfless relationships, broad acceptances of others, tolerance for diversity, and the suspension of judgment in order to sympathetically understand new ideas are difficult or impossible experiences. Add to this dynamic the presumption that adults need not pursue further refinement of their personality and we have set the stage for reinforcing arrested development. What would seem the sensible and preferred attitude of humility is replaced with an invitation to arrogance and self-congratulation.

Jung defines the further pathway of maturation as that of self-realization. By this he means the supra-ego emergence of another locus of personhood, the Self. This culminating complex of associations subsumes the ego as a useful tool in manifesting the will, but does not confuse the ego or any identification with the individual's mature personality.

Self-consciousness in this sense is an expression of an integrative impulse, which is the inclination to freely experience phenomena of many kinds, including those that the ego would set aside. As the Self presumes that there are purposes of cognition beyond identity formation, the attitude is, therefore, to integrate within the individual even those experiences that ostensibly are alien or "other."

This is not an invitation to total relativism; one may still find many behaviors that are morally reprehensible, for example. This attitude does, however, greatly broaden one's acceptance of the world as well as altering the dynamic of experience. Through the Self, the individual takes a leap of hope that he or she is secure in his or her identity and can assume a functioning ego as one element of his or her psyche. This dynamic has implications for useful engagement with society.

One underappreciated alternative route to these kinds of understandings is in the various twelve-step programs. Alcoholics Anonymous and related groups such as Narcotics Anonymous acknowledge in their literature a central debt to Jung's theory. The step programs introduce lifespan development and the possibilities of higher order experience, and if one observes the process and theory of following the steps, the path of self-realization becomes transparently clear. In contemporary society, ironically, only those in crisis tend to employ this well conceived path to growth and maturation.

Obviously the theory requires a high level of confidence on the part of the individual that he or she will not be lost in oblivion if an attitude of differentiation is suspended. For this reason, the individual's evolution of consciousness as outlined here is neither described nor understood as a trouble-free, automatic process.

If an individual does not have a concept that such a developmental process is possible, or if they have not been exposed to concepts of this type at home, at church, in a step program, or at school, the likelihood of discovering and traveling such a path is negligible.

ALIENATION AND EDUCATION

The effects of individual development as described here can manifest themselves in a number of ways. For our purposes, this analysis is being employed to explore the origins and behavior of the contemporary political Right.

Educated elites, like other identifiable peer groups, interact frequently in their own world of the like-minded, tending to have more in common intellectually with parallel professionals around the world than with tradesmen or business-people living next door.

Alienation is a major effect of education that is little explored in contemporary discussions of the school and university experience. A frequent outcome of education is that it loosens family and religious ties and inculcates students into a new and broader world of peers.

It has not been in the interest of the mainstream education establishment to publicize or meaningfully dialogue about this side effect of schooling. Few parents enthusiastically or deliberately sign their children up for such a process. On the contrary, avoiding this socialization is a central motivation of homeschooling and private school initiatives.

In public education, on the way to diplomas and degrees that open up economic opportunity, this quiet subversion of tradition goes on. To a large degree, teachers and professors are trapped in this hostile relationship with convention. The mythic sensibility, as manifested in traditional religion, has rarely been reconciled with the analytic view employed by science, social science, and the world of scholarly inquiry. Professors and scientists neither feel qualified nor motivated to attempt the reconciliation.

Faculty tend to be specialists in their disciplines, certified by the Doctor of Philosophy degree, although the title is to some sense a misnomer. The extent of their study in the philosophy of their respective disciplines is typically far overshadowed by their attention to more narrow disciplinary knowledge. They are not prepared to conduct discussions on the belief systems that form the foundation of what, in an increasingly global and multicultural community, still tend to be Western traditions, and they do not see this kind of persistent self-reflection as part of their role.

The challenges of this type of discourse should not be minimized. Great minds have found frustration in attempts to reconcile philosophy and science with religion. In fact, the modern era left this fundamental challenge unresolved. The dichotomy is one that defines the dynamic and limitations of modernity while creating profound social consequences.

Although the Right may seem to be the aggressor in the culture wars around education, it can therefore be argued that psychologically and culturally their position is a defensive one. Partisans of the Right's politics feel under siege in terms of the legitimacy of their worldview and even their ability to maintain a community of value in their families. There is, in this sense, a great deal of motivation to act out against the forces of the modern, secular state and its schools.

Progressive forces have overridden traditional views in numerous ways, setting a precedent for the use of political power to affect folkways in U.S. society.

The Right remembers when their "sacred cows" were eviscerated: when states' rights and Jim Crow allowed greater (if invidious) individual autonomy in public spaces and businesses; when wives were clearly subordinated to their husbands; when homosexuality was beyond public mention or legal tolerance; when abortion was illegal and birth control and sex education were widely restricted; when schools were a place of Christian prayer and ceremony.

During the past several decades, political operatives have learned to harness this resentment to create voting blocks. The potential of identity politics has been greatly refined in theory and practice and thereby given the means to translate into votes at the ballot box. Additionally, advanced corporate media are mobilized to solidify and propagate the movement. Linked in coalition with Main Street Republicans and market fundamentalists, the cultural or religious fundamentalists found themselves aligned and forming a majority, controlling all major branches of government until they sustained the loss of both houses of Congress in 2006.

Those who take part in the community of scholars have pursued their own agendas, motivated by some combination of material appetite, competitive intensity, and an authentic love for the pursuit of knowledge. In the process, they have left a wake of angry, resentful countrymen who have found their way into communities of mutual understanding. The conservative religious segment of the population was marginalized and forgotten until the New Right mobilized them and gave them political standing. Now that both power and the citizenry are divided, until there is a popular understanding of a new, unifying "social imaginary," we can expect further tearing of society's fabric and damage to public institutions such as schools.

There is a burnt earth aspect to these culture wars, making the stakes for reconciliation high. If there is to be domestic tranquility, society must construct a common view that allows peaceful coexistence, even when the heartfelt views of religious or cultural tradition are not the law of the land. Otherwise, the power of the ballot box will be used to override policies and ideas that scholars have understood were unassailable.

Intelligent design can become the legislated curriculum of life science. Stem cell research is already impeded. Women's rights and those of the gay community may be rolled back, as through banning the morning after pill and defense of marriage legislation, respectively. Vouchers may give full, public funding to sectarian schools, ending the common school. Teaching as a discernible profession, with licensure and formal preparation, may cease to exist.

Given that the relative power of the Right and Left are in delicate balance at the present moment, and given that this democratic principle still is dominant, educators and other progressives face a stark reality. Effective propagation of liberal, humane ideas is an urgent need. Either the political balance must be shifted by a change in the public's mind, or the pendulum, which has begun its backward journey, will sweep exceedingly far.

Further Reading: Erikson, E., 1963 [1950], *Childhood and society,* New York: Norton; Jung, C. G., 1976, *Psychological types,* Princeton: Princeton Bollingen Press; Noddings, N.,

1993, *Educating for intelligent belief or unbelief,* New York: Teachers College Press; Rorty, R., 1998, *Achieving our country,* Cambridge MA: Harvard University Press; Sheehy, G., 1977, *Passages,* New York: Bantam; Taylor, C., 2004, *Modern social imaginaries,* Durham NC: Duke; Wilber, K., 2000, *A theory of everything,* Boston: Shambhala Publications Inc.

Paul Shaker

INCLUSIVE SCHOOLING

Inclusive education is an international movement that aims to have all students educated in general education classes with support and collaboration from specialists, including children with mild to severe disabilities, students considered gifted and talented, and students with other special needs. Inclusive education had its beginning in the efforts of parents of children with disabilities, particularly severe disabilities, and professionals who were concerned about the segregated lives for which these children were being prepared in special education classes and schools. The movement has built on language in laws of countries throughout the world that has required, as in the United States, education in the least restrictive environment for students with disabilities. Over time, advocates of inclusive education for students with disabilities have broadened their focus to include goals of achieving broad-based diversity embracing also those from various cultural and ethnic backgrounds, students considered gifted and talented, second language learners, and others. Similarly, advocates of inclusive education have joined with other initiatives to reform and improve schools overall.

The movement towards inclusive education promoted first by advocates of students with disabilities naturally dovetails with other efforts to improve the capacity of schools and educators to meet the needs of children—particularly related to the education of children considered gifted and talented and the critique of tracking in schools. Educators and parents were concerned with limitations in traditional public schooling for children considered gifted and talented. While some have sought separate classes and programs for these students, others have helped to foster new perspectives on curriculum and instruction in public schools. The movement to create differentiated instruction has sought to provide strategies to allow children with different abilities to learn the same content together without separate and segregated classes while providing appropriate supports and challenges to high functioning children. Having its roots in the needs of children, this approach has been supported by advocates of students with disabilities.

For many years other educators have sought to detrack schools. Tracking is a practice in which separate series of classes are designed for children considered at different functioning levels but not labeled as having disabilities—typically low, average, and above average. While used in many schools, particularly in middle and high schools, many researchers have argued that the practice has only small positive effects on the academic and cognitive achievements of high performing students while often impacting on them negatively socially. For students considered average or below average, the practice is actively harmful, contributing to a watered down curriculum and drawing out high functioning students who act as good models and guides for other students.

Inclusive education, along with differentiated instruction and detracking, is controversial. This controversy takes many forms and is imbedded in many different educational communities. For example, despite a reasonable amount of research related to the value of heterogeneous, inclusive learning for students who are gifted and talented, many concerned with those students continue to believe and argue for separate, pull-out programs as the only viable option for students who are gifted. Similarly, some in the special education and disability community argue that only separate special education programs can serve students with disabilities well.

From another perspective, the debate about inclusive education deals with the roles of professionals in the educational process. For general education teachers, inclusive education requires that they learn how to effectively teach students at very diverse levels of abilities together who may also have other challenging characteristics. Some argue that this is what teachers must do regardless of whether students who are gifted or have disabilities are present in the classroom. These individuals believe that inclusive education helps improve teaching and learning for all children. Others argue, however, that this is an unreasonable and unlikely expectation for teachers.

Perhaps the professional debate is most intense in the professional groups of many specialists who provide support and services in public schools. These include social workers, speech therapists, occupational therapists, physical therapists, special education teachers, gifted education teachers, sign language interpreters, and many more. Inclusive education dramatically changes the roles of these professionals. Traditionally, such professionals work with children in separate clinical environments, most often a room equipped with equipment and tools used by the specialist. In inclusive education, however, specialists work in collaboration with the general education teacher and provide their services in the content of the general education class. Each of these specialists has a professional organization in which the merits of clinical and integrated services have been highly debated. Within each of these professions, however, there is a strong and enduring movement towards inclusive education.

As the inclusive education movement has developed over the last 20 years, it's been interesting to watch the shift of the movement and the way that this is expressed in language. In the United States, early on some called the concept supported education, adapting the language of the field of supported employment, where individuals with disabilities would be trained and supported on a job, rather than in a separate training environment. The term integrated education was used related to having students with severe disabilities attend some general education classes (most often nonacademic subjects like music, art, and physical education) while maintaining their base in a separate special education classroom. However, quickly the term inclusive education came to be used as the predominant term. During a three-month period in 1990, numerous people began to use this term based on a similar thinking process. They had an image of a group of people with their arms around each other who saw individuals outside the group. "Come join us!" the group would say. This was the concept of being included, thus the term inclusive education. Over time, many have used the word inclusive as an adjective to other key words including inclusive teaching and inclusive schooling. These latter terms are most associated with educators, parents, and researchers who see inclusive education as an integral part of effective school reform.

In the mid-1990s a new term for inclusive education came into use: inclusion. This term was most fostered by special educators who felt that inclusive education was a bad idea. It is notable that, for the most part, advocates of inclusive education use the word inclusive as an adjective to words like education, teaching, schooling, and more. However, using the term inclusion as a noun begs a definition and becomes its own entity and program rather than being tied to the integral mission of the school.

What is clear about inclusive education is that it challenges deeply held assumptions about the educational process. The traditional model posits that students of different abilities must be placed in different groups—separate classes, separate schools, separate groups within classes. The assumption is that students cannot learn at their own level well if they are in a heterogeneous group where, for example, a highly gifted student and a nonverbal student with a severe cognitive disability are learning American history together. Interestingly, this oft-used model truly is based on an assumption rather than research. In fact, the available research tends to support an inclusive, heterogeneous approach to education. A recent review of literature failed to find any research support for this practice.

Public education is filled with statements about commitment to diversity. However, the elephant in the living room for schools is the natural distribution of a range of abilities across the human spectrum. We've heard the radio show from Minnesota where "all kids are above average." That's the myth that all parents would like to believe, that their children are above average. Of course, when children are labeled with disabilities, part of what makes this hard for parents is that such a label is an official pronouncement that dashes the belief that their children are above average. In clear, cold, clinical terms they are told that their children are below average.

With all the debates and discussion about education, it's hard to find a realistic discussion regarding how schools deal with ability diversity. However, talk to any teacher and ask the question: "What is the range of abilities of students in your class?" Any teacher anywhere will tell you that abilities range a *minimum* of three grade levels. Most will say six to seven grade levels. One high school teacher told me she had a 10 grade level range—and all this is not counting students with identified disabilities. Several research studies have validated these results in numerous school settings. Despite this reality, however, the closest real discussion you find largely centers on what schools do with those special education students, ignoring the ever-present reality of the wide range of student abilities.

The concept of inclusive education, along with other related educational initiatives and movements, posits a different thesis regarding teaching students with ability differences. This thesis could be summarized as follows:

- Students learn and develop into full human beings when they learn together with students who are diverse in many characteristics including gender, race, culture, language, and ability/disability.
- Educators have developed many strategies for instruction and teaching that will allow such inclusive teaching to be manageable for teachers and effective for all students, ranging from those with severe and multiple disabilities to students considered gifted and talented.

So what *does* the research say about the efficacy of inclusive education—students with mild to severe disabilities, typical average students, students who are gifted and talented, racially and culturally diverse students learning together? As always, of course, research in any meaningful question is never finished. However, here are some conclusions that are clear from the present research base:

- Studies that have systematically compared outcomes from inclusive education and separate programs most often show that academic and social gains are higher in inclusive classes. In some studies, the results were mixed. It is notable that no studies are known that showed segregated education to produce greater academic or social outcomes. It is also notable that research to date does not distinguish between quality of practices in the general education classroom. The only comparison was between inclusive classrooms and separate classes. It would appear likely that *quality* inclusive teaching practices would increase the positive impact of inclusive education even more.
- For students with cognitive disabilities, the more they are included in general education classes, the higher their academic, cognitive, and social functioning.
- Students with mild disabilities make better gains in inclusive than in pull-out programs.
- The quality and outcomes of individualized education plans is improved for students with moderate to severe disabilities
- There is no evidence that academic progress is impeded, but there is evidence that it is increased in inclusive classes for students without disabilities.
- Instruction may be improved for all students at all levels as teachers learn skills of multilevel and differentiated instruction.

- Friendships and social interactions for students with disabilities expand in school and carry over to afterschool contexts.
- Students with mild disabilities are less often accepted and more likely rejected due to behavior than nondisabled students. However, teachers can used numerous strategies for addressing issues of ability diversity that change this impact and create better classroom conditions for all students.
- Students without disabilities view their involvement with peers with disabilities positively. They gain an increased appreciation and understanding of diversity and often improve self-esteem and behaviors.

While research makes it clear that inclusive education is a desirable, effective practice, some argue that educators are neither willing nor able to make inclusive education a reality. Numerous research studies have documented problems that include: (1) poor planning and preparation; (2) inadequate supports for students and teachers; and (3) negative and adversarial attitudes of educators.

Despite the fact that much segregated education exists, the movement towards inclusive education continues to grow—sometimes with major thrusts ahead, sometimes with retrenchment for awhile and with a growth of quiet efforts on the part of individual schools and teachers. Several comprehensive studies have documented case studies of individual schools moving to implement inclusive education, including O'Hearn Elementary School in Boston, Souhegan High School in New Hampshire, and Purcell Marion High School in Cincinnati. The National Center for Educational Restructuring and Inclusion conducted a national study of hundreds of schools throughout the United States who were implementing inclusive education. Sixteen states have engaged in state-wide initiatives for inclusive education. Other researchers and school change agents report that when change efforts involve training, administrative leadership and support, in-class assistance, and other special services, the attitudes of teachers are positive. Some teachers view inclusive education as building on their existing positive teaching practices. Initially, teachers are often afraid of including students with severe disabilities. However, most often as teachers come to know such students as human beings and work with them, they come to value the experience and would volunteer to teach such students again. Finally, most teachers agree with the concept of inclusive education but are afraid they do not have the skills to make it work. As they have positive experiences with good administrative support they become more comfortable and positive.

While some courts have ruled in favor of segregated placements, typically following failed attempts to include a child in a regular class, most have ruled in favor of inclusive education. Courts have upheld the principle of least restrictive environment and have stated that schools must, in good faith, consider inclusive placement of all students, no matter the severity of the disability, and students and teachers must be provided necessary supports and supplementary services. While the courts allow costs, amount of teacher time, and impact on other students to be considered, the standards are so high that denying an inclusive placement based on these issues is rarely supported.

These related concepts—inclusive education, differentiated instruction, and detracking—are being used in an increasing number of school reform models. In some cases, the focus is explicit and clear. In others, it is more implied by the stated values of the approach. The *Coalition of Essential Schools,* for example, has identified 10 principles of effective schooling. Schools move away from the 50-minute class period in high schools and develop larger blocks of instructional time, in which teachers work as interdisciplinary teams to engage students in substantive learning activities. Students demonstrate learning through substantive portfolios and yearly demonstrations to parents, other students, and the larger community. *Accelerated Schools* stimulate the use of challenging and engaging teaching, typically reserved for gifted students, for all students, particularly those with learning challenges. The goal is to accelerate, not slow down, learning for *all* students through exciting, authentic teaching techniques or powerful learning. *Accelerated Schools* engage teachers, administrators, parents, and the community work who work together in teams to develop improved learning strategies for all students. The *Comer School Development Program* brings another important perspective. According to James Comer, a psychiatrist, children need a sense of safety, security, and welcome if they are to learn. In his school development program, schools develop teams to facilitate partnerships with parents and communities and an interdisciplinary mental health team, consisting of teachers, a psychologist, a social worker, and others to deal with holistic needs of both students and families. In each of these models, inclusive education is not specifically articulated as a component. However, the values and visions upon which each model is based often lead schools to incorporate inclusive education as a component of their school reform efforts when they use these models.

Whole Schooling is a school reform framework that incorporates inclusive education as a central component of effective schooling for all children. The model posits that the purpose of public schools is to create citizens for democracy and the achievement of personal best learning for all students. The model is based on eight principles:

1. Create learning spaces for all
2. Empower citizens for democracy
3. Include all in learning together
4. Build a caring community
5. Support
6. Partner with families and the community
7. Teach all using authentic, multilevel instruction
8. Assess students to promote learning

Throughout the world in recent decades, and very recently in the United States, standards-based reform has been initiated with a goal to improve outcomes for students in public schools. The No Child Left Behind Act, passed in 2002, aims to have 100 percent of students pass standardized tests showing their proficiency in math and reading by the year 2014. In the United States, standards-based reform has been touted as a way of improving achievement and outcomes for all students, playing higher levels of accountability and expectations on public schools. In the United States, the NCLB law has come under increasing criticism as unrealistic and punitive, focusing on low levels of learning, limiting creativity and the education of the whole child.

Inclusive education can be viewed as both an extension of and, at the same time, in conflict with the concepts of standards-based reform and the laws designed for its implementation. On the one hand, many schools have decided that, if they are going to be evaluated on the performance of all students in the general education curriculum, students with disabilities need to be learning in general education classes, thus increasing their exposure and likelihood of doing well on standardized tests. On the other hand, standards-based reform identifies one set of expectations for all students. Thus, a fourth-grade student who is highly gifted, functioning on the ninth-grade level, will be expected to perform at the same level as a student with a cognitive disability, reading at the first-grade level. It is clear that, in this scenario, the gifted student is asked to perform far below their capacity, thus making their public school program irrelevant to their needs. The student with a cognitive disability is asked to function at a level far above her capacity. The result will be frustration, humiliation. For this student, no matter what effort she puts forth she will be considered a failure. In this regard, NCLB and inclusive schooling could be seen as at odds with one another.

The movement towards inclusive education is truly international in thrust. In 1994, the country members of the United Nations adopted the Salamonica Statement, which articulated the rights of individuals with disabilities in society. This document particularly focused on schools and supported the concept and practice of inclusive education and called on member nations to use the document to reform their schools in this direction.

The idea of inclusive schooling can be expected to continue as a movement for reform in education. Clearly, the concept is connected at its essence with the concept of democracy. It is not surprising, consequently, to find that inclusive education is most practiced in countries that have a democratic political tradition and that segregated schooling is most firmly entrenched in authoritarian regimes.

One indicator of this trend has been the development of National Inclusive Schools Week in the United States, which has been growing in visibility beginning in 2001 (see www.inclusiveschools.org). According to their Web site:

> National Inclusive Schools Week highlights and celebrates the progress of our nation's schools in providing a supportive and quality education to an increasingly diverse student population, including students with disabilities, those from low socio-economic backgrounds, and English language learners. The Week also provides an important opportunity for educators, students, and parents to discuss what else needs to be done in order to ensure that their schools continue to improve their ability to successfully educate all children.

For those interested in the quality of schooling for students with wide ranges of differences, monitoring the restructuring of schools to incorporate inclusive education as a central component may provide one measure to watch in coming years.

Further Reading: McGregor, G., & Vogelsberg, T., 1998, *Inclusive schooling practices: Pedagogical and research foundations: A synthesis of the literature that informs best practices about inclusive schooling,* Baltimore: Paul H. Brookes; Peterson, M., & Hittie, M., 2003, *Inclusive teaching: Creating effective schools for all learners,* Boston: Allyn and Bacon; Sapon-Shevin, M., 1994, *Because we can change the world: A practical guide to building cooperative, inclusive classroom communities,* Boston: Allyn and Bacon; Tomlinson, C., 2001, *How to differentiate instruction in mixed-ability classrooms,* Columbus, Ohio: Merrill; Vitello, S., & Mithaug, D., 1998, *Inclusive schooling: National and international perspectives,* Mahwah, NJ: Lawrence Erlbaum Associates.

Michael Peterson

INTEGRATED MENTAL HEALTH SERVICES IN SCHOOLS

While the majority of schoolchildren sail fairly successfully through their school years, a significant subset, or 25 percent of children and adolescents, suffers from some degree of psychological, social, or nonacademic concern that interferes considerably in their school life. The vast majority of these affected youth get no help at all from professionals trained to help with specific issues. Children and youth suffering from anxiety, depression, living in violent homes, or living in conditions of poverty are found in today's classrooms struggling to do reading, writing, and arithmetic. Most emotional or social problems emerge in the school years, making schools an important cauldron to capture distress. Educators are well placed to view not only emergent problems of youth but also to be in a position to support intervention in school settings. The issues confronting youth and their families are complex and interrelated; rarely does a student suffer from one problem in isolation of other problems. For example, a child exhibiting poor academic performance at school may return to a home characterized by violence, substance abuse, or the confounding effects of poverty.

Youth in American families suffer higher rates of fragmentation and indicators of at-risk youth behavior than other industrialized nations: higher rates of divorce, teenage pregnancy, suicide, single parent homes, and poverty. Children coming from these homes may need academic direction or supplemental education, health care attention, parenting skills, or a support system that offers what may be difficult to get at home. Families typically suffer complex, interrelated problems that rarely fit tidy definitions or respond neatly to single interventions. Families need integrated and sustained interventions delivered by professionals who recognize and are able to respond to a family's multiple problems and needs. The agencies that offer assistance to families typically are only responsible for their own services and may not be informed of another agency's regulations or qualifications or even ancillary services. Recently these different agencies have sought to find more ways to deliver services based on family and child need rather than an exclusively agency-driven service.

INTEGRATED SERVICES

Mental, physical, and social service programs targeting at-risk children and youth often work in an isolated and fragmented manner, expecting students and their families to seek aid from a variety of disconnected agencies. To achieve both the goals of families needing services and those of service providers, communities from policy analysts to researchers to private enterprise have urged collaboration among the schools and service providers.

Although service integration models are varied, they all suggest collaboration of independent institutions allowing for academic, mental, and physical health services. The assumption is that integrated, comprehensive services will respond more effectively to the interrelated needs of families, reduce overlap of services, and make better use of community resources. The fundamental philosophy is one of cross-disciplinary professionals working as a team to share knowledge about how best to provide services to children and families.

At the very center of service integration is the idea of catering to the whole child. The integrated services approach does not mean a substitution of one service provider for another but rather that each provider contributes a service and/or helps another provider do its job more effectively, and that a child and his/her family receives appropriate services.

Historical Traditions

Elements of integrated service have a long tradition in the United States. Perhaps the first seeds of collaboration between agencies were during the Progressive Era (1890–1917), which was dominated by problems of vast numbers of immigration. With the influx of immigrants came waves of diseases such as diphtheria, scarlet fever, and small pox. Mandatory schooling, child labor laws, and burgeoning numbers of children and adults in close proximity of each other forced the government to combat concomitant problems of infection and contagious disease with preventive medicine. Advocates from many disciplines such as journalism and immigration urged the government to take a strong role in upgrading the health of children by transforming schools from rigid centers of academic training to places where the effects of poverty might be mitigated. Most modern professional community-based services for children were established during this era of reform. Schools were a logical target because (a) the majority of schools were located in local communities, and (b) people had access to these institutions. Beginning in 1870, the health department began to collaborate with state boards of education to provide vaccinations to all school-children. Thus began the first formal collaboration between health services and public schools.

During the Depression of the late 1920s, services in schools were reduced, limited to health inspections, assessment, and first aid. With the onset of World War II, the late 1930s and early 1940s again enjoyed a resurgence of public health at the school site. The Bureau of Child Hygiene and School Health merged with the Bureau of District Health Administration, which placed physicians in the public schools. In the following years, school health services ebbed and flowed depending on the political climate and funding priorities. Programs emerged in response to perceived needs of an increasingly urban society. The idea of "community-school," where academic needs and community activities interacted, began to receive limited attention. Programs tentatively incorporated other agencies and community involvement into school programs, although these did not achieve fruition until decades later. Advocates for children saw early in our history the logic of locating the many helping services at the public school.

The war years and after until the present witnessed a host of social and health-related programs authored by the different presidents who sought integration specifically in the schools: Roosevelt's 1935 Social Security Act and Aid to Dependent Children/Welfare; Eisenhower's 1961 National Institutes of Health; the Kennedy administration's focus on mental retardation; the 1965 amendments to Social Security included Medicaid and Medicare; the 1960s War on Poverty, Head Start, the Elementary and Secondary Education Act (which provided funds for schools with disadvantaged populations), and the Office of Child Development in the Department of Health Education and Welfare (Johnson); and PL94–142 (now called the Individuals with Disabilities Education Act, or IDEA) during the Nixon administration.

A liberal temperament in the years following the Vietnam War in the 1970s fostered a climate in the United States of social activism. Large scale antipoverty programs, preventive programming such as Head Start, and low-cost economic help such as Legal Aid reflected the country's acknowledgment that society needed to respond in concrete fashion to the complex problems facing our country. The federal government, in an acknowledgment of rising social problems and their influence on schools, funded training programs and positions for school counselors.

The Reagan years are perhaps best known for reducing programs in the human services. Decreased programming of the 1980s was a response to failed earlier social programs, a feeling that the "magic silver bullet" did not work, so why bother? There existed a persistent and naive faith that a simple solution would "fix" a complex problem, and when this was found untrue, cynicism towards programs grew.

These programs (with the exception of Head Start) continued to operate from a deficit model, treating problems rather than looking at underlying causes or preventive approaches. Research on the various social programs, however, found that success lay in preventive approaches. The research community learned as much from failed social programs including the tenets of the War on Poverty as well as from the successful programming of Head Start. Family dysfunction was best addressed by preventive programming rather than crisis-oriented, remedial approaches. A proliferation of programs documented the enthusiasm over emerging family support programs.

Need for Integrated Services Programming

Slowly, service providers began to collaborate on delivery of services. This was in response to research that supported preventive programming, the positive effects of a larger, more "ecological" approach to service delivery, and the documentation of increasing troubles experienced by families heading into the twenty-first century.

The problems confronting youth and families in America today are not abating. Achenbach and Howell, two child behaviorists, in 1993 published one of the few investigations that concluded that there are small but pervasive increases in the number of problems and decreases in child competency. The escalating problems of society are being felt in the childhood of our citizens. When we put youth with these challenges in schools, in a relatively sterile, book-learning environment, no wonder the result is low commitment to the education process, a feeling of greater alienation, lowered levels of belief in the validity of social rules and laws, and significant effects on youth competencies.

BENEFITS OF INTEGRATED SERVICE PROGRAMS

Some question whether schools should provide broader services to meet the child's educational, health, emotional, and other general welfare needs or stick to fundamental education (the "basics"). But some services, such as health services, do receive approval from the broader public. For instance, if a child wishes to enroll in a public school, s/he must provide documentation of inoculation against childhood diseases (which have been eradicated to date in the United States). If a child cannot show proof of inoculation, the school can deny entrance to that student. Other signs of the presence of physical welfare programs are vision and hearing screening, head lice treatment and inspection, and nutritionally sound lunch programs. Some schools house medical clinics in an area of the building where a medical staff offers treatment from first aid to the distribution of condoms to complete physical evaluations. What is lacking is the social-emotional programming that an integrated services model would promote.

When students participate in integrated social and mental health programs, preliminary research indicates long-term positive effects on attendance, school retention, achievement, decreased pregnancy and birthrate, and decreased involvement with drugs. Other studies reveal the cost-effectiveness of providing services to those who normally wouldn't get them. Some programs tout the more efficient staffing mix of integrated services. Effective programs include the full participation of family and are empowering. The logic that drives the integrated service format is offering services that are available and close, comprehensive, and appropriate. This philosophy relies on a resiliency model of mental health and development.

Service Delivery Site: Schools or Community?

Many integrated service models offer social and human resource services at the school site. Others choose buildings located conveniently in the community ("school-linked" or "community-based"). There are benefits and barriers to either location for delivery of services, but school-based programs seem a more logical choice.

Delivery of services at the school site has a variety of benefits for both sides. For those delivering the services, the "repositioned" service worker sees the student in a more familiar, "natural" school setting and may get a more complete picture of the specific problem. The worker who has a contextual understanding of the problem may be influenced to choose a particular intervention or goal for treatment. Reciprocally, the school can offer "overhead" (usually office space) to the agency. A holistic approach to intervention is stressed. The problems for the child are interrelated; the services offered in the school are integrated.

Those receiving the services, the students and parents, may view the school as a less threatening and more accessible venue for services than perhaps the traditional setting (hospital, mental health center, social services building, police station). The school setting is, at a minimum, geographically accessible. Most communities have a centrally located school building, typically within walking distance. In the present system of service delivery where different agencies provide different services at different locations, problems abound for the family seeking these services. Transportation to and from offices as well as being able to arrive at established business hours may be problems that are insurmountable.

Barriers

The integration of institutions, disciplines, and services is a formidable task and has not been without problems. There are drawbacks to having schools as the location of services. Many disenfranchised families continue to see schools as a fortress and uninviting. For some, the school represents everything about a system that has been denied to them, despite the rhetoric of education being free to all and a key to future success. If the school serves as the service delivery site, do the problems of service integration remain with the entire program or do these become the school's problems? This problem of perception may turn out to be an insidious undermining factor if not dealt with appropriately.

Funding of programs and mingling of funds can be problematic, if not contentious, with the clash of three institutions: the school system, the medical community, and social service agencies. On the one hand, schools are large, decentralized, public institutions that are funded mostly by individual state dollars (typically 50 percent), local dollars (typically 45 percent), and federal funds (typically 5 percent). Populations (kindergarten through age 16) are mandated to be in attendance. This monolithic system of education differs from health providers, which are largely private and nonprofit, mostly financed through employer-based and other third-party plans. Low-income populations are primarily served through third-party public programs, which are funded mainly by federal and state governments. Typically, providers are used to offering services to individuals who need acute care rather than ongoing treatment. Social services are funded by all levels of government—federal, state, and local. Comprehensive programs for children and families are expensive. It is difficult to secure funding in the current era of budget consciousness.

One question is for what problem(s) to treat/provide service? Who is the identified client/patient? Is the child seen, is the family seen, or are both? Does one problem take precedence over another?

Other obstacles to service integration are equally problematic. The various service providers enjoy an autonomy that is maintained by professional differences in training, management, discipline, and sources of revenue and funding. Jargon and professional ways of doing business are different. The identified problem(s), priority of need or response, assessment of severity, intervention(s), and goal(s) may differ from each professional's judgment. This long history of legislation, payment-for-services, and public approval contribute to "turf" issues: a (perceived) hierarchy of professionals negotiating for their own clientele claiming better or more effective service.

Other issues will need to be addressed; different reporting forms, issues of confidentiality, a lack of training in unknown areas, staffing ratios, physical space, and insurance liability are all important concerns. A final organizational issue that needs to be addressed is one of leadership. Traditionally a school principal's role/priority has been one of education. S/he is empowered in this role by the school board, a recognized extension of state law. The role of the principal will need to be scrutinized: Support for and success of programs can depend entirely on this leadership area, since the principal sets the tone for the school building. If other agencies are to be integrated, to what extent will the authority of community agency boards or other provider governing structures extend? For example, will the foundation president have the same latitude in decision making as the principal? How will conflicts be resolved in the decision-making process?

Very few families fall neatly and consistently into "problem" categories. The possibility that this will become a growing source of friction is great, as the population in the United States increasingly becomes more diverse. Five states will soon have minority majorities (California, Arizona, New Mexico, Texas, and Florida), and in over 30 of the largest school districts in the United States, Caucasian students have become the minority. A system whereby families feel that they are an integral piece can lessen the possibility of disempowerment.

More fundamental will be the conservative forces who support strict academic boundaries confronting more liberal thinkers who maintain that children need social supports in order to benefit from the academic training. Finally, the pressure of immediate "payoff" is at odds with long-term preventive approaches. Collaboration with more systems and more staff typically, at least initially, will use more of a very precious resource: time.

SUMMARY

The last two decades in the education field have been marked by tremendous efforts towards innovations in school reform. One strategy that has attempted to strengthen the school-family relationship and the school-community relationship is service integration (coordination of education, family assistance, mental health and counseling services, and various social service supports). While service integration at the school building is not a new movement, it is enjoying renewed attention partially due to a perceived crisis in children's deteriorating condition of life. This particular aspect of school reform is also influenced by recognition that schools and communities work better together rather than as opponents, and also acknowledges the importance of societal support for the education of today's youth. Prevention researchers have made great strides in increasing awareness of the benefits of prevention programming rather than programs of remediation and crisis-response.

A plethora of barriers to implementation of integrated service programs confronts program developers, including financial constraints, bureaucratic sluggishness, professional turf issues, a history of failed programs, and limited time and personnel resources. Despite these obstacles, the literature is replete with descriptions of integrated service ventures, from single case study programs to broadscale national programs. Emerging criteria of successful programs allows others to capitalize on established programs' strengths. Successful integrated services programs are reporting various program variables that emerge as critical components: a unifying mission, planning time before program implementation as well as intentional periods of planning during the programs, responsiveness to staff needs of authority and cross-disciplinary training, parental involvement, and a mechanism for conflict resolution. Community support is necessary, and the program needs a goal of targeting specific problem behaviors or pandemic prevention. Financial soundness is an extremely complicated objective, but one that needs adherence, as findings are that programs do not increase budget coffers but require coordinated budgets. An evaluation plan reminds participants to be ever-mindful of a client-centered approach, rather than the agency/institutional agenda.

Further Reading: Centre for Academic and Social and Emotional Learning (CASEL) http://www.casel.org; Dryfoos, J., 1994, *Full-service schools: A revolution in health and social services for children, youth, and families,* San Francisco: Jossey-Bass; Ehly, S. W., 2004, *School-community connections: Exploring issues for research and practice,*. San Francisco: Jossey-Bass.

Lynn Miller

INTERNATIONAL COMPARISONS OF STUDENT ACHIEVEMENT

No doubt when comparisons of test scores across nations were first made, a number of people looked at the analysis and asked "Why?" Because a school system is embedded in a larger culture and because the important outcomes of schooling don't show up until after it is over, the process can look meaningless. The comparisons still evoke that attitude in some. University of Namur professor Marc Romainville (2002) expressed it in a discussion of the first Program for International Student Assessment (PISA), from the Organization for Economic Cooperation and Development (OECD):

> Hit parades have been flourishing here (Europe) for some years: the best schools, the world's best universities, the top-performing research centers, etc. Some 30 years ago this sort of ranking would have produced a smile, as we were of the view that the broad and long-term effects of education cannot be reduced to a few trivial indicators and that every education system could be validly understood only by taking account of its history, its aims, and the complexity of its structures.

The "trivial indicators" are test scores. This raises the question, Are they trivial? One could hazard a guess that because they cover a narrow range of education, math and science, and, occasionally, reading, and because they are given to teenagers or younger students, the answer might be yes. But that is not the answer that one hears in most quarters.

The usual answer links test scores directly to international competitiveness. Test scores are, therefore, important. *A Nation at Risk* in 1983 codified this linkage. The U.S. performance in international comparisons was listed as one of 13 indicators of the risk that the nation faced. The commissioners preparing *A Nation at Risk* looked to Japan and saw both a thriving economy and high test scores. The report then made an inference that the high test scores *caused* the economic boom: "If only to keep and improve on the slim competitive edge we still retain in world markets, we must dedicate ourselves to the reform of our educational system."

Thereafter, collective moans and dire predictions about our economic fate greeted the arrival of the various international comparisons. The crescendo of such wailing peaked in early 2005 following the publication of the latest PISA and TIMSS results (TIMSS is the abbreviation for the Trends in International Mathematics and Science Study):

> The fact is that these results signify something real. Think of these assessments as early-warning signals for later economic welfare. Performance on the international math and science assessments directly relates to labor-force quality and has been closely related to national growth rates. (Hanushek, 2005)

> Cause for concern? You bet. You don't have to have the math scores of a rocket scientist to know that in the new high-tech economic world, math and science education is a key asset in global competition. (Carnevale, 2005)

> I'm not here to pose as an education expert. I head a corporation and a foundation. One I get paid for—the other one costs me. But both jobs give me a perspective on education in American, and both perspectives leave me appalled. When I compare our high schools to what I see when I'm traveling abroad, I am terrified for our workforce of tomorrow. (Gates, 2005)

Earlier, headlines in newspaper stories about the study had carried the same assertion: "Math + Test = Trouble for the U.S. Economy" (*Christian Science Monitor,* December, 7, 2004), "Economic Time Bomb" (*Wall Street Journal,* December, 7, 2004). Of course, the results of international assessments had been pretty much the same since the 1960s, so if they are an "early warning signal" the timeline would have to be very long: At the time of these quotes, the World Economic Forum ranked the United States first in global competitiveness among 114 nations. One could also speculate that Mr. Gates' hosts in other countries seldom if ever take him to poorly performing or even average high schools.

The perennial sounding of the alarm over the nation's economic future is analogous to the world seen in the movie *Groundhog Day*, in which the same day repeats over and over but only one person notices. Even as the PISA and TIMSS results arrived in late 2004, not only could the United States boast of the most competitive economy, it could point to a growing economy. In fact, earlier TIMSS results arrived in what turned out to be the longest sustained economic expansion in the nation's history.

While it is impossible to disprove predictions for times that have yet to occur, a recent study using international comparisons from the past through the first TIMSS from 1995 suggests that the impact of test scores on growth is modest at best and is impossible to see in the some decades. Conceptually, we have little reason to expect a large impact of test scores on growth.

Examining GDP and other variables from 1970 to 1990, the impact of math and science achievement on economic growth is positive but modest. When the researchers drop the four "Asian Tiger" nations in their study—South Korea, Hong Kong, Taiwan, and Singapore—the effect remains positive, but much smaller. Much of the achievement effect is attributable to the worst test performers, and therefore the envy of the few countries with the highest achievement scores is questionable.

Also, the effect is not causal. It occurs most in countries that decided simultaneously to focus on economic development and on math and science achievement. The effects were concurrent, not causal.

In the period from 1980 to 2000, there is a positive but statistically insignificant effect, which again becomes even smaller and disappears when the Asian Tigers are removed from the analysis. Restricting the analysis to the decade 1990–2000, there is no effect. In the 1990s, of course, the Tigers turned into pussycats. Their economies fell into free fall and Japan as well stumbled into an almost 15-year period of recession or stagnation.

They also point out that tests don't capture the degree to which schools promote important traits such as creativity, initiative, entrepreneurship, and a host of other variables that have not been amenable to cross-national analysis.

It is unlikely that any single study can turn the tide of fear mongering about America's ability to compete in the global economy. Indeed, in January 2007, Senator Christopher Dodd (D-Conn.) and Representative Vernon Ehlers (R-Mich.) sponsored a forum, "Preparing U.S. Students for the Global Economy." And how would one do that? The answer was: by establishing national standards and assessments in mathematics and science. The two congressmen introduced a bill that would require the National Assessment Governing Board to create such standards and to international competitiveness.

It was noted above that the World Economic Forum ranked the United States first in global competitiveness in its 2004–2005 report. The United States maintained that rank in the 2005–2006 report, but fell to sixth, quite a tumble, in the 2006–2007 report. Had lousy schools at last done us in? No.

The WEF analyzes competitiveness using categories that it has come to call the "nine pillars of competitiveness." The first two of these are institutions and infrastructure. The WEF examines the degree to which public institutions are transparent and operate for the public good, not for private gain. Private institutions must maintain strict standards of accountability and trustworthiness. The pervasiveness of corruption and cronyism in the public sector lowered the rank for this pillar, as did the various scandals in the private sector along with questionable awards of no-bid contracts to preferred corporations.

Infrastructure refers to planes, trains, boats, highways, energy, and telecommunications. The mishandling of the Katrina disaster indicated that the infrastructure was not as robust as it needed to be and called into question institutional (governmental) competence.

The United States also suffered in the pillar of health and primary education not because of schools but because of AIDS, shorter life spans than many less wealthy nations, and inadequate health care despite spending the largest proportion of GDP on it of any nation in the world. The United States spends 15 percent of GDP on health care. The next highest spenders are Germany (11 percent) and France (10 percent). France and Germany, of course, have universal coverage while about one in seven Americans is not covered, some 45 million people.

What bothered the WEF the most though, was the state of the pillar known as macroeconomic stability. The WEF worries when a country spends, as we do, a large proportion of GDP servicing debt, money that could otherwise be available to improve productivity. It equally worries over trade deficits. But what the WEF found most troubling was that the governments had an open ended commitment to coffer-draining spending on war and homeland security while simultaneously planning to reduce the treasury with further tax cuts. On macroeconomic stability, the United States ranked 69th out of 125 nations, just ahead of Armenia, Croatia, and Cyprus; just behind Uganda, Moldova, and the Slovak Republic. The next lowest ranking was 40th for the pillar that combines health and primary education, an improvement from 43rd in the previous year. Most of the remaining rankings were in the top ten.

SAMPLE MATH AND SCIENCE ITEMS FROM PISA

Seal's Sleep

A seal has to breathe even when it is asleep in the water. Martin observed a seal for one hour. At the start of his observation, the seal was at the surface and took a breath. It then dove to the bottom of the sea and started to sleep. From the bottom it slowly floated to the surface in 8 minutes and took a breath again. In three minutes it was back at the bottom of the sea again. Martin noticed that this whole process was a very regular one.

After one hour the seal was

a) at the bottom,
b) on its way up,
c) breathing,
d) on its way down.

Note: Obviously, to answer this question, test takers have to play the "testing game." For instance, they must assume that "very regular" means that it always takes exactly eight minutes to rise up, zero seconds to breathe, and exactly three minutes to dive. Given the speed of a seal in water, Martin couldn't possibly see to the depth it reached after a three-minute descent. One wonders how well children who have never seen a seal would fare with this question.

Chocolate Diet

A newspaper article recounted the story of a 22-year-old student named Jessica, who has a "chocolate diet." She claims to remain healthy, and at a steady weight of 50 kg, whilst eating 90 bars of chocolate a week and cutting out all other food, apart from one "proper meal" every five days. A nutrition expert commented: I am surprised someone can live with a diet like this. Fats give her energy to live but she is not getting nearly enough vitamins. She could encounter serious health problems in later life.

In a book with nutritional values, the following data are applicable to the type of chocolate Jessica is eating all the time. Assume also that the bars of chocolate she eats have a weight of 100 grams.

Protein (g)	Fats (g)	Carbohydrates (g)	Minerals (mg)		Vitamins (mg)			Total Energy (kJ)
			Calcium	Iron	A	B	C	
5	32	61	50	4	—	0.20	—	2142

The nutrition expert said that Jessica "…is not getting nearly enough vitamins." One of those vitamins missing in chocolate is vitamin C. Perhaps she could compensate for her shortage of vitamin C by including a food that contains a high percentage of vitamin C in her "proper meal every five days." Here is a list of types of food:

1. fish
2. fruit
3. rice
4. vegetables

Which two types of food from this list would you recommend to Jessica in order to give her a chance to compensate for her vitamin C shortage?

A. 1 and 2,
B. 1 and 3,
C. 1 and 4,
D. 2 and 3,
E. 2 and 4,
F. 3 and 4.

Note: Most of the information in this "item" is irrelevant to the problem (a second question does ask if all of the energy comes from fat). To get at the question's intent, which is "demonstrating knowledge and understanding of science in life and health," the following stem would do as well: "The doctor tells you that you aren't getting enough vitamin C and that this might lead to health problems later on. Which two of the following foods might you increase to reduce or eliminate your vitamin C deficiency?" One wonders how much students might be distracted thinking about the quirkiness of a girl who eats almost 20 pounds (19.84) of chocolate a week (the story is real, taken from a newspaper account).

INTERNATIONAL TEST RESULTS: AN OVERVIEW

However one feels about the utility of international comparisons, the fact is that since the early 1990s they have constituted a growth industry, supported a number of careers, and assumed increasing importance in the media and among some policymakers. It thus behooves us to take a look at the principal findings.

The principal comparisons carry the acronyms TIMSS, PISA, and PIRLS. PISA stands for Program of International Student Assessment and is conducted from Paris by the Organization for Economic Cooperation and Development (OECD). OECD conducted PISA in 2000, 2003, and 2006. The 2006 results will be available late 2007. PISA tests mostly 15-year-olds in reading, mathematics, and science, with each assessment concentrating on one of the three areas.

TIMSS originally stood for Third International Mathematics and Science Study, but after the 1995 administration, developers decided to repeat it every four years and the "T" now stands for "Trends." The 1995 TIMSS tested students in grades four and eight and in the "Final Year of Secondary School"—which, internationally, is not always comparable to the senior year in the United States. In addition to math/science literacy, the final year study assessed physics and advanced mathematics. After 1995, TIMSS tested only grades four and eight, but another attempt at a final year study of physics and advanced mathematics is scheduled for 2008. TIMSS is administered by the Hague-based International Association for the Evaluation of Educational Achievement, which always abbreviates to IEA. Most of the technical work is done by the TIMSS and PIRLS International Study Center at Boston College (http://timss.bc.edu).

PIRLS stands for Progress in International Reading Literacy Study and is also overseen by the IEA. It assessed reading skills of fourth-graders in 2001 and 2006 with the 2006 results scheduled to be released in December 2007.

On the 1995 TIMSS, American fourth-graders scored above average in math and third in the world in science among the 26 participating nations. American eighth-graders scored slightly below average in math and slightly above average in science among the 41 countries that took part. These results are shown in Table I.1.

We can note that ranks force differences among participants without revealing the size of those differences, which are often quite small. There might be virtually no differences in the *scores* of countries that are ranked, say, first and second. American students correctly answered 58 percent of the items in eighth grade science. This performance, only two percentage points above the

Table I.1   Ranks and Percent Correct, TIMSS 1995

| | Mathematics | | | |
| | Grade Four | | Grade Eight | |
	Rank	% Correct	Rank	% Correct
United States	12/26 (7)	63	24/41(17)	53
International	59		55	
	Science			
United States	3/26 (1)	66	13/41(6)	58
International	59		56	

Note: The numbers in parentheses are the number of countries that had statistically significantly higher scores than the United States. Thus, in fourth-grade math, the United States ranked 12th, but only seven countries had significantly higher scores.

international average, gave them a rank of 13th among the 41 participating countries. Had American students managed to get 63 percent correct—a mere 5 percent more—they would have vaulted to 5th. Had they gotten 5 percent fewer correct, they would have plummeted to 32nd.

American seniors apparently scored at or near the bottom among the 16 to 21 nations participating (the number varied for the various topics). In some instances, though, the operative word was "apparently."

LOCATING THE REPORTS OF INTERNATIONAL COMPARISONS

U.S.-oriented reports on TIMSS, PISA, and PIRLS are available through the National Center for Education Statistics: www.nces.ed.gov. More extensive reports on TIMSS and PIRLS can be found at the International Study Center, Boston College: http://timss.bc.edu. Similarly, more extensive reports on PISA can be found at the Organization for Economic Cooperation and Development: www.pisa.oecd.org.

The apparent downward arc of achievement over the grades gave rise to a cliché as voiced by former secretary of education William J. Bennett: "In America today, the longer you stay in school, the dumber you get relative to your peers in other industrialized nations." However, the final-year study can be characterized as an "apples to aardvarks" comparison. Subgroups of American students most like their foreign peers achieved about the same ranks as in the eighth grade, in the middle of the group (Bracey, 2000). American students were much affected by the fact that so many of them worked so many hours at paid jobs, something uncharacteristic of most countries. One group of American students included "just to see how they'd do" was those who had taken pre-calculus. They scored 100 points lower than American students who had taken calculus. The latter group more closely resembled their foreign peers and also scored in the middle of the group. And, in order to test as near to the end of the school year as possible, the tests—irrelevant to students, teachers, administrators, or parents—were administered in May, maximizing the impact of that uniquely American phenomenon, the "senior slump" (TIMSS is constructed like NAEP with about 140 items, only one-third of which are taken by any given student; as with NAEP, there are no scores for individuals).

One can only conjecture about the reality of the decline in ranks from fourth grade to eighth grade, but it does consistently appear. American textbooks may bear some responsibility—they are about three times as thick as those in other nations. American teachers teach many more topics in the course of a year, and it is quite possible that the "coverage" is too brief and shallow to be effective. In addition, historically, the middle grades have often been viewed as a time of consolidation of material learned earlier in preparation for high school. Other countries are more likely to treat them as high school years in terms of introducing new material.

In the repeats of TIMSS, American eighth-graders gained more than students in a number of other nations. Among the 22 nations that took part both in 1995 and 2003, American eighth-graders ranked 17th in 1995 and 12th in 2003 in mathematics. In science, American eighth-graders ranked 14th in 1995 and 7th in 2003.

American fourth-graders scored the same in 2003 as in 1995, and this caused them to lose a few ranks, from sixth to eighth in mathematics and from second to fifth in science. However, with only 15 nations taking part in both assessments at the fourth grade, it is not clear that this is a meaningful change.

PISA may be an unimportant indicator since American students generally attain average ranks—it is not at all clear what PISA measures. The administrators at OECD contend that it measures the ability of students to apply what they've learned in school to new situations, to "real life" problems. It is obvious from some of the released items, however, that no cognitive scientist would find PISA's notion of "apply" to be either a clear or unitary construct. Different items clearly call for different cognitive skills.

In addition, many of the item stems in mathematics and science are rambling and discursive. This means that they will be heavily affected by reading skills. An acquaintance in Germany has advised that PISA reading and math tests correlate beyond +0.90, above the reliability coefficients of most tests. The stems also sometimes contain information that is irrelevant to answering the question, and it is likely that this information affects the performance of some students.

PIRLS is the successor to the IEA study, *How in the World Do Students Read?* (Elley, 1992). In that 1991 study (published in 1992), American 9-year-olds finished second among 27 nations and 14-year-olds finished ninth among 31 nations, although only one nation had a statistically significantly higher score. It is said that the assistant secretary of education at the time, Diane Ravitch, told the staff at the Office of Educational Research and Improvement to make the data disappear.

PIRLS tested only fourth-graders. American students finished ninth among 35 countries, with three nations having statistically significantly higher scores. Sweden finished first (Finland did not participate) with a score of 562, while the United States came in at 543, and the international average was 500.

In all of the international studies, American students' rankings depend a great deal on the poverty level of the school. For PIRLS, these results are shown in Table I.2. The 13 percent of American students who attend schools with 0 to 10 percent of the students living in poverty score 589, well above top-ranked Sweden. The 17 percent who attend 10 to 25 percent poverty level schools also outdistance the Swedes. The 28 percent in 25–50 percent poverty schools scored 551. If this group constituted a nation, it would rank fourth among the 35 PIRLS countries. Only students attending schools where more than 75 percent of the students live in poverty score below the international average.

It might be argued that this is not a particularly meaningful analysis because poverty exists in other nations. This is true, but not nearly to the extent in other developed nations as in the United States. Other nations have taxes and social programs that transfer wealth to offset poverty that attain significantly greater reductions than the modest efforts here. The proportion of children in poverty in the United States is second only to Mexico and remains quite large after transfers and taxes. For the United States, taxes and transfers cut the poverty rate only from 26.6 percent to 21.9 percent. This contrasts with, say, France, where the poverty rate is actually higher, but transfers and taxes reduce it sharply from 27.7 percent to 7.5 percent (poverty is defined by a family income of less than 50 percent of the median family income in a nation).

WHAT DOES IT ALL MEAN?

As noted at the outset, some people have expressed skepticism about the value of studies such as the ones described here. The resulting "league tables" have been described as a horse race or a "cognitive Olympics," which they most assuredly are not. They are point-in-time snapshots of a long-term process. Questions have been raised about translations, test reliability coefficients, comparability of samples, response rates, and relationship of the tests to the curricula.

Indeed, some would argue that the important outcomes of education are not visible until well after schooling has ended. Thirty years ago, for example, Finland decided to invest a great deal of resources in music education. Today there are proportionately more Finns who play music as a profession or avocation

Table I.2   The Impact of Poverty on Achievement—Data from PIRLS

International Average =	500
U.S. Average =	543
Sweden (highest average)	562

Percent of Students in Poverty	Score	Percent Students Nationally
0–10	589	13
10–25	567	17
25–50	551	28
50–75	519	22
75+	485	20

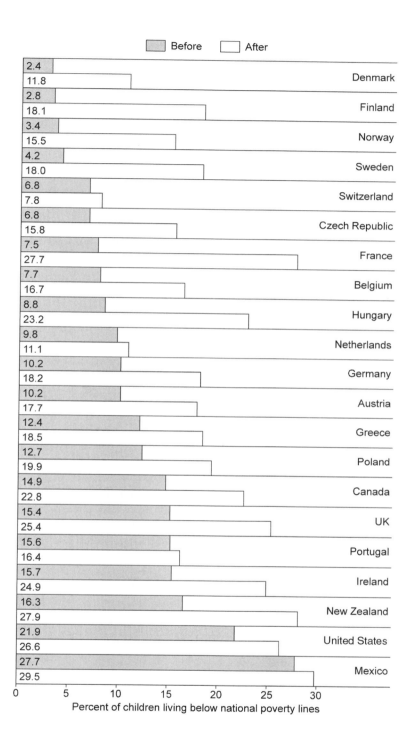

Figure I.1 Poverty in 21 developed nations before and after taxes and transfers.

Source: Child Poverty in Rich Countries 2005. Available at: http://www.unicef.org/brazil/repcard6e.pdf.

than anywhere else in the world. In the classical field, Finland dominates in producing conductors. Finnish conductors lead the Los Angeles Philharmonic, the Minneapolis Symphony, the City of Birmingham Orchestra, the National Orchestra of Belgium, the Ensemble Intercontemporain (Paris), and the Finnish National Opera. Jukka-Pekka Saraste recently returned to Finland from years of leading the Toronto Symphony and the BBC Symphony. This is quite remarkable for a nation of less that 5.5 million people (about the same as the Boston metropolitan area).

Finland's dedication to music is unusual for a nation and said to be due in part to the role of composer Jean Sibelius in springing Finland loose from Swedish and Russian domination and unifying the nation through his first and second symphonies. The United States has had similar programs, formal and informal, applied to technology. Europeans still often cite Thomas Jefferson today as a major influence on the role of science and technology in the nation. Franklin Delano Roosevelt's "Arsenal of Democracy" campaign during World War II can likely be regarded as such a thrust, and John F. Kennedy's determination to land a man on the moon certainly can.

Today, though, no one is taking the long view. Corporate CEOs have their eyes on the quarterly profit, and educators are constrained to Adequate Yearly Progress. Politicians, businessmen, and education reformers speak vaguely, if anxiously, about the "global economy." Someone needs to take the long view.

Further Reading: Bracey, G. W., 2000, May, The TIMSS final year study and report: a critique, *Educational Researcher,* pp. 4–10; Bracey, G. W., 2002, *The war against America's public schools,* Boston: Allyn & Bacon; Carnevale, A. P., 2005, February 2, Education and the economy: If we're so dumb, why are we so rich? *Education Week,* pp. 40–41; Forster, M., 2000, *A policy maker's guide to international achievement studies,* Melbourne, Australia: Australian Council for Educational Research Press, retrieved from http://www.acer.edu.au/research/documents/IntAchStud.pdf; Gates, B., 2005, February 26, prepared remarks for the National Governors Association/Achieve Summit, Washington, DC, retrieved from http://www.nga.org/cda/files/ES05GATES.pdf; Hanushek, E. A., 2005, February 2, Education and the economy: Our school performance matters, *Education Week,* pp. 40–41; Lopez-Claros, A., Porter, M. E., Sala-i-Martin, X., & Schwab, K., 2006, *The global competitiveness report 2006–2007,* Davos, Switzerland: World Economic Forum; Ramirez, F. O., Luo, X., Schofer, E., & Meyer, J., 2006, November, Student achievement and national economic growth, *American Journal of Education,* pp. 1–29; Romainville, M., 2002, Du bon usage de Pisa, *Revue Nouvelle,* 115(3–4), 86–99.

Gerald W. Bracey

K

KNOWLEDGE

TEACHING AND LEARNING FOR OUR FUTURE

Contemporary society is rife with text messaging, podcasts, Blackberries, web sites, and e-mail, all which have dramatically changed the way we, and especially our children, communicate and think. Music and movie downloading, chat rooms, and video games have become an essential part of everyday life. For many of our children, it is simply impossible to imagine life without a cell phone that doubles as a camera, music player, and Internet browser. We have many more educational and entertainment options than ever before and they are pulling us in many different directions. Yosemite National Park, known for its majestic views, mystical waterfalls, and the magnificent Half Dome, is experiencing steadily declining attendance for the first time in over a decade. This decline is blamed, in part, on the fact that Half Dome is now competing with PlayStation and Xbox for people's attention.

Technology impacts nearly every aspect of our lives, yet its impact on teaching and learning is, at best, modest and, in many cases, negligible. Even with impressive corporate and governmental investments resulting in billions of dollars being spent to build digital learning networks in schools, teaching and learning at the beginning of the third millennium remains relatively unchanged from the early days of the twentieth century when the country was in the throes of the industrial revolution. Almost 100 years after the industrial revolution, we are moving away from an industrial age to an information society. Today's centralized control, standardization of the curriculum, top-down administration of courses, and high-stakes testing reflect a model of schooling inconsistent with our era of information. Our current system of public education was created for an industrial age and is no longer adequate to address the challenges of our twenty-first century society (Brown, 2006).

LIFE IN 1900

To understand the speed and impact of change, it is useful to look back a little over a century ago to gain some perspective. The United States was emerging as a nation of fantastic opportunity. Over 1,500,000 people per year were leaving their homes in other countries and arriving in the United States. Most immigrants were leaving grinding poverty in Europe, and were better off upon arriving in the United States. However, most immigrants were consigned to become the legions of "have-nots" whose only choice was to take the worst and most dangerous jobs for the lowest pay. Foreign-born persons and their children were in the majority, but prejudice was common and social class determined how people were treated.

In 1900, wealthy families were considered to be "upper class." The upper class comprised 1 percent of the population, but they owned 99 percent of the country's wealth. Young upper class girls were tutored at home until they were about 13, and then they were sent off to "finishing schools" to learn homemaking and intricacies of social etiquette. Females entered society and became eligible for marriage at about age 16, and their goal was marriage to a husband from the same class as their own. Boys of the upper class were home-tutored and sent off to "preparation school," followed by college or university, most commonly to prepare them to run the family business.

In 1900, middle class citizens worked as shop owners or employees in factories. This was a time that was unique. Members of this new middle class had many opportunities to build their fortunes. Depending on when middle class children started school, they usually dropped out about the time they were 12–13 years of age. Then they had to find full-time jobs, but some of the more affluent members of the middle class (mostly children of small business owners) were able to attend a college or university.

The largest class in 1900 was the lower class, and it was they who struggled daily to survive. Many were immigrants who lived in large cities or on farms in rural areas in unhealthy, unsanitary living conditions. In the city, it was common that several families often occupied a cramped, dingy apartment intended for a single family. Most could not read and many spoke very limited English. They usually worked 10- and 12-hour factory shifts, six days a week, in dangerous working conditions for paltry wages. It was common for eight-year-olds to work on farms and in factories instead of attending school. Many children worked at jobs that adults were unable to do, such as crawling into small places to fix or change machinery parts. Many children were injured or killed doing this work. It was common for families to have more than five children who could work and bring home money so that the family could survive. If one child happened to be killed in their work, the survival of the family was not put in jeopardy. Many children lived on their own, away from their families, selling newspapers, sewing, cleaning chimneys, and the like. Those children who were more fortunate developed a skill or trade as an apprentice with a blacksmith, carpenter, seamstress, or other skilled worker.

New York City in 1900, with a population of 3.4 million people (its current population is 17 million) was the nation's largest and most exciting city; Los Angeles, with a population of 102,000, was not even in the top 20 cities in the United States. Great Britain was the most powerful country in the world, with Queen Victoria, its longest reigning monarch. Life expectancy of people in the United States was 47 years of age. One in seven persons graduated from high school ion 1900. Forty-two percent of the workforce was involved in farming; the average worker, toiling in dangerous conditions and long hours, earned $9.70 per week. One in 13 homes had a telephone and the vast majority of homes had no electricity or indoor plumbing. There were fewer than 1,000 miles of paved roads throughout the United States. Wilbur and Orville Wright were still three years away from their first flight. Horses, railroads, and travel by foot were the main forms of transportation. There were 4,000 cars on the road, worldwide, with speed limits of 20 miles per hour. There were more lynchings (116) than auto deaths (96) in the United States in 1900. The three largest companies in the United States were United States Steel, Standard Oil, and the American Tobacco Company. John D. Rockefeller, leader of the Standard Oil Company, was to become the single most important individual in shaping the rise of the modern corporation. These companies not only were the driving forces of the Industrial Revolution, they also represented the ruthless pursuit of profit, more often than not in direct defiance of the law.

Progressive education was emerging, and at the University of Chicago, John Dewey established the first elementary school. Progressive ideas, rooted in democratic practice, were quite popular, but in 1900 their impact on schools was minor. The annual teacher salary was $350. Italian educator Maria Montessori was becoming widely known for her new teaching method. Due to the influx of immigrants, the biggest problem for education was the lack of room in schools for the rapidly expanding population.

The development and change that the world has seen since 1900 is remarkable, and to the person living in 1900, the change to come was unimaginable. The fundamental connection between then and now is revolution. In 1900, the revolution was steeped in manufacturing and rapid social change, and now, ours is borne of technology and information. This information revolution provides a set of challenges—not unlike those in 1900—in which we must consider how best to prepare students for their future, how best to develop schools that are responsive to our future, and what it means to be educated persons in our rapidly changing world. The task is difficult and it requires that all of us imagine a future into which our students are entering. The potential is limitless, and what results most likely will impact our society for the next 100 years and beyond. Planning for an education in an era that may hold some of the most profound changes of our time may prove to be among the most important challenges facing our society this century. In order to move our thinking into the realm of the future, it is important to consider the generation of students who comprise our immediate and long term future.

TOP 20

In 2007, the National Academy of Engineering listed the top 20 achievements of the twentieth century:

1. electrification
2. automobile
3. airplane
4. water supply and distribution
5. electronics
6. radio and television
7. agricultural mechanization
8. computers
9. telephone
10. air conditioning and refrigeration
11. highways
12. spacecraft
13. Internet
14. imaging
15. household appliances
16. health technologies
17. petroleum and petrochemical technologies
18. laser and fiber optics
19. nuclear technologies
20. high-performance materials

THE MILLENNIALS

Born after 1980, the millennials—also known as the Echo Boom, Generation Y, Generation XX, Generation 2K—are more than 60 million strong in the United States. These are the sons, daughters, and grandchildren of the "baby boomer" generation. The millennials grew up in a time of uninterrupted economic prosperity and are among the most protected generation in history in terms of government and safety regulations. They are used to being consulted regarding family decisions. As a result, they tend to exhibit strong bonds with their parents. According to one survey, 75 percent of millennials said they share their parents' values. They are more racially diverse; one in three are *not* Caucasian. One in four lives in a single parent household, and three in four have working mothers. Diversity is the embodiment of the millennials. They encounter messages on a daily basis that reflect a stunning array of political viewpoints, consumer choices, and cultural perspectives. The global reach of the Internet has made it possible for persons who have similar interests to talk with one another, provide immediate assistance and aid, and share divergent points of view irrespective of their national boundaries, ethnic differences, or cultural chasms.

The millennials who sit in our elementary and secondary classrooms are getting a vast majority of their news from such nontraditional sources such as Jon Stewart's "The Daily Show" and a wide array of blogs. An estimated 32 million people have read a blog, while 8 million have created their own blogs. When the millennials use these blogs and other technologies, they are encountering a mind-boggling assortment of issues, at once complex and contradictory. For example, issues that are facing the millennials are: determining the moral implications of fighting the "war on terror," balancing the rights of the logging industry to make a profit with the rights of those who wish to preserve the environment for the sake of future generations, the uncertainty of not being able to think of one political party as exclusively conservative or liberal, and global warming; and these are but a few of the issues that the millennials are bumping into on a daily basis.

In the world of the millennials, technological communications have the capacity to transmit billions of messages simultaneously to almost anywhere on the planet. News of a tsunami in Indonesia, a civil war in Darfur, or an earthquake in California reaches the millennials literally minutes after the events occur and places our students in a virtual world where they are "on the scene" as the event unfolds. With this myriad of messages, one must ask: Do these messages that the millennials receive on a daily basis help them form a perspective that accurately reflects the world? It is critical that teaching and learning help millennials and future generations answer this question so that they can gain a reliable and valid sense of world conditions. With the unprecedented resources that are generating huge amounts of information about the state of the planet and its people, there is a need for teaching and learning that provides for the sharing and processing of information to help the millennials—and those that follow them—to gain a sense of important patterns, divergent points of view, and future trends.

COLLEGE MINDSET

Beloit College annually publishes its "College Mindset List " for students entering each fall. Below are some cultural touchstones that have shaped the lives of college students who were born in 1988.

- They have known only two presidents.
- The Soviet Union has never existed and therefore is as scary as the student union.
- "Google" has always been a verb.
- "So" as in "Sooooo New York," has always been a drawn-out adjective modifying a proper noun, which in turn modifies something else.
- They are wireless, yet connected.
- They always have been able to watch wars and revolutions on TV.
- They have always had access to their own credit cards.
- DNA fingerprinting has always been admissible evidence in court.
- Bar codes have always been on everything from library cards to snail mail and retail items.
- Ringo Starr has always been clean and sober.

THE CHANGING LANDSCAPE OF KNOWLEDGE

For millennials in the information age, knowledge has become more un-settled, less predictable, and rapidly changing. Alvin and Heidi Toffler in their book, *Revolutionary Wealth,* talk about the "law of obsoledge," where as change continues to accelerate, the knowledge that we currently possess rapidly be-comes obsolete, hence the term "obsoledge." For example, our knowledge of our own solar system forever was changed with the demotion of Pluto from its sta-tus as a planet, while our vocabulary was enhanced with the American Dialect Society's 2006 Word of the Year—plutoed—meaning "something that has been devalued."

With knowledge having a more limited "shelf life," the need increases for students to change from memorizing facts to problem solving augmented by a community of groups and learning teams. To overcome a growing sense of anxiety and uneasiness about our own "obsoledge," we need to develop cognitive tools that will help us visualize concepts as variations of larger themes. Big con-cept thinking, systemic analysis, and model building will replace the less useful memorization of disconnected facts. Sophisticated online search engines will lead learners to specific facts and details that students will discard after their use and resurrect when necessary. Unlike the end-of-chapter, recall-based questions students answer in today's textbooks, the ever-changing landscape of knowledge will demand that learners in the future engage with knowledge rooted in prob-lems that are contextual, complex, and messy. For example, students will learn to access specific knowledge related to the Bill of Rights because it is essential to helping them complete a problem centered task, rather than to receive a high score on a Monday morning quiz or a standardized test. Software will track an individual's learning proficiency and generate a personal learning profile that will help teachers to provide support and guidance for all students. Knowledge in the future will emphasize students probing, questioning, and learning *how* to do something, as opposed to memorizing facts for a standardized examination.

Millennials want to engage in authentic, real life activities that connect the curriculum to their lives while challenging their creativity. But most importantly, teaching our children and preparing them for their future means acknowledg-ing the unique technological and communicative abilities they currently possess so that they can connect these skills with the knowledge they need to know for tomorrow's world.

A Glimpse into Our Future

Forecasting the future can be fraught with problems. Once predictions of the future included a world where we were destined to a future replete with flying cars and robots that would serve our every need. However, forecasts of the fu-ture should not be interpreted as predictions of what the future *will* be; rather, a forecast is a glimpse of what *may* happen, or proposals for what *should* hap-pen. Futurist Eric Garland argues that the skill of predicting the future helps to expose our assumptions, blind spots, and ignorance. *The Futurist,* a journal that forecasts trends and ideas about the future, provides an annual outlook for the future. This forecast, combined with other perspectives on the future, clearly presents some significant implications for education during the next 100 years.

BUSINESS AND ECONOMICS

- The ratio of total income of people in the United States in the top five percent and bottom five percent of income has grown from 6 to 1 in the 1980s to 200 to 1 in 2006. Disparities between rich and poor will continue to grow.
- An estimated 3.3 million high-tech service jobs will move out of the United States over the next 15 years; the shift of high-tech jobs may be a permanent feature of economic life in the twenty-first century.
- The development of nanotechnology will result in breakthroughs in food, agriculture, more powerful computers, and alternative energy systems.
- Workers over the age of 55 will grow from 14 percent of the labor force in 2005 to 19 percent by 2012. Companies will see the age range of its workers span four generations.

SCIENCE

- Biotechnology, nanotechnology (molecular manufacturing), and closed-environment agriculture will efficiently feed the world's population.
- Thousands of people will work in space communities in orbit, on the moon, and on Mars.
- Hydrogen, fusion, third-generation fission plants, solar powered satellites, and renewable energy sources will provide a safe and abundant mix of energy.
- By 2030 the use of fossil fuels for power and transportation will be all but eliminated.

ENVIRONMENT

- Water supplies and energy choices will make or break the Chinese and Indian economies with sustainable sources of energy critical for their economic survival.
- Costs of global–warming-related disasters will reach $150 billion per year worldwide in 10 years.
- By 2100, coastal fisheries along Florida's coast and estuaries could be lost to flooding related to global warming.
- By 2025, 75 percent of U.S. residents will live on the coasts. The impact of hurricanes and global warming will impact more people than ever before.

TECHNOLOGY

- Computers will have artificial empathy for users, picking up on body language, facial expressions, and tone of voice.
- Computers will be one billion times more powerful in 30 years, rivaling the human brain.

- Wireless technology will be incorporated into our thought processes by 2030, allowing us to boost memory and thinking capacity and moving us beyond the basic architecture of the brain's neural regions.

EDUCATION

- Education will become more portable and on-demand via downloading. Teachers will upload information, lectures, and other educational resources to students to access at their own convenience.
- Content will change from disciplines to a broader interconnectedness of information, with digital learning that will promote multidisciplinary thinking, multiple perspectives, and nonlinear thinking.
- Interactive, virtual learning rooms that can be adapted to whatever is being learned will replace the classroom—virtual trips will be taken to any part of the planet and to the communities in space and allow students to view and question scientists and other professionals as they do their daily work.
- Students will have individual, lifetime web sites that provide information, feedback, and updating regarding their individual learning styles and that will guide students to resources that fit their specific learning needs and interests.

A FUTURE ORIENTED PERSPECTIVE

In the next 100 years, radical changes in social and political mores, education, cultural awareness, medicine, and transportation will be part of everyday life. Simply put, we cannot imagine all that the future holds for us. By focusing on the future as we think about, plan, and develop our schools and their curricula, we must consider what society might be like for millennials and their children, and the essential knowledge and skills they will need to be successful 50 to 100 years from now.

A future oriented perspective assumes that the schools and curriculum we develop will not be static and mired in standardized accountability measures that inhibit creativity. Schools need to be structured so that they are able to quickly adapt to the changing world in which our students live. One can often hear the phrase, "if only schools were run like businesses..." as a call to change and innovation for schools. This simplistic phrase is an indication of a fundamental misunderstanding of how businesses *and* schools work in our society. Businesses are *always* thinking toward the future, and in order to do this, they have created structures that are flexible and easily changed. Profits are the ultimate measure of accountability for businesses, and businesses are never hesitant to throw out old notions and change rapidly to meet the demands for profits from their stockholders. Unlike schools, businesses have *never* established a rigid accountability system that is difficult to change, prescribes their every movement for years to come, and limits their ability to respond to future problems. The current system of accountability in our schools was developed primarily by persons outside of education (e.g., politicians, policymakers, and business leaders) that is not only antithetical to a business accountability model but is difficult to change and is not responsive to the current or future needs of students.

Currently, we are confronted by issues that raise complex and perplexing problems that have no obvious answers: How will the free world address terrorism without infringing on human rights? What will be the role a free and open press in a world heavily influenced by multinational corporate control? How do we address the rights of all people with respect to marriage? How will we feed a world population that will more than double in 60 years? The answers to these questions will be found in our future. They will involve thinking that we can only imagine. If we are to prepare our citizens to make thoughtful decisions, now and in the future, our schools must be open to thinking about unfathomable and uncertain outcomes. A future oriented perspective will need to constantly monitor and forecast change—and its costs and consequences—in order to guide our progress more wisely. And future oriented planning will result in change that focuses on where we are going, as well as where we have been, so that the decisions and plans we make today will position us for success in our uncertain future.

A future oriented perspective demands rigorous, research based curricula and planning involving higher education, public school personnel, parents, and community leaders. We know more about teaching and learning that we knew 20 years ago. We know that we must connect knowledge to the lives of the students, and we know that it takes citizens who question and who are imaginative to keep our democracy healthy and strong. However, we cannot hope to reform the schools without a future oriented perspective that involves all of us working more closely with schools. This means thinking and working with those who are in schools on a daily basis: administrators, teachers, students, staff, and community members. Through working together, there is an infinite universe of possibility regarding how knowledge can be taught and delivered. Curricular redesign efforts that focus on qualitative and quantitative research-based best practice can help jump-start a sweeping reform of the teaching and learning.

Some educators are beginning to use "scenario planning," to help prepare for the future. This is a process that helps planners create "plausible realities" that are most likely to influence our future by analyzing trends in the surrounding environment, interpreting how these trends might interact with each other, and theorizing how these trends will impact and shape the future. An example of one school district that is actively planning for the future is the School District of Kettle Moraine, Wisconsin. The superintendent has convened a task force whose goal it is "to transform the educational delivery system to better and more efficiently meet the needs of all students." The task force is engaged in activities such as scenario planning to understand the changes the district may encounter in future decades.

As we consider the future, we should not move rashly to adopt a singular, national perspective that is driven by ideology and special interests. Rather, we need to take the time to conscientiously consider a wide array of perspectives that could help to reinvent schools and curriculum and make them relevant and flexible to meet the unknown demands of the future. Perhaps we will discover that a curriculum should be regional rather than national to better serve the diversity of the nation. Whatever the forum and its outcome, the time has come for educators to discuss how its schools meet the needs of future generations of learners, unlock the learning potential of each student, and ensure an exciting, engaging, and rigorous course of study.

Just as those who lived in 1900 would marvel at our world, the world in 2110 will be one that many adults living today would not recognize or understand. More emphasis may be placed on what Richard Samson calls "hyper-human" skills such as caring, judgment, intuition, ethics, inspiration, friendliness, and imagination. Jobs of the future may have titles such as: bioaesthetic coach; intercommunity farmer; personal genome optimizer; telemedicine technician; underwater hotel manager; offshore outsourcing coordinator; manager of diversity; skycar mechanic; or transhumanist technician. However, no amount of research and educated forecasting makes the future wholly knowable. What we do know is that untold social, political, economic, and cultural problems will be facing our citizens 100 years from now and beyond. Social problems in the future such as overpopulation, disease, threats to individual freedom, and ecological disasters may be avoided or at least better addressed through recognition of their dangers and discussion of their consequences. A reasoned and intelligent view of the future is more likely when there is a willingness and ability for educators to develop schools that can adapt to change. Futurist Arnold Brown poses the future as a choice between being carried helplessly into the future or controlling it, by "getting people to forget what they think they know, and open their minds to what they now need to know."

Fundamentally and most importantly, societal impetus may be affected by a future oriented perspective in planning our curriculum and our schools. We can no longer continue with schools, curriculum, and instructional approaches that are based upon twentieth-century assumptions and perspectives. Since all predictive techniques may influence the perception of reality, a future oriented perspective will play an important role in the education of our citizens. The decisions that we make about schools today will inevitably impact how curriculum is developed and delivered in the next 100 years and beyond. Undeniably, if the schools are not attentive to the future, our schools and their curricula may be "plutoed," thus failing our citizens and the very democracy that we all so deeply cherish.

Further Reading: Brown, A. 2006. The Problem Is Not What You Don't Know, It's What You Think You Do Know, *Futures Research Quarterly*, Spring 2006, Vol. 1; Toeffler, A., & H. Toffler, 2006, *Revolutionary Wealth*, New York: Alfred A. Knopf, 2006

Perry M. Marker